ISBN 978-1-331-87728-8
PIBN 10248406

Similar Books Are Available from
www.forgottenbooks.com

Travels in the Interior of Africa
by Mungo Park

Via Rhodesia
A Journey Through Southern Africa, by Charlotte Mansfield

A Visit to India, China, and Japan in the Year 1853
by Bayard Taylor

Italian Castles and Country Seats
by Tryphosa Bates Batcheller

Captain Cook's Third and Last Voyage to the Pacific Ocean, Vol. 1 of 4
In the Years 1776, 1777, 1778, 1779 and 1780, by James Cook

Travels in Peru and Mexico
by S. S. Hill

A Handbook for Travellers in Southern Italy
Comprising the Description, by John Murray

The Handbook for Travellers in Spain, Vol. 1
by Richard Ford

A New Collection of Voyages, Discoveries and Travels
by John Adams

The Sacred City of the Ethiopians
Being a Record of Travel and Research in Abyssinia in 1893, by J. Theodore Bent

The Outgoing Turk
Impressions of a Journey Through the Western Balkans, by H. C. Thomson

Travels in the Old World
Illustrated, by J. M. Rowland

The Travels of Marco Polo, the Venetian
The Translation of Marsden Revised, by Marco Polo

Travels in Arabia
by Bayard Taylor

From the Gulf to Ararat, an Expedition Through Mesopotamia and Kurdistan
by G. E. Hubbard

From Occident to Orient and Around the World
by Charlton B. Perkins

The Periplus of the Erythræan Sea
Travel and Trade in the Indian Ocean By a Merchant of the First Century, by Wilfred H. Schoff

Five Years in a Persian Town
by Napier Malcolm

Central Asia, Travels in Cashmere, Little Tibet, and Central Asia
by Bayard Taylor

The Bondage and Travels of Johann Schiltberger
A Native, by Johannes Schiltberger

Hastily gobled up in five Moneths travells in France, Savoy, Italy, Rhetia commonly called the Grisons country, Helvetia alias Switzerland, some parts of high Germany and the Netherlands ; Newly digested in the hungry aire of Odcombe in the County of Somerset, and now dispersed to the nourishment of the travelling Members of this Kingdome

By

VOLUME II

Glasgow
James MacLehose and Sons
Publishers to the University
MCMV

THE TABLE

	PAGE
Observations of Vicenza, ...	2
Observations of Verona, ...	16
Observations of Brescia, ...	41
Observations of Bergamo, ...	49
Observations of Rhetia, commonly called the Grisons Country, ...	63
An Oration by Hermann Kirchner in Praise of Travel in Germany, ...	71
Observations of Chur, ...	88
Observations of Helvetia, otherwise called Switzerland, ...	92
Observations of Zurich, ...	94
Epistle from Thomas Coryat to Gaspar Waserus,	113
Epistle from Thomas Coryat to Gaspar Waserus,	121
Epistle from Gaspar Waserus to Thomas Coryat,	122

THE TABLE

PAGE

Epistle from Thomas Coryat to Rodolphus Hospinianus, ... 123

Epistle from Thomas Coryat to Henry Bullinger, 127

Epistle from Thomas Coryat to Marcus Buelerus, 130

Epistle from Marcus Buelerus to Thomas Coryat, 135

Observations of Baden, ... 137

Observations of Basle, ... 152

Observations of Some Parts of High Germany, 178

Observations of Strasburg, ... 181

Observations of Lower Baden, ... 199

Observations of Turlowe, ... 205

Observations of Heidelberg, ... 207

Observations of Spires, ... 231

Observations of Frankenthal, ... 252

Observations of Worms, ... 255

Observations of Mayence, ... 269

Observations of Frankfort, ... 287

Observations of Bingen, ... 295

Observations of Bonn, ... 309

THE TABLE

	PAGE
olphus	
.	123
ullinger,	127
Bœlerus,	130
Coryat,	135
	137
.	151
Germany, .	178
	181
.	199
.	205
.	207
.	231
.	232
.	255
.	269
	287
.	295
.	309

	PAGE
Observations of Cologne, ...	311
Observations of Nimeguen, ...	357
Observations of Gorkum, ...	362
Observations of Dordrecht, ...	364
Observations of Flushing, ...	373
Posthumous Fragments of the Poems of Rev. George Coryat, ...	377
Index, ...	409

ILLUSTRATIONS

PAGE

A Delineation of the Amphi-Theater of Verona,   24

A True Figure of the Famous Clock of Strasburg,   192

A Sciographie or Modell of the Great Tun of
    Heidelberg, ...   224

Frederick IV., Count Palatine of the Rhine,   .   232

The Pembroke Dragon, ...   392

THE SECOND VOLUME

OF

Coryat's Crudities

Containing his Observations of Vicenza, Verona,
Brescia, Bergamo, Rhetia, commonly called
the Grisons Country, Helvetia, Some
Parts of High Germany, Stras-
burg, Heidelberg, Worms,
Mayence, Frankfort,
Cologne and
Gelderland

CORYATS CRUDITIES

VOLUME II

I Departed from Venice in a Barke to Padua about eight of the clock in the evening the eighth day of August being Munday, after I had made my aboad there sixe weekes and two dayes, and came to Padua about nine of the clocke the next morning. Here I was very graciously used by my Lord Wentworth. For he invited me most *Lord* kindly to dinner to his owne table, which courtesie the *Wentworth.* very course of humanity doth injoyne me thankfully to remember. After dinner I walked with him to the Santo, where I observed divers things that I have already mentioned in my observations of Padua: as an exorcisme performed by a Priest for the expelling of the divell out of a man possessed: a monument of one of our English Earles of Devon-shire: another of Petrus Bembus, &c.

I departed from Padua about two of the clocke in the [p 292.] afternoone the same day, being conducted in my way by my kinde friend Mr. George Rooke, of whom I have made mention before in my discourse of Padua, and came to a solitary house thirteene miles beyond, about seven of the clocke in the evening, where I lay that night. When I was out of Padua I observed that there are no woods, *Woods cut* groves, shrubs, or any manner of trees growing neare to *down.* the citie, as there were in former times. For all of them have beene cut downe within these few yeares. I noted a singular point of policy in this. For the Venetians who are the Lords of Padua, have caused this to be done, to the end that there shall be no place of shelter for the enemies to shroude themselves in, if any should happen to approach to the citie, with an intent to assault it. All

Guasto, a
waste plot. that space which is so voyd of trees, is called the Guasto,
that is, the waste plot; not because it is altogether waste
and unprofitable, as bearing no commodity at all. For
it beareth great store of Melons and other fruites: but
because there grow no trees there. This Guasto is
extended about some three miles in length, before I could
come to any trees. The like Guastoes they have also
about their other cities in Lombardy, &c.

I departed from the solitary house about sixe of the
clocke the next morning being Wednesday, and came to
Vicenza about eight of the clock. The distance betwixt
that house and Vicenza is five miles.

[p. 293.] My Observations of Vicenza, in Latin Vincentia
and Vicetia.

Julius Cæsar Scaliger hath written these verses upon
Vicenza.

Scaliger's
verses on
Vicenza. BAcche pater, Ceres alma bonæ bona numina pacis,
    Quæ patulos agros, qui juga curva tenes.
Quid rerum, quid amicitiæ cum Marte cruento
    Vobiscum? vestrum ut vexet utrumque furor?
Pulchra racemiferos domitat Vicetia colles,
    Lætaque spicilegi jugera findit agri.
Cædis amor, cædis germanæ insana cupido:
    Nec patrius nato est tutus ab hoste cruor.
Nusquam iter est: vastata jacent latrone protervo
    Ruscula, corruerunt ignibus hausta suis.
Parce (nefas) scelerare manus Gens debita cœlo,
    Imbueque ignoto pectora digna deo.
Divinæ facies, regio cœlestis: at hujus
    In cœli medio tartara dira vigent.

This city was built about three hundred twenty foure
yeares before Christs incarnation, by the people called
Euganei, whom Antenor the Trojan expulsed from that
place, where he built Padua, and not long after it was
much inlarged by those Gaules that were called Galli
Senones, which followed Brennus in his warres. There

alled the Guasto,
; altogether waste
idity at all. For
ither fruites: but
This Guasto is
gth, before I could
es they have also
&c.

: about sixe of the
resday, and came to
he distance betwixt

a Latin Vicentia

these verses upon

bona numina pacis,
rva tenes.
ne cruento
emque furor?
lles;

pido:
e cruor.
rrone protervo
1 suis.
ebita cœlo,
o.
us

ndred twenty four
r the people called
expulsed from that
t long after it was
were called Galli
his warres. These

are two rivers that run through it, whose names are
Bacchilio and Eretinus, whereof Bacchilio is the fairest,
over the which are built seven bridges, partly of stone
and partly of timber. On the left hand of the bridge,
which leadeth into the citie from Padua, I told sixteene
pretty water-mils, which are very commodious to the *Water mills.*
citie: it is thought to be about some foure miles in compasse with the suburbes, being seated in a plaine at the
foote of the hill Bericus, and built in that manner that
it representeth the figure of a Scorpion. For it extendeth [p. 294.]
it selfe much more in length then breadth. And about
the West end it is so slender and narrow, that it resembleth
the tayle of a Scorpion: it is invironed round about with
a bricke wall, wherein are eight gates: many goodly
Palaces and stately buildings, both publique and private I
saw in this citie. In the first street as I came in from Padua
I observed a very beautiful palace of a convenient heigth,
in the front whereof I read this inscription: Has ædes
quanta celeritate ignis consumpsit, tanta feré M. Antonius
Walmarana Stephani Equitis clarissimi filius â fundamentis
erexit anno M.D.XCIII. In the great market-place is
erected a stately pillar of freestone of some twenty foote
high with the winged Lion upon it. The Prætorium *The*
of the citie standeth at the north side of this market-place, *Prætorium.*
which is a very sumptuous and magnificent building, but
much inferiour to that of Padua. It is in length fifty sixe
paces, and in breadth twenty two: at the higher end there
is a Tribunall, above the which the winged Lyon is placed,
richly gilt. Betwixt the Lyon and the Tribunall I read
this inscription, written upon a ground of gold. Antonio
Bernardo Jurisron. & patri optimo ob rempub. domi
forisque fæliciter administratam, urbe pontibus, carcere,
foro, templis exornata, Judæis & noxiis ejectis, civitate in
pristinam dignitatem studiis & sanctis moribus restituta,
monte Pietatis fundato, grata Vincentia posuit, M.CCCC.
LXXXVI. The roofe of this Praetorium is hollow as that
of Padua, having many yron beames that come athwart
or a crosse from one side to the other, as that of Padua.

The outward roofe is covered with lead. In each side above is a faire gallery adorned with goodly pillars: likewise each side beneath hath a walke garnished with marveilous faire great pillars, sixe being compacted together in one, which doe make a faire arch: of which arches there are nine: one of these lower walkes is thoroughly finished, viz. the northerne by the market-

[p. 295.] place: but not that in the South side; when I was in Vicenza, they were building very diligently every day to end the same: which without doubt will be a most beautifull walke when it is once brought to perfection, and it will yeelde a great ornament to the Praetorium. So then of all these faire walkes high and low, which belong to the Palace there are foure. Also there are two or three paire of stately staires that leade up to the hall.

A marvellous Neare unto this Palace there is a Tower of a marveilous *slender tower.* heigth, as high (in my opinion) as that famous Tower of Cremona or St. Markes of Venice, but so exceeding slender that I never saw any Tower in all my life so high of such a slendernesse.

There are foure very memorable things to be seene in this citie: the Monastery of the Dominican Fryers, the Palace of the Count or Earle Leonardus Walmarana, his Garden neare to the west gate that leadeth to Verona, and

The monastery a famous Theater, built anno M.D.LXXXIIII. In the *of the* Monastery of the Dominican Friers is to be seene the *Dominican* thorny crowne of our Saviour Jesus Christ (as they say) *Friars.* which St. Lewes King of France, anno 1259. bestowed upon his brother at Paris, who hapned afterward to be Bishop of Vicenza, and a Dominican Frier. They report that he was the man that bestowed this crowne upon the Monastery. In my notes of Paris I have written something of this crown. For in Paris they say that they have the thorny crown: and here in Vicenza the Dominicans most constantly affirme, that none hath it or can have it but themselves: eyther they must prove that Christ had two severall crowns of thornes put upon his head (which is contrary to the history of the Evangelists) or else it must

ES

1. In each side
dly pillars: like-
garnished with
being compacted
e arch: of which
lower walkes is
e by the market-
when I was in
ently every day to
t will be a most
ught to perfection,
to the Praetorium.
gh and low, which
Also there are two
ade up to the hall.
wer of a marveilous
at famous Tower of
, but so exceeding
n all my life so high

: ngs to be seene in
min ican Fryers, the
dus Walmarana, his
deth to Verona, and
XXXIIII. In the
is to be seene the
Christ (as they say
no 1259. bestowed
ed afterward to be
Frier. They report
is crowne upon the
e writ ten something
that they have the
e Dominicans most
or can have it but
hat Christ had two
his head (which is
sts) or else it must

OBSERVATIONS OF VICENZA

needes follow that one of these crownes is false. Never-
thelesse I went thither to see it for my mindes sake, but I
could not possibly obtaine the favour, though the Friers
otherwise used me very courteously, affirming that it was
never shewed to any man whatsoever but upon Corpus [p. 296.]
Christi day, and that it was kept under three locks. One
of the Monkes shewed me a very memorable thing in this
Monastery. For he brought me into their kitchin, and *The monastery kitchen.*
told me, that where the chimney is, even where their
meate is wont to be rosted and sodde, certain Arrians
heretofore lived, their principall Master reading from a
chaire that stood in the same place, the Arrian doctrine
to his disciples and followers: but at last the holy Bishop
Bartholomew (of whom I have already spoken) chaced
them out of the Citie, and in their roome placed the
Dominicans.

The Palace of the Earle Leonardus Walmarana seemeth *Earl Leonard's palace.*
to be a very magnificent building, if the inside be correspondent to the front next to the street. For that front
is very beautifull, having much pointed diamond worke
about the bottome, and about the toppe many pretty
histories curiously cut in stone. Under one history is
written, Ars superat naturam: under another where grey-
hounds are most exquisitely carved, these two Greeke
wordes are written κάλλιστος πόνων, whereby is meant that
hunting is the most generose and noble exercise of all
others. Both these emblemes are made on the right
hand as you go into the house. On the left hand this
under a fine historicall worke. Ubi periculum, ibi
festinandum. Againe over the dore this noble and most
remarkable inscription is written very faire in stone:
Maria Austria Augusta, Caroli Quinti, Maximiliani
Secundi, Rodolphi Secundi Imperatorum filia, uxor, mater,
à Philippo fratre Hispaniarum Rege Potentisimo, ad
regendum Lusitanorum quondam Regum Imperium nuper
partum, è Germaniâ accita per Italiam iter faciens, in his
aedibus, quòd ipsa ob veterem Austriacorum Principum
erga hanc domum clientelam maximè volvit, cum Mar-

garita Maximilianoque filiis Archiducibus, á Leonardo Walmarana Comite eodemque Philippi Regis Pensionario, splendidissimo apparatu accepta fuit. Anno. M.D. LXXXI. IV. Kal. Octobris.

[p. 297.]
*Earl
Leonard's
garden.*

The third is the Garden of the foresaid Earle Leonardus, which is so delectable and pleasant that it seemeth a second Paradise. At the entrance of it over the first gate I read this inscription in Capitall letters.

Civis. Amice. Advena.
Qui loci amœnitate cupis oblectarier,
    Securus huc ingredere,
Teque largitèr recrea.
Nullus intus canis, nullus Draco ;
Nullus falce minaci Deus.
Omnia sed tuta, benigneque
        Exposita.
Sic volvit Comes Leonardus
    Walmarana Hortorum Dominus,
Modestiam quòd tuam & Con-
    tínentiam Custodem fore fi-
dat optimum. Anno M.D.XCII.

After I came into the garden I turned on the right hand, and descended into a very pleasant and delicious walke,

*The second
inscription.*

at the entrance whereof I read this second inscription made in stone over a faire gate.

Si te imprudentem graviores
        Fortè
Huc usque insequutæ sunt
        Curæ,
Eas velint nolint procul
Nunc ut abeant facito.
Hilaritati namque & Genio
    Pars hæc potiss. dicata est.

Againe, having passed through that gate and walke which was but short, I entred into a third walke of a notable length (for it was at the least two hundred paces

6

long) beset with most delightfull trees on both sides. At the entrance of this walke there standeth another stately gate, over the which I read this third inscription, which indeede is most witty and elegant. *The third inscription.*

> Cedros hosce qui dempserit,   [p. 298.]
> Floresve carpserit,
> Is Sacrilegus esto ;
> Vertumnoque & Pomonæ,
> Queis sunt sacri,
> Pœnas luito.

In both sides of this walke I saw Cedar trees, Orange, *Fruit trees.* Lemmon, and Pome-citron trees, and fruits of all these kindes ripe. Amongst the rest I observed passing faire Citrons, which made my mouth even water upon them, and caused me almost to transgresse his law. One side of the walke is invironed with a goodly wall, by the which the fruits doe grow. About the middle of the walke there is built a pretty convenient house, wherein tame connies and divers sorts of fine birds are kept, as Turtles, &c. In the middle of the garden is built a faire round roofe, supported with eight stately pillars of white stone, it is said that it shall be all covered with lead, but it was not when I was there. Also I saw a fine Labyrinth made *A fine* of boxe, but the dore was locked that I could not get in. *labyrinth of* And many lofty Pine trees, but some of them were so *Box.* nipped with the cold frost and snow that fell the winter before, as those were in the king of Frances garden at the Tuilleries, that they were even starved. Also for the more addition of pleasure to the place, there is a sweet river full of fine fish running by that fruitfull walke, wherehence is ministred store of water to moisten the garden in time of drougth. Finally to conclude, such is the affluence of all delights and pleasures in this garden, that it is the most peerelesse and incomparable plot for the quantity that ever I saw.

The fourth and last memorable thing of this City is a *The Theatre* stately faire Theater, which was built by certaine Scholars *of Vicenza.*

7

in the yeare M.D.lxxxiiii. that were called Academici
Olympici, but why so called I know not. It hath an
Orchestra made in it according to the imitation of the

[p. 299.] Roman Orchestraes, which is at the lower end of the
degrees, or (as I may more properly terme them) benches
or seates, whereof there are fourteene, each above another,
compassing something more then halfe the Theater, and
contrived in the fashion of an halfe Moone. In that
Orchestra none sit but Noble and eminent persons. He
that shewed me this Theater told me that the Orchestra
and fourteen benches would containe about some three
thousand persons. The Scene also is a very faire and
beautifull place to behold. In this Theater was acted a
play for many yeares since with divers goodly shewes
before William Gonzaga Duke of Mantua, father to the
present Duke Vincentius Gonzaga. Againe, afterward

Muscovite
Ambassadors
entertained.

certaine Moscovite Ambassadors that came from Rome,
were very honourably entertained in this Theater with
musicke and a banquet. And after them certaine young

Japanese
noblemen.

Noblemen of that farre remote region in the East called
Japan or Japona, being descended of the bloud royall of
the Country, were received here with great state, at what
time Livius Pajellus a singular Orator pronounced an
eloquent Oration in praise of them. But one of the latest
great shewes that was made here was presented before the
forenamed that famous Earle Leonardus Walmarana, in
the yeare 1585. For at that time the Tragedy of
Sophocles, which is intituled Oedipus, was most excellently
acted in this Theater. The history of the acting whereof
is finely painted in the Court wal at the very entrance to

Inscription in
the Theatre.

the Theater. Over the three dores of which Court I read
these three inscriptions, written in Capitall letters.
    This over the first.
        Olympicis Excitamento.
    This over the second.
        Civibus Oblectamento.
    And this over the third.
        Patriæ ornamento.

8

OBSERVATIONS OF VICENZA

alled Academia
iot. It hath an
imitation of the
ower end of the
ne them) benches
.ch above another,
the Theater, and
Moone. In that
aent persons. He
that the Orchestra
about some three
s a very faire and
Theater was acted a
ers goodly shewes
antua, father to the
Againe, afterward
came from Rome,
this Theater with
hem certaine young
a in the East called
the bloud royall of
great state, at what
... pronounced in
But one of the latest
...sented before the
... Walmarana, a
the Tragedy of
was most excellently
the acting whereof
very entrance to
which Court I read
pitall letters.

ento.

to.

In the front of the Scene, directly opposite to the [p. 300.]
Orchestra, this is written:

Virtuti ac Genio
Olympicorum Academia
Theatrum hoc â funda
mentis erexit, Anno
M. D. LXXX. IIII
Andrea Palladio Architecto.

Without the City also are two most stately and goodly
things to be seene. Whereof the first is a very magnificent
arch built about the end of the City, southward as you
goe up to the hill Bericus. The other is the Palace of *The palace of*
the Earle Odoricus Capra. The arch certainly is a very *Earl Odoric.*
sumptuous monument being of a lofty heigth, and supported with foure portly marble pillars, two on one side,
and as many on the other. At the top standeth the winged
Lyon in white stone, and at both the endes of the toppe
two statues also of white stone are erected. In the front
of the outside of the arch, this is written under the
Lyon.

Deiparæ Virgini Berici
Montis
Jacobus Bragadeno Am
bross. F. Præf. Religionis
& urbis amantiss. D.
M. D. XCV.

After I was entred within this arch, I ascended a mar- *Marvellous*
vailous high paire of staires, much higher then those that *high stairs.*
I have mentioned in my description of Lyons. For they
are of that heigth that they will make a weake body utterly
weary before he can attaine to the toppe. For they containe no lesse then a hundred and fifty greeses. And you
must ascend by five greeses at a place till you come to the
toppe, the severall partitions being in number thirty.
Truly they are the highest staires that ever I trode in my
life out of a Church or house. At the left hand of the [p. 301.]

ascent a little after I was entred within the arch, I read this inscription in a stony pillar.

Quis ascendet in montem sanctum tuum?

In another pillar on the right hand, this ·

Innocens manibus & mundo corde.

After I was come almost to the toppe, I found this inscription in a stony pillar on the left hand.

Franciscus Bernardinus
Saracenus
Scalas fecit ex stipe
publicè privatìmque
Collata,
& viam reliquam
ad Mariæ templum usque
silice promovit.
c I ɔ I ɔ c.

And this inscription in another stony pillar on the right hand.

Hospes si properas,
Paulúm sistito,
Urbis, collium, fluminum,
Agrorum, Alpium aspectu
Laborem lenito.
Abi. perge pius,
Dei matrem Virginem
Salutato.
Stratæ viæ commodum
Piis precibus rependito.

The Temple of the Virgin Mary. After I had ascended those staires I went to the Temple of the Virgin Mary, seated upon the toppe of the hil, and about a mile distant from the City. All the Monkes that dwell here are meerely lay-men. In the Moneth of August when I was there, this Monastery was exceedingly frequented with people, and so it is every yeare in the same Moneth. For they hold this opinion and doe very confidently maintayne it, that by the prayers which godly [p. 302.] people doe make in the Church of that Monastery that Moneth, one soule shall be redeemed out of Purgatory forsooth. Infinite are the votive tables that I saw hanged about the walles of this Church. I saw many indeede at the Altar where our Lady is worshipped at the Arsenal, and in other places of Venice, but never a quarter so many in one place as here. I walked into the Cloyster of the Monks, and into a high gallery at the toppe of the Monastery, where they have a passing sweet prospect. Surely they dwell in as convenient a place for a retired life as any I saw in Italy, nay none comparable to it. They say that many miracles are shewed in this Monastery.

The other memorable thing without the City, is the sumptuous Palace of the above named Earle Odoricus Capra, which is a little mile distant from the City. It is built upon a prety eminent hillocke, and is round (in which respect it is called in the Italian Rotonda) having foure very beautifull fronts, which doe answere the foure parts of the world. At the East front as I ascended to *The arms of* the house, I saw three white statues erected, and under *Earl Odoric.* them the picture of a blacke Goate which is his armes. Under the which I read this.

> Scriptum
> Memoriæ perpetuæ
> Mandans hæc
> Dum sustinet & abstinet.

At the West end under another scutchin this is written.

> Qui ædes has arctissimo
> Primogenituræ gradui
> Subjecit.

At the North side this under a third scutchin.

> Una cum omnibus censibus,
> Agris, vallibus, & collibus
> Ultrâ viam magnam.

11

[p. 303.] In the South side this under the fourth scutchin.

Marius Capra
Gabrielis F.

Every front hath sixe most stately great pillars, and two paire of staires to ascend to the same, each contayning eighteene faire greeses. The roofe of the house is round, and very pretily adorned partly with curious pictures, and partly with statues, which worke was contrived by the *An open roof.* elegant pensill of Alexander Magantia. Also the roofe is open for the raine to descend into a very convenient place made of purpose in the hall for the receiving thereof. In one of the higher chambers there is the fairest chimney for clavy and jeames that ever I saw, saving that of the King of France at his Palace of Fountaine Beleau before mentioned. For it was made of an extraordinary fine coloured marble, beautified with faire veines of divers colours. This marble came from Verona. In another chamber I saw a clavy and jeames of touch stone, and a *A stately* table boord of the same : also there is a stately celler under *cellar.* the Palace, the roofe whereof is vaulted. At the farther end of this cellar as you go forth of it into a faire vineyard, this impresse is written over the dore in great letters.

Antrum non Cumæum
Neque Homericum videbis,
Sed Bacchi ;
Hospes ingredere,
Lætior abibis ;

But I found not the words of the inscription true ; for I went not out more merily then I came in, because the cellarer had not the honestie to bestowe as much as one draught of his wine upon me.

The Bishop's I was at the Palace of the Bishop of Vicenza whose *Palace.* name is Dionysius Delphinus. In this Palace is the towne prison.

This City was much annoied by the army of that *[p. 304.]* mercilesse Barbarian Attila, with many other famous cities

12

scutchin.

at pillars, and two
; each contayning
the house is round,
rious pictures, and
s contrived by the
in. Also the roofe
a very convenient
ie receiving thereof.
s the fairest chimney
, saving that of the
ntaine Beleau before
n extraordinary fine
re veines of divers
erona. In another
f touch stone, and a
a stately celler under
··· At the farther
··to a faire vineyard,
: in great letters.

debis,

··ption true; for I
··e in, because the
··e as much as one

of Vicenza whose
Palace is the towne

··he army of that
··ther famous cities

of Italy, after hee came out of his country of Scythia to spoyle the Europæan Cities. Also the Emperour Fredericke the second besieged it about the year a thousand two hundred and forty, and afterward having entred it by force of armes, he defaced a great part of it with the furie of the fire.

For the sight of most of these notable things that I enjoyed in this faire citie, I doe acknowledge my self exceedingly beholding to two Italian yong Gentlemen *Two courteous* that were Vicentines borne, whose names were Thomas *Italian* de Spanivellis, and Joannes Nicoletis; especially to one *gentlemen.* of them, who kept me company almost all that day that I spent there, and conducted me from place to place till he had shewed me all the principall things of the citie. For surely many Italians are passing courteous and kinde towards strangers, of whose humanitie I made triall in divers other cities in Italie, as Padua, Venice, Verona, Brixia, Bergomo, &c. Therefore I will ever magnifie and extoll the Italian for as courteous a man to a stranger as any man whatsoever in Christendome. For I have had a little experience in my travels of some of every principall nation of Christendome.

The first that converted this Citie from Paganisme to Christianitie, was Prosdocimus that preached the Gospell first at Padua, as I have before mentioned.

The Vicentines were first subject to the Signiorie of Venice about the yeare 1404. at what time they submitted themselves of their own accord to the Venetians.

That day that I came forth of Vicenza, being Thursday and the eleventh day of August, I saw a franticke and *A frantic* lunaticke fellow runne up and downe the citie with a *lunatic.* gowne about him, who kept a very furious stirre, and drew many people about him.

The West gate of the Citie that leadeth to Verona, hath a very lofty Towre of a goodly heigth, and without [p. 305.] the same on the left hand, I saw a marvailous sumptuous gate made of free-stone, and newly built, but not fully finished. All the front is contrived with pointed diamond

13

CORYAT'S CRUDITIES

worke. At that place there is nothing at all built but only this gate. This charge me thinkes might have beene well saved, for it serves for no other purpose but onely for a beautifull entrance into a faire meadow.

Vicenza famous for counts and knights.

I will now conclude my observations of Vicenza with two memorable Italian sayings, the one of the Counts and Knights of Vicenza, which is this:

Quanti hâ Venetia ponti e Gondolieri,
Tanti hâ Vicenza Conti e Cavallieri.

That is, looke how many bridges and Gondoleers Venice doth yeeld, so many Counts, and Knights doth Vicenza.

The wine of Vicenza.

The other, of the wine of Vicenza, which is in a manner proverbially spoken of, as other commodities are of other Italian cities, viz.

Vin Vicentin,
Pan Paduan.
Tripe Trevizan.
Putana Venetian.

That is, The Wine of Vicenza,
The Bread of Padua.
The Tripes of Treviza.
The Cortezans of Venice

Thus much of Vicenza.

I Departed from Vicenza about tenne a clocke in the morning, the eleventh day of August being Thursday, and came to Verona the next day about nine of the clocke in the morning: The things that I observed bewixt Vicenza and Verona are these. Most of the horsemen that I met were furnished with muskets ready charged, and touch-boxes hanging by their sides full of Gunpowder, together with little pouches full of bullets; which is a thing so commonly used in most places of Italie, that a man shall scarce finde a horseman in any place riding without them. I heard that this is the reason of it· because the people of the country are so given to villainies,

Armed horsemen between Vicenza and Verona.
[p. 306.]

14

ᴛES

? at all built but
might have beene
purpose but onely
adow.

is of Vicenza with
of the Counts and

Gondolieri,
Cavallieri.

1 Gondoleers Venice
ghts doth Vicenza
which is in a manner
modities are of other

∴a
∴ce
∴za

∴e a clocke in the
∴t being Thursday,
∴: nine of the clock
I observed bewitt
∴: of the horsemen
∴ers ready charged,
∴full of Gunpowder,
∴bullets; which is a
∴es of Italie, that a
∴n any place riding
the reason of it:
∴given to villainie,

that they will rob, rifle, and murder passengers, if they are not sufficiently provided to defend themselves against them. At every miles end by the way for the space of tenne or twelve miles, I saw certaine pretty stony pillars* *Pillars erected* erected by the high way side, such as we call in Latin *by the wayside.* cippos, whereof some had Inscriptions, some had not, which I suppose were set up for many yeares since, even in the time of the Roman Monarchie to limit their miles. whereupon many auncient Latin authors whensoever they would mention a place of Italie distant certaine miles from a citie, would say, decimo &c lapide ab urbe distat. Some of the Inscriptions of these pillars were so auncient and even eaten out with time, that I could hardly reade above two or three letters of them: Perhaps they were set up before, or not long after, Christs incarnation. Againe some had crosses on them as being erected by Christians. On the right hand as I travelled to Verona, I saw three very stately and strong castels upon hils, adorned with goodly battlements, &c. whereof one, which stood almost in the middle way betwixt Vicenza and Verona, was built by the Princely familie of the Scaligers of Verona, as a certaine grave Gentleman tolde me that I overtooke riding upon the way, who discoursed with me very familiarly of many matters in Latin: the same castle is now possessed by the noble Contarens of Venice.

The territories of Vicenza and Verona doe confine and meete together about a place called Turre, which is but *Turre.* one solitarie inne, so called because the signe thereof is a tower. This is thirteene miles beyond Vicenza. About [p. 307.] nine miles on this side Verona I sawe a most magnificent Palace not about half a mile distant from the way on the left hand. I was told that it belonged to a Venetian Clarissimo, called Peter Gritti.

That day about five of the clocke in the afternoone *A violent* there fell a marvailous violent showre after I was past *shower.* about some two miles beyond Villa nova, which is seven-teene miles from Vicenza, that continued almost for the

* These kinde of pillars Plutarch doth call σημεῖα in Vita Gracchi.

15

space of three miles, even till I came to my lodging, and made me wet to the very skinne, that I did even rigere frigore.

I observed great abundance of vineyardes on both sides of the way, and exceeding fertile Champaines, goodly meadowes, pastures, corne fieldes, and arable groundes both betwixt Padua & Vicenza, & also betwixt Vicenza and Verona. Onely I saw one speciall commodity wanting, wherwith (God be thanked) England is so abundantly furnished, as no place (I think) in al Christendome more, being indeed a thing exceeding necessary for the sustentation of mans life, as any other thing whatsoever that God hath given unto man, viz. sheepe. For I remember I saw but three little flockes in all the way betwixt Padua, and Verona, which are forty eight miles distant.

Sheep wanting.

Within a mile of Verona on the left hand of the way there is a faire little Monastery that belongeth to the order of those Monkes that are called Camaldulenses, which doe weare white gownes and cowles of the same. There are but eight of the Fraternity, their Church is very faire, and they have a Cloyster that invironeth almost their whole Monastery, round about adorned with many beautifull pillars, whereof I told twenty eight of a great bignesse.

[p. 308.]

My Observations of Verona.

Julius Cæsar Scaliger hath written these verses upon
Verona.

Scaliger's verses upon Verona.

ITaliæ canimus semper florentis ocellum,
   Calliope nequeat grandiùs ulla loqui.
Aucta deis, auctura poli Verona Quirites;
   Quot cives, tot habens sydera digna Jove.
Non animi, non ingenii vigor acrior usquam,
   Nulla creat plures Martia terra duces.
Transferre in cœlum volvit sibi Jupiter, atquI
   Clarior in nostris malvit esse locis.

The antiquity of Verona.

This citie is of that antiquitie, that some do write it was first founded by the ancient Hetruscans and hath

16

my lodging, and
I did even rigen

.rdes on both sides
aampaines, goodly
d arable grounde
so betwixt Vicenza
ll commodity want-
and is so abundanth
Christendome more,
ary for the sustenta-
whatsoever that God
For I remember I
way betwixt Padua,
miles distant.

left hand of the way
xelongeth to the order
Camaldulenses, which
of the same. Then
: Church is very faire,
;:::::::h almost this
!.: with many beauti-
!:: of a great bignesse.

Verona.

these verses upon

l:s ocellum,
l.!'a loqui.
[Q::ir:tes;
d:gna Jove.
=or usquam,
{ duces.
l-:piter, atqui
r.:.,
'ocis.

l some do write t
t truscans and hath

beene in times past accounted one of their twelve cities
on this side the Apennine mountaines. But afterwards
in processe of time, the Gaules that are called Senones,
having passed over the Alpes under the conduct of their
Captaine Brennus, came into this part of Italy, and ejected
those Hetruscans out of the possession thereof, and greatly
amplified and enlarged the same. So that it was called
Verona quasi Brenona, from their Captaine Brennus. But
there are some that write, that it had the denomination of
Verona from Vera, the name of a noble familie amongst
the Hetruscans. Surely it is a very delectable, large, and
populous citie, and most sweetely seated: for the noble
river Athesis runneth by it which Virgil calleth amœnus,
as   §————Athesin ceu propter amœnum.

It issueth out of the Alpes not far from the city of Trent.
This river yeeldeth a speciall commoditie to the citie. *The river Adige.*
For although it be not able to beare vessels of a great
burden, yet it carrieth pretty barges of convenient quantitie, wherein great store of Merchandise is brought unto [p. 309.]
the city, both out of Germany and from Venice it selfe.
In one side of this river, I told nineteene water-mils, which
were like to those that I saw upon the river Rhodanus at
the city of Lyons. There are foure bridges which joyne
together both the bankes of the river, whereof one is very
faire and beautifull above the rest. By the sides of that
bridge that I passed over when I entred into the city from
Vicenza, I observed two faire stones of white marble *Stones of white marble.*
opposite to each other, with armes and scutchins in
them: in that which is on the right hand I saw this
inscription.

Qui fluminis vim passus
annos plures jacuerat,
Civitatis ornamento,
& commodo
Pons tandem est restitutus.

§ Ænei. 9.

And under the same this:

Andrea Gritti Principe,
Francisco Foscaro Prætore,
& Hieronymo Zano prefecto.
an. Salutis M.DXXIX.

In that on the left hand this·

Fluminis impetu disjectum pontem
diligentiâ Joannis Æmi Prætoris
penè restitutum, Francisci Foscari
Successoris cura perfecit.

Also I noted a third stone of white marble, in which are
written certaine auncient characters of that antiquity that
I thinke no man can reade them; because indeede they
are partly defaced. A certain Italian young Gentleman,
unto whom I was much beholding for the sight of many
noble antiquities of this citie, told me that this river
The inunda- Athesis doth sometimes so extremely swell, that it hath
tions of the utterly overwhelmed all the bridges, and much annoyed
Adige. the citie. For testimony whereof he shewed me this
[p. 310.] memorable inscription written in the corner of a certaine
wall not farre from the river, which mentioneth a very
strange and unusuall inundation thereof.

Viator hæc hìc tabula
posita est ut perpetuò
sciri possit summas
nostri fluminis
aquas huc usque
pertigisse.
die xxx. Octobris
anno M. D. L xvii.
& siccitate &
diluviis infausto.

This Table is placed about twenty foote higher then
the bridge, according to my estimation, which argueth so
strange an inundation of the Athesis, that I doe not

remember I ever read of the like, saving once of the Tyber in the time of the Emperour Mauricius when S. Gregory was Pope. For then the Tyber so far exceeded his usuall bounds, that he overflowed the very walles of Rome.

The forme of the building of this citie is something like to that of Turin in Piemont : for it is almost square. The greatest part of it standeth in a plaine, and some part of it that bendeth to the South, is situate upon a hill, whereon are built two stately Castles, the one of S. Fælix, the other of S. Angelo; also it hath one more in the plain that standeth neare to the river : that of St. Felix is invironed with a faire bricke wall, which is adorned with battlements that yeeld so faire a shew, that from the west it is seene a great way off. All these Castles, especially those two on the hill, are passing well furnished with munition and artillery for the defence of the citie against the invasion of the enemy. The wals of the citie are the fayrest of all the Italian cities that I saw, and indeede fayrer then any I ever saw before in all my life. For they are of a marveilous heigth, in some places forty foot high, according to my estimation, built all with bricke, and fairely beautified with battlements. Also there are five gates in them of great antiquity, whereof some are garnished with curious carvings, images, and marble pillars. The compasse of the whole citie together with the suburbes is thought to be betwixt sixe and seven miles. Within these few yeares it is become very strong; for the Venetians doe daily strengthen it with wonderfull strong fortifications, rampiers, and bulwarkes, which they have incompassed with deepe and broad Trenches, so that it seemeth to be almost impregnable.

So many notable antiquities and memorable monuments are to be seene in this noble city of Verona, as no Italian citie whatsoever (Rome excepted) can shew the like. But the worthiest and most remarkable of all is the Amphitheater commonly called the Arena, seated at the South-west end of the city where cattell are sold; whereof I

The Castles of Verona.

The walls and gates.

[p. 311.]

The amphitheatre

19

have expressed a picture ın this place, according to the forme of it, as it flourished in the time of the Roman Monarchy. This word Amphitheater is derived from these two Greeke words ἀμφὶ which signifieth about, and θεῶμαι to behold, because which way soever a man doth view it, he findeth it of a circular and round forme. So that herein an Amphitheater differeth from a Theater, because an Amphitheater is every where round, but a Theater (according to the forme of the auncient Roman building) is but halfe round, being made in the fashion of an halfe circle or halfe Moone. The model of these kinde of Amphitheaters which the auncient Romanes built in Rome, and other places of Italy, was derived from the *Amphi-theatres first built by the Athenians.* Athenians, who were the first that erected an Amphitheater. Certainly this present building, whereof I now speak, is a most stupendious masse of worke;

> Non opus, at moles, qualem neque tota vetustas
> vidit, & haec ætas non habitura parem;

[p. 312.] To use those verses of it that one wrote in praise of the King of Spaines Palace at Escuriall in Spaine. For indeed it is such an admirable Fabricke that it draweth all strangers into admiration thereof : and I am perswaded that the beauty thereof after it was first built and throughly consummated, was so glorious, that it no lesse drew spectators from most of the principall places of the world to contemplate the excellency thereof, then that famous Temple of Vespasian in Rome, dedicated to Pallas, which is so highly commended by Josephus the Jew. It was reported unto me by Gentlemen of good note in this citie of Verona, that the like Amphitheater is not to be seene at this day in all Italy, no not in Rome it selfe. Neyther doe I thinke that antiquity could ever shew a fayrer piece *Verona amphitheatre very ruinous.* of worke for an Amphitheater; but it is very ruinous at this time. For the principall ornaments thereof are demolished and defaced. So that it hath lost more then halfe of its pristine glory : it is uncertaine who was the first founder thereof. That it was built by one of the

20

OBSERVATIONS OF VERONA

; according to the
ime of the Roma
:r is derived from
ignifieth about, and
soever a man doth
d round forme. S
:th from a Theater
where round, but i
the auncient Roma
nade in the fashion of
model of these kinde
nt Romanes built it
was derived from the
.t erected an Amphi
...ng, whereof I now
:f worke;

eque tota vetustas
).tura parem;

wrote in praise of h
:n Spaine. For indee
· that it draweth al
nd I am perswaded th
:: built and through
hat it no lesse dis
all places of the worl
:of, then that famou
:.red to Pallas, whic
:.s the Jew. It wa
good note in this citi
ter is not to be seen
:.e it selfe. Neythe
:r shew a fayrer pro
it is very ruinous a
iaments thereof as
hath lost more then
ertaine who was th
built by one of th

Roman Emperours every man beleeveth, but by whom no Chronicle, Annals, or auncient History doth certainly record.   But Torellas Sariana, a learned man borne in Verona, who hath written certaine bookes of the antiquities of this citie, is drawen by certaine arguments and conjectures to affirme, that it was built by the Emperour Augustus, and that in the two and fortieth year of his Empire, which was that very year that our blessed Saviour was borne into the world.   Were such a building to be made in England, I thinke it would cost at the least two millions of our pounds, that is, twenty hundred thousand pound, even as much as tenne of our fayrest Cathedrall Churches.   For it is all built with redde marble : which *Red marble.* although it were a very chargeable piece of workemanship ; yet they could build it as cheape there as in any part of al Italy.   For in the territory of Verona they have divers marble quarries, and that of sundry colours, as white, blacke, redde, &c.   It was dedicated to Janus, and hath as [p. 313.] yet many notable things to be seene, which do argue the singular beauty thereof when it flourished in his prime. For it was invironed with two round walles, whereof the outward was a thing of rare magnificence.   Which by the invasion of many barbarous people, as the Gothes, Hunnes, (who under the conduct of their King Attila sacked this city) and Longobards under their King *The* Alboinus, hath beene so ruinated, that there is but a little *amphitheatre* part thereof standing, the marble stones being pulled *destroyed* downe, and removed therehence, partly for the garnishing *by the* of the private houses of the city, and partly for other uses. *barbarians.* This, together with all the other partes of the machine, was built with redde marble, all the pieces being cut square which doe very excellently garnish the worke. That which remaineth at this day of the outward wall, though it be but little, doth testifie that it was a wondrous architecture.   For there are now standing three rankes or rowes of arches, and each row doth containe three severall degrees of arches more, built one above another, and raised to a wonderful heigth, at the least one hundred and

21

The arches. fifty foot high, according to my estimation. These arches were heretofore distinguished with stately pillars of redde marble answerable to the rest: and the highest degree of the third was most gloriously beautified with faire statues made of Corinthian worke, which were placed betwixt the pillars and the arches; every arch having two severall statues, so that to double the number of the arches, which are in al seventy, there were erected one hundred forty two statues: which yeelded a passing ornament to the wall. Again, these three degrees of arches were built of as many distinct formes of workmanship, namely the Corinthian, the Ionicke and the Doricke. Also above these foresaid degrees there was a fourth ranke of building, which was erected at the very toppe of all, viz. a degree of windowes made all open, without either glasse or any other thing in

[p. 314.] it. These corresponded the number of the arches, even seventy two, and served for the people to sit in, to the end they might the more conveniently behold the games

The outer and inner walls. and exercises in the Amphitheater. All this outward wal, whereof now there is but a little fragment left, onely those three ranks of three severall arches that I have already mentioned, did round about inviron the whole building (as I have before said) being some twenty foote distant from the inner wal. But the inner wal it selfe doth stand pretty well, and yeeldeth a most stately shew, though some parts of the toppe be something blemished. For all the arches doe as yet remaine, even seventy two; for I walked round about them, and tolde them all. Now whereas of the outward wal there were three degrees of arches, there are not above two in this outward wall, which stand directly one above another, so that the number of those above doth answere them beneath. And for the better grace of the worke there is inserted betwixt every arch a goodly pillar of red marble, the base whereof being made of the same matter, is five foot thicke, and the distance betwixt every couple of pillars is sixteene foote. The lower arches are now converted to very base and sordid uses. For they serve partly for stables to put horses and hay in, and partly

22

for tipling houses for poore folkes to sell wine in, and other necessaries. After I had exactly viewed all the outward parts, I was admitted into the inside by a fellow that gets his living altogether by shewing the same to strangers, and as soone as I came in, I was driven into great admiration. For I saw so many things as will make a stranger not a little wonder. There I observed the seates, or benches, made of redde marble, incompassing *Benches of red* the cavea, or plaine within it round about, and ascending *marble.* by degrees one above another to the very toppe, which are in number forty two: but the greatest part of the marble of these benches hath beene (to the great blemish of the work) carried away for many yeares since by those [p. 315.] barbarous people that have much eclipsed the glorious beauty of this building. Yet the gentlemen of Verona have within these few yeares something repayred it againe. For they have bestowed so great charges in mending them on both sides with new marble benches correspondent to the former, that those on the right hand cost them three-score thousand crownes, and those on the left sixe thousand, as a Gentleman of Verona told me that shewed me the particulars of the Amphitheater. These threescore *Great charges* and sixe thousand crownes being not the fiftieth part of *for mending.* the charge (as I thinke) that the whole building would cost, were it now to be built from the foundation, may give a man some conjecture what an infinite and excessive masse of money it cost in those dayes when it was first founded, though I beleeve their building was then much cheaper then now. Also these Gentlemen of Verona doe daily beautifie it with new addition of marble benches, because they have oftentimes great shewes exhibited here to the people upon festivall dayes, as running at Tilt, and other noble exercises, especially upon their Carnivall day, which is observed amongst them in the same manner as our Shrove-tuesday with us in England, being called Carnivall from the two Latin words, Caro and Vale, that is, farewell flesh, because after that day they eate no more flesh till Easter. These foresaid two and forty benches have in

23

The benches contained 23,000 people. former times contained three and twenty thousand people that were the spectators of the games played therein, a foote and halfe and no more being limited to every particular person. The higher bench is esteemed a hundred fourescore and three pearches in compasse, and that in the middle, namely the one and twentieth, a hundred and two and forty. Every pearch being ten foote long. Likewise from north to south it is thought to be three hundred and threescore foote long: and from east to west three hundred and forty foote broad. All that open and [p. 316.] void space at the toppe was wont to be covered over wholly with curtaynes at the time of their publique games, to the end to keepe off the scorching beate of the sunne, which otherwise would very much annoy the people. The galleries in the inside are contrived after a very strange manner, not unlike unto Labyrinths. For there are three degrees of them vaulted one above another, through the which both those that were above upon the benches did descend to goe forth of the roome, and they beneath *The rooms for the beasts.* ascended to their seates. Also I observed certaine roomes where the beasts were kept, with whom the Gladiatores were to fight. These roomes have at one end certaine little open places to let in the aire for the refreshing of the beasts, such as we call in Latin spiracula. The cavea or greene plaine in the middle is made in the forme of an egge, sharpe at the ends, and broade at the sides, very like to a pond that I have seene in one of Sir Francis Carewes gardens in Middlesex: and it is in length nine & thirty pearches, in bredth two and twenty and halfe. For I did exactly observe the length and bredth of it. Now it is divided in the very middest by a certaine kind of pale, like to that of our Tilt-yard at Whitehall, where the Venetian Gentlemen and Nobleman of Verona doe sometimes encounter at justs and tornaments. In the middest of this plaine divers spectacles and games were wont to be shewed in former times to the people, whereof some con- *Bloody fights.* sisted especially of a most bloudy kind of fight betwixt men and beasts, which was performed by their Gladiatores.

24

q
a
2
p

[

OBSERVATIONS OF VERONA

For according to the auncient custome of the Romans certaine enormous malefactors that had committed some capital crimes, being condemned to fight for their lives with wilde beasts, were in this place and such other (whereof Rome had many, as the Circus maximus, &c.) exposed with their swordes and targets, and such other weapons to the fury of savage beasts, as Lyons, Beares, Tigres, &c. if fortune favoured them so well that they slew [p. 317.] those beasts, then both their lives were saved, and also they had some reward bestowed upon them, which was commonly called brabium, in token of their victory. But if they were slaine by the beasts, it was esteemed as a just recompence for their wicked deserts. But to conclude this discription of the Amphitheater of Verona, it is a worke of such admirable magnificence that as I never saw the like before, so I thinke in al my future travels (which I determine God willing to undertake hereafter both in Christendome and Paganisme) I shall never see a fairer

Thus much concerning the Amphitheater.

ALso I saw the rudera of an auncient Theater which was *An ancient* a distinct building from the foresaid Amphitheater, *theatre.* upon a hill on the farther side of the Athesis, neare to the gardens of the Dominican Friers.

The Palace which doth now belong to the Capitano, was *The Palace of* heretofore the habitation of the Princely Scaligers: at the *Verona.* left hand of the porch whereof, which is a very magnificent and stately building, are three very faire arches made with free stone, and adorned with diamond worke. In the front of this building which is newly built, & looketh towards that goodly walke where there is a great meeting of Gentlemen and Merchants twise a day, this inscription is written over a dore betwixt two scutchins. Regia hujus superiorem utramque partem longâ incuriâ ruinam ita minitantem, ut penè reparationis desperationem cunctis adferret, Justinianus Contarenus Prætor, Franciscus Priulus Præfectus ab extremo vindicârunt occasu, & in longé splendidiorem faciem pristinâ restituêrunt c I ɔ. I ɔ. c I I.

25

Againe, betwixt two other dores neare unto this, there is written this also over the scutchins in the same front.

Virtuti & Honori

Julii Contareni Prætoris, & Bernardi Marcelli Præfecti, quorum singularis prudentia ut in regendâ urbe mirificè

emicuit: sic in maximâ rerum perturbatione bellicis apparatibus vacando, amborum vigilantia, celeritas, diligentia fuit suspicienda. c I ↄ. I ↄ. cvi.

Besides in the inside of the Palace I read this inscription written in a new wall that includeth part of the court betwixt two golden scutchins over the dore. Atrii hujus quod conficiendum supererat, ne suo ornamento destitutum squaleret, Justinianus Contarenus Prætor, & Daniel Delphinus Præfectus, unanimes omni cultu perfectum D. M. D. CIII.

In another wall of the court right opposite unto this, many Noblemens armes are very gallantly painted, amongst the rest the spread-Eagle about the toppe of the wall, under which this is written. Aquilæ bicipitis pectori Justinianorum prisci stemmatis quæ cernis affixa insignia. Mapheus Justinianus dum pro Veronensibus contra Bebracenses strenué pugnat, parto hostium vexillo hæc sibi bellicâ virtute vendicavit, M. C C. L.

In a lower roome which is on the right hand of the court as you come in from the street, I observed great store of munition, especially great pieces of Ordinance upon wheeles, and lesser, as sakers, &c. that roome being wholly replenished with furniture for war-fare.

The Piazza or the publike walke without the Palace is a faire place, paved al with bricke. In length it is threescore and seven paces: in bredth five and forty. And it is on every side inclosed with goodly buildings. At the East with the Prætors Palace, at the West with a certaine goodly auncient building that serveth for publique uses. At the South with the Præfectus Palace, at the North with the Councell house, which is a very faire building, having foure beautifull windowes in the front, and a goodly walke

: unto this, there i
the same front.

ı Marcelli Præfeɛ
egendâ urbe mirin
batione bellicis app
ı, celeritas, diligenʃ

: I read this inscripti
eth part of the cow
the dore. Atrii huiʃ
ı ornamento destitutæ
Prætor, & Daniel Dɛ
‒‒‒ perfeɛtum D. Yʃ

ʒhɛ opposite unto th
ʌery gallantly painteɛ
ɛ about the toppe of tl
Aquılæ bicipitis pastœ
‒ɛ ɛɛmis amica insigni
‒ɛɛɛɛɛbus contra Belœ
‒ɛ‒ vexillo hæc sl
ɛ L.
ɛ ‒ʃɛ hand of the cow
ɛ ʃerved great store ɛ
ɛ ɛf Ordinance upʌ
ɛ ɛɛ roome being whilʃ
ɛ ‒ɛ‒
ɛ ʌithout the Palace is
ɛ In length it is three
ɛ and forty. And it i
ɛ ʃildings. At the Eaʃ
ɛ Veʃt with a certain
ɛ ʃh for publique use
ɛ ɛe, at the North wɛ
ɛ ʃire building, havinɛ
ɛ and a goodly walɛ

adorned with nine stately pillars of blew and porphyrie marble that make eight faire arches.   Over the gate of the Councell house this inscription is written above two golden scutchins :   Ubique simul.   [p. 319.]

And againe, this under the same in golden letters upon an azure ground.   Pro summa
                                                   fide
                              Summus amor
                              M. D. XCII.

Also the higher part of the front is garnished with five *Five beautiful* beautiful marble statues of certaine famous learned men *statues.* borne in this noble City, who with the excellent monuments of their wit have much ennobled their Country. The first is of Marcus Vitruvius, who hath written ten bookes of Architecture, being next to the Palace wall of the Prætor.   Next to him, Valerius Catullus the Poet. The third Caius Plinius the Historiographer.   The fourth Æmylius Macer the Poet that wrote certaine poems of hearbes.   The last, Cornelius Nepos an eloquent Poet in the time of Cicero.   Also there is another of Hieronymus Fracastorius, erected over a stately arch that standeth at the west end of the Councell house.

I saw the monuments of two of the noble Scaligers of *Monuments of* Verona in a little Churchyard, adjoyning to the Church *the Scaligers.* called Maria Antiqua, but a little way distant from that Palace, where they lived in former times, which now belongeth to the Venetian Capitano, as I have before said. The fairest whereof is that of Mastinus Scaliger, standing at one corner of the Churchyard, which is such an exceeding sumptuous Mausoleum that I saw not the like in Italy. It is supported with six stately pillars of porphyrie marble, without the which are six sumptuous pillars more very curiously wrought with pretie works and borders.   At the toppe of which outward pillars are certaine little pinnacles, each whereof sustaineth an image of an armed man made in alabaster.   Also above those six pillars there is a marvailous rich worke made of alabaster, whereon

27

[p. 320.]

there stand more images very exquisitely carved. Upon the toppe of all, even upon a little pinnacle standeth the statue of Mastinus Scaliger himselfe on horsebacke made of alabaster. It doth very neare represent the living shape of him. For it is said that it was made in his life time. In the lower part of the monument this Epitaph is written.

Mastinus Scaliger.

S Caligera de gente fui, celebrique ferebar
  Nomine Mastinus, claras dominabar in urbes.
Me Dominum Verona suum, me Brixia vidit,
Parmaque cum Luca, cum Feltro Marchia tota.
Jura dabam populis æquo libramine nostris
Omnibus, & fidei, & Christi, sine sorde secutor.
Occubui primò post annos mille trecentos
Et decies quinque, heu, lux ibat tertia Juni.

The other monument is of Canis Grandis, or Magnus Scaliger, which standeth in another corner of the same Churchyard right opposite unto this, the same being a very magnificent thing adorned with many pillars and statues of marble, but something inferiour to this. There also is this Epitaph.

Magnus Scaliger.

S I Canis hic grandis ingentia facta peregit,
  Marchia testis adest quam sævo Marte subegit,
Scaligeram qui laude domum super astra tulisset,
Majores si Parca dies infida tulisset ·
Hunc Julii geminata dies undena peremit,
Jam lapsis septem quater annis mille trecentis.

Also there is a third monument of another Scaliger Prince, called Canis Signorius; which is erected directly over the Church dore, the Epitaph whereof I could not perfectly reade.

This City in the time of the Roman Monarchy was a long time subject to the Romans. Afterward it was possessed by the Ostrogothes, and after them by the Longobardes, whose first King Alboinus kept his Court here. At last they gave place to the successors of Carolus Magnus, as Pipin his sonne, Prince Berengarius and

The possessors of Verona.

28

others, that kept their Court here. After them, it came [p. 321.]
into the hands of the Tyrant Ezzelinus: who being again
dispossessed, these Scaliger Princes (of whom I have before
spoken) and others of the same family had the soveraigne
dominion of this City for the space of two hundred yeares,
till Joannes Galeatius Viscount of Milan abrogated their
governement in the time of Antonius Signorius Scaliger
about the yeare 1396. After which time the said Galeatius swayed Verona eighteene yeares. But as soone as he
was dead, one of the Scaligers recovered it againe. The
same being made away with poyson, Francis Carrarius
enjoyed the Principality halfe a yeare. But the Venetians
being exasperated against him for Scaliger's unnaturall
death, deposed him againe about the yeare 1405. and
governed the same till the yeare 1509. Then it was seven
yeares subject to the Emperour Maximilian, who in the
yeare 1517. restored it to the Venetians, that have continually from that time to this present day enjoyed the
possession thereof.

The principall market place of the City is very faire, *The principal market place.*
which I take occasion to mention by reason of a notable
thing that I observed there tending to idolatry. For on
the front of a faire house adjoining to this market place,
there standeth the image of the virgin Mary, made in
white marble with Christ in one arme, and a booke in one
of her hands. Under the which this superstitious inscription is written concerning the adoration of the same
image.

Quisquis
Sacram hanc B. M. Imaginem
Sole occidente
Comprecatus fuerit,
Huic
Centum dies
Ex eâ pœnitentiâ
Quam acturus erat,
Indulgentur. [p. 322.]
Francisco Veritate Com. Prætore. cIɔ.Iɔ.c.vii.

29

A little above this inscription this is written in gold letters.

Diplomate Pauli V. Pontificis Maxi.

Againe on the right hand of the image this.

Mariæ
Quæ est maxima,
Virgini, Christi matri,
Auxiliatrici, Conservatrici,
Placidæ, propitiæ, secundæ,
Quam quotidiè statâ horâ
Prostrati homines adoranto ;
Incorporati omnes negociatores
Stipe collata
Signum hoc marmoreum,
P. Paulo Malaspina Præt.
Inchoatum
Vincentio Manuello Juriscon. Præf.
Perfectum
Poni curaverunt
Reverendissimi

Joannes Baptista Arnoldus, Joannes Baptista Tachetus, Joannes Pona, Franciscus Lutiascus, Natalis Roccaius, Laurentius Tudeschinus, cIɔ.Iɔ.c.vii. Cal. Augusti.

A pleasant fountain. Also I saw about the middle of the same market place a marvailous pleasant fountaine, adorned with a very ancient marble image, wearing a crowne upon her head; that is said to be a representation of Verona. From divers spouts of this statue, jugis aquæ fons doth incessantly flow. Besides, at the higher end of this market place there is erected a very stately marble pillar with the winged Lyon advanced upon it. And in a Gentlemans house of the City but a little way from that, I saw a very beautifull paire of winding stayres, made by that singular architect Andreas [p. 323.] Palladius, which by reason of the curious workemanship thereof are much shewed to strangers.

There are some Jewes in this city, though not so many as in Venice or Padua, who are shut up from the Christians

30

OBSERVATIONS OF VERONA

in their Ghetto by three gates; upon one whereof, which *The Ghetto of the Jews.* standeth at one end of their street, I read this inscription. Auctore Patre nostro piissimo Augustino Valerio Cardinali optimo, Judæi hunc in locum publico Municipum Principisque decreto conclusi sunt: Julio Cæsare Nogarola Comite Antonio Fontanelo Jurisconsulto Gratia-Deo Rambaldo Cur. cIɔ.Iɔ.Ic. Catharino Zeno Prætore, Petro Mauroceno Præfecto. At another end is erected another gate right opposite unto this, at the toppe whereof this is written. Religionis ergô septum hoc ex Decurionum placito Senatusque Veneti authoritate decretum optimo savente Deo ac Augustino Valerio Cardinali amplissimo Pastoralibus officiis, adjuvante Catharino Zeno Prætore, Mauroceno Præfecto. Julii Cæsaris Nogarolæ Com. M. Antoni Fontaneli I c. Gratia-Dei Rambaldi Præsidum curâ perfectum conspicitur, cIɔ.Iɔ.Ic.

The buildings of this city, especially those that belong *The buildings of the city.* to the Gentlemen, are very faire, being for the most part built with bricke: though I have seene some of the Gentlemens houses built with passing faire stone, and richly adorned with many goodly marble pillars; the pentices or eavisses of their houses being much broader then I have observed in other cities. Also many of their outward walles and their chimneys are very fairely painted, which giveth great ornament to their houses. I observed one Palace amongst the rest beautified with a passing faire front, which was contrived wholy with pointed diamond worke. The like whereof I have before mentioned both in one of the outward bulwarks of the castle of Milan, & in the east front of the Duke of Venices Palace. But that diamond worke was made only in a little part of each front, [p. 324.] even about the lower end. But this whole front was adorned with it from the bottome to the very toppe, which yeelded admirable grace to the edifice.

In another front of one of their houses I read this prophesie of Christ, written under the picture of Sybilla Tyburtina. Virgo concipiet. *The Cathedral Church.*

I was in their Domo, which is their Cathedral Church

31

dedicated to our Lady; a very aunciént and goodly building, wherein are shewed some notable monuments. But that which is most of all esteemed and reverenced of the Citizens, is the Sepulchre of Pope Lucius the third of that name, which I saw. This Lucius died in Verona, Anno MCLxxxv. when he came thither to proclaime a generall Councell, Urban the third being substituted in his place. But that elegant Epitaph which is written upon his tomb I did not observe, being afterward bestowed upon me by a friend of mine, even this:

Luca dedit lucem tibi Luci, Pontificatum
Ostia, Papatum Roma, Verona mori.
Imò Verona dedit tibi verè vivere, Roma
Exilium, curas Ostia, Luca mori.

The fairest Organs that I saw in Italy or in any other country, are in this Domo.

The Bishop of Verona. The name of him that was Bishop of Verona when I was there, was Albertus Valerius, being successor to Augustinus Valerius, that was afterward made Cardinal. His Palace is neare to the Domo, the front whereof is very faire, having foure stately pillars of marble at the entrance, which are supported with two great square bases of the like marble, in one whereof this inscription is written:

Probis
Improbisque
Par aditus;
Dispar
Exitus.

[p. 325.]
Eupropius first preached the gospel in Verona. This city first received the Gospell by the preaching of Eupropius, who was sent thither from Rome by Saint Peter. Since which time they have had many godly and learned Bishops, whereof thirty sixe have bin canonized for Saints, by reason of the great holinesse of their lives. The chiefest of them all being Saint Zeno, the numen tutelare or protector of Verona, who was a godly Bishop of this citie, and a faithfull Martyr of Christ, who suffered

OBSERVATIONS OF VERONA

in the seventh persecution of the Church under the Emperour Decius, unto whom King Pipin above saide built a very sumptuous Church at the West end of the Citie, which is beautified with many goodly ornaments. In the front thereof about the entrance of the same many religious histories are presented in Alabaster. Also the first gate is a worke of great sumptuousnesse, being decked with many pretty little peeces of brasse, wherein many notable histories of the bible are passing curiously described : likewise at the sides of this gate there are carved two exceeding great Lyons in red Marble, that sustaine two goodly pillars. Within the Church there is an extraordinary great front made of porphyrie. In a low crypta or vault of this Church I saw the monument of Saint *Monument of* Zeno, & againe above neare to the quire his statue made *S. Zeno.* in stone with a miter upon his head. He is pourtrayed laughing and looking very pleasantly, in his left hand he held a reeden rod, the top whereof was pretily made with bone finely wrought, which indeed was nothing else but the top of his Crosier : at the ende hanged a counterfeited Trowte, in token that hee was much delighted in taking of Trowtes, as a Benedictine Monke tolde me. There I read this inscription, Anno Dom. trecentessimo primo Beatus Zeno moritur duodecima Aprilis.

I saw the monument of King Pipin whom I have before *Monument of* mentioned, the sonne of Carolus Magnus, in a little Cell *King Pipin.* adjoyning to this Church ; this sepulchre is supported with foure pretty pillars of marble. All strangers that are admitted to the sight of this tombe, doe first enter by a dore [p. 326.] that is most commonly locked, into a greene rude Court, and so descend by a paire of staires of some tenne or twelve greeses. There is great store of water oftentimes hard by the monument issuing out of the spring in the same place, as there was when I was there, which certaine Monkes tolde me is of great vertue to cure sundry diseases. This King dyed in Milan (as I have before said in my description thereof) but his body was afterward removed hither, and interred in this place, according to his owne

request in his death-bed. For Pipin so dearely loved
Verona, that he kept his royall Court sometimes therein.

A marble tabernacle.

In the quire of this Church I observed an admirable faire
marble tabernacle that belongeth to the Benedictine
Monks, the fairest that ever I saw made of marble. It is
beautified with two exceeding rich marble pillars, which
although they are but little, yet by reason of the admirable
curiosity of the worke formed therein by the hand of Dame
Nature her selfe, and distinguished with passing variety of
fine colours; they are esteemed so precious, that for them
and the tabernacle it selfe a certaine Gentleman of Venice
offered three thousand crownes, as one of the Monkes
told me.

Church of S. Anastasia.

I was in the Church of Saint Anastasia that belongeth
to the Dominican Fryers, a building of notable magnificence. In the body of the Church I observed twelve
exceeding huge pillars of marble which were the greatest
that ever I saw, even greater then those two famous pillars
of Phrygian marble in Saint Markes place in Venice, neare
to the Adriatique gulfe, which I have before mentioned in
my description of Venice. Sixe of these stand in one side
of the Church, and as many in another. At one side of
the Church I saw a marvailous faire monument of Janus
Fregosius Prince of Genua, adorned with foure most

[p. 327.]

sumptuous pillars of Alabaster, and an excellent image of
himselfe made of the same matter, with a trunchion in his
hand, and a crested helmet upon his head. At the top of
the monument this epitaph is written in Touchstone.

Deo Opt. Maxi.
Janus Fregosius Ligurum Princeps,
Ac Venetæ reipub : terrestrium copiarum
Omnium Præfectus, ubi fortissimi Ducis officia
Domi forisque præstitisset; Sac. H. T. F. I.
Hercules filius paternæ pietatis memor. F.

I observed foure passing beautifull pillars of a flesh-
coloured marble at one of the Altars of the body of this
Church, which are estimated at three hundred crownes a
peece.

34

OBSERVATIONS OF VERONA

In the Monastery of the Olivetan Benedictine Monkes which are attyred with white vailes made of a kinde of Say and copes of the same, I saw a most sumptuous paire of Organs, and a very admirable workemanship in certaine wainescot pillars in their closet, where their priest did put on his roabes for the celebration of masse.

Sumptuous organs.

Also I visited the Monastry of the Bartholomæan Monkes seated upon a hill on the farther side of the Athesis, and I observed their fountaines which they told me are of singular efficacie for the curing of certaine infirmities.

I was admitted into the most magnificent Palace of Count Augustinus Justus, but not without some favour. There I saw stones with very ancient inscriptions, which I could not reade by reason of the antiquitie of them. Also I was shewed a certaine higher roome in the Palace which was a place of that singular glory, that I saw not the like in any private house of Italy, the beauty thereof consisting especially of pictures which hanged round about the roome, beeing in number one hundred fifty nine, and such as represented some of the worthiest and most eminent persons of the world in divers ages. There I saw many of the Roman Emperours most exquisitely painted, and some of the German Emperors, and Kings of Spaine: also Kings of France: many Dukes of Venice, and divers Popes: of our English Kings but one, and that was King Henry the eighth. But the Italian painter erred, for the picture more truely represented Henry the seventh, then H. the eighth. There I saw the three famous Scaligers of Verona, whom I have before mentioned, Mastinus, Grandis Canis, and Canis Signorius; the pictures of sixe of the most renowned great Turkes. Of Totylas King of the Gothes. Of Alchitrof King of Æthiopia. Of Muleamet Scirisso King of Marocco. Of Scanderbeg. Of David de Degli Abissini the present Presbyter John. Of Tamberlan. Of Gattamelita the Generall of the Venetians land forces. Of Sinan Bascia a famous Captaine of the great Turke, and many other fine pictures representing

Palace of Count Augustinus Justus.

[p. 328.]
Many portraits.

Six great Turks.

35

persons of both sexes that will much delight a curious traveller. Therefore I counsell thee whatsoever thou art that meanest in thy travels to see Verona, to make meanes to bee admitted into the Palace of Count Augustinus Justus, and to see this noble and glorious roome before thou dost come forth of it: for many English gentlemen have seene it, as the Italian told me that shewed it to me.

The Palace garden. Also the Italian shewed me his garden, which is a second Paradise, and a passing delectable place of solace, beautified with many curious knots, fruites of divers sorts and two rowes of lofty Cypresse trees, three and thirty in a ranke. Besides his walkes at the toppe of the garden a little under St. Peters Castle, are as pleasant as the heart of man can wish; being decked with excellent fruites, as Figges, Oranges, Apricockes, and with Cypresse trees. In one of these walkes is a delicate litle refectory: at one side whereof there is a curious artificiall rocke, adorned with many fine devices, as scollop shels, and great variety of other prety shels of fishes brought from Cyprus: and mosse groweth upon the same as if it were a naturall rocke.

[p. 329.] This place certainely is contrived with as admirable curiosity as ever I saw, and moystened with delicate springs and fountaines conveighed into the same by leaden pipes. I have seene in England one place something like to this, even in one of the gardens of that noble knight Sir Francis Carew of Middlesex, who hath one most excellent rocke there framed all by arte, and beautified with many elegant conceits, notwithstanding it is somewhat inferiour unto this. Againe in another walke I saw his fine chappell, wherein his Chaplaine doth often say Masse to him.

A mournful spectacle. I observed a very mournefull shew performed by Monkes in Verona. For I saw eighteene couples of them accompany a corse of one of their Fraternity to Church, being attired with blacke buckram vailes, and marked with the signe of the starre on the left side of their breasts, girt with a blacke girdle, their heads covered with a blacke hood that came over all their shoulders, and hid all their face. Before their eyes were made two holes to looke out:

36

OBSERVATIONS OF VERONA

each of them carryed a burning candle in his hand of virgin wax, and some of them three candles, and there was put into every candle two peeces of their little tin money called gazets.

This citie was besieged by the Emperour Charlemaine shortly after the battell betwixt him and Desiderius the last King of the Longobardes neare the citie of Vercellis, whereof I have before made mention. At what time Adalgisius the sonne of the said Desiderius having escaped by flight from the foresaid battell, fortified himselfe herein together with Queene Berta the Wife of Carolomannus, who was the eldest brother of the Emperour Charlemaine. *The Emperor Charlemagne.*

But Charlemaine without any long siege got the citie into his possession, because the citizens yeelded themselves unto his mercy. Also it was besieged about one hundred and fourteene yeares after that time by the Emperour Arnolphus, who by Berengarius Duke of Forum Julii, now called Friuli (a Prince that sometimes in those daies kept his court in this city) was sollicited to come into Italy with an army of men to aide him in his warres against his great æmulus Guido Duke of Spoleto who contended with him for the Kingdome of Italy : but the citie received no great hurt by his siege ; for it quickly yeelded it selfe into the hands of the Emperour, as it did before to Charlemaine. [p. 330.]

Neare this citie was fought a great battell, anno 778. betwixt the Emperour Charles the second surnamed the Bald, and the two sonnes of his brother Lewes surnamed Germanicus, whose names were Caroloman and Charles : in this battell (which was fought about two years after the great battell waged at the towne of Andernach in Germany, which I will hereafter mention in my notes of the same place, betweene the said Emperour and his Nephew Lewes another of these Princely brethren) was the Emperour conquered by his Nephewes, and shamefully put to flight, shortly after the which he died in Mantua, as I have before written. *A great battle A.D. 778.*

Here Philippus Arabs, the first Christian Emperour was

37

CORYAT'S CRUDITIES

slaine by Decius the Captaine of his forces in Illyricum,
and afterward his successor in the Empire. Here also
Death of Alboinus the first King of the Longobards died an' un-
Alboinus. naturall death.   For whereas the said King, after he had
taken the famous citie of Pavie by a long siege out of
the hands of Longinus the first Exarch of Ravenna, kept
his court in this citie of Verona, and solaced himselfe
with feastes and banquets: he compelled his wife Rosa-
munda to drinke one day at table out of the *skull of her
father Cunimundus, whom a little before he had slaine:
for the which his Queene intending to be revenged upon
him for that most inhumane and barbarous injury, con-
spired with one Helmichildus a noble Longobard, to kill
the King her husband, with promise both to marry him
if he would execute the matter, & to bestow the Kingdome
of Lombardy upon him.   Whereupon Helmichildus being
[p. 331.] tempted with this faire offer, murdered Alboinus, as he
was asleepe in his bedde.   And so by this meanes he
obtained indeede the marriage of the Queene, but not
the possession of the Kingdome.   For being constrayned
to flie away presently after he had committed this bloody
Queen assassination, he came with his wife Rosamund to Ravenna
Rosamund. to the Court of Longinus before named, where after they
had remayned a little while, Longinus falling in love with
the Queene, perswaded her, to the end he might the sooner
enjoy her in marriage, to poyson her new husband Helmil-
childus.   The Queene shortly after delivered her husband
a poysoned cup as he came one day out of a bath, which
when he had greedily dranke, and now perceived the
violent effect of the poyson, he compels Rosamund to
drinke the rest; so that she died presently with her
husband.   Here Ludovicus King of Italy, the sonne of
Boson King of Province, by his wife Hermingardis

* The like example I have read of the skull of the Greeke Emperour
Nicephorus who succeeded the Empresse Irene, and divided the Empire
with Charlemaine.   For after he was slaine by the Bulgarians the King
of Bulgaria did set his skull in a plate of silver, and commonly dranke
in the same at his banquets instead of a cuppe. Carion. Chronic. lib. 4.

38

OBSERVATIONS OF VERONA

s forces in Illyriam
Empire. Here a
igobards died an t
id King, after he b
f a long siege out
arch of Ravenna, b
. and solaced him
npelled his wife Ro
ut of the * skull of a
: before he had slan
iz to be revenged up
barbarous injury, ca
oble Longobard, to b
~ se both to marry E
· bestow the Kingdo
-pon Helmichildus be
·dered Alboinus, a
so br this meanes
·· the Queene, but t
For being constray
i committed this blo
'i Rosamund to Rave
ramed. where after th
·n:s falling in love w
end he might the soa
i new husband Hele
r delivered her husb
ir out of a bath, wh
nd now perceived t
compels Rosamund
id presently with h
of Italy, the sonne
s wife Hermingil

ll of the Greeke Emp
it, and divided the Em
y the Bulgarians the b
·er, and commonly di:
Carion. Chronic. lib.

daughter to the Emperour Charles the second surnamed the Bald (whom I have before mentioned) had his eies plucked out of his head by Duke Berengarius before named.

Besides those famous learned men borne in Verona, that I have above mentioned, with many other most excellent wittes, that it hath ever bredde from time to time, I have often read of two most worthy women borne in this city, *Two worthy women.* whereof each was esteemed the Phœnix of her time for learning, with mention of whom I will end this description of Verona; the one was called Isota Nogarola a *virgin, who attained to so great knowledge, that she was very eloquent in the Greeke and Latin tongues, and wrote many excellent Latin Epistles to Nicolas, the fifth Pope of that name. Also she composed an elegant Dialogue, wherein she disputed the matter, who committed the greatest sinne Adam or Eve. The other was †Genebria, who in the time of Pius the second of that name Pope, wrote sundry Latin Epistles with a most elegant stile; which two women have no lesse ennobled this famous citie, with their learning then Aspasia, and Diotima, did [p. 332.] Athens, Cornelia, Rome, Cassandra Venice, or Hilde gardis the citie of Bing in Germany.

Thus much of Verona.

I Remained in Verona all Friday after nine of the clocke in the morning, all Saturday, and departed therehence upon Sunday being the fourteenth day of August, about one of the clocke in the afternoone, and came to a little towne called Desensan, in Latin Desentianum, which is *Desensan.* subject to the Venetians, and two and twenty miles beyond Verona, about eight of the clocke in the evening. In this space I observed onely a faire Fortresse of the Venetians at a towne called Peschiera, fourteene miles from Verona : *Peschiera.* the other things were ordinary, as faire Vineyards, &c.

* Fulgosus lib. 8. cap. 3. Memorabilium.
† Gesnerus Biblioth.

39

This towne Desentianum is situate neare to the goodly lake Garda heretofore called Benacus, which Virgil mentioneth in these wordes:

Fluctibus, & fremitu assurgens Benace marino.

The first name Benacus was imposed upon it from a towne so called, and also the new name Garda from a towne situate neare to it, which retaineth that name at this day. *Lake di Garda.* This lake is called in the Italian Lago di Gardo; it is said to be thirty five miles long, and in some places fourteene broad. I heard that it is commonly esteemed the noblest Lake of all Italy, and some doe not sticke to preferre it before the famous Lacus Larius, now called Lago di Como. The faire River Mincius that runneth by Mantua (of whom I have before made mention) issueth out of this Lake: it is oftentimes very rough and boysterous, inso much that at sometimes of the yeare it is very dangerous for passengers to passe that way. The cause of which roughnesse is ascribed unto the high cliffes that inclose it [P. 333.] on both sides, and interclude the windes, who having not the liberty there as in the open sea, doe extremely tosse *Golden sands.* up and downe the waters. It yeeldeth golden sands like those of Tagus by Lisbone, and Pactolus by Sardis in Lydia. Also it aboundeth with fish, especially Carpes, Troutes, and Eeles. This lake is very memorable for one thing, to wit, for a famous victory gotten near unto it of the Germanes, by that worthy and victorious Emperour Flavius Claudius the successor of Galien, of whom the Historians do write he partly slew and partly tooke captive two hundred thousand.

I departed from Desentianum the next day being munday, and the fifteenth day of August about seven of the clocke in the morning, and came to Brixia, commonly *Brescia.* called Bressa, being eighteene miles beyond it, about two of the clocke in the afternoone: in which space I observed nothing memorable, but onely some few ruinous Castles, which seeme to be buildings of great antiquity.

40

OBSERVATIONS OF BRESCIA

My Observations of Brixia.

Julius Cæsar Scaliger hath written this Hexastichon upon
Brixia.

QUæ pingues scatebras speculâ despectat ab altâ
Postulat imperii Brixia magna vices.
Cœlum hilarum, frons læta urbi, gens nescia fraudis.
  Atque modum ignorat divitis uber agri.
Si regeret patrias animis concordibus oras,
  Tunc poterat Dominis ipsa jubere suis.

Scaliger's verses upon Brescia.

This citie standeth in that part of Lombardy which is
called Longobardia Transpadana, because it is beyond the
river Po, and is situate in a plaine at the foote of a hill,
being in compasse three miles. It was first founded by
the auncient Gaules called Cenomani, though some doe
write it was a Colony of the Romans. I heard that there
are some notable antiquities and inscriptions in this citie,
but I must intreat thee (gentle Reader) to pardon me
although I doe not communicate them to thee. For I
made so short aboad in the Citie, that I could not observe
halfe so much as I would have done if I had remained
there but one whole day.

Brescia founded by the Gauls.

[p. 334.]

It is invironed with strong walles, wherein there are
five gates, and fortified with a most impregnable Castle
that standeth upon a hill, built all with free-stone. Also
it is well watered with pleasant springs and sweete foun-
tains, as any citie I saw in Italy, nay none the like. Which
flow incessantly from many fine Conduits in sundry
market-places, and it is moystened with a river called
Garza, which indeed is but little, yet very commodious
to the Citie.

The Palace wherein the Venetian Praetor and Praefectus
doe lie (for here both have but one Palace, though in
other cities they have two) is a sumptuous building, and
furnished with great store of munition and artillery. At
the west gate thereof, which is most commonly guarded
with a guard of Souldiers that doe attend there all the day

Palace of Brescia.

41

with Partizans in their handes, I read this inscription over a Scutchin on the right hand as I went into the court.

Dux, Heros, Scriptor Paruta,
Regis, geris, edis,
Urbem, res, libros,
Imperio, arte, manu.

And this a little under the same,

Fide, Virtute, Integritate, spectatissimo viro
Paulo Parutæ hujus urbis Praefecto
Optimè merito, anno Dom. M.D.Lxxxxi.

The Palace The Palace court is thirty sixe paces long and forty broad,
court. and all the wals round about are adorned with sundry
armes of the Venetian Gentlemen. Also in the middle of
[p. 335.] the court there is an exceeding pleasant Conduit that
spowteth out water in three degrees one above another;
in the second degree are sixe prety pipes, out of the which
the water doth most abundantly flow: also the higher
part doth exceeding pleasantly powre out water. At the
west end of the Palace in the outside of the wall, this is
written under the winged Lyon.

Æternæ pacis, justitiæ, libertatisque Defensor.

Over the dore of the Praetors chamber I read this impresse.

Diligite justitiam qui judicatis terram.

Armour. I went into one of the Prætors inner roomes, which I
saw furnished with armour round about all the walles, as
helmets, costlets, and other armour for armes and thighes,
which served only for horsemen. The like armour also
was on both sides of the entry within that roome, which
leadeth to the lodgings of the Præfectus. Under which
armour I saw on both sides launces and speares for horsemen. At the north side there is a goodly brasen dore
made like a latteise window, through the which I saw five
faire roomes more, passing well furnished with armour.
At that gate are exceeding faire pillars of blacke marble,

42

ITIES

this inscription on
nt into the court.

,

spectatissimo viro
Praefecto
1. M.D.Lxxxi.

s long and forty fou:
t adorned with sum:
Also in the middle
: .... Conduit t
rees one above anoth:
' : :e·: c·.: of the wl:
· ::·:: .:so the hig:
·=·: :.: water. A:
.::ie of the wall, thi

::::sc: Defensor.

::er I read this impres

:: ::::-::

; :rner roomes, whid
about all the walles;
· ::r ::::es and thig:
T:e l:ke armour 2:
hun that roome, wb:
fectus. Under wh:
and speares for har:
: goodly brasen de
the which I saw b:
:ished with armou:
·s of blacke marl:

interlaced with prety white vaines. Many fine pictures of armed men are made by the sides of that northerne dore. Opposite unto this roome is another faire chamber, the roofe whereof is curiously adorned with excellent pictures.

Their principall market place is very faire, at one corner *Principal* whereof there standeth a goodly high pillar of free-stone, *market place.* whereon the winged Lyon is advanced according to the custome of the Venetians, who have erected such a pillar in the principall market place of every Citie subject to their dominion, as I have before mentioned in Vicenza and Verona. At the west end of this market place there standeth a most stately Councell house, which was very faire, and covered with lead before it was burnt. But they have reedified and marvailously beautified it beneath [p. 336.] with goodly pillars, and above round about with borders and workes in great arches, and with marble pillars and images of admirable curiosity, representing some of the auncient Roman Emperours, so passing faire that I have scarce seene a more curious and artificiall architecture in Italy, saving the Amphitheater of Verona, the Palace of Padua, and some few of the Venetian buildings.

In the Domo which is dedicated to our Lady I saw a *Cathedral* very faire monument of Francis Maurocenus their last *Church.* Bishop, who was also Cardinall. His statue is erected above a most beautiful stone wherein his Epitaph is written: and above the same his Cardinals hat and armes. His Epitaph is this.

D. T. V.

Joanni Francisco Mauroceno
    Patricio Veneto
Prisca gentis nobilitate, vitæ sanctitate,
Religione, omnique virtutum genere,
    Ac rerum gestarum gloria clarissimo.
Qui post amplissimas in Sabaudia, Gallia,
Hispania, Polonia, Constantinopoli reipub. nomine
Singulari cum integritate, fide, prudentia,

43

CORYAT'S CRUDITIES

Animi excelsi atque invicti magnitudine,
  Ac denique omnium approbatione,
    Obitas legationes;
A Gregoria XIII. ultró designatus,
  Mox â Sixto V creatus
    Brixiensis Episcopus,
Et ab eodem in Gallia iterum ad Henricum III.
Summa cum potestate difficillimis temporibus missus
  Re felicitèr gesta, absens extra ordinem
    S. R. E. Cardinalis
Ingenti cum omnium bonorum acclamatione factus est,
  Et simul
    Legatus â Latere.

[P. 337.] Ad extremum omnibus vitæ ornamentis cumulatus
  In Ecclesiæ suæ gremio incredibili ejusdem
Ac totius Venetæ atque adeò Christianæ Reipub.
    Mærore,
Verus Gregis Pastor, ac liberaliss, pauperum Pater,
  Ex hac vita ad æternam demigravit,
    Anno cIɔ. Iɔ. Xcvi. Men. Janu. die xiiii.
Pauperes hujus Civitatis Brixiœ
  Hæredes ab eo ex asse instituti.
Ope Marini Georgii ipsius Cardinalis Consob.
  Et in Episcopatu Successoris
Parenti optimo grati animi monumentum P.
    Vixit Ann. lviii. Men. iii. Di. xv.
      Sedit Ann. x. Men. i. Di. ix.

The Emperor Constantine's cross.   In this Domo is kept a very memorable monument (if that were true which the Brixians do report of it, as without doubt it is absolutely false) namely the Crosse that was presented unto the Emperour Constantine in the south part of heaven, about the going downe of the sun, at what time he marched with his army towards Rome, to joyne battell with Maxentius. In which Crosse these characters were plainly seene: In hoc signo Constantine vinces. The Brixians doe call this Crosse whereof they so much boast, Oroflamma, which signifieth the golden Flame, &c. and they affirme that it representeth the colour

44

of heaven. Albeit I hold this tradition to be a meere, yea, a very grosse figment (for what wise man that hath his wit in his head and not in his heele, will beleeve that this should be the very same heavenly Crosse? seing we reade that Constantine himselfe could not have the same, but in steede thereof made another Crosse the next day after of gold and precious stone, which was borne before him in steede of a standard, Euseb. de vita Constant. lib. 1.) yet for the satisfaction of my mind I made meanes to see it, but I could not obtayne the sight thereof, because it is shewed but at certayne times.

The Bishop of Brixia hath many temporall dignities [p. 338.] added to his spirituall, so that he is intitled a Duke, Marquesse, and Earle.

I visited the Church of the Dominican Friers, which *Church of the* is a very fayre building, the Quire being beautified with *Dominican* many goodly ornaments, amongst the rest their new taber- *Friars.* nacle is a very glorious piece of worke. One of the Friers told me that they keepe a bone of one of Mary Magdalens armes here: but I could not obtaine the sight of it, because it is shewed but at certaine times.

The nunnery which is dedicated to the holy Martyr St. Julia, is a building of great antiquity. For it was built by Desiderius the last King of the Longobards in the time of Carolus Magnus, about the yeare 750. The Church thereof hath beene lately renewed and beautified at the charges of the Nunnes. Upon the front I read this inscription.

Relicto Templo quod Desiderius
Rex Salvatori erexerat,
Hoc nobilius Deo & Sanctæ Juliæ
Dicatum Sacræ Moniales
Construxerant. An. Sal. cIↃ.IↃ.Ic.

This Nunnery hath beene in times past a receptacle of *Nunnery of* many royall Ladies, who after their entrance into the same *S. Julia.* spent all the remainder of their lives there in divine medi

45

tations, under the rule of St. Bennet: as Ansilperga the sister of the foresaid King Desiderius the founder thereof, and Hermingarda his daughter: and Hermigranda the wife of the first Emperour Lotharius, and Angilberga the sister of the Emperour Charles the third, and Berta the daughter of King Berengarius, and many other Noble Matrons and Virgins. One miraculous or rather prodigious accident that hapned once in this City in the time of the Emperour Ludovicus the second, I will mention here, to wit, that it rayned bloud here for the space of three dayes together, which was as red and lively as if it had newly flowen out of the body of any man or beast. A portent so exceeding strange, that as I never read or heard of the like in any place of the world before, so I doubt whether there was ever the like accident either before or since of the like continuance; my Authour of this was a learned man of this City, whom I found to be a man of excellent learning.

A rain of blood.

[p. 339.]

This city was first converted to Christianity about the yeare 119 by St. Apollinaris Bishop of Ravenna.

SS. Faustinus and Jovita.

One of their churches is dedicated to two Saints namely Faustinus & Jovita that were heretofore citizens of the same City of Brixia, and constant Martyrs of Jesus Christ: who suffered martyrdome in the persecution of the Emperour Adrian, whose great torments one Calocerius perceiving that they endured with great patience, he cryed out with these words: Verê magnus Deus Christianorum. For which he was also martyred in the same place.

They have one principall tower above the rest commonly called Pallada, wherein the fairest bels of the City doe han .

Palaces of the gentlemen.

The Gentlemens Palaces of the City are very faire, most of them being built with free stone, not with brick, as in many other Italian Cities. One amongst the rest I observed of great magnificence, in the front whereof an Eagle was so exquisitely pourtrayed, that it much graced that part of the building. Also their pentices are as broad as those of Verona. Many of their streetes are beautified

46

as Ansilperga the
he founder thereof,
Hermigranda the
and Angilberga the
third, and Berta the
many other Nobles
us or rather prodigy
s City in the time of
will mention here,
or the space of three
nd lively as if it had
nr man or beast. &
s I never read or hear
d before, so I doubt
ident either before or
Author of this was to
. . . to be a man of

. . . . y about the
. Ravenna.
. . . Saints named
. . fore citizens of the
. . . Martyrs of Jesu
. . the persecution of
. . . s one Calocerus
. . patience, he cried
. Deus Christianorum
. . same place.
. . e the rest commonly
. . s of the City are

r are very faire, most
. . t with brick, as is
. . mongst the rest I
. e front whereof is
. . at it much grace
. . ntices are as broad
. . etes are beautified

with such open galleries to walke in, and garnished with faire pillars, as those of Mantua, Padua, and Venice, above mentioned.

This City is one of those that Attila King of the Hunnes grievously wasted, when he entred into Italy after his overthrow in France by Ætius Generall of the Roman army. Many hundred yeares after which time it was so much inclined to factions and mutinies, that in the time of Ludovicus the third of that name Emperour and one of the Othoes, it changed her governement no lesse then seven times in the space of eight and twenty yeares; but at this time after so many revolutions and alterations of their state, it is subject to the noble Signiory of Venice. [p. 340.]

The Cutlers of this City are accounted very excellent workemen for making of knives, targets, and swordes of a singular temper: also the trade of making silke and linen doth much flourish here. *Excellent cutlers.*

It happened that the same Munday that I was in Brixia, was Barthelmew day. At what time there was a most solemne and ceremonious dedication of a new image to the Virgin Mary with Christ in her armes, which I saw performed in a certaine little Chappel with many superstitious rites. For they attired the image with a great many several roabes, as of sattin, taffata, lawne, &c. and there was a great multitude of litle waxen idols brought to the Chappell, whereof some were onely armes, some thighes, some presented all the parts of a mans body: although these toyes were no novelties unto me. For I saw many of them before that time in divers Italian Cities. Yet I had a marvailous itching desire to finger one of them, only to this end, to bring it home into England, to shew it to my friends as a token of their idolatry: but I saw there was some difficulty in the matter. Howbeit I gave the venture upon it in this manner. I stood at one corner of the Chappel while many women were at their divine oraizons prostrate before the image, and very secretly conveighed my fingers into a little basket (nobody taking notice thereof) where the images were laid; and *Dedication of an image.*

47

so purloyned one of them out, and brought him home into England. Which had it been at that time perceived, perhaps it might have cost me the lying in the Inquisition longer then I would willingly have endured it.

Thus much of Brixia.

[p. 341.] I Departed from Brixia about eight of the clock in the morning the sixteenth day of August being Tuesday, *Bergamo.* and came to Bergomum commonly called Bergomo the last City of the Venetian Signiory about seven of the clocke in the evening. The distance betwixt these two Cities is thirty miles. I observed in this space great abundance of goodly vineyards, which at that time yeelded ripe grapes passing faire and sweet. For I did oftentimes borrow a point of the law in going into their Vineyards without leave, to refresh my selfe with some of their grapes. Which the Italians like very good fellowes did winke at, shewing themselves more kinde unto me then the Germans did afterward in Germany, as I will hereafter declare in my observations of their country. For they will not graunt a stranger that liberty to goe into any of their vineyardes without leave, as the Italians doe. The *Pleasant* greatest part of the way betwixt these Cities is as pleasant *travelling.* as any I travelled in Italy. For it is very plaine and even; one spacious lane, on both sides whereof the goodly vine-yardes grew, extending it selfe about eighteene miles in length. All that day I saw great abundance of people going to and fro, but especially forward towards Bergomo, because there was a great faire there at that time; most of the horsemen being well appointed with muskets or pewternels ready charged, according to that custome of the Italians that I have before mentioned.

My Observations of Bergomo.

Julius Cæsar Scaliger hath written these verses upon Bergomo.

INgenium, corpus, mores, obtutus, amictus,
 Tecta, cibus, gressus, guttura, sermo, sonus:
Omnia crassa modis insignibus, omnia dura,
 Sic valeant silices ut superare suos.
Ista domi: sed vicinus si aspergat acetum,
 Artibus atque dolis vincitur ipse suis.

Scaliger's verses on Bergamo. [p. 342.]

This City was built about a hundred and fifty yeares before the incarnation of our Saviour Christ, by one Cirinus King of Liguria. It standeth on the side of a hill, having in the east and south the pleasant plaine of Lombardy before it. So that from many places of this City there is as sweet a prospect as any place of Italy doth yeeld. In the north and west are great hils that leade towards the Alpes. It is devided into two parts, the higher and the lower. Unto the higher there is a long and tedious ascent. It was my chaunce to be here at the time of their fair the next day after Barthelmew day, which lasteth a whole weeke; being kept in a large plaine a little way distant from the lower part of the City. This was the greatest faire that ever I saw in my life, except that of Franckford in Germany, whereof I will hereafter speake. For there was a great concurse of people not onely from the Cities of Lombardy, but also from many other principal Cities of Italy: besides many Germans both out of the Grisons country and Switzerland repaire hither at this time: exceeding plenty of all manner of commodities being there sold.

S. Bartholomew's Fair.

The first that planted the doctrine of Christian religion in the City, and chaced idolatry and Paganisme out of it, was St. Barnabas, who preached the Gospell first also at Milan.

The Cathedrall Church is dedicated to our Lady, and standeth in the higher part of the City: a very notable

Cathedral Church.

faire building though but little. At the entrance of the north gate there are two faire pillars of red marble, supported with two huge Lyons of the same matter. At the toppe over an arch which is above the dore, is advanced a gallant fellow on horsebacke made in alabaster. One part of this northerne front on the right hand as you enter into the gate, is passing beautifull, being compacted wholly of sundry sorts of marble and alabaster, which doe yeeld a very glorious shew. The greatest part of it is made of checker worke. In the middest of this front is a faire round window garnished very excellently with many prety pieces of marble, at the sides whereof are erected the statues in alabaster of two famous Roman Emperours. Julius Cæsar on the left hand, under whom this is written in great Roman letters: Divus Julius Cæsar. And above him this: Imperavit annis V. On the right hand the effigies of Trajan, under whom is written: Divus Trajanus Augustus. And above: Imperavit Annis XVIII. But I perceive that they calculate the time of his raigne within compasse. For al the historians write that he raigned nineteene yeares and halfe. These statues are made to the middle part of their breast and no further. I told certaine Italian Gentlemen that observed me writing, they were much to blame to erect the images of prophane heathen men upon their Church. For although it were good to keepe such antiquities, yet they ought not to be placed upon Churches where Christ is worshipped; but rather upon their Councell houses, or their private buildings. This part of the frontispice is passing faire, and worthy to be noted by an industrious traveller.

[P. 343.]

After I entered the north gate I observed in a faire litle chappell on the right hand of the Church, an exceeding sumptuous monument of Barthelmew Coleon the General Captaine of the Venetians land forces, as I have before mentioned in my discourse of Venice. They say it was made in his life time by his owne appointment. He is represented on horsebacke, all in glittering gold in his complete armour that he wore in the field, and his military

Monument of Bartholomew Coleon.

50

OBSERVATIONS OF BERGAMO

the entrance of t
of red marble, s:
ume matter. At t
he dore, is advanc
e in alabaster. O.
ght hand as you en:
g compacted wh:
ister, which doe p:
:st part of it is m:
of this front is a fr
lently with many pr
hereof are erected t
us Roman Emperor
er whom this is writ
ius Cæsar. And al:
On the right hand t
...ten: Divus Traia:
1.· Annis XVIII. l:
:: his raigne wi:
:s write that he raig:
:ex statues are mad:
:::: no further. I t:
::::d me writing, t:
::: images of prop:
For although it w:
::: they ought not t:
::: is worshipped; t:
::: their private hu:
::: is passing faire, t:
:us traveller.
:observed in a faire E:
Church, an exceed:
:r Coleon the Grea:
:res, as I have bef:
::. They say it is:
appointment. He:
littering gold in t:
:eld, and his milit:

trunchion in his right hand. All this monument is made of pure alabaster, wherein are represented many notable histories done in the pretiest litle images and works that [p. 344.] I saw in any City of Italy. The whole worke is supported with four alabaster pillars, at the foote whereof are expressed the heads of Lyons. At the toppe of all is advanced his helmet and crest with his armes, at the sides are hanged two auncient banners which are grievously rent and torne with antiquity. A little from his Tombe there is hanged up a faire cloth of arras, in the middest whereof his armes are finely wrought, which are three testicles. The reason is, because nature gave him three stones, one more then other men have, as I have said before in my description of Venice. The monument it selfe is a worke of that admirable sumptuousnesse, that I esteeme it the fairest I saw in Italy, saving that of Mastinus Scaliger in the little Churchyard at Verona. The Epitaph *Coleon's* it selfe is this. *epitaph.*

D. O. M.

Bartholomæus Colleonus de Andegavia, virtute immortalitatem adeptus, usque adeò jure militari fuit illustris, ut non modò tum viventium gloriam longè excesserit, sed & posteris spem eum imitandi ademerit. Sæpiùs enim â diversis Principibus, ac deinceps ab illustrissimo Ven. Senatu accepto Imperio tandem totius Christianorum exercitus, sub Paulo Secundo Pontifice Maximo, delectus fuit Imperator: cujus acies 14. annis ab ejus obitu, solo jam defuncti Imperatoris tanquam vivi nomine militantes, jussa cujuscunque alterius contempserunt. Obiit 4. Nonas Novembris, Anno Domini 1475.

There are two very sumptuous Pulpits on both sides of the Quire without, made of blacke and white marble, having faire winding staires to ascend to them, with a very rich rail at the edge made of brasse, and adorned with many curious and fine workes.

One of the Priests of the City told me that there are *Admirable* forty Masses said every day in this Church: An admir- *devotion.* able devotion certainly. The greatest part of them is

51

celebrated in two little Chappels on both sides of the Quire. Where I noted two exceeding curious railes at the entrance of them, the pillars whereof are made of white and blacke marble, and the upper part ex versicolore marmore.

The roof of the Choir.

The roofe over the Quire is very beautifully concamerated, and richly gilt. Round about the upper end of the Quire there is as exquisite a peece of worke as ever I saw of that kinde. For a certaine cunning artificer called Franciscus de Ferreo monte hath with extraordinary curiosity contrived the history of the creation of the world, and many other histories of the old Testament in wainscot. So rare a worke that it is most admirable to behold. There are also two very rich paire of Organs on both sides without the Quire, most sumptuously gilt, and imbossed with many very excellent workes.

The Baptistery.

At the west end of the Church right opposite to the Quire, I saw a passing faire and auncient Fabricke, built of sundry kinds of marble, wherein are baptized the children of Noblemen onely. It is an admirable architecture, raysed unto such an heigth that it doth even touch the roofe of that part of the Church where it standeth. It is built round and adorned with six partitions of little marble pillars, whereof many are Porphyrie, each partition contayning fourteene severall pillars. At the toppe there standeth the image of an Angell. Againe betwixt every partition prety images are made in redde marble: Also about the middle of the worke six alabaster images round about the same, being distant asunder by an equall distance. The dore at the entrance is made of brasse, and contrived like a Latteise window. I observed in a redde marble stone, which is about the foot of this rare worke, a notable thing which is not to be omitted, even the true resemblance of a serpent, formed more exquisitely in the stone by the hand of nature her selfe the most cunning architect of all, then the most curious artificer in the world could possibly have done. A thing that was shewed me by an Italian, as a matter very worthy my observation.

52

OBSERVATIONS OF BERGAMO

a both sides of t
ing curious railes;
thereof are made t
per part ex versicol

beautifully concam
t the upper end of t
of worke as ever I s
unning artificer cal
.. with extraordin
f the creation of t
y the old Testament:
.i is most admirable;
rv ..th paire of Org
.. sumptuously g
.....t wickes.

ch right opposite to
: l... ent Fabricke, h
..... are baptized t
... an admirable an
.. tha r doth even tru
... where it stand:
.. partitions of it
?... each parte
... .t the toppe t
... betwixt ev
... marble: f
... images m
.. by an equall t
.. made of brasse, r
I observed in a n
.. of this rare wor
omitted, even the m
are exquisitely in e
.lie the most cunni
s artificer in the wo
tiat was shewed t
thy my observatio

This piece of marble may be very properly called Ophiti-call (of which I have written before in my notes of Venice) because it doth so truely present τόν όφίν, that is, a Serpent.

The Arras and hangings about this church are as faire as I saw in any Church of Italy.

Bishop's Palace. The Palace of the Bishop of Bergomo, whose name is Joannes Baptista, doth joyne to our Ladies Church, but is the basest and most beggarly Palace for a Bishop that I saw in Italy.

I was at the Prætorium, which is in this higher part of the citie, a very obscure and meane Palace, and inferiour to all the other Palaces of the Venetian Praetors that I saw. The name of the Praetor when I was in Bergomo was Vincentius Barocius.

The Exchange. Hard by our Lady Church there is a stately walke, which I take to be their Exchange, and a place where they meete about their civill affaires. It is fairely roofed, & sumptuously vaulted, and supported within with two degrees of pillars. It is square; for it is but thirty two paces every way. In the middle of the easterne wall, which is at the upper end of the walke, I read this inscrip-tion upon a large table of Touch-stone.

> Andreæ Gussono Prætori,
> Viro virtutibus omnibus
> Atque inprimis in hanc patriam
>   Charitate insigni.
> Qui pauperes præ fame deficientes
> Ingenio quidem, liberalitate
>   Autem maxime sustinuit:
> Qui ne ab ea ampliùs premerentur,
> Ad rem frumentariam
>   Viam invenit.
> Qui montem pietatis ad multos
> Annos derelictum, honestiùs
>   Quâm anteâ erexit.
> Qui utriusque fori juribus
>   Consulens, sua cuique

[P. 347.]

53

CORYAT'S CRUDITIES

Hactenùs confusa, distinxit.
Qui hæc levia existimans
In commodis nunc altioribus
Vires suas omnes contendit.
B. B. B. D. D. An. P. Chr. Nat. M. D. Lxxxix.

Church of the
Augustinian
Friars.

I visited the Church of the Augustinian Friers which is situate in the middle of the hill, betwixt the higher and the lower citie. A little within the entrance of the Church there are two faire Fonts of blacke marble that serve for their holy water. Their Tabernacle upon their high altar is a very costly thing. For it cost them two thousand duckats, which is two hundred thirty three pound six shillings eight pence sterling. Within that Altar there is a marvailous rich table, that covereth almost all the wall of the higher Chappell where their high Altar standeth, even from the toppe to the ground, being adorned with the picture of S. Augustine, and some other Saints. Also they have a wonderfull rich paire of Organs lately made, and decked with exceeding faire pillars, made indeede but of Wainscot, but so curiously handled, that it yeeldeth a very faire shew: it is said it shal be all gilt. There are twelve Altars in this Church, one against another, sixe in each side, made in so many severall Chappels; in one

Ambrose
Calepine.

whereof there lyeth the body of famous Ambrose Calepine heretofore one of the Friers of this Monastery. This is he that made that notable Latin Dictionary so famous over all Christendome, which hath beene since his death so inlarged and augmented by the studious labours of other learned men, that were he now alive he would scarce know his own worke. It grieved me to see how obscurely he was buried: For he hath nothing but a flat stone upon him, without Epitaph or any other memoriall that might derive the fame of so worthy a mans name to future ages.

[p. 348.]

All that space of the wall which is betwixt every one of those foresaid twelve Chappels, is beautified with a rich Taffata hanging: on which there hangeth one of the pictures of the twelve Apostles: the whole twelve being

54

ITIES
it.

oribus
tendit.
at. M. D. Lxxxix.

ustinian Friers which
betwixt the higher a
: entrance of the Chu
te marble that serve i
de upon their high ai
.ost them two thous
thirty three pound i
V.thin that Altar then
ereth almost all the r
near high Altar stand
... being adorned v:
: some other Saints. A
·· y' Organs lately m:
: p. is, made indeede?
...... it it reedeth
al be all gilt. There a
or against another, sur
everall Chappels; in v
famous Ambrose Cale;
the Monastery. This
Dermeary so famous or
here since his death:
studious labours of oth
we he would scarce kne
o see how obscurely!
· but a flat stone up
· memoriall that mig
s name to future ag
betwixt every one i
beautified with a ri:
hangeth one of the
· whole twelve bein

placed upon the twelve severall hangings. Also each of
these hangings differeth from another in colour.

Over one of the dores of the Trinity Church, which is *Trinity*
in the lower part of the citie, these verses are written : *Church.*

> Aurea perpetuò funduntur ab æthere dona
> His adytis : si quidem Romana sacraria Clemens
> Explicuit, sociasque animas effecit & aras.

Also over the same dore there is an arch, about the edge
whereof without the same arch, this following is written
in a round compasse :

> O summè excellens cælestis gloria regni,
> Quam pius ecce Deus si velit ipse dabit.

Againe, under that, this is written within the arch, a little
above the picture of the Virgin Mary, holding Christ in
her armes :

> Angelicas inter mentes, superasque phalanges.

Under the same directly over the dore as you enter into
the Church, this Tetrastiche.

> Filia, nupta, parens, magni rectoris Olympi,
> Idem qui natus virque paterque fuit.
> Adsint ut cæptis quæ sunt tria numina & unum,
> Hæc tria Virgo roga Filia, Nupta, Parens.

The Gentlewomen of this city doe weare very strange *Counterfeit*
kinde of chaines about their neckes. A stranger at the *Chains.*
first sight of them will imagine they are very precious
ornaments, worth three or foure hundred duckats, and
made of pure gold : as indeede I did. But after better
consideration he will find them counterfait. For indeed
they are but copper, as an Italian told me. They hang
very large about their necks, being about three times
double, and have extraordinary great linkes. Also I
observed that their attire doth much differ from the habits
of the Italian Gentlewomen in other cities of Italy. For [p. 349.]
whereas most of their gownes are of Sattin or Taffata ;
the sleeves of them are exceeding great in the middest,
and so little at the hands, that they cannot weare them

55

upon the sleeves of their other garments. So that they alwaies hang loose and flapping. This fashion they have borrowed from the Spaniards. For I saw it much used by the Spanish Gentlewomen at Turin, and by a woman Mountebanke in Venice that imitated the Spanish attire.

A rude dialect.
The language of this City is esteemed the rudest and grossest of all Italy, as the Bœotian dialect was the basest of all Greece. In so much that one of our English men Thomas Edwards in his Monostiches that he hath composed of the Italian Cities, hath written this verse of Bergomo.

Bergomum ab incultâ dictum est ignobile linguâ.

The governement of it is as the rest of the Cities subject to the Venetians. Heretofore it was subject to the Roman Empire, when the same flourished in his glory. But after the downefall thereof it was spoiled by Attila when he destryed Brixia, Verona, and other famous cities of Italy. Then the Longobardes had the dominion of it for a long time: then again the Kings of Italy made it tributary to them. In the time of whose sway thereof it hapned to
Bergamo besieged A.D. 900.
be once very straightly besieged by the Emperour Arnolphus about the yeare of our Lord 900. much about the time that he besieged Verona also, as I have before mentioned. But he had not long girt it with siege before he expugned it by force of armes. And having entred the same, he apprehended and hanged one Ambrose Earle of the City, who fortified and defended it in the behalfe of Guido (whom I have before mentioned) Duke of Spoleto against Berengarius Duke of Friuli. After the Kings of Italy the Turrians and Vicounts of Milan succeeded in
[p. 350.]
the government thereof. Also the Scaligers of Verona and the Frenchmen. But at last it subjected it selfe voluntarily to the Venetians, under whose protection it enjoyed tranquillity and peace at this day.

This City yeelded me the worst lodging for one night that I found in all my travels out of England. For all

ITIES

nents. So that th
his fashion they ha
'or I saw it mu
o at Turin, and l
:t that imitated t

tecmed the rudest a
I dialect was the bea
ne of our English a
.hes that he hath os
, written this verse i

est ignobile lingui.

: rest of the Cities subj
was subject to the Rom
[...] But th
[...] by Attila whm!
[...] famous cities of Ital
[...] it for a ki
[...] it tributary
[...] it baptsed:
[...] Emperour Ani
[...] much about th
[...] as I have before no
[...] siege before!
[...] having entred th
: one Ambrose Earle
[...] it in the behalfe
[...] Duke of Spole
[...] After the Kings c
i Milan succeeded t
: Scaligers of Veron
i: subjected it sel
whose protection t
[...]
[...] for one nigh
England. For a

OBSERVATIONS OF BERGAMO

the Innes were so extreme full of people by reason of
the faire, that I could not get a convenient lodging though
I would have given two or three duckats for it. So that
I was faine to lye upon straw in one of their stables at the *A hard*
horse feete, according to a picture that I have made of it *lodging.*
in the frontispice of my booke. Where (notwithstanding
my repose upon so uncouth a pallate) I slept in utramque
aurem, even as securely as upon a bedde of downe, because
of my long journey the day before. And it was long
before I could obtayne this favour, which was at last
granted me by the meanes of an honest Italian Priest who
had beene a traveller. Unto whom I was not a litle
beholding for some curtesies that I received at his hands in
Bergomo. He promised to revisit me the next morning,
to the end to shew me the antiquities of the City. But
he was prevented to my great griefe by the villany of a
certaine bloud-thirsty Italian, who for an old grudge he
bare to him, shot him through the body in his lodging
with a pewternell.

Also a certayne Dominican Frier of this City called *A courteous*
Vincentius de Petrengo, who was the chiefe reader of the *Dominican*
Prædicatory family, and stiled himselfe de Conventu *Friar.*
Basellæ, did so greatly gratifie me in this City, that I
cannot conveniently let him passe in this Treatise of
Bergomo, without some kinde of mention of his name.
For I received a speciall favour at his hands, which was
this. When I was to goe forth of the City towards the
Grisons country, and so into Germany, being ignorant
of the way, I repaired to the Augustinian Friers to crave
some directions of them for my journey. But none of
them could direct me themselves, though very kindly they [p. 351.]
brought me acquainted with this foresaid Dominican, to
the end he should satisfie me about the matter, because
he had lived within these few yeares in the territory of
the Grisons, as a Chaplaine to a certaine Clarissimo of
Venice that was sent Ambassador unto them, at what time
he preached against the Calvinists of their country, as he *Friendly*
himselfe told me. Truly he gave me as friendly councell *Counsel.*

57

as any Protestant could have done. For he told me what daungers there were betwixt that and Germany, and the meanes how I might avoid them : that I was a Calvinist, he said he was fully perswaded, because I was an English man. Notwithstanding he would willingly give me the best counsell he could, in regard I was a stranger in those parts. Therefore he signified unto me that it would be very dangerous for me to passe in one place of the Grisons country within a few miles after the entrance thereof, if I were not very circumspect. For he said there was a certaine Castle seated by the lake of Como which was possessed and guarded by a garrizon of Spaniards, by which if I should happen to take my journey, they would *The Spanish* lay their Inquisition upon me, as soone as they should *Inquisition to* perceive that I was an Englishman, and so consequently *be feared by* torture me with extreme cruelty, if they saw me constant *Travellers.* in the profession of my religion, till they might compell me to abjure it, which if I would not doe by the violence of their punishments, then at last they would put me to death, and excarnificate me after a very bitter and terrible manner. For the avoiding of which dangers he counselled me to leave the Castle on the left hand of my way, and so to passe on the right hand towards a towne called Chiavenna. Thus by the kind advice of this honest Frier I tooke such a way in the Grisons country, that I shunned the Spanish Inquisition, which otherwise would not (I beleeve) have given me leave to bring thus much newes [p. 352.] out of Italy into England, except I would have renounced my religion, which God forbid I should ever doe, not-withstanding any torments of Spaniards or any other enemies of the Gospell of Christ. I am sure all kinde of Friers will not give Protestants the like counsell to eschew the bloudy Spanish carnificina, (which is almost as cruell a punishment as Phalaris his brasen bull, or the exquisitest torments that the Sicilian Tyrants were wont to inflict upon offenders) but on the contrary side endevour rather to intrappe them therein.

Angry flies. Those angry flies called cimices, which are generally

58

OBSERVATIONS OF BERGAMO

For he told me wh
d Germany, and th
at I was a Calvini
use I was an Engli
willingly give me th
as a stranger in the
me that it would h
the place of the Grisa
the entrance thereof;
e he said there was,
: of Como which w
rizon of Spaniards, h
my journey, they wou
s soone as they shou
... and so consequent
i they saw me contin
... they might comp
c ev doe by the viole
ir they would put me t
a very bitter and terrib
... keepes he counsell
... of my way, w
wards a towne call
true of this honest fre
country, that I shun
otherwise would not l
bring thus much new
I would have renounc
should ever doe, at
... niards or any othe
I am sure all kind
s the like counsell t
ma, (which is almos
us brasen bull, or th
Tyrants were woo
the contrary sid
erein.
which are generally

dispersed over all places of Italy in the sommer time, did very much offend me in this City, as they did also in every City of Italy. They will shrewdly bite a mans skinne, and leave their markes behind them, yet they will doe no great hurt to a man.

I observed a strange phrase both in this City and all other Italian cities where I was, that whensoever any Italian doth discourse in Latin with a stranger or any man else, he will very seldome speake to a man in the second person. As for example he will not say, Placet ne tibi : but Placet ne dominationi tuæ or vestræ. So that they doe most commonly use that circumlocution, even to the meanest person that is.

I observed another thing also in the Italians pronouncing *Italian pro-* of the Latin Tongue, which though I might have men- *nouncing of* tioned before in the description of some of the other *Latin.* Italian Cities; yet seing I have hitherto omitted it, I will here make mention thereof, rather then not at al, because this is the last City of Italy that I shall describe in this journey. The Italian when he uttereth any Latin word wherein this letter i is to be pronounced long, doth alwaies pronounce it as a double e, viz as ee. As for example : he pronounceth feedes for fides : veeta for vita : ameecus for amicus, &c. but where the i is not to be pronounced long he uttereth it as we doe in England, as in these wordes, impius, aquila, patria, Ecclesia : not aqueela, patreea, Eccleseea. And this pronounciation is so generall [p. 353.] in all Italy, that every man which speaketh Latin soundeth a double e for an i. Neither is it proper to Italy only, but to all other nations whatsoever in Christendome saving to England. For whereas in my travels I discoursed in Latin with Frenchmen, Germans, Spaniards, Danes, Polonians, Suecians, and divers others, I observed that every one with whom I had any conference, pronounced the i after the same manner that the Italians use. Neither would some of them (amongst whom I was not a little inquisitive for the reason of this their pronounciation) sticke to affirme that Plautus, Terence, Cicero, Hortensius,

59

Cæsar, and those other selected flowers of eloquence amongst the auncient Romans, pronounced the i in that sort as they themselves doe. Whereupon having observed such a generall consent amongst them in the pronounciation of this letter I have thought good to imitate these nations herein, and to abandon my old English pronounciation of vita, fides, and amicus, as being utterly dissonant from the sound of all other Nations; and have determined (God willing) to retayne the same till my dying day.

Two famous men of Bergamo. Amongst other learned men of great note that this city hath bred, I will name two famous persons that after they had a long time lived here in the profession of Popery, being at last truly illuminated with Gods holy Spirit abandoned this Citie which was their native soile, and went into Germany, where they undertooke the profession of the Gospell of Christ, and afterward persevered in the Protestants religion til their last breath. These were Hieronymus Zanchius, and Gulielmus Gratarolus. Whereof the first was a most singular Divine, and a zealous Preacher of Gods word in the renowned Cities of Strazbourg, Heidelberg, and other places of Germany. Besides he hath exceedingly edified the Christian common-weale, [p. 354.] especially that which doth most sincerely professe the true doctrine of Christ, by those manifold and most solid workes of Divinity, that he hath published to the world, which will continue a sacred memory of his name till the worlds end. The other though he were by profession a Physition, and an excellent man in that faculty; yet he applied himselfe to the study of Divinity also, which doth appeare by one notable Treatise that he wrote de notis Antichristi. At last he died in the famous University of Basil, where he spent the greatest part of his life after his conversion.
Thus much of Bergomo.

I Remained in Bergomo all Wednesday, and departed therehence the next day being the eighteenth of August, about eleven of the clocke in the morning, and

60

wers of eloqu
ounced the i in t
pon having observ
in the pronouncia
imitate these nati
th pronounciation
rely dissonant fr
and have determi
ill my dying day.
great note that t
s persons that ab
profession of Pop
with Gods holy Sp
native soile, r
oke the professi
and persevered in t
These were He
Cervulus. Whe
scelus Pred
Cities of Strasbu
mans. Besides
Christian common-w
ly professe the t
catholi and most s
ptised to the wo
ory of his name till t
x were by professi
in that faculty; yet
trinity also, which he
that he wrote de act
amous University
part of his life de

romo.

esday, and depart
the eighteenth a
n the morning, as

came to a village called St. Johns in the valley Brembana, about sixe of the clocke in the evening. This was sixteen miles from Bergomo. The first village that I passed through was Zogno, which was twelve miles beyond Bergomo: and St. Johns foure miles beyond that. Al the villages both of the valley Brembana and of the Grisons country are commonly called by the name of terræ: every severall village a terra. There runneth a very swift river through this valley called Brembus, wherehence the valley hath the name of Brembana. Most of this valley is an ascent leading towards the Alpes. At the entrance it is something pleasant way, but after I had passed some sixteen miles it was very laboursome and painfull to travell, as well in regard of the steepnesse, as of the extreme hard stones wherewith the greatest part of the way is pitched.

The village of St. Johns.

I departed from St. Johns about seven of the clocke in the morning, the nineteenth day of August being Friday, and came to a terra, upon the mountaine Ancone called Mezolt about sixe of the clocke in the evening. This dayes journey was but eleven miles. I passed through two villages of Terraes betwixt St. Johns and Mezolt. Whereof the first was Allapiazza, where I dined with certaine Sclavonians, who told me that about five daies before that, there were thirty Bandits taken about eight miles beyond that place, who lay in waite in certaine privy corners of the mountaines, to spoile the passengers that were to travell that way towards Bergomo faire. These Bandits are banished men, who for some notorious villany that they have committed in their owne countries, doe voluntarily flie away for feare of punishment, and being afterward very poore and destitute of maintenance, they live by rifling and spoyling of travellers. The other of the two Terraes is called Ulmo, three miles on this side Mezolt. Within halfe a mile after I was past Ulmo I beganne to ascend the Mountaine Ancone, which is otherwise called Montane de S. Marco, a very high Alpe and difficult in ascent. There lay at the same Inne at Mezolt,

[p. 355.]
Mezolt.

Thirty Bandits taken.

61

CORYAT'S CRUDITIES

where I did, a certaine Grison called Joanne Curtabatus borne in Chiavenna, with whom I had much good discourse. For he spake prety good English. And lived many yeares heretofore in Cambridgeshire with Sir Horatio Palavicino an Italian, whom he served. He told me he was a Protestant: I found him a man of very courteous behaviour, and indeede he did me a certaine kindnesse, in which respect I thought it fit to name him in my journall.

I departed from Mezolt about sixe of the clocke in the morning the twentieth day of August being Saturday, and came about eight of the clocke in the evening to a Terra called Camp three and twenty miles beyond it, in the fruitfull valley Telina commonly called Valtulina in the Grisons country. From Mezolt to the toppe of Saint Marks Mountaine it is foure miles. There standeth an Inne built upon the toppe of this Mountaine which is the farthest bound of the Venetian Signiory, which extendeth it selfe in length from the City of Venice to this place, no lesse than an hundred threescore and fourteene miles. In all which space the Venetian money is current. Over the dore of the foresaid Inne the golden winged Lion is erected, under whom this inscription is written in blacke letters upon a golden ground.

Via hæc ab urbe Bergomi Morbinium tendens
Temporis injuria & montium ruinis interrupta,
Atque penitùs interclusa, ad communem usum et commodum non modò aperta fuit & instaurata, sed etiam planior ac latior effecta, insuper extructa præsenti rerum vectigalium taberna. Quæ opera ab Aloysio Priolo Prætore inchoata, & a Joanne Quirino Præfecto ex Serenissimi Senatus decreto perfecta
fuerunt atque absoluta Anno cIↄ. Iↄ. Xciv.

The end of my Observations of Italy.

OBSERVATIONS OF RHETIA

My Observations of Rhetia commonly called the Grisons Country.

Etwixt the foresaid Inne and Morbinio it *Morbinio.* is nine miles. In all which space there is a continuall descent from the Mountayne. This Morbinio is seated at the very foote of the hill, and is the first Towne of the Grisons country, situate in the foresaid valley Telina, which is famous for wines. For indeed it yeeldeth the best wines of al the Grisons country, which are esteemed so good, that they are therehence carryed to all the principall and remotest places of the Grisons territory. As to Curia the Metropolitan City *Curia.* of the country threescore and seven miles off. None of those wines are carryed in Carts. Because the narrownesse of the waies is such that no Carts can passe there: [p. 357.] but al upon horses backs. In this Towne and all other places of this valley they speake Italian, but such rude and grosse language as in the City of Bergomo, or rather worse.

The name of Rhetia commeth from Rhetus a certayne *The country of* King of Tuscia, who being expelled out of his owne *Rhetia.* country by Bellovesus the Gaule about 587. yeares before the incarnation of Christ, at what time he conquered the Insubres, and built the City of Milan, came with many of his subjects into these valleys seated betwixt the Alpes, where they built Castels and fortifications for their defence. And after his time the country had his denomination from him as I have already said.

This country of Rhetia is at this day divided into two parts, the higher and the lower: all that Tract which beginneth from the farther edge of Switzerland, and includeth some part of Lombardy as farre as the lake of Como, (the inhabitants whereof are commonly called the Grisons) is the higher Rhetia. The lower deriveth his beginning from the river Lycus, which divideth this from the higher, and extendeth it selfe as farre as the river Ænus, which boundeth Rhetia and Bavaria.

Great abundance of sheep.

I observed a special commodity in this countrey that I could not see in Italy. For I saw great abundance of sheepe here, which I met driven in the way in many great flocks, all the sheepe being according to my estimation at the least foure thousand: but I heard they were not the sheepe of the countrey, but the citizens of Bergomo, which were kept here about the Alpine mountaines almost al the yeare, and at that time of the yeare the sheep-beards doe use to drive them home every yeare to their Masters.

Frogs.

Also I noted marveilous abundance of little hip-frogges in that part of this valley Telina, where I travelled. I never saw the hundreth part of them in so short a space in all my Life: Most of their meadowes being so full of them, that I could not step five or sixe steps but I should finde a little frogge; a thing that I much wondred at, because I could not search out the naturall reason why there should be more store of them there then in other Countries. In my journey betwixt Morbinio and Camp where I lay that night, I left that castle on the left hand whereof the Dominican Fryer Vincentius of Bergomo told me, which is guarded by a Garison of Spaniards. Also I saw the noble lake of Como, upon the brinke whereof the foresaid castle standeth: this lake is called in the Italian Lago di Como from the city of Como seated by it, which grieved me that I could not see, because it is possessed by the Spaniards. For there I should have seene two notable things the one a worthy elogium of Plinius Secundas, who was a citizen of Como, though borne in Verona, as I have before said; that elogium I heard is written upon our Lady Church dore: the other the famous study of Paulus Jovius that excellent Historiographer and citizen of this citie also. That study is to this day shewed standing in a little Peninsula neare to the city which was once very elegantly adorned with the images of a great multitude of famous men, especially such as excelled in any faculty of learning, a learned elogium being added to

[p. 358.]

The Lake of Como.

TIES

s farre as the riv
avaria.
this countrey the
great abundance :
le way in many pa
ng to my estimate
heard they were to
citizens of Bergom
tne mountaines alon
yeare the sheep-head
yeare to their Maste
x of little hip-frogs
, where I travelled
... in so short a spa
adowes being so full
... me steps but I shou
... I much wondred a
the naturll reason of
next there then in oth
r.n Morbinio and Ca
x castle on the left ha
... s of Bergomo the
... of Spaniards. Also
... a tire brinke where
... lake is called in th
city of Como seated b
... see, because it i
here I should have seen
... elogium of Plini
Como, though borne
... elogium I heard
... the other the famo
it Historiographer a
r is to this day shewe
to the city which w
le images of a gre
such as excelled t
rium being added t

every one by the same Jovius. This lake is otherwise called Lacus Larius from the Greeke word λάρος, which signifieth gavia, that is, a Sea-mew or Sea-gul, because there is wonderfull plenty of them about this Lake. The foresaid Jovius hath most elegantly described this lake in a peculiar Treatise thereof.

That night that I lay at Campe, which is a Terra, situate *Campe.* by the goodly lake of the Grisons, distant about foure miles from the lake of Como, and in some places at the least two miles broad, there happened such a horrible thunder, lightning and raine all that night, that it caused an exceeding fluxe of waters from sundry places of the mountaines on both sides of the valley, that the next morning I could not goe by land to the next village, by reason of the extreme inundation, but was constrayned to [p. 359.] row thither in a boat. I departed from Camp about seven of the clocke in the morning, the one and twentieth day of August being Sunday, and came to a Terra called Candolchin being eighteene miles beyond it, above five of the clocke in the afternoone, where I lay that night. In this space I observed nothing memorable ; only I passed through the towne Chiavenna, in Latin Clavenna, situate *Chiavenna.* at the farther end of the valley Telina, standing in a valley of the same name, in which I travelled full twenty miles. This towne ministred some occasion of comfort unto me, because it was the first Protestant town that I entred since I went out of Italy, yet not wholly Protestant. For some part of it embraceth Popery, and heareth daily masse. The Protestants that are here professe the Calvinian not the Lutheran religion, who had a very learned Preacher when I was there, called Octavianus Mejus, who was brought up in Geneva, his parents being Italians of the city of Luco in Tuscanie. In this towne dwelt Joannes Curtabatus, of whom I have before spoken, who refreshed my heart with a cup of excellent wine. This towne is rich, and inhabited with many wealthy merchants; also it hath great store of goodly vineyards growing about it.

CORYAT'S CRUDITIES

Rough ways. The wayes both in the valley Telina some few miles
before I came to Chiavenna, and also in the ascent of the
valley Candolchin, are very offensive to foote travellers.
For they are pitched with very sharpe and rough stones
that will very much punish and grate a mans feete.   I
observed that the poore Alpine people dwelling in the
mountaynous places of the Grison territory, doe send their
children abroad into the high wayes with certaine hoddes
tyed about their necks, to gather up all the horse-dung
that they can finde, which (as I take it) serveth onely for
the dunging of their Gardens.   The like I saw many doe
[p. 360.] in the valley Brembana, and in some few places of Lombardy a little before I came to Bergomo.
    I passed through a delicate great meadow a little on
this side Candolchin, contayning at the least forty acres
by my estimation, which was a thing that I much wondred
at, by reason that the countrey is so extreme stony and
barren, invironed with such huge steepe mountaines on
both sides, and for that the Terra is situate in a marvailous
high place, having very high mountains both at the ascent
unto it, and the descent.
    The houses in the poore Terraes of the Grisons that
are situate about the mountaines, are so made, that both
the endes and the sides doe consist of whole pine trees,
compacted together in steede of stony wals, though in
many places their walls are stony also, especially in their
faire townes, as Chiavenna &c.
A cheerful A certaine Priest of this country cheered me with very
priest. comfortable wordes at mine Inn at Candolchin, because
he saw I was a solitary man and a stranger.   For he told
mee that because the fare of some places of the country
was hard and the ways bad, hee would endeavour with
cheerfull termes to rowse up my spirits, and to be as merry
as a solitary man could, as I travelled in as honest
a country as any in all Christendome.   For had I a
thousand crownes about me, I might more securely travell
with it in their country without company or weapon, then
in any other nation whatsoever : affirming that he never

66

heard in all his life of any man robbed in that country. This his speech was afterward confirmed unto me in other places: which if it be true, I attribute more to the honesty of this nation, then to any other that I could ever see, reade, or heare of under the cope of heaven; but whether I should ascribe this their innocencie to the severitie of the lawes of their Country inflicted upon robbers, (whose examples perhaps may terrifie others, and deterre them from committing the like offences,) or to the inherent and natural vertue of the people I know not, onely this I say, [p. 361.] that I never heard of such rare honesty before in all my life, in any people whatsoever before or since Christ.

I Observed in Candolchin and other places before I came thither, both in the valley Brembana and Telina, a strange kinde of wooden cuppes like pailes, in which they *Wooden cups.* bring up Wine to their Ghestes, with prety convenient pipes about a foote long, to powre out the Wine into the Glasse or cuppe, these are used also in most places both of the Grisons country and Switzerland.

I departed from Candolchin about eight of the clock the next morning being Munday, and the two and twentieth of August, and came that night to a towne called Tossana situate at the foote of a hill, twenty five *Tossana.* miles beyond it, about seven of the clocke in the evening; The language in the valley of Candolchin is Italian.

After I was past Candolchin, I did continually ascend for the space of eight miles till I came to the toppe of a certaine high mountaine called Splugen mountaine. Betwixt all this valley of Candolchin, which beginneth a little on this side Chiavenna, and extendeth it selfe to the top of the foresaid mountaine, there runneth a very swift lake called Lir. I travelled sixteene miles in this valley of Candolchin. From the toppe of the Mountaine to the descent it is sixe miles. At the foot of the hill there is a town called by the name of the Mountain, viz: Splugen, which is wholy Protestant. From this place *Splugen.* forward all the Grisons speake Dutch. Here at Splugen I entered into a third valley of the Grisons country,

namely the valley of the Rhene, which is so called
because a little arme of the noble river Rhene runneth
through it. In this valley of Rhene I travelled tenne
miles. The Rhene which runneth through this valley,
flowes with such an extreme swiftnesse, that the water
thereof in certaine places where it falleth downe from steepe
cataractes, raiseth a certaine reaking mist to a great heigth,
[p. 362.] which proceedeth from the greate violence of the torrent.

From Splugen to another towne of the same name
Westward it is a mile, from that to a towne called Sassam
five miles, from Sassam to Tossana seated at the foote of
a mountaine at the farther end of the valley of Rhene,
five miles more. I meane not five miles of the Grisons
A Grison mile country. But I reduce their miles to our English com-
is five English putation, one of theirs being five of ours. All those
miles. foresaid towns professe the Protestant Religion. I
observed a custome in this country that is not used (I
thinke) in any place in Christendome, that whensoever a
stranger or any other of the same country, doth aske one
of them upon the way how many miles it is to any place,
he will not answere so many, but will tell you in so many
howers you may be there. Which yeeldeth a very uncertaine satisfaction to a traveller, because the speede of all
is not a like in travelling : For some can travell farther in
one howre, then others in three.

In many places of Rhetia, till I came into that part of
it which is almost wholy Protestant, I saw many little
Chappels built by the high way side (as in Savoy) tending
to Superstition ; as the picture of Christ, the Virgin Mary,
and sometimes of some Saints above the Altar.
Thick The trenchers in most places of this country are so
trenchers. strange, that although perhaps I shall seeme ridiculous to
the reader to mention so meane a matter ; yet howsoever
by reason of the noveltie of them, they shall not passe
unmentioned. They are for the most part at the least an
inch thicke, and as large in compasse as a cheese of my
country of Somersetshire that will cost a shilling.

The tyle of most of their houses is made of pieces of

68

OBSERVATIONS OF RHETIA

wood as in Chambery in Savoy, not of earth as in France, Italy, and England.

The Windowes of their houses are exceeding little in all their Terraes and in most of their townes, the greatest part whereof are covered with little boordes in the outside.

In sundry places of their country I observed divers Castles and Forts of great antiquity built upon high rockes, and eminent hils. But now they are much ruinated, and of reparations: it is likely that these were built either by the followers of King Rhetus that inhabited this Country after he was ejected out of his Kingdome of Hetruria in Italy by Bellovesus the Gaule (as I have before said) or by the People of the country for meanes of defence against the armies of the Romans, that under the conduct of Julius Cæsar and many other noble captaines of Rome, made themselves a way through this country by force of armes into Germany.

[p. 363.]
Many castles and forts.

They built a great multitude of little cottages upon the very toppes of the steepe Alpine Mountaines, as in Savoy, and have many little plottes there also, as in Savoy.

Although the greatest part of this country doth yeeld very poore people: yet I have observed some few places passing wel furnished with all manner of necessary commodities for the sustentation of mans life: as Oxen and Kine, Sheepe, Goates, many goodly meadowes and pastures, indifferent corne fields, and abundance of wood that groweth upon the sides of the Mountaines. Their drink is not beere, but wine, the greatest part whereof the valley Telina doth minister to the remoter places, as I have before said. Also they are competently stored with hempe, which they doe not strip with such laborious difficultie as we doe in England by the meanes of their fingers, but by certaine wooden instruments made for the same purpose that do very easily sever the stranne from the scale. Their fare is good in many places and very cheape. Amongst many dishes that come to their table Martelmasse beefe is very frequent.

A well furnished country.

But seeing I am now come into that part of the Grisons

69

country which speaketh Dutch, I wil here interrupt my [p. 364.] description of it by the addition of a most elegant Latin Oration that I have annexed unto this discourse written in praise of the travell of Germany by that learned German Hermannus Kirchnerus, the author of the first Oration that I have prefixed before my booke, and according to my meane skill rudely translated into our mother tongue by my selfe : which although perhaps it may seeme unto some a meere impertinent matter to my present discourse :

Rhetia a German country. yet in regard that Rhetia is a member of Germanie, whose language a great part of it speaketh, and my first introduction that conveighed me into this noble country of Italy, after my survay of some parts therof ; I hope the candid reader wil not miscensure me for inserting this into my Observations, especially seeing the elegancy of it is such, that it cannot be but pleasant to all readers whatsoever, but more particularly unto travellers, & most of all unto those that either have already seene some parts of Germany, or intend hereafter to see it. As I for mine owne part have superficially observed some few principall Cities thereof, and determine by the gracious permission of the Almighty to see most of the famous Cities and greatest Princes Courts both of all the higher parts of Germany & the Netherlands, which are places that to an industrious traveller will yeeld infinite both experience and delight. To detayne thee long with preambles of praises of this most imperiall and renowned Region out of my little experience of the same, were a matter very superfluous, seeing this most eloquent Oration doth as lively paint her out in her true colours as ever Apelles did his Venus ἀναδυομένη. Onely the better to encourage thee to see her glorious beauty, whereof I my selfe have to my unspeakable joy and comfort perceived a little glimpse, I say with Kirchnerus, that Germany is the Queene of all other Provinces, the Eagle of all Kingdomes, and the Mother of all Nations. Therefore omitting farther introductions I present unto thy gentle and favourable censure this excellent Oration it selfe.

70

I here interrupt
most elegant Lat
his discourse writt
that learned Germ
of the first Orati
ke, and according :
to our mother tong
ps it may seeme ne
my present discours
er of Germanie, whi
:h, and my first into
this noble country o
... thereof; I hope th
me for inserting th
eeing the elegancy of
... to all readers wh
... travellers, & most p
... some pri
... As I for m
... some few princip
... ... permissi
... the famous Cities &c
... the higher parts o
... are places that m:
... both experience an
... preambles of priv
... Region out of e
... a matter very sup
Oration doth as firs
is ever Apelles did h
... to encourage th
I my selfe have to r
... a little glimpse
is the Queene of l
Kingdomes, and h
mitting farther into
d favourable censu

Another Oration made by the foresaid Hermannus
Kirchnerus, a Civil Lawier, Orator, and Poet,
&c. And pronounced in the noble University
of Marpurg above named, by a worthy Schollar
of his Henry de Stangi, a Silesian, upon this
Theme. That the travell of Germany is to be
preferred before all other travels.

OF those things which seeme greatly to tend *Hermann*
to the knowledge of common affaires, to *Kirchner's*
the information of a right judgement, to *oration in*
the wisdome of a civill life, and the perfect *praise of travel*
understanding of good counsels, are to be *in Germany.*
earnestly commended and diligently delivered unto youth, which shall be hereafter
advanced to the helme of publique authority : surely there
is no reason why I should doubt but that the most laudable
custom of travelling, and the desire of knowing the
manners of forraine countries and nations, the lawes of
Cities, and formes of common-weales abroad should be
both esteemed very profitable and pleasant, and also be
furthered to the uttermost with all manner of helpes, and
accounted the most necessary thing of all others for youth,
according to that excellent speech of Apollonius which is
every where extant amongst the ancients concerning this
matter, that a yong man ought to travell out of his
country no otherwise than if he were destitute of house
or home. Which custome of travelling if we have read
to have beene at any time frequented and used of any
nation whatsoever, certes we may most plainly perceive
as it were at noone-tide that it is at this day most famously
exercised by the men of our Germany, even by the
common and almost daily endevour of our Princes and
noble Personages that travell into farre countries, so that
there is scarce found a man of any note and fame in the
courtly life, in the politique conversation, and civill society,
which hath not both learned the manners and languages of

71

forraine nations, and also seene abroade in the world the
state and divers governments of Kingdomes, that hath not
with eyes and feete made use of England, Italy, France,
and Spaine, and observed whatsoever is memorable in
remote nations, and worthy to be seene in every place of
note.

Germans'
travelling
greatly to be
commended.
Now as no man doth doubt but that this custome of
our Germanes travelling out of Germany beyond the Alpes
and the Seas, is greatly to be commended especially if they
prescribe unto themselves a just and laudable end of
travelling: so againe who will not say but that this
preposterous order of our men is justly to be condemned
which they observe in the course of their travels, when
as most of them after they have with great diligence sought
out the Roane, the Seine, the Tyber, and the Po; and
not only curiously searched for the ruinous theaters of the
ancient Romans, and the rubbish of their decayed buildings, but also crept into all the stewes, all the brothell
houses, and burdelloes of Italy, after I say all these things,
have so omitted the sight of the most beautifull Cities of
Germany their country, the most elegant Townes, the well
governed Common-weales thereof altogether unknowen
unto them, that they are not able as much as to name the
principall ornaments of Germany. Which thing truly is
not only unworthy a Citizen that loves his country but
also an argument of notable negligence, & most unbeseem-
ing a German man, not to know, not to see, not to search
out Germany wherein he was borne and brought up,
wherein he hath all his wealth and all his estate, and for
whose sake (if neede should require) he ought not doubt
to powre out his vitall bloud. And why so? are you not
all constrayned (my fellow Academicks) to subscribe to this
my opinion that the knowledge of no nation is so necessary
as the searching out of a mans owne country, and the
manners thereof, and the right understanding of that
common-weale whereof each of us is a part and member?
the Lamiæ that are a certaine kinde of Monsters, are
laughed at in the Poeticall fables, in that they were so

72

IN PRAISE OF TRAVEL IN GERMANY

...de in the world...
...omes, that hath...
...land, Italy, Fra...
...er is memorable...
...ere in every place

...that this custome
...y beyond the Al...
...especially if the
...laudable end...
...say but that...
...y to be condem...
...their travels, wh...
...igence some...
...and the Po; r...
ruinous theaters of...
...decayed bu...
...all the brid...
I say all these thi...
...beautifull Citie;
...zant Townes, the r,
...together unknow...
is so...al as to name...
...thing true...
...oves his country...
...ce, A most unbese...
...to see, not to sea...
...re and brought...
...all his estate, and...
...he ought not do...
whie so? are you...
...to subscribe to...
nation is so necess...
ne country; and...
...derstanding of th...
a part and membe...
of Monsters, ...
that they were s...

blinde at home that they could not see their owne affaires, could foresee nothing ; but when they were once gone from home, they were accounted the most sharpe-sighted and curious searchers of all others: so who doth not thinke that the eyes of our Germans that gadde into Italy, France, and I know not whither, are very ridiculous, when as by taking long voyages unto farre remote people, after they have curiously sought out all matters amongst them, are ignorant of the principall things at home, and know not what is contayned within the precincts of their country, and are reckoned altogether strangers in their native soile. What is there nothing (saist thou) at home that is worthy to be seene and knowen, and for whose sake a journey ought to be undertaken? I that am a stranger in mine owne country will contend with thee in this Oratorian field concerning this subject, and will produce most apparant reasons to prove that the travell of Germany is more excellent then of all other nations, and to be preferred before all others. Wherefore I intreate you to entertaine my Oration with gentle eares, yea I earnestly request and beseech you for the love sake of your country, to receive my speech with your wonted favour and indulgence, while I give you a tast of the principall ornaments of our common country.

Therefore that my Oration may derive her beginning *What travel* even from this, I will aske this first question: how many *means.* travellers there are that when they undertake any voyage do rightly understand what travell meaneth. Since many doe fondly imagine that it is nothing else then a certayne gadding about, a vaine beholding of sundry places, a transmigration from one country to another, whose feete doe only move from place to place, and whose eyes are conveighed from one field to another. Of whom thou mayest very rightly use that knowen speech of the Poet.

> The climate, not their minds they change,
> That sayling over every Sea doe range.

But we will say that he is the man that visiteth forraine

73

Kingdomes and doth truly travell, and that according to
the censure of all learned men, the consent of Historians,
and the opinion of politicians, he I say, who whither
soever he directeth his journey, travelleth for the greater
benefit of his wit, for the commodity of his studies, and
the dexterity of his life, who moveth more in minde then
body, who attayneth to the same by the course of his
travel, that others doe at home very painfully and with
great study by turning of bookes. Will you have me
(my worthy Auditors) speake more plainly to you? it is
travell that stirreth up wisdome, purchaseth fortitude,
confirmes it being purchased, gives light unto us for the
instruction of our manners, makes us from barbarous to
be gentle and milde natured: it rooteth out a fond selfe
love, it availeth to suffer labours, to undergoe dangers,
and with a valiant and manly minde to endure them, and
sheweth us the nearest way to the solid learning of all
things. What need many words? let travell be the plentifull institution of all our life. For histories doe teach
us that men of old time did travell to that end. So that
Ancient Solon travelled into Asia, Plato into Egypt, Pythagoras
travellers. into Italy, the Romans to Marselleis, Mithridates into
Cappadocia, and others undertooke very long and tedious
voiages to this end, that they might gather together the
lawes and ordinances of their common-weale out of the
divers decrees of sundry nations, and that the best of them,
after they had gathered them, might convert them to the
use of their country, that whatsoever excellent things they
did reape abroad amongst others, they might bring them
home, and at home instruct their countrymen therein. If
thou undertakest the desire of travelling with that minde
and intent, to what end dost thou goe forth of thy country?
whither dost thou bend thy course? to what end dost
thou travell with the swallow leaving thy nest? doth not
Praise of Germany in respect of the plenty and commodity of those
Germany. things, by many degrees excell all other nations? who as
the Queene of all other Provinces, the Eagle of all
Kingdomes, the Mother of all nations, doth shee not most

74

IN PRAISE OF TRAVEL IN GERMANY

plentifully impart unto thee all those thinges which may tend as well to the happy institution of a common-weale, as to integrity of manners, purity of religion, and piety of life, the ornament of wit, and the elegancy of speech? for if thou desirest to know the formes of common-weales, and the governement of a Monarchie, if thou wouldest understand the manner of an aristocraticall rule, and of the popular state, where shalt thou better and more exactly learne these things then in Germany, which is as it were an abridgement of the world? pray goe with me (my courteous Auditors) and consider the most goodly Common-weales and Cities of our Germanie. What I pray you, will you finde wanting in that most stately Common-weale of Strasbourg, in that most plentifull Norimberg, in most elegant Auspourg, in spacious Colen, in most beautifull Lubeke, in that worthily commended Breslaw? In which cities according to the testimony of Scaliger in his booke intituled of the praise of Cities, equitie her selfe doth reigne, all iniquity is banished, justice doth governe, for unjustice no place is left, good men are called forth with rewardes, and evill men called backe from vice and punishments. If thou desirest to behold the most happy state of an Empire that can be devised in the world, namely of our most sacred Emperour, our most potent Electors, our illustrious Princes, our Earles, Barons, Nobles, and other rankes knit together with a most admirable bond, thou shalt not see it any where but in Germany, but onely in Germany, I say. In Germany thou shalt behold the steppes of the ancient Persian Empire, and a certaine lively image thereof : in Germany, the power and liberty of the Grecians : in Germanie thou shalt observe the possession of the ancient Romanes. Wouldest thou with Cyneas the Ambassadour of Pyrrhus crave such a Senate of the Empire, wherein should be all Kings, all like to auncient Pyrrhus? In no place of the earth shalt thou finde it but onely in Germany. Wilt thou heare consultations of the weightiest matters of all the world?

75

No where shalt thou heare them but in the Diets of
Germany. Wilt thou have Captaines of the great Empire
mightier then the successors of Alexander himselfe? No
where shalt thou find it but in Germany. Dost thou crave
the most famous Tribunall in the whole Empire, the shop
of the auncient Roman justice, and as it were the Sessions
of the old Amphictyones of Greece? No where shalt thou
behold it but in Germany. Good God, if for the beholding of this most sacred meeting those ancient heads of the
civill law could be recalled to the fruition of this vitall
breath, Papinianus, Paulus, Ulpianus, Pomponius, Caius,
Julianus, and all other sacred Masters of the lawes could
returne into this world out of their ashes, truly I beleeve
they would travell into the middle of Germany from the
Elysian fields, yea I will say that Astræa her selfe the
Goddesse of justice would descend with them from heaven
to place her habitation there also amongst mortall men.
But what shall I say of the other fruits of travell?
where shalt thou more happily and studiously attaine to
all the liberal sciences then in Germany, which doth excell
the auncient Egyptians in the study of Geometrie, the
Hebrews in Religion, the Chaldæans in Arithmeticke, the
Grecians in all arts, the Romans in discipline, and in variety
of mechanicall trades, constancy, and fortitude, all other
nations. Which the very strangers themselves how much
soever they envy us, are constrained to confesse maugre
their hearts. Bodin wrote this though he were very
sparing of the German praise, the very truth it selfe
wresting the speech from him, he wrote it I say, and
proclaimed it of the Germans with an open voice, out of
the Kingdome of France, Neither can any other man
write otherwise of it. Let them behold so many learned
The German Athenæ in Germanie, so many noble Universities, as that
universities. of Vienna in Austria, of Heidelberg in the Countie Palatine, of Colen by the Rhene, of Prage in Bohemia, of
Erdfurt and Jene in Thuringia, of Leipzick, of Rostock,
Louan, Friburg, Ingolstat, Basil, Gripswald, Tubingen,
Mentz, Wittenberg, Franckford, Konigsberg, Julia, in the

IN PRAISE OF TRAVEL IN GERMANY

ut in the Diets
of the great Emp
nder himselfe? }
IV. Dost thou co
ole Empire, the de
s it were the Senat
No where shalt tho
rod, if for the beho
se ancient heads of t
fruition of this ve
us, Pomponius, Ca:
::: of the lawes co,
: :hes, truly I beli
· ·" Germany from t
:: A:=za her selfe t
: wra them from hence
k" age: mortall men
· · E:s of travel
.t. s:l usly attaine
· · · :: :ich doth exa
· · · : Geometrie, ti
· · · : Arithmetike, ti
:::: and in vare
::: ':':nde, all ele
· :: ::=:es how ma:
·:: : : confesse magn:
:::: he were m
· · ·:: truth it sel
· · z:e it I say, a:
::: :: open voice, out i
· :: any other ma:
·:::: so many learned
[::versities, as the
in the Countie Pal
·:e in Bohemia, t
· ::pzick, of Rostox,
·.:=wald, Tubinge,
·:berg, Julia, in the

Duke of Brunswicks dominion, Strasbourg, Altorph. Let them also behold this our famous seate of all the Muses, which hath nourished that opinion of a most happy genius and nature amongst all strangers even from her first beginning, that even as Ammianus hath written of the University of Alexandria, that it never dismissed any from it but endewed with learning; so out of this noble Academie there have sprung Counsellors for Kings over all the world, and for our sacred Emperor himselfe, and governors and teachers for all common-weales, Churches, and Schooles. What also shall I say of those other Universities like unto ours? unto whom I would not doubt but that all the Sages of the Grecians, all the wise Romans, and all the famous Orators would travell into Germany, if they should happen to enjoy the benefite of life againe.

No where shalt thou find so many Archimedes, so many Vitruvii, so many Nasicæ, so many Ciceroes, so many Horaces, so many Virgils, so many Scævolæ, so many Papiniani, as in Germanie. Which also Argyropylus the learnedst of the Grecians confessed at Rome in the Popes Court, when he cryed out that all the graces, all arts, and good letters were fled beyond the Alpes into Germany.

The day would fail me if I would make a Catalogue of the most famous wits that are in this one Province of Hassia, and especially in this University wherein we live, how many and how great lights it doth yeeld that may compare with that admirable antiquity of the auncient Grecians and Romans. Here could I point out to thee with my finger Caians, Lælians, Mutians; here Galens, here Platoes, here such as Socrates, here Tullies, here Virgils, here also (which is the most to be wished for thing of all) the Chrysostomi, the Epiphanii and Athanasii.

Wilt thou go to know military discipline? where I pray thee shalt thou finde the Schoole of Mars but amongst the Germans, amongst whom it was thought in former times that Mars himselfe dwelt? for which cause Alexander that both in substance and name was great, very wisely

Germans famous in wars.

77

thought it was not good for him to provoke the Germans into the field. Also C. Caligula, and Augustus stoode in such feare of them that when they heard a rumour of their comming into Italy, they doubted much of their safety, so that both of them fled beyond the sea: what can be more gloriously spoken of the Germans Mars? what more worthily reported? no man by force of arms recalled the Gothes when they invaded Spaine, no man expulsed the Saxons when they surprized Brittaine, no man kept out the Vandals when they subdued Africk, no man repelled the Francks when they vanquished Gallia, no man repressed the Ostrogothes when they conquered Italy. Most incredible hath been the strength of our warlike valour, and our military arts have been admired by all nations wherewith our Germany hath excelled in all ages, and with which it hath gotten the prize from all nations, and the Empire and praise of the victory even from the Romans themselves which were the conquerors of all other people. Most justly is Germany to be called the shop of Mars, which hath ministred most valiant Captaines, and expert souldiers and forces to all famous battels that were ever waged in any parts of the earth, from the time of the great voiage of Xerxes. For what skirmish, what fight, what notable campe was there ever in the field in the time of our forefathers without Germans? what sea, what country is so remote unto whom the gleaves and halberts of our Germans are at this day unknowen? as for those warres which are waged at this day in the Netherlands and in Hungarie, are they not managed by the helpe and industry of our Germans? what sayest thou to the most mighty Tyrant of the east which most earnestly attempted with fire and sword to destroy the whole world, have not the armes of the German Mars brought him into those streights that he was compelled humbly to crave peace, and having craved it could hardly obtaine it? moreover in no place of the world are there to be seen stronger munitions, greater fortresses, better fortified Cities then in Germany. No where can a man see greater provision of

IN PRAISE OF TRAVEL IN GERMANY

rovoke the Germ
Augustus stood
ard a rumour of t
much of their sol
the sea : what ca
ans Mars ? what a
x of arms recalled
, no man expulsed
une, no man kept c
drick, no man repe
ed Gallia, no man
conquered Italy. M
f our warlike vale
admired by all nat
ted in all ages, and t
in nations, and
* *** from the Rom
: all other pee
the shop of Ne
*** Caranes, and equ
that were g
the time of
what ty
r in the field in
what sea, t'
sleeves and halbe
as for the
in the Netherl
by the helpe a
thou to the m
earnestly attemp
world, have
him into the
to crave pee
it ? moreov
to be seen strong
Cities that
greater provision

peeces of Ordinance, engins and warlike instruments then *Famous forts in Germany.* in Germany. I could name unto thee the principall Forts, Castels, garrizons, and armouries of our most potent Dukes, Princes, and Common-weales over all Germany, whereof part I know with mine eies, and part have heard with mine eares. I could shew unto thee Vienna the most invincible Fortresse of Christendome, that hath beene so often assaulted by the frustrate attempts, and great enterprises of that most cruell enemy : I could point out unto thee Dresden a place of incredible strength and puissance : I could name Custrinum the strong seate of Brennus : I could speak of the fortifications and rampiers of Meidenburg : the wals, and lofty battelments and towers of Strasbourg : also I could mention the Castels and strength of Norimberg : the greatnesse of Colen : the puissance of Ulm : the force of Auspurg : withall I could make relation of this most auncient Province of the valiant Catti, which is strengthned with most invincible fortifications, even to the great admiration of the eyes and eares of all strangers : besides I could tell thee of a great many other strong fortifications of Germany, whose number doth exceed the gates of the Thebanes, were it not that in this place I make my speech unto those that know their country of Germanie more exactly then my selfe.

I passe over the exercises of the frequent tilts and horsemanship used in the Courts of so many mighty Princes, I speake not of their manners and grave discipline which doe much confirme the science of military vertue. Goe thy wayes now, and see whether thou canst seeke for in any other part of the earth a greater opportunity of understanding warlike affaires. But perhaps thou wilt say that a man may reape more pleasure in the travels of Italy and France. How so I pray thee ? for truly I see not, I understand not how that should be true. Whom will not the magnificence of Palaces in Germany delight, the beauty of so many royall buildings, and most artificiall architectures ? which heretofore Æneas Sylvius an Italian borne, and the most learned of all the Popes when he

79

made his aboade in Germanie, affirmed that he could not sufficiently admire.

The counterfaited and painted delights of Italy are much carryed about the world, but pray how can they compare with these our pleasures and commodities? those present themselves only to the outward eies and pleasure of the body : but these bring great pleasure of the minde accompanied with singular profite. Pray what can Italy, France, England, or Spaine shew unto thee that Germany hath *The fertility* not? art thou delighted with the pleasure of fields, the *of Germany.* fertility of trees, the plenty of vineyards? thou needest not run into Campania for that purpose, or visit the Florentine gardens, or goe beyond the Alpes to see the Orchards and famous Paradises of Cardinals. Germany will afford thee farre more elegant both gardens and fields not only of our soveraigne Princes and noble Peeres, but also of our most wealthy Citizens of Norimberg, Auspourg, and else where. The Rhene, and Neccar, will shew thee that abundance of vineyards, that plenty and excellency of wine, the Mœne will yeeld thee that amœnity, and so will the Ister, that neither the Adriatique gulfe, nor the Seine, nor Tyber can compare with those places of Germany. What need I report unto thee our woods and groves, wherein nature her selfe doth take pleasure to inhabite? in what country shalt thou find the same more fruitfull, and better replenished with all pleasures & delights then in Germany? the pleasure of hunting which many doe preferre before all other recreations of this life, thou mayest enjoy in Germany to thy very fill. Dost thou delight to behold the sea? and to see the ebbing and flowing of the armes thereof, to goe aboord great ships, and to exercise thy selfe with navigation? then goe to the maritime cities of lower Germany, and to their most elegant mart Townes. Desirest thou to know the fashions, habits, and languages of sundry nations? Germany will shew thee in the havens of Hamborough and the Baltical Cities, Russians, Italians, Frenchmen, Englishmen, Spaniards, Polonians, Danes, Suecians, and also the farthest

Portingals. Besides so many plentifull mines of copper, yron, silver, and gold, in Germany, in Bohemia, (which is also a great part of the German Empire) in Misnia, in Moravia, in Saxony, in Silesia: for the knowing whereof who would not be drawn from the farthest boundes of the whole world? I well know that Cornelius Tacitus would returne into Germany from the infernall parts, if the fates would permit him, that he might behold all these things, and illustrate them with new writings.   Doe thou not passe over the most holsome and pleasant bathes of Germany, unto the which when Poggius the Florentine came, he thought that he was arrived at a new Paradise, in so much that he wrote that nothing in the whole compasse of the earth could be found more pleasant, more sweet, then the bathes of Baden: for he said that there was the seate of the Graces, the bosome of love, and the Theater of pleasure.   Art thou delighted with most witty fabricks and inventions?   In no place of the world shalt thou finde more witty engins and excellent peeces of worke-manship, then in Germany.   Which all strangers are constrained to graunt, in so much that they say, the Germanes have their wit at their fingers ends.   By the Germanes wit the art of printing was first invented, of all arts that ever were as the most profitable, so the wittiest invention, so that it seemeth to be ascribed not so much to mortall men, as to the immortall God, which is mani-fested by the testimony of a certaine Poet that saith thus.

O Germany first foundresse of that skill
Then which time passed hath nought more useful found,
Teaching the Presse to ease the writers quill.

To what end should I advance the other inventions of the Germans? what shall I name unto you their Gunnes? which although they were invented to the destruction of men, yet for the goodly invention they are worthily commended.

The art of making clocks that were in the time of *Clock making.* Carolus Magnus brought into Germany by the munificence of the Persian Ambassadors, which at that time were a great miracle to our people, the East, and Persia her selfe that first gave them, having now received them againe from the hands and wits of the Germanes, doth greatly admire them, according as Augerius hath certified us.

But perhaps thou wilt say that Italy will shew thee more auncient monuments, and more images of antiquity. Report I pray thee (for I desire to hear it) the ruines of auncient Theaters, the decayed pillars of the auncients, and the fields where Troy was, as Virgil speaketh.

German antiquities. But (good God) Germany will present unto thee many more reliques of auncient things, which was a very flourishing Kingdome with Cities and Villages above a thousand years before Rome was built. For what can Italy shew answerable to the antiquity of the German Trevirs? if thou dost looke upon the old ruines and mortar, the auncient stones that have continued there even from the time of the old Babylonian Ninus, doe present unto thee the most true signes of walles built with pitch and slime. If it pleaseth thee to behold the townes and buildings of the ancient Romans, looke upon Colen, Auspurg, and other most ancient Cities. If thou wouldest see tombe stones with auncient inscriptions and statues, thou hast the monument of Drusus, neare Mentz, upon a hill by the Rhene, which the auncient historians have so often mentioned. There is nothing in all the Italian antiquities that can be preferred before those of Germany. Can the sight of Cannæ, of Trebia, and Thrasimenus, that are so famoused for Annibals victories and his slaughter of the Romans, more delight thee then the Rhene and Danubius, which for the space of three hundred years bare the brunt of the Roman forces? Can those auncient places of Italy minister more pleasure unto thee where heretofore the Volsci, the Veientes, the Sabini, the Hetrusci, inhabited, then those, where the auncient conquerers of so many Kingdomes, and the vanquishers of Italy it selfe, even those victorious people of Germanie, the Gothi, the Longobardi, the Catti, the Suevi,

82

IN PRAISE OF TRAVEL IN GERMANY

the Sicambri, the Bructeri, the Angrivarii, the Bavari, the Treviri, the Nervii, the Nemetes, the Triboci, the Vangiones, the Ubii, the Frisii, the Cimbri, the Franci, and other innumerable most glorious nations dwelt? Doth the memory of Scipio, Metellus, and Julius Cæsar, more delight thee then the statues of most valiant Ariovistus, warlike Harminius, invincible Charles, couragious Roland, glorious Henry, and of other heroicall Worthies? but why doe I call up dead men to the stage? why doe I speake of those that lie in the graves? admit that all these things so worthy to be seene and heard, were wanting unto us, yet the hospitality of the Germans, the excellentest vertue of all others (the praise whereof derived from their parents they doe most worthily maintayne) whom would it not incite to travell into Germany, whom would it not allure, whom would it not draw? which it is written the famousest amongst the auncient Romans to have done, namely Pliny, Tacitus, Julius, Augustus, Tiberius, who vaunted that he travelled nine times out of Italy into Germany. But what a kinde of solitarinesse was there then of old Germany, what an unshapen face, what a roughnesse, so that if it be compared with the present Germany, it seemeth to be made a golden and marble country out of a leaden and wooden, even as Sylvius hath testified, whose eyes the brightnesse of the Empire and the German nation did so dazell, that he wrote this to the men of his owne nation. Let us endevour that we may be called rather Germanes then Italians, but although we cannot prevaile to bring that matter to passe, yet howsoever let us direct our studies to that end, that we may alwaies obey that famous nation. Adde unto all these things the Germans faith and integrity, and the most safe seate of travelling. Italy is full of a thousand treacheries, of a thousand dangers, and Spaine also is as full of them, whereof a man may most truly use that speech.

Mourning and dread in every place,
And deaths fell image shewes her face.

83

Since therefore these things are true, why should any man wonder that from the remotest regions of the southerne world the Antipodes, and those whom all the age of the Romans knew not, and whose being to have beleeved it was accounted a most haynous crime and deadly offence, have of late yeares arrived in Germany, after an infinite length of travell to see our most valiant Netherlanders? Againe, why should any man wonder that not only in the time of the Empire of Charles the Great, but *Persianambas-* also no longer then seven yeares since, the Ambassadors *sadors visit* of the King of Persia came to our most Soveraigne Prince *Germany.* Mauritius to Cassels (which Peter Ramus commended at Paris out of the Kings Professors chaire of the University, and which in his writings he stiled by the name of a second Syracusæ where Archimedes dwelleth) being moved with the fame of so worthy a Prince, whom all forraine Nations and People doe admire and honour for the Phœnix of his time, and from thence to have travelled through the middle of Germany to our most invincible Emperour Rodolph. It is even incredible to be reported how much they admired the Cities and Townes of Germany, our Princes territories, and the large bounds of the Empire, the strong Cities and Fortresses. I thinke there are some in this company, that when they were commorant in this Province with our most noble Prince for some certaine dayes, and saw those Ambassadors, they heard how greatly they commended the munition of Cassels, affirming that there was not the like in all Persia. With what wonder and astonishment they beheld the armoury, the rampiers and trenches there, how they observed the magnificence of the Palaces and Gardens, and how they commended the pompe and regall glory of the Court. For these things from their report came afterward to our eares. Moreover why should a man wonder, that men being so often publiquely sent from the innermost desarts of the Russians and Moschovites came into Germany to behold the glory of the imperiall Diet, the might of the Empire, the elegancy of the Cities, and the most noble institution of

84

the common-weale. Also we understand by the report of Augerius Busbequius a most true Writer, that when as in the memory of our fathers, the Ambassadors of Solyman the great Turke came to Franckfort to the assembly of the Princes, being conducted thither through the middle of Germany, they were even amazed and astonished with wondering at the most populous Cities, the multitude of Castels, most beautifull Provinces of the most potent Electors and Princes. Also it is manifest that the like hapned to the Polonians and Frenchmen, when they guarded King Henry out of the Kingdome of France through the middle of Germany; so that they affirmed they then understood with what great power and glory Germanie did excell all other Kingdomes. *An eloquent panegyric.*

Let others therefore goe according to their affections whither they list, let them travell into England, remaine and dye in Italy, let them waxe tawnie in Portingall, and be dyed with the Sunne and soile of Spaine, let them travell into France, saile into Scotland, and let others againe goe to other places; for mine owne part I have resolved that I will never alter my opinion, but will ever thinke that the travell of Germany is to be preferred before all others, and to be more profitable and pleasant then others: and as Plato is said to have given thanks to the Gods in that he was an Athenian born and not a Theban, so let us most worthily congratulate our good fortunes in that we are not strangers, but Germans borne. And surely I doe even promise my selfe (my gentle Auditors) that there is not one of you all but after he hath considered the reasons of this my opinion, and weighed my arguments with an equall and indifferent judgement, he will be of the same minde that I am, and approve my speech.

We beseech the almighty God that is the founder of *A prayer for Germany.* all Regions and Provinces, with all possible earnest prayers, that he would protect, save, and defend our common country Germanie, being the Mother and soveraigne Queene of all other Kingdomes, adorned with the imperiall roabe of dominion and glory of the Cæsarean

Majesty above all other Empires and Kingdomes, most
purely illuminated with the light of Gods holy word above
all other nations, decked with victories and most glorious
triumphes, endowed with most mighty, happy, and wise
Emperours, Princes, and Governours, enriched with all
gifts of humane blessings and prosperity, against all the
assaults of our enemies : and finally that he would embrace
it even to the worlds end with the sweetnesse of his
inexhausted goodnesse and clemency ; but most especially
that he would everlastingly preserve in a most flourishing
estate this Province of Hassia, which is the most beautifull
of all Germany, wherein I am a sojorner for learning sake,
Hassia I say, which heretofore brought forth the most
potent Macedonian Philip of Germany, William the most
wise Solomon of Germany, and now the Prince Maurice
the only miracle of all vertue and learning : also I beseech
him that he would make our Church and Academie
fruitfull like a fertile vineyard, and perpetually
protect it against wolves and beares, and all
the attempts of our adversaries, that
we may sing and cry out with the
Kingly Prophet, He hath
not done thus to
every nation.

FINIS.

OBSERVATIONS OF RHETIA

HAving imparted unto thee this most excellent Oration in praise of the travell of Germanie, the reading whereof cannot be but very delightfull unto thee, I will now returne unto that part of the Grisons country wherehence I digressed, even to Tossana, where I entred a fourth valley which is called by the same name as the other *Tossana.* immediately behind it, namely the valley of Rhene, because that river runneth through this also where it inlargeth it selfe in a farre greater bredth then in the other valley. Also some doe call it the valley of Curia from the citie of Curia the metropolitane of the country, standing in the principall and most fertil place thereof.

I departed from Tossana about seven of the clocke in the morning, the three and twentieth of August beeing Tuesday, and came to Curia tenne miles beyond it, which is the head citie of the country (as I have before said) about one of the clocke in the afternoone.

I observed many wooden bridges in this valley, made *Bridges made* of whole pine trees (as those of Savoy) which are rudely *of pine trees.* clapped together. One of those bridges is of a great length, about one hundred and twenty paces long, and sixe broad, & roofed over with timber. Also it hath foure very huge wooden pillars in the water. This bridge is made over the river Rhene, about five miles on this side the citie of Curia, over the which every stranger that passeth payeth money.

I observed this country to bee colder by halfe then Italie, the ayre beeing heere as temperate as with us in England.

The abundance of Peares and Apples in many places *Abundance of* of Rhetia, especially about the citie of Curia, is such that *fruit in Rhetia.* I wondred at it: For I never saw so much store together in my life, neither doe I thinke that Calabria which is so much stored with peares, can yeeld more plenty for the quantitie or space of ground, then this part of Rhetia [p. 367.] doth. Their trees being so exceedingly laden, that the boughes were even ready to breake through the weight of the fruite.

The Alpes on both sides of this valley are farther distant a sunder, then in the other parts of Rhetia that I had before passed, by meanes of which distance, the space betwixt them being exceedingly enlarged, doth yeeld many fairer meadowes then I saw in the other places of the country: amongst the rest I passed one very goodly and pleasant meadow about a mile on this side Curia, which in my opinion contained about two hundred Acres.

My Observations of Curia,

Commonly called Chur, the Capitall Citie of Rhetia.

Chur.

CUria is of some antiquitie, for it was built about the yeare after the incarnation of Christ 354. at what time Constantine the Emperour when he made warre against the Alemannes, lodged his campe in this valley, and in the same place where the citie now standeth, kept a kinde of court or Sessions for the debating of the common affaires, wherehence the citie being built a little after his departure, had the name of Curia, but it was often after that called by the name of Augusta Rhetorum or Rhetica, as I have before written in my notes of Turin. It is seated under an high Alpine Mountaine, and built in a triangular forme, having on the east and south the steep Mountaines, whereof those on the East are well planted with vineyards; on the west and north side is a goodly spacious plaine, especially that on the North, wherin the river Rhene runneth, being about an English mile and halfe distant from the citie. It is invironed with a faire wall,

[p. 368.] having three gates therein, and adorned with certaine pretty turrets that doe much beautifie the same. It was converted to the faith of Christ shortly after the first

TheCathedral building thereof. The Cathedral Church is dedicated to
Church. S. Martin, and was built by one Thello a Bishop of this city, in number the seventeenth, about the year 770. This Church belongeth to the Protestants, the whole citie indeed being Protestant (but of the Calvinist religion) saving onely some little part, which in a Church that is

88

built in the higher part of the Citie hath daily masses celebrated. In that Church I saw one very auncient monument of a certaine Bishop of this citie, but destitute of an Epitaph, so that the citizens could not tell me what his name was that lay buried there. Also I observed in the same Church many images, superstitious pictures, and Papisticall vanities, as an exceeding great and long picture of Saint Christopher, carrying Christ upon his shoulders, and the image of an Asse with extraordinary long eares, and Christ sitting upon him bare-legged and bare-footed. I was in the Bishops Palace which standeth in the higher part of the citie, beeing a very faire and goodly building, and of great antiquitie. For the Bishopricke of Curia *The Bishopric* is esteemed one of the antientest Bishopricks of all *of Chur.* Germany. For it beganne in the yeare 452. The first Bishop being one Asimo, who was one of the number of those Bishops that were assembled together at the Councell of Chalcedon in Greece. Since which time there hath beene a succession of some eighty Bishops unto him that was Bishop when I was there, whose name was Joannes Flugius, but a Papist. He lived not in the City, but in another place of Germany in voluntary banishment. For about some twelve moneths before I was in Curia, there was a tumult raised in the City, whereof I heard he was the principall Authour. Whereupon because he feared that the Citizens would have punished him, he went voluntarily into exile, so that now he liveth a very obscure and private life. There is great trafficke exercised in this [p. 369.] City, being the place where they lade and unlade their merchandise. For whensoever they send any merchandise beyond the Mountaines, they lay two packes upon each horse. For they use only horses in this country, not carts, by reason of the narrownesse of the waies, as I have before said. And the same horses when they returne home, bring backe that noble wine that I have above mentioned of the valley Telina otherwise called Valtulina.

I was in their Councell house, in the principall roome *The Council* whereof they hang the picture of the present Duke of *House.*

89

Saxony Christian the second. The reason why they so much grace him, is, because he was a great benefactor to the City when he passed that way into Italy. In this Councell house the Magistrates of the State which are sent from the townes of Rhetia, one from every Towne, doe keepe their Sessions thrise every yeare about criminall and civill matters. They have two Councels, the greater and the lesser. The greater consisteth of threescore and fourteene Magistrates, which deliberate and consult about publique matters touching the whole state. The lesser consisteth of fourteene Magistrates which determine matters concerning the city Curia only. Againe, the whole State of Rhetia is devided into three leagues, which are nothing else than Fraternities or Communities that elect and send Magistrates for the execution *The Rhetian* of the affaires of the common-weale. These leagues *Leagues.* were contracted amongst themselves at several times for the better defence of the country against the forraine invasion of strangers, who before that confederation did often oppresse them with many villanies and enormous injuries. The first, wherein the Bishop of Curia, the Deane and Chapter, and the City are united together, was begunne and confirmed in the yeare 1419. The second in the yeare 1424 in a towne called Trontz, and concluded by the Abbot of Disertinum, the Earle of [p. 370.] Masauc, and the Baron of Rezuns. At what time the Abbot added this condition, that the same league should not be made to the prejudice either of the Roman Empire whose Prelate he was, or of the Lordes of Milan whose Earle he was. The third and the last was concluded in the yeare 1470, amongst ten jurisdictions of those that live in a part of Rhetia called Prettigoia. And at last all these three leagues linked themselves together in one forme of union and confederacy for the better strengthning of their common-weale against the violent incursions of forraine forces. Moreover they are at this day united with the Switzers. He that will be farther instructed in the popular governement of the Grisons, let him read a booke

OBSERVATIONS OF CHUR

written by that learned Josias Simlerus of Zurich in Switzerland, who (as a learned man told me in Curia) hath written a peculiar Treatise of the common-weale of the Grisons.

In this City there is a mint where they stampe money *A mint in* of gold, silver, and tin that serveth for the whole territory. *Chur.* This mint I saw together with their armoury house, but I had not the opportunity to enter into either of them.

Here was Magnentius (whom I have before mentioned in my notes of Lyons) proclaimed Emperour by his Souldiers against Constance the second sonne of Constantine the Great, at what time the same Magnentius was generall Captayne of the Roman legions in Rhetia, and afterward he slew the same Emperour Constance as he slept in his bed in a towne called Helena not farre from the Pyrenean mountaines.

In the principall market place which is opposite to St. *The principal* Martins Church before mentioned, there is a goodly faire *market place.* conduit with a faire statue of an armed man standing upon the toppe thereof, a thing very excellently handled. The Citizens bestowed great charges that year 1608 that I was in the City in repayring this conduit, so that they [p. 371.] have greatly beautified it.

I read these verses following written upon a rich citizens house of this City, even upon the outside of the wall over the dore.

Deus.
Stant dextrâ lævaque undæ, procede Viator
transi, rumpe moras, anteriora vide.
Viator.
Duc me, nec sine me, per me Deus optime, duci,
nam duce me pereo, te duce salvus ero.

Thus much of Curia.

I Departed from Curia about six of the clocke in the morning the foure and twentieth of August being Wednesday, and came to Walastat a towne of the country of Helvetia, now called Switzerland, foure Helvetian *Helvetia.*

91

miles, that is, twenty of our English, beyond it, about seven of the clocke in the evening.

The King of France hath built a most magnificent Palace in Rhetia, within a mile and halfe of the citie of Curia neare to the river of Rhene, where a French Ambassador made his residence when I was in the country, being sent to the state of the Grisons from the King of France.

The end of my Observations of the Grisons Country.

[p. 372.]   The beginning of my observations of Helvetia, otherwise called Switzerland.

Ragatz.

He name of the first towne of Switzerland that I entred is Ragatz, ten English miles beyond the citie of Curia.   There Rhetia, and Helvetia doe confine.   I travelled in Rhetia seventy three English miles betwixt Morbinium at the entrance of the country, & this towne of Ragatz at the *The bounds* entrance of Switzerland.   This countrey of Switzerland is *of Switzer-* situate betwixt the Mountaine Jura, the lake Lemanus *land.* (which is otherwise called the Lake Losanna) Italy, and the river Rhene : and it is bounded on the East with the Earledome of Tyroll, on the West with Savoy and Burgundy, on the South with the Coctian Alpes now called mount Senys (as I have before mentioned in my notes of Savoy) Lombardy, the Dukedome of Milan, and the Territory of Piemont on the North with the river Rhene. Againe, the bounds of Switzerland extend themselves about two hundred and forty miles in length, according to the computation of Cæsar, which appeareth to be true at this day ; but in bredth it containeth not above eighty miles, though Cæsar inlargeth the breadth of it to a greater distance.

Within a quarter of a mile after I entred into Switzerland I passed through a very goodly meadow, which I thinke contained at the least five hundred acres.   That day they mowed some part of the same meadow, and

OBSERVATIONS OF SWITZERLAND

carryed away hay ready made out of some other part thereof. I wondred to see their hay harvest so late, being *Late hay* about two moneths later then with us in England. For *harvest.* that was Barthelmew day in Switzerland. But I attribute that harvest to the fatnesse and fertility of the ground. For I beleeve they have two hay harvests, one about that [p. 373.] time that ours is in England, and this I take to be their second hay harvest. The first Rhenish wine that I dranke *Rhenish wine.* was at Walastat, from which place downward, till I entred into Holland, I had continually Rhenish wine in all the Helvetical and German townes and cities. But not that only: for in some places of Switzerland I had good redde wine also: but after I was out of Switzerland I tasted no other wine but onely Rhenish.

I departed from Walastat about three of the clocke the next morning being Thursday and the five and twentieth of August, and passed in a Barke upon the goodly Helvetian lake twenty English miles that day, and about seven of the clocke in the evening arrived at a solitary house by the water side, where I lay that night. The diet *The diet of* of Switzerland is passing good in most places; for they *Switzerland.* bring great variety of dishes to the table, both of rost and sodde meates: and the charge is something reasonable; for my Spanish shilling did most commonly discharge my shot when I spent most.

This Helvetian lake that runneth through a good part of Switzerland betwixt the Alpes, is in many places of a great breadth, at the least two English miles broad. Our barke passed one wooden bridge made over this lake, of an extraordinary length, the longest that ever I saw, even as long as the lake is broad, viz. two miles, so that it joyned together both the bankes of the lake.

I departed from that solitary house about tenne of the clocke that night in the same barke, and came to Zurich fifteene English miles beyond it, about foure of the clocke the next morning being Friday, where I solaced my selfe all that day, and the better part of the next day with the learned Protestants of the citie   I passed thirty five

93

English miles upon the Helvetian lake betwixt Walastat and Zurich.

My observations of Zurich, in Latine Tigurum, the Metropolitan Citie of Switzerland.

Zurich.

SUch is the antiquity of this citie, that it is thought it was built in the time of Abraham (which was about two thousand yeares before the incarnation of Christ, and thirteene hundred yeares before the foundation of Rome) as Rodolphus Hospinianus that glittering lampe of learning, a most eloquent and famous Preacher of this citie tolde me; together with two more, Solodurum an other faire city of Switzerland, & Trevirs in the Netherlands, which by reason that they were built about one time are called the three sister cities of Germany. In the time of Julius Cæsar this citie was but an obscure village: so that he called it Pagus Tigurinus, but in continuance of time *A pleasant* it grew to be a beautifull citie. It is most delicately *site.* seated in a very fertile soile that yeeldeth great plenty of corne and wine. Also it is most pleasantly moystened with water, partly with the noble Helvetian or Tigurine lake that washeth one side thereof, being of a goodly breadth, almost two English miles broad; partly with the river Sylla which runneth by the west side of the city, into which the ashes of Witches, Sorcerers, and Heretiques are cast, after their bodies are burnt, as I will hereafter farther declare in my notes of this citie; and partly with the pleasant lake Limacus mentioned by Cæsar. This is derived out of the Tigurine lake, and runneth through the middest of the citie, so that it maketh two severall cities the greater and the lesser: having three faire bridges over the same, but built with timber, where the citizens doe *The Lake of* usually walke. This lake imparteth two speciall com-*Zurich.* modities to the citie, the one that it yeeldeth abundance of fish, and those passing good; the other that it carrieth *[p. 375.]* many pretty little Barkes, and such like vessels of a meane burden that serve for the conveying of corne, and many other necessaries forth and backe for the use of the citizens.

94

!TIES

.e betwixt Wales

Latine Tigurum,
Switzerland.

... that it is thoug
... (which was abou
...tion of Christ, t
...dation of Ro:...
... lampe of lear...
...eacher of this ci...
...turum an oth
...n the Netherland
...bout one time a...
...... In the time...
...re village: so th...
...mance of the...
... is most delicate
... great plenty...
...ry moysters
...lan or Tigurin
... ing of a good
...., partly with th...
res side of the city
erers, and Heretiqu
... as I will hereafte
...and partly with th
...r Cæsar. This is
runneth through the
b two severall obs
x faire bridges one
re the citizens the
two speciall com
eeldeth abundance
her that it carrieth
vessels of a mean
corne, and many
se of the citizens.

In this lake they have two great wooden wheeles neare to the bridges, each by a severall bridge, made in the forme of water-mils, which are in continuall motion, so cunningly and artificially composed, that they doe incessantly spout out water through a great multitude of pipes. Truely it is a very delectable sight to beholde. Likewise I observed that upon both the sides of the lake which extendeth it selfe very near fifteene English miles in length, there groweth great abundance of delectable vineyardes. This city is walled round about with very goodly wals, *Goodly walls.* built with exceeding strong stone of great antiquity, and beautified with faire battlements. Also there are sixe very magnificent and stately gates in the wals, built wholy with square stone, and made in the forme of strong bulwarkes, which doe greatly beautifie the citie; and they are garnished with the armes of the citie displayed thereon, which are two Lyons and a coate of white and blew. In these wals are many strong and auncient Towers, which served heretofore for fortifications against the hostile force, whereof sixe are in that part of the wall which is in the west side of the citie, being built with a pretty kinde of stratagematical invention. For the first of these sixe is so artificially contrived, that some part of it runneth a litle into the wall, so that almost the whole Tower butteth out from the maine wall into the ditch adjoyning to it, saving that little which is inserted into the wall. The next Tower entreth farther into the wall, and so every other by degrees one after another farther and farther till the last, which is the sixth, is inserted wholly into the wall, that no part of it at all butteth out towards the ditch. A certaine learned young man of the citie called Marcus Buelerus, unto *A learned* whom I was exceedingly beholding for the sight of most *guide.* of the principall things of Zurich (being appointed to [p. 376.] keepe me company by the meanes of that singular learned man Rodolphus Hospinianus) tolde me, that the reason why these Towers were built after such a strange and extraordinary forme, was this, because if the towne should happen to be assaulted or besieged by the enemy, the

95

CORYAT'S CRUDITIES

presidiarie souldiers which for the defence of the citie
should watch in those Towers, might the more commodiously see one another, and so give watch-word to each
other as occasion required.   Hard by the wall where these
foresaid Towers are built, there runneth a little muddy
The lake of lake, which by the auncients was called the lake of frogs,
frogs. which name it continually retaineth even to this day, by
reason of the great abundance of frogs therein.   There is
a marveilous pleasant walke for the citizens to walke in
hard by that lake.   Also there are five more of those
Towers made in other parts of the wall, so that in the
whole wall there are eleven Towers, and five Gatehouses
or Bulwarkes before mentioned, which doe yeeld a speciall
grace to the whole Citie.   About the East-side of the
Citie, unto the which from the lower parts you have a
pretie easie ascent, there is another exceeding pleasant
The Trench. and delectable greene walke hard by the Trench (for the
whole wall of the Citie is invironed round about with a
Trench) of a quarter of an English mile long.   That
part of the Trench is a very pleasant greene, where the
Patricians and Gentlemen of the Citie doe keepe Deere,
having built there sundry little pretie houses wherein
they use to feede them with hay in the winter time.
    The Citie hath his name of Zurich from two King-
Zurich signi- domes;   for the Dutch word Zurich signifieth two
fieth two cities. Kingdomes: the reason thereof is this, because in times
past one part of it, even that which is on the farther banke
of the River Limacus, belonged to a certaine Kingdome
called Turgovia, which retaineth that name to this day,
part whereof belongeth to the state of Zurich, the other
[p. 377.] part which is on the hither banke of the river belonged to
a Kingdome or Province called Ergovia, which yet keepeth
his name, and now belongeth to the Tigurines.   Also the
Latine name was heretofore Turegum, before it was called
Tigurum, and it was so called, *Quasi duorum regum
civitas.*   That name of Turegum was very auncient, for
so it was called in the time of Julius Cæsar as well as
Tigurinus pagus.   For testimonie whereof this verse was
96

OBSERVATIONS OF ZURICH

defence of the c
the more commod
watch-word to ex
the wall where th
ineth a little m
ed the lake of fr
even to this day,
gs therein. Th
citizens to walk
: five more of th
t will, so that in
b, and five Gatehou
ich doe yeeld a spe
the East-side of t
wer parts you hav
er exceeding pleas
.. the Trench (for t
et round about wid
.sh mile long. T
sat greene, where f
... doe keepe Dee
c..le houses when
he winter time.
... from two K
...ch signifieth m
..., because in tim
s on the farther back
a certaine Kingdom
... came to this day
.f Zurich, the othe
he river belonged to
a, which yet keepet
igurines. Also th
before it was calle
si duorum regum
very auncient, fo
Cæsar as well as
eof this verse we

heretofore found in one of the gardens of the Citie, as
my foresaid friend Marcus Buelerus told me, being written
there by the appointment of Julius Cæsar himself, and
continued there a long time after, even this.

Nobile Turegum, multarum copia rerum.

There are foure Churches in the Citie, whereof the fayrest
was built by Clodoveus King of France, and dedicated to
Saint Felix, and Saint Regula, by whose names it is called
at this day : These Saints, Felix and Regula, are highly
esteemed amongst the Tigurines, but not in that superstitious manner as Saints are amongst the Papists : the
reason why the Tigurines doe honour them, is, because
they were the first that preached the Gospel in the Citie,
as my foresaid friend Buelerus told me, and for their bold
confession of the Christian Religion were martyred in the
Citie in one of the first persecutions of the Primitive
Church : their manner of death was beheading. For the
place where they were beheaded was shewed me neere to
one of their Bridges on the farther side of the Limacus,
viz. a very auncient faire building, which is called in
Latine aquatile templum, because it is built altogether
in the Limacus : this place was heretofore in time of
Paganisme a temple of idolatrie, but now it is altogether
alienated from holy and Religious uses, though it bee
continually called by the name of a Temple, and serveth
as a publicke house for secular affaires. Without the
edifice, almost round about halfe the compasse, there is a
pretie walke paved with stone, the edge whereof is garnished with ten huge stonie Pillars. In this place three
Martyrs suffered Martyrdome together : Namely the foresaid Felix and Regula who was his wife. The third was
a Priest called Exuperantius. Two of these three, viz.
Felix & Regula, craved before their execution, that they
might be buried in a certaine place of the Citie that they
themselves appointed ; which I saw in this foresaid
Church, where there is a plaine Stone laid over their
bodies. The like Miracle is reported of them as is written

*Church of
S. Felix and
S. Regula.*

[p. 378.]
*Three
martyrs.*

C. C. II   97   G

of St. Denis in France, as I have before mentioned, that
they carried their heads in their hands after they were
strooken off from their bodies, to the place where they
desired to be buried. How true or false this is, I will not
dispute the matter, because I never read the Historie in
any authenticke writer, onely I heard it of the learned
men of the Citie. In the Cloyster of this foresaid Church
of Saint Felix and Regula, I saw to my great comfort the
Sepulchres of Sepulchers of sundry famous and learned men, who were
famous men. singular ornaments and most glorious bright-shining
Lampes of Christs Church, since the reformation of
Religion began in Switzerland, and such as by their holinesse of life, sinceritie of doctrine, and the manifold
Monuments of their most learned workes, have infinitely
benefited the Church of God, and purchased themselves
eternitie of name till the worlds end. These are the men
whose bodies lie enterred in this Cloyster, Peter Martyr
the Vermilian, Henricus Bullingerus, Rodolfus Gualterus,
Theodorus Bibliander, Conradus Gesnerus, Ludovicus
Lavaterus, Josias Simlerus, Joannes Gulielmus Stuckius,
&c. Truely it grieved me to see so many rare men so
meanely buried. For none of them had any more than
a flat stone laide upon them without Epitaph, or any maner
of inscription to preserve them from oblivion ; in so much
that a stranger cannot know one Sepulchre from another,
except one of the Citie shew him the particulars. Surely
[p. 379.] the memorie of these worthy men would quickly be
extinguished among the Tigurines, if they had not in
their life time immortalized the same by their learned
writings. For the Tigurines honour none of their citizens
that are buried in the citie, of what facultie, dignitie, or
merit soever they are, either with faire monuments, or
beautified by Carolus Magnus, who upon the yeare 810
bestowed great charges upon the same. For a monument
of whose imperiall munificence the Tigurines have erected
a goodly stonie statue to the honour of his name in the
South side of one of the towers of the Church, which is
therehence called the tower of Carolus Magnus. This

fore mentioned, t
nds after they w
he place where t
alse this is, I will
read the Historie,
ard it of the lear
f this foresaid Chr
my great comfort
armed men, who w
orious bright-shin
e the reformation:
such as by their l
ne, and the manif
...kes, have infini
d purchased themsel
... These are the m
..., Peter Mar
..s Rodolfus Gualter
Gesnerus, Ludovi
es Gulielmus Stuckii
: so many rare me
em had any more th
: Epitaph, or any na
...tion; in so m
epulchre from anoth
particulars. Such
en would quickly l
s, if they had not t
ame by their learn
r none of their citi
t facultie, dignitie, e
faire monuments, a
upon the yeare he
e. For a monum
igurines have erect
of his name in th
he Church, which s
lus Magnus. Th

statue is made according to the full proportion of a mans
bodie with a golden Diademe upon his head, a Scepter in
the right hand, and a golden sword in the left.

The second Church is dedicated to Saint Peter, whereof *Church of S. Peter.*
part is reported to be of that antiquitie, that it was built
in the time of Abraham, and at the first building thereof
was consecrated to the worship of the Paynime gods : for
the lower part of it toward the foundation argueth the
ancientnesse thereof, being built in the outside with
pointed diamond work like unto certain buildings that I
observed in Italie, as I have before mentioned. The
citizens were bestowing great charges in repairing the
steeple of the Church when I was in Zurich. The third
is the Abbesse Church which Ludovicus King of Germanie,
and the nephew of Carolus Magnus founded in the yeare
853. neere unto which he built a faire Nunnerie, whereinto
none were admitted but onely noble women. Both the
Church and the Nunnery were built indeed by the appointment of the foresaid King Ludovicus, but Rupertus Duke
of Alemanny disbursed the greatest charge thereof, and
Ludovicus contributed something to the same. The first
Abbesse was the Lady Hildegardis King Ludovicus
daughter. This Nunnery is now converted to a Schoole [p. 380.]
which hath beene a most fruitfull seminarie of many *Nunnery converted to a*
excellent learned men. Ex quo ludo tanquam ex equo *school.*
Trojano (to use *Ciceroes words that he spake of Isocrates
schoole in Athens) multi eruditissimi viri prodiêrunt.
For this schoole hath beene the nurse of all the famous
Tigurine divines that have florished in this citie, and so
ennobled the same by their learned writings since the
reformation of religion began. Herein are ever brought
up 16 striplings of the most exquisite and pregnant wits
that can be selected out of the whole citie, and when
they have accomplished the foure and twentieth yeare of
their age, they are transplanted therehence, and enter into
the Ecclesiasticall function. In all that space they are
brought up in the studie of humanity and divinitie at the

* 2 Lib. de Orat.

publike charge of the citie. The fourth and last Church is that which heretofore belonged to the Predicatores or Dominican Friers.

I was in their armory unto the which I had accesse by the meanes of a worthy learned man of the citie, a great professor of eloquence, a singular linguist. For he spake seven languages, being very skilfull in the Hebrew and Greeke tongues, and a famous traveller. For besides Italy, Germany, and France, which he had well travelled over, he had been also in England, Scotland, and Ireland, a man of so rare and excellent gifts, that he hath attained to that which the Grecians call ἐγκυκλοπαιδείαν, that is, an exact knowledge in the seven liberal sciences. His name is Gaspar Waserus. When I came afterward to Frankford at the time of the Mart, I saw a most singular Latine Oration made by him upon the life and death of that famous Pastor of Zurich, Joannes Gulielmus Stuckius, who died in this citie not long before my being there. This foresaid Waserus sent a scholer with me to the Tigurine Prefect, a noble man of the citie, whose name was Hortmannus Eselerus, who used me very graciously, discoursed with me in Latin, sent a Mandato under his hand to the keeper of the armory to shew me the same. Truly I have seene farre greater armories then this, as that of Milan, but especially those of the Arsenall of Venice. Also our owne in the Tower of London yeeldeth more store of munition then this: but never in my life did I see so well a furnished place for the quantity. Amongst the rest of those things that this Armory doth present, it yeeldeth more notable antiquities then ever I saw in any armorie before. For heere I saw those arrows which the ancient Helvetians used in the time of Julius Cæsar, when they fought with the Romanes. They are very short, but exceeding big, being above two inches in compasse, and headed with great three-forked heads. Of these arrowes I saw a great quantity: Likewise the banners & ancients that the Helvetians displaied in the field against the Romanes, which are almost eaten out with antiquity: And

Gaspar Waserus a famous traveller.

[p. 381.]

Armoury of Zurich.

Weapons used by the Helvetians against the Romans

100

many of the Romans ensignes with their armes in them, even the eagle, which the Helvetians wonne from them in fight. These banners are something lesse then those that are used in this age. Also I observed many shields which they used in their skirmishes with the Romanes, being made of sinews, one whereof I saw exceedingly mangled, and hackled with stroakes of swords, &c. All these things are shewed in one of the higher roomes of the Armory. For it consisteth of many faire roomes most curiously kept. Also there is shewed another most worthy monument in the same roome, even the sword of William Tell an Helvetian of the towne of Swice, who about some three hundred years since was the first author of the Helveticall confederation which hath been ever since retained in their popular government, by reason of a certaine notable exploit that he atchieved. Therefore I will tell a most *History of* memorable history of Will Tell before I proceede any *William Tell.* further, being very pertinent to this purpose, which was this, as I both heard it in the Citie, and afterward read it in the third booke of Munsters Cosmography. When as [p. 382.] the Germane Emperours being the Lords of the principall Cities of Helvetia constituted forraine Prefects and rulers about three hundred yeares since as their deputies over three townes, especially above the rest, namely Sylvania, otherwise called Underwald, Urania, commonly called Uri, and Swice, it hapned that the Prefect of the towne of Swice behaved himselfe very insolently, abusing his authority by immoderate tyrannizing over the people. For amongst other enormous outrages that he committed, this was one. He commanded one of his servants to compell all travellers that passed such a way, to doe *Travellers* reverence to his hat that was hanged upon a staffe in the *compelled to do* high way. The people unwilling to offend the Magis- *reverence to a* trate, did their obeysance unto the hat. But one amongst *hat.* the rest, even this foresaid William Tell, being a man of a stout courage, refused to doe as the rest did. Where-upon he was brought before the Magistrate, who being grievously incensed against him for his contumacie,

101

injoyned him this pennance: that he should shoote an
arrow out of a crosse-bow at an apple set upon his sonnes
head that was a little child, whom he caused to be tied to
a tree for the same purpose, so that if he had fayled to
strike the apple, he must needs have shot through his
sonne. This he commanded him because this Tell was
esteemed a cunning archer: At the first he refused to doe
it: But at last because he saw there was an inevitable
necessity imposed upon him, he performed the matter
greatly against his will, and that with most happy successe.
For God himselfe directing the arrow, he shot him so

The apple cunningly shot by Tell. cunningly, that he strooke off the apple from the childs
head without any hurt at all to the child. And whereas
he had another arrow left besides that which he shot at his
sonne, the Prefect asked him what he meant to do with
that arrow: he made him this bould and resolute answere.

[p. 383.] If I had slaine my child with the first, I would have shot
thee through with the second. The magistrate hearing
that, commanded him to be apprehended, and carried away
in a barke. And when he was come betwixt the towne
of Urania, and a certaine village called Brun, having by
good fortune escaped out of the boate, he ranne away with
all possible expedition over the difficult places of the
mountaines, where there was no common way, and so
came to a place neere to the which he knew the tyrant
would passe, where he lay in ambush in a secret corner of
the wood till he came that way, and then shot him through
with his other arrow. It hapned that this Tell did weare
the foresaid sword about him when he atchieved these
worthy actes, in regard whereof the Switzers have ever
since that time hanged up the same in their Armory for a
most remarkable monument, though me thinks it had
beene much better to have reserved the arrow with which
he shot through the tyrant, then the sword that he wore

Tell's exploit the original of the Helvetic confederation. then. This noble exploit was the first originall of the
Helveticall confederation. For shortly after these matters
were acted, those three foresaid townes of Underwald, Uri,
and Swice united themselves together in a league by a

solemne forme of oath about the year 1316. to the end to shake off the yoake of those forraine tyrants. And afterward the other Cities of the Province imitated them, so that in the end all the Cities of Helvetia combined themselves together in a league of unity, which though it hath beene often assayed since that time to be dissolved and violated by the forraine forces of mighty men, as by some of the German Emperours, by Leopold, and Fredericke, brothers and Dukes of Austria, by the Earles of Kyburg, &c. yet it hath continued firme and inviolable to this day. As for the name of Switzers it grew upon this foresaid occasion, even because the above mentioned William Tell the first author of this league was borne in the towne of Swice. For before that time all the inhabitants of the country were called Helvetians. Having now reported [p. 384.] this notable history, which I could not conveniently omit, I will return againe to the armory. I saw also in the *An Ancient* foresaid higher roome, an Ancient that the Switzers got *won from* in the field from that famous Charles Duke of Burgundy. *Charles Duke* For there were most bitter warres waged betwixt the *of Burgundy.* Helvetians and this Duke Charles for the space of three yeares, in which space they fought three very hot battels in as many severall places, the Helvetians ever carrying away the glory of the field from him, and in the last skirmish about the City of Nancey in Lorraine they slew him (after he had lived three and fortie yeares, one moneth, and five and twentie daies,) with three grievous wounds, upon the Epiphany which we commonly call twelfe day, Anno 1477. But to returne once more to this higher roome of the armory; besides these foresaid antiquities, heere I observed a marvailous multitude of costlets, and head peeces, and a great deale of complete armour of proofe, for the whole body, which is so finely disposed in order, and so elegantly kept, that it yeeldeth a wondrous faire shew.

At the upper end of this roome I saw two artificiall men *Two artificial* standing a pretie distance from each other, even at the *men in armour.* corners of the roome, armed with their complete armour of proofe, and crested helmets upon their heads, which a stranger at the first entrance of the roome would conjecture to be living, and very naturall men standing in their armour; this also giveth no small grace to the roome. In another roome I saw most terrible swords made according to the imitation of those that the ancient Helvetians used in their warres against Julius Cæsar, being two-edged, and of a great length, above two yards long, having many steelen pranges, or sharpe hookes at the sides. In another roome I saw onely speares and launces, whereof there was a goodly company. Againe in another, axes and mattocks

[p. 385.]

for pioners to use about digging of trenches. In the lowest roome of all, which is the fourth, I noted an exceeding

All sorts of ordnance.

multitude of pieces of ordinance of all sorts, as culverins, demiculverins, demicannons, sacers, basiliskes, &c. whereof some were taken as trophies from the foresaid Duke of Burgundy, being indeed pieces of admirable beauty and value, adorned with his armes, and many curious borders and works contrived in the same. Amongst the rest I saw one passing great murdering piece, both the ends thereof were so exceeding wide, that a very corpulent man might easily enter the same. This also was wonne in the field from the same Duke. Besides, I saw seven huge and very sumptuous brasen pieces equalling at the least, if not exceeding the length of the longest piece I saw in the Citadell of Milan, above named. All these things I saw kept very daintily, and in passing good order. Although

Arms for 10,000 men.

this armoury be well able to arme ten thousand men, yet if there should happen any occasion of warres, they neede not use any of it: because every private man of the citie, together with the rest in the other townes, villages, and hamlets of the country are privately very well furnished in their owne houses: onely if they hire any strangers then they use it, but not else. The Tigurines are able to furnish fortie thousand armed men in their whole territory; but the Citie it selfe armeth two thousand onely and no more.

Thus much of the Armoury.

104

I Saw their campus Martius, where both in ancient times they were wont to muster their souldiers, and so do at this day. It is a very goodly greene plaine, where I observed five exceeding massy pillars of stone, which serve only for this purpose, that souldiers may in the time of muster discharge their peeces at them for the better triall and proofe of them. I noted every one of the pillars to be much battered with the force of their bullets. *The Campus Martius.*

There are two prisons in the City, whereof one standeth in the water, being built in the manner of a Tower, unto the which none can come but by water : herein capitall offenders and debtors are kept. The other is one of those six Towers in the westerne wall of the City already mentioned, unto which they are committed that have done some small and veniall crime. *[p. 386.] Two prisons.*

There is one very delectable greene in an eminent and high part of the City, where there grow many goodly trees that doe make a pleasant grove. Here stand many stony tables of a convenient bignesse with benches about them for their archers to sit at their refection, after they have exercised themselves with shooting, which is an exercise much used amongst them. Neare unto this place dwelt one of their Consuls when I was in Zurich. For they have two Consuls in the City, which doe not change every yeare as the Romans did, but when they are once elected into the Consulat, they keepe that consular dignity while they live, except upon some just desert they are degraded. *A delectable green.*

Their Lictores or Serjeants doe weare party-coloured cloakes, which are of a blew and white colour according to the armes of the City.

Their houses both publique and private are very faire. Their private houses of a goodly heigth, many of them foure stories high. Their matter of building is partly free stone, and partly timber. For they have no bricke at all.

The habits of the Citizens doe in some things differ from the attyre of any nation that ever I saw before. For *Attire of the citizens.*

105

all the men doe weare round breeches with codpeeces. So that you shall not finde one man in all Zurich from a boy of ten yeares old to an old man of the age of a hundred yeares, but he weareth a codpeece. Also all their men doe weare flat caps and ruffe bandes. For I could not see one man or boy in the whole City weare a falling band.

[p. 387.]

Many of their women, especially maides doe use a very strange and phantasticall fashion with their haire that I never saw before, but the like I observed afterward in many other places of Switzerland, especially in Basil. For they plait it in two very long locks that hang downe over their shoulders halfe a yard long. And many of them doe twist it together with pretty silke ribbands or fillets of sundry colours.

Strange beds.   The beds of the Innes of this City and of all the other Helvetian and German Cities are very strange, such as I never saw before. The like being in the private houses of every particular Citizen as I heard. For every man hath a light downe or very soft feather bedde laid upon him which keepeth him very warme, and is nothing offensive for the burden. For it is exceeding light, and serveth for the coverled of the bedde. In the refectory of that Inne where I lay which was at the signe of the two Storkes, there is a stove, such a one as I have before mentioned in my Observations of Padua, which is so common a thing in all the houses of Switzerland and Germany (as I have before said) that no house is without it. I found them first in Rhetia, even in the City of Curia.

Fat soil.   The soile round about this City is so exceeding fat, that it yeeldeth wonderfull plenty of corne, which is every weeke sold here in so great abundance that it doth not only suffize for the maintenance of the City, but also is communicated to their neighbouring Townes, being conveighed unto them partly in Barkes upon the Helvetian lake, and partly with carts and upon horses backs. Also the City is served with such passing store of provision of all sorts whatsoever, that a man may live as cheape here as in any City of Switzerland or Germanie. For I observed

TIES
| ... with codpec...
... all Zurich from:
...e age of a hundre...
...o all their men d...
...r I could not s...
...re a falling bac...
...es doe use a ve...
...their haire the...
...erved afterward...
...ly in Basil. Fo...
...hang downe ove...
...many of them de...
...ds or fillets of...

...and of all the othe...
...tinge, such as I...
...e private house...
...For every mr...
...table laid upo...
...nothing othe...
...and serve...
the refectory of the
x of the two Storks:
before mentioned i
so common a thin
Germany (as I hav...
it. I found then
uia.

, so exceeding fa...
one, which is ever...
that it doth no...
he City, but als...
g Townes, bein...
on the Helvetia...
ses backs. Also
of provision of
s cheape here as
For I observed

at my Inne, which was at the signe of the two Storkes, more variety of good dishes then I did in any Inne in my whole journey out of England, our ordinary being sixe battes, that is, fifteene pence English. Every bat countervailing two pence halfe peny of our English money.

About an English mile directly beyond the Citie Westward, I saw a place where malefactors are punished. Which is a certaine greene place, made in the forme of a pit, neere unto the which there standeth a little Chappell, wherein some Clergie man doeth minister ghostly counsell unto the offendour before he goeth to execution. In that Chappell I sawe wheeles. If they should happen to tremble so much that they cannot stand upright (as sometimes offendours doe) they are punished in the Chappell. As about some fourteene yeeres before I was at Zurich, three Noble Tigurines were beheaded in that Chappell because they were so inclined to trembling that they could not stand upright. The punishments that are inflicted upon offendours are divers, in number five, whereof the first is beheading, which punishment they onely do sustaine that are incestuous men or high-way robbers. The second is the Gallowes, upon the which those are executed that commit Burghlarie or burne houses. The third is the water, which incestuous women doe suffer, being drowned therein. The fourth is the fire wherewith Witches, Sorcerers, and Heretickes are punished; and after their bodies are burnt, their ashes are cast into the River Sylla aforesaid. The fifth and last punishment is wheeling, which is onely for murderers. This Citie hath suffered great alteration and change of Governement. Heretofore it was governed many yeares by the Dukes of Almannie or Suevia till about the yeare 1083. it was againe freed from them. After that, about the yeare 1136. it was recovered againe by Fredericke Duke of Suevia, who was afterward made Emperour of Rome, and excluded Conrad Duke of Zaringia out of the possession of Zurich. About the yeare 1336. on the seventh day of June, there rose a sedition in the Citie, so that the whole Senate was removed

[p. 388.]
Place of punishment.

Five punishments.

Witches burnt with fire.

A sedition in the city.

107

[p. 389.]

or rather expulsed out of Zurich, and another substituted in their place, which caused great tumults and confusion in the Citie. For there were many Noblemen and Gentlemen of the Senate, which being united together by a mutual affinitie, governed the whole state according to their pleasure, and executed many unjust and wrongfull judgements to the great prejudice and oppression of the Citizens. At what time the greatest part of the old Senators retired themselves to a place called Rapperswyl to John Earle of Habspurg. For the Tigurines slew one of the Earles of Habspurg, for whose death John aforesaid that succeeded his father in the Earldome, determined to be revenged upon the Citizens. Whereupon certaine Souldiers that promised the Earle to betray Zurich to him, approched privily by night to the Citie. But the Tigurines being forewarned of the conspiracie, very providently prevented the matter, and slew many of the souldiers, tooke the Earle prisoner, and tortured the traytors with the torment of the wheele, in the yeare 1350. About some two yeares after that, Albert Duke of Austria besieged Zurich both with the best forces he could make of his owne, and the auxiliaries of the Earle of Wirtemberg, and the Bishops of Strasbourg and Basil. The Cities of Berne and Friburg aided him also. But the Tigurines being confederated with the inhabitants of the Townes of Swice, Underwald, Uri, and Lucerne defended themselves very valiantly against their enemies, till at last there was a peace concluded on both sides, with condition that the Tigurines should set John of Hapspurg at libertie. Many other bitter brunts also this Citie hath often endured both before the time of the confederation and since, having beene tossed to and fro from one Lord to another, as if shee had beene Dame Fortunes tennis ball. But at this day by the gracious indulgence of the heavenly powers, it enjoyeth great peace and a very halcedonian time with the rest of the Helveticall Cities under that happie league of union,

[p. 390.]

being subject neither to King nor Kaysar. And if warres should happen, it hath so fortified it selfe in time of peace

Zurich besieged by Albert Duke of Austria.

with store of munition and provision for warfare, that it is well able to defend it selfe against any forraine forces.

Here might I make mention of the forme of their Aristocraticall state, their severall and distinct Magistrates, the manner of the election of them, and such other memor able particulars touching the administration of their commonweale. But I must needes confesse I did not use such curious inquisition for these matters as I might have done: contenting my selfe rather with these foresaid matters (which I learned partly by the observation of mine own eies, partly by the instructions of my learned friend aforesaid Marcus Buelerus; and partly by reading of Munsters Cosmography, unto whom I acknowledge my selfe beholding for some of these above mentioned histories) then with the exact knowledge of their government, which I could not possibly attaine unto by reason that I made my abode there, but a day and halfe. Wherefore I intreat thee (gentle Reader) to pardon me though I cannot informe thee of their aristocratie according to thy expectation, promising thee that I will as well as I am able supply that in my next journey into this country (for I determine by Gods heavenly assistance to see hereafter all the thirteene principall townes of Switzerland) which I have now omitted in the observation of their government. I received much kindnesse in this Citie of one Master Thomannus the Prefect of the corne market, whom I could not but mention in this discourse gratitudinis causâ. A sonne of his called Gaspar Thomannus a man of good gifts, and a lover of learning hath beene many yeares commorant in our Universitie of Oxford.

Amongst other learned men that I conversed with in this Citie, Henry Bullinger was one of the chiefest, a man of very singular learning, the nephew of that famous preacher and writer of godly memory Henry Bullinger the successor of Zuinglius in the Ecclesiasticall function of Zurich. This man is a very vigilant preacher of this Citie, and a painefull labourer in the Lords Vineyard. He shewed himselfe very debonaire and courteous

A confession.

A kind Prefect.

Henry Bullinger.

[p. 391.]

109

unto me. For he led me into his studie, which is exceedingly well furnished with divinitie bookes, and much augmented with many of his grandfathers. Amongst the *Bullinger's* rest, he shewed me a manuscript of his grandfathers never *manuscripts.* yet printed, which was an historie of the Popes lives; and a manuscript Epistle of Theodorus Beza unto him, wherein he delivered his opinion of the said worke. Also he shewed me one most execrable booke written by an Italian, one Joannes Casa Bishop of Beneventum in Italy, in praise of that unnaturall sinne of Sodomy. This booke is written in the Italian tongue, and printed in Venice. It came first to the hands of this mans grandfather aforesaid, who kept it as a monument of the abhominable impurity of a papistical Bishop, to which end this man also that received it from his grandfather, keepeth it to this day.

A strange I observed a strange Latin phrase amongst the learned *Latin phrase.* men of this Citie, which is likewise used in most Cities and Universities of Germany (as I have heard) at the least in all those where I have bene. Whensoever any of them discourseth in Latine with a stranger, he will not speake to him in the second person, as to say, Ut vales Domine? but alwaies in the third person after a stranger maner then ever I observed before. As, Ut valet Dominus? cujas est Dominus? quamdiu commoratus fuit Dominus in Italia? in quam regionem jam tendit Dominus? placet ne Domino? By this word Dominus meaning your selfe to whom he speaketh, though at the first time I heard that phrase, I conceived that they meant a third person. After I had duly considered this pretie Germanisme, and com-pared it with a phrase that is frequent in the holy *[p. 392.]* Scriptures, I perceived that they borrowed this forme of speech from the very Scriptures themselves. Which made me much the more applaude the same: As for example, when Jacob brought a great drove of Ewes and Kine to present to his brother Esau for a gift, he spake thus unto him: I have sent it that I might finde favour in the sight of my Lord. Genesis cap. 33. verse 8. Meaning Esau himselfe to whom he spake, although indeed he seemed to

-, which is excee
-ookes, and mu-
-rs. Amongst th
grandfathers nev-
-e Popes lives; a-
-unto him, where-
-worke. Also h-
-en by an Ital-
-in Italy, in pr-
-booke is writt-
-e. It came fir-
aforesaid, who ke-
-of a papis-
received it fro-

the learne-
most Citie-
at the lea-
-any of the-
not speak-
vales Domin-
stranger maner th-
-r Dominus? cap-
-it Dominus i-
Dominus? placet a-
-ning your selfe t-
time I heard th-
urd person. Afte-
-anisme, and con-
-tent in the hol-
red this forme o-
-es. Which mad-
As for exampl-
-ies and Kine t-
spake thus unt-
-ur in the sigh-
Meaning Esa-
-d he seemed to

speake of a third person : The like phrase being used twise in the same Chapter, and very often in many other places of Scripture.

It is a matter very worthy the consideration to thinke how exceedingly God hath blessed this citie with a great number of most rare wits, and passing learned men within these foure score yeares. *Zurich blessed with many learned men.* For though it be no Universitie to yeeld degrees of Schoole to the students : yet it hath bred more singular learned writers (at the least in my poore opinion) then any one of the famousest Universities of all Christendome, especially Divines, and such as have consecrated their name to posterity even til the end of the world by their learned works. For the writers of this City have bene no ordinary or triviall men that have divulged to the world triobolary pamphlets, but such as have published bookes both of the greatest volume, and of the most excellent & solid learning, being men endewed with those admirable gifts as have made them equall, if not superiour *Profound Scholars.* to the profoundest Scholers of Christendome ; and such men they are as may very truly apply unto themselves that speech of Saint Augustine : Nos sumus ex illorum numero qui scribendo proficiunt, & proficiendo scribunt. Yea many of them have bene such as have shined like most glittering blazing starres, not onely in their owne country of Switzerland, but also in all other regions and kingdomes of the Christian world that doe sincerely embrace the doctrine of the reformed Church. For what Doctors can we name in any Universitie of all Europe that excelled these men, Huldrichus Zuinglius, Henricus Bullingerus, [p. 393.] Theodorus Bibliander, Rodolphus Gualterus, Ludovicus *Famous* Lavaterus, Conradus Gesnerus, Josias Simlerus, Joannes *Doctors.* Jacobus Frisius, Gaspar Megander, Joannes Gulielmus Stuckius. Whose writings being replenished with most sweete and exquisite learning doe as mute witnesses very sufficiently testifie and confirme the truth of my speech. Neither doe I thinke that any man which doth judicially reade their bookes will dissent from my opinion : Besides many more of an inferiour ranke that have partly bene borne in this Citie, and partly professed there: Men of excellent parts, and well knowen unto the world by their learned volumes, whom notwithstanding I will passe over unnamed, that the reader may not deeme me ambitious in reciting the names of learned men. At this day that worthy man Rodolphus Hospinianus with whom I conversed in Zurich (as I have before said) hath much illustrated this Citie with his manifolde bookes full of great learning.

Praise of Zurich not derogatory to Oxford and Cambridge. Howbeit I doe not by this praise of Zurich derogate from the learned men of mine owne country. For I am perswaded that our two famous Universities of Oxford and Cambridge do yeeld as learned men as any in the world; but for the quantity (not the quality) of writing the Tigurines without doubt have the superioritie of our English men. To conclude this narration of Zurich: I attribute so much to this noble citie, that for sweetnesse of situation, and that wonderful exuberancy of all things whatsoever tending both to profite and pleasure, I compare it at the least even with Mantua herselfe, in Italy, whom before I have so highly extolled, if not preferre it before the same: though indeed that be greater in compasse then this. For that is foure Italian miles about, but the circuite of this comprehendeth no more then halfe an Helvetian mile, which is but two English miles and a halfe.

Thus much of Zurich.

[p. 394.] HEre I have thought good to adde to my description of Zurich before I proceed any further with my observations of my travels, certaine Latine Epistles that I sent to some of the learned men of the Citie; partly because thou mayest read a briefe epitome in my first Epistle of my ensuing observations betwixt that Citie and the farther end of Germany where I was imbarked for England, and partly because my friends that shall happen to read my booke, may understand that it was my good *A league of* fortune to enter into a league of friendship with some of *friendship.* the profound schollers of this worthy Citie; a thing that hath ministred no small joy and comfort unto me. This

EPISTLE TO GASPAR WASERUS

first Epistle following is to that rare Linguist and famous traveller Gaspar Waserus. My superscription was this.

Clarissimo viro
Domino Gasparo Wasero

Eximio Philologo, & politioris literaturæ in cele-
berrimâ Civitate Tigurinâ apud Helvetios
Candidato, amico suo dilecto.

The Epistle it selfe is this.

Ubitabis arbitror (clarissime vir celeber-
rimeque Musarum antistes) aliquid sinistri
mihi accidisse in profectione meâ Germanicâ inter vestram civitatem Tigurinam
& patriam meam, quoniam in tanto isto
temporis intervallo ad te haud scripserim,
proùt fideliter tibi promisi. Veniam mihi
des quæso. Nam tot tantisque negotiis districtus fui
statim post appulsum meum in patriâ, ut vix respirandi
tempus mihi fuerit, nedum scribendi otium. Quod ad
peregrinationem meam Germanicam attinet post discessum
meum â Tiguro, jucundissima sanè atque faustissima fuit
tota illa profectio, & secundis ventis mare trajeci, donec
mihi contigit Angliæ

———— κάπνον ἀποθρώσκοντα νοῆσαι,

Ut Homerus de suo Ulysse canit, ac tandem exopta-
tissimum patrii mei soli littus auspicatò appellere. Sed
quandoquidem tibi pollicitus sum, si mihi contingeret in
patriâ pedem figere, literas tibi scribere non tantùm signi-
ficantes gratitudinem meam ob tuam eximiam erga me
benevolentiam pari conjunctam humanitate (quam gratâ
quâdam prædicatione semper prædicare soleo τοῖς φιλομού-
σοις atque eruditis meis amicis, & cujus gratiâ tibi ingentes
gratias reddo ab intimis cordis mei recessibus dimanantes)
sed etiam aliquem tibi gustum præbentes mearum Ger-
manicarum observationum ; ecce hasce crassâ Minervâ

Epistle to Gaspar Waserus.

CORYAT'S CRUDITIES

contextas observatiunculas tibi mitto ὥσπερ ἐν τῇ ἐπιτομῇ, quoniam epistolaris ista brevitas cogit me illas coangustare, & in multo succinctius compendium reducere, quâm in meo ἀυτογράφῳ exemplari exaravi. Has ut æqui bonique consulas, donec in publicum fusiùs scriptum meum hodœporicum divulgaverim post meas longinquas peregrationes, Belgicam, Saxonicam, Danicam, Alemannicam, Suecicam, Polonicam, Hispanicam, alteram etiam Italicam, Siculam, Scoticam, Hibernicam, Germanicam, Ægyptiacam, ac denique Hierosolymitanam (nam omnes istas regiones si non peragrare, saltem invisere θεοῦ διδόντος decrevi) te impensè rogo.

A Badenâ igitur vestrâ Helveticâ exordium sumam. Ibi sacellum quoddam prope basilicam mortuorum calvariis atque ossibus adeò refertam vidi, ut alterum Golgotha vocari non immeritò possit.   Profectò

> Obstupui, steterúntque; comæ————

Quando primò infinitam illam congeriem animadverti. Reor equidem die mundi novissimo totam myriada animarum illa ossa resumpturam. Badenses illos superstitionibus Papisticis & idolatricis cultibus supra modum addictos observavi. Nam plurimas imagines ad idololatriam spectantes in basilicâ vidi. Hinderhoviæ, quæ exiguo intervallo distat â Badenâ lustravi vestras Helveticas thermas, quò magna populi multitudo â multis locis circumcircâ partim τῆς διατριβῆς ἕννκα, partim morborum curandorum causâ tunc confluebat. Particularia balnea non minus sexaginta illic numeravi. Peculiare σύνταγμα de illorum virtute scripsisse celeberrimum illum tum medicum tum philosophum Henricum Pantaleonem Basiliensem retulit mihi quidam quem in balneo quodam sese lavantem vidi sacerdos. Sed de errore meo in viâ antequam in illa balnea incidere possem, scripsi in Epistolâ meâ ad Dominum Hospinianum, quam, si placuerit, legas. In Kiningsfeldiano Monasterio propè civitatem Brooke, quod jam pertinet ad Dominos Bernenses, observavi monumentum Leopoldi ultimi ejus nominis Austriæ Ducis, qui multotiès Helvetios infestis armis oppugnavit, & in templi choro picturam suam unâ cum suis viginti septem proceribus graphicè depictam. Basileæ cultissimæ, splendidissimæ, atque munitissimæ civitati multa mihi apprimè arriserunt. Cathedralis Ecclesia divæ Mariæ dedicata magnificentissima est, & microcosmo quodam insignium tum antiquorum tum neotericorum monumentorum egregiè ornata. Illic in penitiori quâdam æde, scilicèt scholâ Theologicâ, familiaritèr versatus fui cum præstantissimo illo & Theologo & Philologo Joanne Jacobo Grynœo, cujus eruditum commercium me valdè oblectavit. Suavissimus meherclè ac ἐπαφρόδιτος senex est in suis colloquiis, de quo meritò potest illud Homericum prædicari

$$\text{τοῦ καὶ ἀπὸ γλώσσης μέλιτος γλυκίων ῥέεν αὐδή}$$

atque illud

$$\text{Αἰὲν ἀριστεύειν, καὶ ὑπείροχος ἔμμεναι ἄλλων.}$$

Ibi etiam celeberrimum illum Theologum Basiliensis Academiæ τὸν ἀστέρ ἀρίζηλον (ut Pindaricis verbis utar) Amandum Polanum â Polensdorf. in scholâ Theologicâ prælegentem audivi. Nec non Dominum Zuinggerum summi illius Philosophi Theodori Zuinggeri Basiliensis filium, virum profectò elegantissimum, ac publicum Græcæ linguæ in illâ Academiâ professorem unam ex Homeri Iliadibus publicè interpretantem. Munacii Planci Luguni fundatoris statuam ligneam affabrè exstructam, intra prætorii Basiliensis atrium observavi, cum pluribus aliis memorandis rebus quas illa inclyta civitas suppeditat. Argentina, quò advectus eram â Basileâ secundo Rheno, non parum solatii mihi præbuit. Turrim illam exquisitissimam Cathedralis Ecclesiæ unâ cum famigerato illo horologio penè ad stuporem sum admiratus. Urbis situs, ædium tum publicarum tum privatarum splendor atque elegantia sensus meos voluptate quadam novâ titillavit. Badenæ inferiori, quæ ad Marchionem ipsius Principem pertinet, balnea adeò calida sunt, ut vix illorum scaturientem aquam nudis manibus attrectare possem; aiunt Aurelianum Imperatorem horum fuisse inventorem.

CORYAT'S CRUDITIES

Ista civitas cum alterâ Badenâ religione consentit, nimi-rùm Papisticâ. Tamen princeps illorum, qui religionem profitetur reformatam, sed â vobis Tigurinis atque nobis Anglis parùm discrepantem (etenim Lutheranus est) non residet hìc, sed Turlaci. Ubi multâ quidem difficultate intra civitatis portas admissus fui. Sed nullis rationibus veniam ingrediendi Principis aulam impetrare potui. Tamen prænobilis quidam generosus, qui fuit primarius aulæ ipsius Præfectus, perhumanissimè me tractavit. Inde Heidelbergam profectus sum Palatinatus inferioris Metropolin atque florentissimam Academiam. Hìc Comitis Palatini ad Rhenum Frederici quarti qui religi-onem vestram & nostram amplectitur, augustissimum palatium non sine diffcultate quadam intromissus vidi, & in quadam cellâ vinariâ vas quoddam vinarium stupendæ ac portento sæ capacitatis, ad cujus summitatem ligneâ scalâ ascendebam. Locupletissimæ illius Bibliothecæ, quæ extructa est in quadam parte primariæ Ecclesiæ dedi-catæ S. Spiritui, tam copiosâ supellectile librorum & impressorum & manuscriptorum admiraculum usque in-structæ, mihi copiam fecit Principis Bibliothecarius eximius ille politioris literaturæ Candidatus Janus Gruterus. Sed repentinus duorum adolescentulorum Principum Anhaltinorum ingressus me impediebat, quò minus bibliothecam ex voto lustrarem. Postquam deliciis Heidelbergæ oculos atque animum satis pavissem, Spiram illam Imperialem per deserta nemorum me contuli. Hìc collegium Jesuitarum adii, cum quibus αψιμαχίαν seu velitationem quandam habui, quoniam Munsteri Cosmo-graphiam, cujus Spirensem descriptionem in ipsorum bibliothecâ legi, malignè depravârunt ; expungentes non-nullos locos, hoc scilicèt prætextu, quoniam adversus fidem Catholicæ Romanæ Ecclesiæ faciebant. Saluta-tionem divi Bernardi Abbatis Clarevallensis ad beatam virginem Mariam in basilicâ hujus urbis observavi æneis literis in tribus rotundis marmoribus incisam, O clemens Maria, ô pia Maria, ô dulcis Maria. Ista verba illum loquutum fuisse ad lapideam imaginem ipsius stantem

116

ad dextram introitus Chori asserunt Spirenses Papistæ, ac tum imaginem edidisse vocem; Bernardum autem bisce verbis illum increpasse: Dominatio tua sui ipsius oblita est. Non decet enim fœminam loqui in congregatione. Multa prætereà alia notatu dignissima hic vidi. Hinc mihi Wormaciam contendenti, inter ambulandum in viâ publicâ casus quidam infaustus infestusque contigit. Nam forte ex tritâ semitâ in vineam quandam ad carpendos paucos uvarum racemos deflectens, quibus sitim meam merendæ tempore restinguerem, quia tam liberè ac impunè me illic id facturum speravi, quod anteâ in nonnullis Longobardiæ vinetis factitavi; repentè â quodam rustico bipennifero apprehensus eram, qui subitaneo suo incursu metum sanè non vulgarem mihi, utpotè inermi, incussit. Detraxit enim capiti meo petasum, atque Alemannicis suis verbis, quæ ego prorsus ignorabam, minas mihi intentavit. At ego inscius idiomatis sui, æquè ac βάτραχος Σερίφιος, obmutui. Tandem verò interventu quorundam qui Latinos meos sermones intellexerunt, & pro me ad illum Germanicè interpretati sunt, ac mollibus suis dictis ferocientes ipsius spiritus placârunt, lis ita composita est, ut minuto precio galerum redimerem. Wormaciæ totam istam historiolam quibusdam Evangelicis ministris, & aliis facetis congerronibus narravi, qui ex illâ relatione in effusissimos cachinnos soluti erant. Civitas ista Wormaciensis non mediocritèr mihi adblandita fuit. Quadrata turris Basilicæ S. Petri è longinquo conspicua, superba ædificia, præcipuè Episcopale propè Ecclesiam extrinsecus insignibus gentilitiis, & picturis duodecem Sibyllarum, quibus particularia illarum vaticinia de Christo subscribuntur; Prætorium in cujus frontispicio Fredericus tertius Imperator depingitur, ampla fora, spatiosæ plateæ, firmi muri fossis circumfusi, propugnacula, omnia denique voluptatis materiam peregrinis præbent. A Wormaciâ per Openheimiam in latere montis instar Jerusalem sitam, Moguntiam perrexi Electoris Archiepiscopi dignitate, & typographiæ tot ingenuarum artium fœcundæ matris invento celebrem. Hìc in

CORYAT'S CRUDITIES

Epistle to Gaspar Waserus. Jebusitas rursùs sive illos Romani Pontificis Hierarchiæ Janisarios, & ὑπερασπίστας Ignatianæ colluviei fratres incidi, cumque Nicolao Serrario eorum Patriarchâ, qui tam virulentis convitiis in Lutherum (edito quodam de Lutheri magistro libro) debacchatus est, congressus sum. Compluribus vetustis monumentis tam sacris quàm profanis Moguntia abundat. Inter cætera propè Monasterium Benedictinorum in quodam edito colle vineis consito observavi lapideum Colossum Drusi privigni Octaviani Cæsaris, ingentem sanè molem, à formâ glandis Germanicè Aichelstein appellatam. Hìc Drusum cum Germanis dimicasse, ac post insignem victoriam de eis reportatam, gloriosum trophæum eum erexisse perhibent. Hinc per Rheni & Mœni confluentem navigio Francofurtum advectus eram, ubi nundinis illis autumnalibus totius Europæ celeberrimis interfui, multosque meos conterraneos ad summum meum gaudium vidi. Populorum diversorum, præsertìm prædivitum mercatorum, ex plurimis Christianismi partibus, non tantùm ex omnibus ferè opulentissimis Germaniæ vestræ urbibus, sed etiam ex Italiâ, Galliâ, Daniâ, Angliâ nostrâ, Poloniâ, Scotiâ, &c. confertìm huc confluentium ingentem concursum hic sum conspicatus.

* Non, mihi si linguæ centum sint, oráque centum,

Infinitas harum nundinarum divitias narrando percensere possum. In bibliopolarum plateâ admirandam omnigenorum librorum copiam animadverti, & inter reliquos elegantissimam tuam orationem in obitum immortali memoriâ digni vestræ Tigurinæ Ecclesiæ summi Antistitis Joannis Gulielmi Stuckii. A Francofurto terrestri itinere Moguntiam redii, & indè exiguâ cymbâ Rhenum usque ad Coloniam Agrippinam sulcavi. In isto spatio multas præclaras civitates atque oppida in utrâque Rheni ripâ elegantisimè sita præterivi. Colonia ista magnificentissima atque frequentissima civitas est omnium quas in Germaniâ vidi, & situm amœnissimum habet. Nihil non splendidum & nitidum hìc: tantùm fæce & sordibus

* Ænei. 6.

EPISTLE TO GASPAR WASERUS

Pontificiarum superstitionum tota contaminatur. Multas egregias & non contemnendas antiquitates hìc perlustravi. Integram historiam trium Regum, quorum sepulchrum adeò ostentant Colonienses, ex typographicâ quâdam tabulâ extra sacrarium appensâ (in quo fertur illorum ossa recondi) excripsi. Sed totam illam narrationem nugatorium commentum esse plurimi Orthodoxi censent. Sancti Gereonis templum visitavi, ubi ossa Thebæorum atque Maurorum Martyrum reponuntur; Sanctæ etiam Ursulæ meæ conterraneæ templum. Hic magna multitudo ossium & craniorum asservatur, quæ thecis vel operculis byssinis ac bombycinis aureis stellulis distinctis cooperiuntur. Coloniâ relictâ liquidam viam Rhenanam per Clivensem ditionem, Geldriam, & Hollandiam semper tenui, in multis inclytis urbibus, Novi omago, Gorcomo, Dordraco pernoctans. A Dordracenâ illâ urbe Virginali (tali enim epitheto cives illam insigniunt, partim quod semper invicta steterit, partim etiam quòd Virgo illam fundaverit) & clarissimo Emporio Euripum usque ad Armurum primum Zelandiæ oppidum tranavi, â quo per Middleburgum Zelandiæ Metropolin Flishingam deveni, quæ peregrinationis meæ Germanicæ extimus erat terminus. Hinc plenis carbasis per cæruleum elementum vectus Londinum appuli, ubi paucos dies inter amicos meos, (qui obviis ulnis me post longos terræ marisque labores amplexi sunt,) corporis & animi reficiendi causâ commoratus, tandèm in exoptatissimam patriam meam in Comitatu Somersetensi, qui jacet in occidentali Angliæ parte, lætabundus perveni. Hic fuit ultima periodus longinquæ meæ peregrinationis quæ â Venetiis ad patrios lares millenis viginti quinque milliariis Anglicis constabat.

Habes jam (Ornatissime Vir) συντόμως descriptam meam Germanicam itinerationem â vestro Tiguro. Sed hoc censeas velim nullam Germanicam civitatem majore solatio ac voluptate me affecisse quâm vestram. Nam omnia illìc adeò mihi arrisere, ut copiosiorem illius descriptionem in meo ὁδοιπορικῷ libro quâm ullius alterius Germanicæ urbis (exceptis tantùm Basileâ, Heidelbergâ, Spirâ, & Coloniâ)

Epistle to Gaspar Waserus.

CORYAT'S CRUDITIES

fecerim. Armamentarium vestrum omnimodo apparatu bellico instructum, antiquis Aquilis & vexillis Romanorum, nerviceis clypeis, oblongis atque ancipitibus ensibus utrinque, plurimis praeacutis cuspidibus armatis, gladio Gulielmi Tell Suitensis confœderationis vestræ Helveticæ authore, excusso Præfectorum vestratium externorum jugo, qui immani ac plané barbaricâ in civitates vestras tyrannide grassati sunt, variisque aliis insignibus antiqui tatibus summè decoratum, & exquisitissimo decentissi moque ordine excultum, hyperbolicis ad multos meos con terraneos præconiis extuli. Nec non elegantem civitatis situm, amœnum Limaci interfluxum, nitida templa, turrita ac pinnata mœnia profundis vallis circumcincta, firmissima propugnacula, pulchras plateas, elegantia ædificia, excellentem vestram aristocraticam politiam, summam in exteros humanitatem, maximam rerum omnium tum ad utilitatem tum ad voluptatem conducentium exuberantiam, nihil non summis laudibus ad sydera evexi. Vestræ denique civitati tantum tribui, ut paradisum deliciarum, fertilissimum ingeniorum totius Germaniæ seminarium, & ipsissimum Musarum domicilium non immeritò appellaverim. Unum tantùm hoc vobis deesse affirmavi, nimirùm cohonestationem virorum Tigurinorum tam Martis quam Musarum ornamentis illustrium statuis, Mausoleis, & honorariis virtutum eorum epitaphiis atque elogiis, quæ ubique in omnibus cœteris Germaniæ civitatibus observavi, præcipuè verò Basileæ, Heidelbergæ, Spiræ, ac Moguntiæ. Sed omnia hæc unâ cum Gallicis, Italicis, & Rheticis observationibus quas jamdudum collegi, & Hispanicis, Polonicis, Danicis, Saxonicis, Turcicis, quas posthàc (Christo duce) collecturus sum, tandem divini numinis auspiciis in unum corpus redacta, copiosè explicata, ac certo quodam ordine ac methodo digesta & typis excusa videbis. Intereà impolitis bisce lineis extremam coronidem imponens, te oro atque obtestor, in amicorum tuorum album referre digneris tibi addictissimum (etsi
Sit penitùs toto divisus ab orbe Britannus)
Thomam Coryatum Odcombiensem.
Londini pridie Calendas Augusti : Anno Regis θεανθρώπου 1609.

EPISTLE TO GASPAR WASERUS

To the same also I wrote this poore Greeke Epistle.

ΚΑὶ ταύτας ὀλίγας γραμμὰς Ἑλληνικὰς ἀναγνῶναι (Ἀνερ᾽ ἀξιώτατε ταὲ καὶ φιλομουσότατε) σοῦ δέομαι. κἄ᾽ν γαρ ἀπαιδευσίας καὶ ἀπειροκαλίας γέμωσι, ἀλλ᾽ ὅμως τῆς ἐμῆς πρὸς σὲ εἰλικρινεστάτης εὐνοίας τεκμήρια οὐκ ἀφανῆ τυγχάνουσιν οὖσαι. ὄντως ἐμαυτὸν εὐδαιμονίζω, ὅτι ἐμοὶ ἐν ὑπερθαλασσίαις χώραις τῆς περισπουδάστου σῆς φιλίας τυχεῖν συνέβη, τῆς πολὺ μᾶλλον ἐμὲ εὐφρακυίας ἢ ἀλλῆ τὶς ἡδονὴ ἧς ἀπέλαυσ᾽ ἐν ταῖς ὁδοιπορίαις ἐμαῖς. ὅτι δέ κατα τὸν Δημοσθένη, τὸ φυλάξαι τἀγαθὸν τοῦ κτήσασθαι πολλῷ χαλιπώτερον εἶναι δοκεῖ, τῆς φρονήσεως σημεῖον ἡγοῦμαι τὴν σὴν φιλίαν κτησάμενον παντὶ τρόπῳ πειρᾶσθαι αὐτὴν φυλάξαι. μηδένα δὲ λόγον βελτίω πρὸς τοῦτ᾽ ἐξευρισκειν διος τ᾽ ἦν, ἡ ἐπιστολὴν σοὶ πέμπων, γνοὺς ἐπιστολὰς εἶναι οἱονεὶ ὀργανικάς αἰτίας, δι᾽ ἃς εἰώθαμεν ὡς τὰ πολλὰ τὰς φιλίας βεβαιοῦν. ἵνα δέ αὐτὴ ἡ φιλία παρ᾽ ἡμῖν ἀλλήλοις αὐχθῆ, τοῦτο σοὶ εὔχομαι (τῶν Μουσῶν λαμπρότατον κλέος) ὥστε ἀντιτέμπειν ἐμοὶ τὰ γράμματα ἐκ τοῦ τιγουρου, ὧνπερ οὐδὲν μοὶ χαριέντερον ἢ ποθεινώτερον συμβάιη. τὸ δὲ μάκρον τόπου διάστημα οὐδέν ἐστιν ἐμπόδισμα πρός τοῦτο· ῥαδίως γὰρ δύνη ἀποστέλλειν αὐτά πρὸς Ἀγγλίαν ἀπὸ τοῦ φραγκοφούρτου τῷ τῶν πολυθρυλλητῶν ἐκείνων ἀγορῶν καιρῷ. ἐὰν ταύτης τῆς φιλανθρωπίας ἐμ᾽ ἀξιώσης, δήπου ἀλύτῳ τῆς φιλίας συνδέσμῳ ἐμὲ σοὶ ἀεὶ συσφίγξεις. ἔρρωσο ὁ τῆς παιδείας φωστήρ, ἕως ἂν πάλιν ἴδω, σὲ, ὁ μοί συμβήσεσθαι ἐλπιζω ἐν τῷ ἐρχομένῳ θέρει. δέομαὶ σοῦ προσειπεῖν παρ᾽ ἐμοῦ ἐκεῖνον εὐγενῆ Τιγουρίνον Κύριον Ὀ῟ρτμαννον Ἀισέλερον, ὃς φιλανθρωπότατα μοῦ ἐχρήσατο αὐτῶ ἀντὶ τῆς ἑαυτοῦ εἰς ἐμὲ φιλανθρωπίας χάριν ὡς οἶον τε μεγίστην ἀποδίδωμι.

Εὐμενέστατος σοῦ φίλος, σοὶ ἀεὶ ἕως τῆς τελευτῆς συνεσφιγμίνος
Θωμᾶς Κοριατὸς Ἄγγλος ὁ ἐκ της Ὀδκομβίας.

Λονδίνοθεν πρώτῃ ἱσταμένου Σκιροφριῶνος τῷ ἔτει μετὰ τὴν ἐνσάρκωσιν Σωτῆρος τοῦ κόσμου χιλιοστῷἑξακοσιοστῷ ἐννάτῳ.

Having about some three quarters of a year since received an answer from this learned man, I have thought it not amisse to insert it into this place, as an argument

of his love unto me; but I will not expresse his superscription, as I have done those of the Epistles that I
wrote unto all my foure learned friends of this Citie of
Zurich, because he ascribeth such titles unto me, as I
never did, nor shall deserve in my life. The Epistle
itselfe is this.

S. P. D.

Epistle from Gaspar Waserus.

Iteræ tuæ (Doctissime Vir) quas ex ultimis
nundinis autumnalibus ad me dedisti,
mihi redditæ, & longè gratissimæ fuerunt
multis nominibus. Nam, præter iter
tuum, quod graphicè & luculentèr admo-
dum descripsisti, clarè ex eis perspexi
eximiam tuam benevolentiam, quâ me
licèt absentem, & longissimè â vobis dissitum egregiè
sanè prosequeris, & ad eam perpetuandam proporrò te
quasi devincis. Quæ causa est, cur non noluerim isthoc
Epistolium tibi reponere, & eandem tibi de me quoque
polliceri. Iter egregium profectò est, quod ab eo tempore, ex quo â me discessisti, felicitèr Dei gratiâ confecisti:
& optandum esset, ut multi tui similes extârent, qui non
transcurrendo tantùm corpora aspicerent, sed introspicerent
etiam animos, rerum momenta, non margines aut superficies. Tum major profecto hominum politicorum &
prudentum, quibus etiam in Ecclesiâ habemus opus, sine
dubio extaret numerus. Hoc si diligentiori curæ mihi
fuisset in Angliâ, Scotiâ, Hiberniâ, Belgio, Galliâ, Germaniâ, Italiâ, & alibi, quum provincias illas florentissimas
peragrarem, paulò meliùs res se meæ haberent. Præclarè
igitur tu, qui omnia ista quâm diligentissimè observare,
scrutari, connotare voluisti. Etenim meminisse tandem
hæc tanta juvabit.

De rerum statu nostrarum pauca habeo ad te scribere.
Rex Galliæ recèns in Helvetiis conscribi curavit sex millia
peditum; quæ ad redigendos ducatus Juliacensem, Clivensem & Montensem in potestatem Principum Brandebur-
genis & Palatini, in Galliam hìnc proficiscentur. Quòd si

EPISTLE FROM GASPAR WASERUS

Serenissimus Rex vester, (uti facturum credunt & optant omnes boni) sua quoque conjungat auxilia, magnam sanè jacturam faciet Antichristus. Apologiam ejus cum præfatione monitoriâ refutatam esse â Bellarmino, haud dubiè jam cognovisti. Regerit is Crambem Pontificiam millies â nostris refutatam magnâ suâ ignominiâ. Vestrûm jam est Regis vestri causam contra Lanistam istum Purpuratum in manus sumere, & masculè propugnare; prout per Dei gratiam virorum generosissimorum & in hac palæstrâ exercitatissimorum apud vos ingens est copia. Deus optimus maximus vestris laboribus prolixè benedicat; cujus clientelæ, seu λιμένι ἀσφαλεστάτῳ, te commendo corditùs mi Thoma optime, & amicissime. Tiguri 16 Mart. 1610

Tui studiosissimus Gaspar Waserus,

Professor sanctarum linguarum in scholâ Tigurinâ.

Epistle from Gaspar Waserus.

This Epistle following is to M. Rodolphus Hospinianus a learned Preacher and writer of controversies of the Citie of Zurich. The superscription whereof is this.

Epistle to Rodolphus Hospinianus, Preacher.

Reverendissimo viro Domino Rodolpho Hospiniano præstantissimo theologo, vigilantissimoque animarum pastori in inclytâ civitate Tigurinâ Helveticarum urbium Metropoli.

The Epistle it selfe is this.

Tsi non ut hominem perfrictæ frontis, audacis tamen genii seu ingenii fortassè (Vir Clarissime) me redargueris, quòd ad te ausim scribere, & Musas tuas severiores hisce intempestivis lineis interpellare. Condones quæso meæ audaciæ. Nam talem opinionem tuæ humanitatis ac egregii candoris imbibi, quippè quòd familiarissimo tuo commercio in ædibus tuis Tiguri me dignatus fueris, ut non omninò ingratas tibi istas literas fore mihi penitùs persuaserim, præsertìm cum proficiscantur â grato animo

123

Epistle to
Rodolphus
Hospinianus,
Preacher.

gratias tibi singulares reddente ob tuam summam erga me
benevolentiam, quam satis abundè demonstrasti, quando
illum eruditum, suavitèr moratum, ac lætæ indolis juvenem
Marcum Buelerum mihi ut comitem conciliasti toto illo
tempore quod contrivi in vestrâ civitate. Juvenis ille, cui
plurimis nominibus me devinctissimum ingenuè agnosco,
idoneus & index & dux mihi fuit. Nam insignitèr mihi
gratificatus est tum indicando mihi precipuas maximâque
observatione dignissimas res, quas vestra suppeditavit
civitas, ut templa, arces, propugnacula, scholas, celeberrimum vestrum armamentarium omni munitionum genere
ac πανοπλία instructum, nihil visu dignum omittens:
tum etiam ducendo vel potius deducendo me in viâ meâ
Badenam versus, & quandò nobis mutuò valediximus, vim
lachrymarum (ô tenellum & liquidum cor) profundendo.
Ejus humanitati atque τῇ ἀναμνήσει omninò tribuo,
quòd tam copiosam historiolam vestræ civitatis scripserim.
Multò enim pleniorem narrationem feci in meo ὁδοιπορικῷ
Tiguri ac rerum Tigurinarum, quâm ullius aliæ civitatis
in Germania, exceptis duntaxàt quatuor, Basileâ, Heidel-
berga, Spirâ, & Coloniâ. Parvi (reverende vir) tuo consilio unâ quadam re. Nam si memineris, consuluisti mihi
digredi parùm ex viâ ad videndum balnea propè Badenam
vestram Helveticam. Sed in multis profectò diverticulis
& ignotis callibus erravi, antequam illa invenire potuerim,
hâc præcipuè de causâ, quoniam inscius vestræ linguæ non
potui Germanicè percontari viam. Tantùm hac phrasi uti
solius eram. Her ist das der raight stroze auf balnea.
Sed Germani, præcipuè rustici illi Corydones quibus
obviam dedi, existimantes præ rudi meâ atque imperitâ
verborum Teutonicorum pronuntiatione me peregrinum
fuisse, & vestræ linguæ ignarum, mihi interroganti semper
annuerunt, & gestibus quibusdam subobscuris viam in quâ
progrederer, mihi indigitârunt, sed non viam ad balnea.
Non enim intellexerunt quid sibi vellet meum verbum
Balnea. Tandem post multam deambulationem Kininfs-
feldianum Monasterium veni, ubi â quodam docto juvene,
qui linguam Latinam mediocritèr calluit, sciscitatus sum

124

EPISTLE TO R. HOSPINIANUS

ubi essent balnea Badensia. Respondit, me illa præteri-
isse, & â tergo reliquisse per totum Germanicum milli-
arium. Quare efflagitationum mearum instantiâ illam &
oravi & exoravi, ut ad balnea me comitaretur. Quod
humanitatis officium benevolentissimè mihi præstitit, atque
ita post multos errores balnea illa lustrare & eorum virtu-
tem explorare mihi contigit. Juvenis ille quoniam
eandem quam ego religionem professus est, familiari sua
societate, & blandis facetiis me valdè recreavit. Inde profectus sum Brookam, Rheinfeldiam, ubi iterùm lenitèr ac
amœnè labentem vestrum Limacum observavi, ac tandem
Basileam. Hìc genialitèr biduum contrivi versando cum
plurimis egregiis viris, Musarum & rei literariæ candidatis.
Sed recensere tibi omnes meas Germanicas observationes,
quas in illis inclytis civitatibus curiosiùs collegi, esset tum
prolixum tum superfluum, præcipuè quoniam in Epistolâ
meâ ad celeberrimum illum Dominum Gasperum Waserum concivem tuum, quâ fieri potuit maximâ brevitate illa
omnia succinctè attigi, quam (si tibi visum fuerit) legas.
Amicos illos tuos, quos ut â te salutarem me orasti, viros
reverendissimos, atque egregiis virtutum & eruditionis non
vulgaris laudibus excultissimos, Academiæ Oxoniensis ful-
gidissima luminaria, Dominum Doctorem Hollandum
regium Theologiæ apud Oxonienses professorem, & Dominum Doctorem Rivium novi Collegii ibidèm Gardianum
(ut vulgo vocant, Anglicè the Warden) haud quaquam
vidi, ex quo domum redii. Sed salutem tuam illis trans-
misi per conterraneum tuum Dominum Gasparum Thom-
annum Tigurinum, qui multos annos Oxonii literis operam
dedit. Cum illo familiaritatem nuper inivi. Nam literas
illi à patre suo viro honestissimo sanè (ut mihi videtur) &
pientissimo tradidi, cui gratias quæso maximas des meo
nomine, quòd me Tiguri humanissimè tractaverit.
Quinetiam hoc oro te, ut illi significes, filium suum adversâ
fortunâ apud nos uti; nam tantâ inopiâ & paupertate
laborat, ut συμπάθειαν quandam in me commoveret
utque vicem ejus maximè dolerem. Proinde sicuti ego
illi consulvi ut in patriam rediret, ubi cum parentibus,

CORYAT'S CRUDITIES

propinquis, & necessariis reliquum ætatis conterat, præcipuè quum patria sua eruditissimis viris abundet, quorum
societas illi tum adjumento in conficiendo doctrinæ suæ
studio, & levamento in sublevandâ suâ egestate futura sit;
sic etiam pater ipsius φιλοστοργίαν suam declarabit, &
paterni erga illum amoris specimen egregium edet, si
literas ad illum scripserit, quibus eum ad penates suos
Tigurinos revocet, quò tandem aliquandò post diuturnum
istud quasi voluntarium exilium ex dulci suâ patriâ sibi in
canicie suâ adminiculum, & veluti idoneum ad senectutem
suam suffulciendam baculum sit. Tum patris tum patriæ
suæ causâ opto ei ex animo magis secundam fortunam
quâm apud nos fruitur. Nam patriam ipsius tanto amore
amplector, ut (si Deus mihi vitam prorogaverit) in prox-
imâ meâ Germanicâ profectione totam vestram Helvetiam
perlustrare decreverim, præcipuè tredecem vestros Can-
tones, Tigurum & Basileam iterum, Bernam, Scafusium,
Solodurum, Lucernam, Friburgum, Swiciam, Uraniam,
Sylvaniam, Tugium, Glaream, & Abbatis cellam.

Sed quò tandem excurrit vel expatiatur calamus meus?
ignoscas quæso prolixitati meæ (dignissime vir) nam tuâ
humanitate fretus (quam re ipsâ non ita pridem expertus
sum) calamo meo nimis laxas habenas dedi, quas jam
restringere expedit, ne tibi in pulcherrimo tuo Theologico
studio impigrè currenti ista levicula πάρεργα sint impedi-
mento, quò minus ad extremam curriculi metam per-
venias. Promisit mihi (egregie vir) ingenuus ille juvenis
Marcus Buelerus se sollicitaturum te ut mihi rescribas, si
priùs ad te scriberem. Quo me favore si dignatus fueris,
usque ad extremum vitæ halitum obstringes

Tibi deditissimum, tuæqúe doctrinæ haud
minimum præconem

Thomam Coryatum Odcombiensem.
Londini pridie Calen. August. Anno 1609.

The third Epistle I sent to M. Henry Bullinger aforesaid, the superscription is this.

Viro ornatissimo amico suo Henrico Bullingero, celeberrimi illius viri Henrici Bullingeri summi Tigurinæ urbis quondam antistitis nepoti, eruditissimo ac vigilantissimo apud Tigurinos in Helvetiâ Ecclesiastæ.

The Epistle it selfe is this.

Via inter reliquos meos Tigurinos amicos non ultimum locum tenes (clarissime charissimeque mi Bullingere) à me paucis compellandus & salutandus es. Ne si intellexeris me ad Dominum Hospinianum & Dominum Waserum literas dedisse, teque omisisse, ingratitudinis notam mihi inuras, quum tam benevolè, tam humaniter, tam comitèr multò suprâ tum expectationem tum meritum meum domi tuæ Tiguri ultimo autumno me tractaveris. Nam tam benigno ac dulci alloquio me ignotum ac peregrinum in ædibus tuis dignari, manifestum liberalis animi argumentum fuit ; sed in bibliothecam tuam, in illud tam variè copioseque instructum Musæum (quod multò majus erat) me introducere, librorum tuorum elegantissimorum copiam mihi facere, avi tui beatæ memoriæ manuscripta volumina ostendere, humanitatis tuæ singularis ut insigne indicium & prædicavi meis doctis conterraneis, nonnullis aulicis viris, celeberrimarum Academiarum nostrarum alumnis, & equestris ordinis generosis ; & prædicare non supersedebo,

*Dum memor ipse mei, dum spiritus hos reget artus.

Proinde facere non potui quin paucis hisce lineis te salutem, partìm ut turpem ingratitudinis labem subterfugiam ; partìm etiam ut amicitia nostra firmiùs coalescat, quod summoperè expeto.

* Virg. Ænei. I.

CORYAT'S CRUDITIES

Epistle to Henry Bullinger. Antequam vidi Musæum tuum, tum fando accepi, tum in duobus probatis authoribus legi, Joannem Casam Episcopum Beneventanum in Italiâ de Sodomiæ laudibus libellum conscripsisse. Authores illi apud quos illius fit mentio, sunt isti, Joannes Juellus ille noster Phœnix Anglicus, Episcopus Sarisburiensis, in suâ elegantissimâ doctissimâque Ecclesiæ Anglicanæ Apologiâ, & clarissimus ille tuus conterraneus Conradus Gesnerus in suâ Bibliothecâ, qui bisce verbis illum librum memorat. Impurissimus hic nebulo edidit poemata quædam Italica, in publicum Venetiis excusa, in quibus (proh scelus) Sodomiam laudibus extollit. Istorum authenticorum scriptorum authoritate nixus, sæpiusculè Papicolis in Angliâ & alibi retuli quendam Papisticum Episcopum Italicum tam spurcum librum scripsisse, eumque typis imprimendum curasse, ut nullus nostræ reformatæ religionis professor vel audire illum patientèr ferret, ne dum talem conscriberet. Refragati mihi sunt Papistæ de isto libro verba facienti, & tam pertinacitèr affirmarunt nullum ejusmodi librum â Casa fuisse scriptum, ut aliquantum dubitaverim utrum verum esset quod de illo libro memoriæ prodiderunt gravissimi isti authores. Sed quum jam tandem hisce oculis illum intueri in tuo Musæo mihi contigerit, non video cur execrandam illius consceleratissimi Episcopi spurcitiam excusent Pontificii. Etsi autem ille immundissimus liber sit dignus qui aut Thetidi, aut Veneris tradatur marito (ut elegantèr politissimus ille Politianus loquitur de Homero â se translato in quâdam Epistolâ ad Jacobum Cardinalem Papiensem) tamen tibi consulerem reservare potiùs in Bibliothecâ tuâ illud detestandum monumentum ad perpetuum Papisticæ immundiciei dedecus & infamiam. O vos terque quaterque beatos Tigurinos, qui per totum penè Christianum orbem, præcipuè religionem reformatam & verè Christianam profitentem, pro fidei vestræ puritate, assiduâ & indefessâ in scribendo industriâ, singulari & incomparabili doctrinâ, & eximia pietate, suprâ reliquos, etiam in extremis oris plagisque totius Christianismi celebramini. Ita enim Deus vestræ civitati & incolis bene-

ι fando accepi, ις
innem Casam Ερι
Sodomiæ laudib
apud quos illug :
ille noster Phar:
o suâ elegantissi
ιlogiâ, & clariss.
nerus in suâ Εκ
memorat. Impus
quædam Italica, :
proh scelus) Sodo:
nticorum scriptore
is in Angliâ & ab
n Italicum tam spu
nprimendum curare
· professor vel auti
n conscriberet. It
ro verba facienti, ι
ejusmodi librum i
dubitaverim utro
emoriæ prodidene
ι jam tandem his
mini contigerit, æ
...ratissimi Episco;
iutem ille immundi
aut Veneris tradam
Politianus loquitur
Epistolâ ad Jacobu
onsulerem reservat
ιdum monumenta
...fecus & infamis.
rinos, qui per totan
gionem reformation
dei vestræ puritate,
ustriâ, singulari ἐ
ite, cuprâ reliquos,
Christianismi cele:
ti & incolis bene-

EPISTLE TO HENRY BULLINGER

dixit, ut nulla sit Christianismi pars tam longè dissita, quò non nominis vestri celebritas pervaserit, præsertìm ex quo puriorem Evangelii doctrinam amplexi estis. Nam tempore illo tenebrarum, quo crassis illis superstitionibus & idolomaniâ Papisticâ immersi estis, non memini vel unum clarum virum vestram civitatem peperisse. Sed ex quo Papismo nuncium remisistis, & repurgatam doctrinam filii Dei, sacrosanctum ejus Evangelium in cordibus vestris plantastis, prædicastis, in circumjacentibus regionibus, disseminatis, & tam vocibus quàm accuratissimis vestris scriptis eam propugnastis, Deus bone quot strenui & heroici Jesu Christi athletæ, quot imperterriti veritatis Evangelicae πρόμαχοι Tiguri exorti sunt, qui pro orthodoxâ & veteri Catholicâ doctrinâ verè Apostolicâ, verè Christianâ contra ementitum Romanæ Ecclesiæ Catholicismum, & commentitium Papalis tyrannidis primatum calamis suis, & spirtualibus gladiis pugnantes, sibi & patriæ suæ immortalem gloriam nullâ temporis injuriâ intermorituram pepererunt? nam tot egregios verbi divini assertores contra novitias & spurias Cacolycæ Romanæ Synagogæ traditiones apud vos intra octoginta annorum spatium natos arbitror, quot nullam aliam totius Christianismi Academiam vix peperisse reor. Ut autem cæteros Tigurinos Doctores taceam, Henricus Bullingerus avus tuus piæ memoriæ instar omnium erit, qui doctrinam sinceriorem Jesu Christi purissime ut θεόπνευστος & θεοδίδακτος Doctor & docuit, & promovit ad insignem Christianæ reipub. utilitatem, & elaboratissimis suis lucubrationibus vestram civitatem, non minùs quàm Smyrnam suam Homerus, aut Mantuam Virgilius maximè nobilitavit ; cujus libris Theologicis, præsertìm Decadibus suis tantum authoritatis tribuimus nos Angli, quantum Sibyllinis oraculis antiqui Romani ; usque adeò ut publicè in Ecclesiis nostris eas asservari authoritate Regiâ mandatum sit, quò plebeii homines iis concionibus in sacrosanctis Christianæ fidei mysteriis faciliùs informentur. Hunc si imiteris (doctissime mi Bullingere) hujus vestigiis si inhærescas, & tam vitæ integritate quàm doctrinæ puritate si illius genium exprimas (quod te summis conatibus facere accepi) verè te avissare dicam. Quod ut facias, nos Angli (qui avi tui sanctissimam memoriam veneramur) præcipuè ego, qui tecum aliquam saltem externam si non intimam amicitiam contraxi, ardentibus votis exoptamus.

Macte igitur virtute tua, sic itur ad astra (Egregie vir,) & istam quam nactus es Spartam orna, hoc est, istam sacram facultatem Theologicam quam suscepisti, excole, ut tandem consummatissimus Theologus & Ecclesiæ Christi fulgida lampas, sicut Luna inter minores Stellas, evadas. Vale doctissime mi Bullingere, & hunc animulum meum verè & ἀψευδῶς tui amantem ut redames te instantèr oro. Tui studiosissimus

Thomas Coryatus Odcombiensis.
Londini Pridie Calendas Augusti, Anno 1609.

The fourth and last Epistle I sent to my friend Marcus Buelerus above named.

The superscription is this.

Egregiæ indolis & optimæ spei juveni Marco Buelero Musarum alumno, ac benè merito suo amico, Tiguri Primariæ Helvetiæ Civitatis rei literariæ & bonis artibus operam danti.

The Epistle it selfe.

Andem aliquando (clarissime mi Buelere) post longas moras hasce literas tibi mitto, non sine dolore profectò ablatam fuisse mihi ad te scribendi opportunitatem toto isto tempore ex quo patriam meam appuli; præpedîtus nimirùm magnâ negotiorum mole, quæ statìm post meum in patriæ fines ingressum me undique circumvallârunt. Sed præstat serò scribere quâm non omnino. Non possum satis amplas gratias tibi reddere (mi Buelere) ob tuam insignem humanitatem ultimo autumno Tiguri mihi præstitam,

TIES

is conatibus fac
t facias, nos dr
eneramur) praeq
iam si non intum
xoptamus.

itur ad astra

is Spartam orna
cam quam suscep
s Theologus & E
Luna inter more
B....gere, & h
amantem ut redim

...issimus
...us Odcombiens
...ii, Anno 1615

...t to my frien
e named.

is this.

.eni Marco Buele
' suo amico, Tigu
en literariæ & bon

..e.

..ssime mi Buelere
sce literas tibi misisse
fectò ablatam fuisse
opportunitatem non
...am meam appuli
magnâ negotiorum
st meum in patria
irunt. Sed præstat
possum satis ampliss
b tuam insignem
mihi præstitam,

quam quoâd vixero gratâ atque tenaci memoriâ complectar, &, si in Helvetiâ aliquod tempus conterere mihi iterum contigerit (quod fortassè aliquandò accidet præ amore illo quô uberrimam tuam patriam amplector) aliquod sanè gratitudinis specimen edam, quod tuam in me benevolentiam aliquâ ex parte rependet. Nam tuâ potissimùm ope adjutus plurima memoranda in vestrâ Civitate Tigurinâ observavi, quæ forsan posthac typis excusa unâ cum Gallicis, Italicis, & Germanicis meis observationibus videbis.

Memini (mi Buelere) in mutuis nostris colloquiis inter deambulandum me sciscitatum fuisse te an Græcam linguam calleres, teque respondisse, quòd etsi adhuc ejus imperitus esses, tamen divino numine aspirante eam addiscere decreveris. Ego illâ occasione impulsus, in laudem præstantissimæ illius linguæ aliquantum digressus fui, promisique (si unquam ad te scriberem) ad illius studium te seriò cohortari velle. Proindè non abs re erit, si paucas lineas exarem, quibus tanquam stimulis seu calcaribus quibusdam ad elegantissimæ illius linguæ cognitionem imbibendam te incitem. Quum multa sint (mi Marce) quæ te ad Græcam linguam perdiscendam exacuere possunt, tum hæc duo potissimùm. Primò exempla omnium vestratium celeberrimorum Tigurinorum, qui doctrinæ laude floruerunt. Nam quum multos clarissimos immortalique memoriâ dignissimos viros vestra civitas produxerit, Huldicum Zuinglium, Henricum Bullingerum vestri Bullingeri egregii Theologi jam apud vos viventis avum, Theodorum Bibliandrum, Conradum Gesnerum, Rodolphum Gualterum, Ludovicum Lavaterum, Rodolphum Collinum, Josiam Simlerum, Joannem Jacobum Frisium, Joannem Guilielmum Stuckium, cum plurimis aliis præstantissimis viris, qui in vestro Helvetico orbe tanquam splendidissima luminaria refulserunt, omnes istos Græcè non mediocritèr doctos, sed eâ linguâ ad amussim excultos, ad ejusque summum quasi apicem et fastigium pervenisse reperies; quippe cujus adminiculo veritatem indagare, errores refutare, & Pontificiorum prava dogmata atque

CORYAT'S CRUDITIES

ἑτεροδιδασκαλίαν evertere faciliùs possent. Nam ex omnibus illustribus viris quos vestra aluit civitas, ne unum quidem nominare potes qui Græcâ linguâ non imbutus fúerit. Secundò consideratio crassæ inscitiæ nonnullorum, qui etsi famam aliquam ob superficialem quandam doctrìnam in repub. literariâ adepti fúerint, tamen quia hujus linguæ cognitione destituti fuêre, in multos putidos ac fœdos errores prolapsi sunt, & scriptis suis perridiculas quasdam absurditates ipsis etiam pueris irridendas & reprehendendas mandârunt. Nam Petrus Comestor Ecclesiæ Trecensis presbyter, qui vixit anno 1206. & præstantissimus sui temporis theologus existimatus fuit, hoc vocabulum Eunuchus derivare non dubitavit ab ἐυ quod significat benè, & Nuche, victoria. Nimirùm quòd egregia & penè cœlestis victoria ei visa fuerit. Quum re verâ dedicatur ἀπὸ τῆς ἐυνῆς quod significat cubìculum, & ἔχειν habere, id est, sese in cubiculo connere, quia eunuchi ad cubiculorum & gynecæorum custodiam curamque comparari solebant, quòd ancillis expeditiores essent, & ob exemptos testiculos ad coitum inepti. Nicolaus etiam Lyranus egregius apud nos Anglos theologaster, & Minoritanæ familiæ summum decus, qui floruit anno 1310. hypocritam appellari affirmavit ab hypos quod est sub, & crisis aurum. Quia sub auro scilicèt exterioris conversationis habet absconditum plumbum falsitatis : anile profectò delirium, & puerilibus sibilis excipiendum. Alius etiam Theologus non infimæ apud Pontificios classis, diabolum traxisse nomen scribit â dia quod est duo, & bolus morsus (ô lepidum & perfacetum caput, ne dicam plumbeum) quòd duobus scilicèt morsibus totum hominem devoret, uno corpus, altero animam. Sed constat ἀπὸ τοῦ διαβάλλειν potiùs deduci diabolum, quoniam quum sit humani generis hostis, homines apud Deum calumniatur. Nonnè subsannas nasoque suspendis adunco istas pueriles etymologias? quare ne ejusmodi crassa errata committas, quæ ex Græcæ linguæ ignorantiâ oriri solent, tibi amicè consulo

―――― Exemplaria Græca

Nocturnâ versare manu, versare diurnâ.

EPISTLE TO MARCUS BUELERUS

Ut cum Horatio loquar. Nam (ut idem affirmat)

> Graiis ingenium, Graiis dedit ore rotundo
> Musa loqui.

Memoriæ proditum est Joannem Capnionem quem aliâs vocabant Reuchlinum, authorem hujus apoththegmatis fuisse : Hebræos quidem bibere fontes, Græcos verò rivos, Latinos autem paludes. Quare rivulis istis limpidissimis temet proluas, rivulis inquam qui in carminibus Homeri,

> (———— a quo ceu fonte perenni
> Vatum Pieriis ora rigantur aquis)

abundè scatent, in Demosthenis et Isocratis orationibus melle Hymettio dulcioribus. Crede mihi mi (Buelere) etsi salebrosa sit & spinosa via ad Athenas Græciæ acropolin, tamen illuc si semel perveneris, infinitis deliciis & quâdam voluptatum affluentiâ animum tuum pasces. Rudimenta fortasse Græcæ linguæ aspera & acerba sunt, tamen postquam sedulitate & Vigilantia industriâ eorum acerbitate superaveris, singularem quandam jucunditatem indè percepturus es. Memento illius non tam veteris quàm veri dicti ; χαλεπά τὰ καλά, & pervulgati illius versiculi.

> Dulcia non meruit qui non gustavit amara.

iisdem penè verbis te alloquor (mi Buelere) quibus Helenus Virgilianus Æneam affatus est.

> ——————————*Via prima salutis

(inquit Helenus,) sed gloriæ atque felicitatis, inquam ego,

> (Quod minimè reris) Graiâ pandetur ab urbe.

à Græcâ videlicêt linguâ potissimùm petenda est illa cognitio quæ te meritò beare potest. Brevem istam parænesin ad politissimæ illius linguæ scientiam comparandam æqui quæso bonique consulito, exemplis nimirùm nixam tum multorum Doctorum qui in vestra civitate Tigurina floru-

* Æneid 3.

erunt, quorum fama propter summam atque ferè incomparabilem eorum in omni doctrinarum genere præcipuè Theologiæ scientiam in totum Christianum orbem emanavit, & quos non modò non abhorruisse à Græcâ linguâ sed etiam ad ipsum illius culmen aspirasse manifestum est; tum etiam absurditatum quarundam, quæ ex illius linguæ inscitiâ profectæ sunt.

Quod mihi promisisti Tiguri vehementissimè te oro prestare. Nam pollicitus es mihi, si scriberem ad tres illos pereruditos atque egregios viros, Dominum Waserum, Dominum Hospinianum, & Dominum Bullingerum, te illos sollicitaturum ut mihi rescribant. Quare quum ad illos scripserim, obsecro te ad me literas dare ut illis persuadeas. Quam mihi humanitatem si præstiterint, me illis Gordiano quodam amicitiæ nodo perpetuò devincient. Porrò hoc te rogo, ut gratias maximas meo nomine Domino Thomanno rei frumentariæ apud vos præfecto pro suâ erga me benevolentiâ haud vulgari agas, eiquè significes me tradidisse filio suo literas quas ab eo accepi Tiguri, nec non filium suum secunda valetudine perfrui, sed jam

Non fiavit velis aura secunda suis.

Hæ sunt quas tamdiu abhinc tibi promisi literæ, quas æquo atque benevolo animo te accepturum spero, præsertìm missas âtui ἀκιβδήλως amantissimo amico; aliquam etiam â te Epistolam vicissìm expecto, quam mihi pergratam fore tibi penitùs persuadeas. Vale bellissime mi Buelere.

Tibi obstrictissimus tuæquè incolumitatis cupidissimus,
Thomas Coryatus Odcombiensis.
Londini pridiè Calendas Augusti 1609.

FRom my friend Marcus Buelerus, unto whom I wrote this Epistle, I received in answere of mine at the same time that my learned friend Mr. Waserus sent me that before mentioned, which for the love sake I beare unto him, in regard of the great courtesies he did me in Zurich, I have thought good to communicate to the world, though

EPISTLE FROM MARCUS BUELERUS

indeede it be but plaine, and wanteth that elegancy that I expected from him. The titles that he attributed unto me (because I will not acknowledge them, as being altogether unworthy of the least of them) I have omitted, as I have done those of Mr. Waserus before.

His Epistle is this.

Tanè literæ â te (vir clarissime & charissime) tandem? Quod in gaudio improviso, vix credidi ipse meis oculis cum legerem, manibus cùm tenerem. Deum ego testor, ut in solo nomine tuo lecto exsilii. Officium mihi fuit tua scriptio, imò beneficium, quia ἀντιφιλήσεως est index; quia etiam, quam sermone benevolentiam tu ante biennium, eam nunc affatim ostendit Epistola tua venusta, lepida, & pro re ipsâ bella, quâ me summo studio, pro amore, pro familiaritate nostra, pro candore denique tuo singulari ad Græcas literas exhortaris, multis rationibus firmissimis allicis, persuades, delectas; ab hoc enim tempore, quo ad me tuæ literæ venerunt, & antè, omnem meam operam & laborem in hoc studio collocavi, quoad potui diligentissimè; ἀ μή δὲ μεμάθηκα προστλήψομαι ταῖς ἐπισήμαις. πολὺ γὰρ κρεῖττον μοί δοκεῖ περὶ τῶν χρησίμων ἐπιεικῶς δοξάζειν, ἢ περὶ τῶν ἀχρήστων ἀκριβῶς ἐπιστασθαι. πάσης δέ τῆς περι τὴν φρόνησιν ἐπιμελείας εἰκότως σὺ αἴτιον εἶναι νομίσεις. Διάγε ἐκεῖνο δικαίως ἄν ἐκ καρδίας χάριν ἔχρω μεγάλην. Convictu Domini Beumleri usus sum eo tempore, cum adfuisses, nunc verò Domini Henrici Bullingeri, ad quem etiam literas dedisti, quem ego propter mirificam φιλανθρω-πίαν & singularem erga me benevolentiam & amo & colo. Videbis fortassis aliquando alios libros multos, quos Dominus Beumlerus præstantissimus Theologus edidit, (si modò nostrorum Tigurinorum Theologorum libros evolvere cupias) multa enim volumina scripsit contra D. Heilbrunnerum, Pistorium, Bellarminum, Jacobum Andreæ, Philippum Nicolai, Faustum Socinum, & alios hæreticos recentiores. Ex tuis literis denique conjecturam

135

Epistle from
Marcus
Buelerus. facere potui te incolumem in patriam rediisse; gratulor itaque tibi reditum illum prosperum in patriam tuam, & (ut debeo) vehementèr gaudeo, post longinquam tuam in regionibus transmarinis peregrinationem. Plurimùm tibi arridet nostra ¦Helvetia, & φιλανθρωπία, quâ gens ista prædita est, insignis; contrâ ego Angliam in pectore amo, cùm ob religionem sinceram, tum propter Doctores (ut audio) fato quôdam natos ad optimas artes, & erudiendam rudem nostram ætatem. Itaque si Deus vitam et vires aliquas, viæque securitatem in hâc æstate annuerit, studiorum causa Heidelbergam vel Steinfurtum proficiscar, et in reditu in patriam, me vestra etiam Anglia per aliquot menses habebit quod tam benè Deus (aveo) quâm ego avidè. Plura adderem, sed quoniam inclusas has volvit suis literis Clariss. Scholæ nostræ Rector Dominus Waserus, fasciculus ne supra modum cresceret, hìc subsisto, plura quidem addere jussit amor, qui magnus mihi in te & sanctus. Valdè de valere cupio, (optime vir) καὶ φιλοῦντα ἀντι φιλεῖν. Si respondere velis, ad nundinas Francofurtenses autumnales Tigurum mitte literas ad Dominum Waserum, qui mihi (si Tiguri adhuc immorer) reddet,

[p. 395.] sin minùs, ad me transmittet. Iterum vale. Tiguri in patriâ 8. Cal. April. Anno ultimi temporis 1610.

Tui Studiosissimus Marcus Buelerus
Tigurinus SS. Theologiæ studiosus,
ἐιλικρινὴς καὶ ἀνυπόκριτος φίλος.

BUt now at length I will returne to my observations againe. I departed from Zurich upon a Saturday being the seven and twentieth of August, about two of the clocke in the afternoone (being conducted about two miles in my way by my friends Mr. Thomannus and Marcus Buelerus, who at our final departing bedewed his cheekes with teares) and came to a place nine English *Maristella.* miles beyond it called Maristella, which is hard by the river Limacus, about eight of the clocke in the evening. I passed the river in a boate, and lay that night in a solitary house by the river side. Betwixt Zurich and

Maristella I observed a passing faire and spacious country full of excellent faire corne fields. About eight miles beyond Zurich I passed by a certaine Chappell standing by the high way side wherein was an exceeding massy multitude of dead mens bones and skulles heaped together. These are said to be the skulles of the Souldiers of Charles *A multitude* the great Duke of Burgundie, (whom I have before mentioned *of bones.* in my notes of Zurich) and the Switzers, who not farre from this place fought a great battell, in which there was great slaughter on both sides.

I departed from Maristella the next morning being Sunday and the eight and twentieth of August about seven of the clocke, and came to the City of Baden commonly called ober Baden, two English miles beyond it, about eight of the clocke.

My Observations of Baden. [p. 396.]

THis City is of some antiquity. For it is mentioned *Baden.* by Cornelius Tacitus, that famous Historiographer that lived in the time of Tiberius Cæsar. I passed a bridge over the river at the entrance of the City. It standeth in that part of Switzerland which is called Ergovia, and on the farther side of the river there lyeth the territory of Turgovia. On one side of the towne are certaine hilles, and on the other the river Limacus aforesaid that runneth by Zurich, on which river they doe usually passe in boates betwixt Zurich and this City. Againe, the City is so built that it standeth on both sides of the Limacus. It lyeth in the very meditullium of Helvetia, which is the reason that the confederates doe celebrate all their publique assemblies that concerne the whole state in this City. There standeth a Castell upon the toppe of the hill which doth now suffer great dilapidations. One thing I observed in the German Cities that I could not perceive in any place of France, Savoy, Italy, or Rhetia. Namely, the heads of boares nailed upon the *Boars' heads* dores of dwelling houses of Cities and Townes. The *nailed upon* first that I saw in Germany were in this City of Baden. *doors.*

137

For here I saw many of them hanged upon the dores both at the entrance into the City, and in the fairest streete. These heads are of certaine wilde boares that the people doe kill in hunting in the forrests and woods of the country. Which hunting of wilde boares is more exercised by the Germans then by any other Christian nation. And it is the custome of the country whensoever they have killed any great boare to cut off his head, and erect it in that manner as I have already spoken. The like I observed afterward in many other German Cities. I was in the fairest Church of the City which is dedicated to our Lady, where I saw a great many pictures and images (for this City is wholly Papisticall) and one very curious Altar made of wainscot. On the south side of the Church there standeth a little Chappell, wherein I saw an exceeding multitude of dead mens bones and skulles laid together at the west end thereof. I never saw so many dead mens bones together in all my life before. For the number of them was so great, that I thinke at the day of judgement at the least ten thousand soules will challenge them. Surely for what cause they heape together these bones (I confesse) I know not.

[p. 397.]

A chapel heaped with bones and skulls.

The Earldom of Baden.

This Citie in times past was subject to a proper Earle of her owne, who was intitled the Earle of Baden. But about the yeare 1180. Henry their last Earle of Baden being dead, the Earledome was translated by the meanes of a certaine Lady to the Earles of Kyburg. Againe, after the death of Hortmannus the last Earle of Kyburg, who died about the yeare 1260, there rose a great contention about this Earledome. But at last Rodolphus Earle of Habspurg that was afterward elected King of the Romanes, got the possession of it, and after his death it was continually possessed by the Dukes of Austria till the Councell of Constance. At what time the Helvetians by the commandement of the Emperour Sigismund first seised upon it, who have ever kept it from that time till this day.

Thus much of the Citie of Baden.

138

THE BATHS OF BADEN

I Departed from this City about tenne of the clocke the same Sunday, and tooke my journey directly towards the Bathes which are within halfe an English mile of the Citie. For Master Hospinian of Zurich did earnestly counsell me to see them, as being a place very worthy my observation. But there hapned such a sinister accident unto me upon the way, that it was very difficult for me to find them out; whereby I verified the old speech, though indeed the same be properly spoken in another sense; Difficilia quæ pulchra. For by reason that [p. 398.] I was ignorant of the Dutch language, those that met me by the way could not understand my speeches, and so gave me no certaine directions to finde out the place. Whereupon I went five English miles beyond it before I *A happy acci-* could learne any newes of it, even to the famous Monas- *dent.* terie of Kiningsfelden neere the Citie of Brooke. Which accident ministred occasion unto me to see certaine memorable monuments in this foresaid Monasterie, which I had not seene, if this occurrent had not driven me thither. Here I hapned to insinuate my selfe into the acquaintance of an honest sociable Scholler, who very courteously walked with me five miles back to the bathes. For I was stroken with such an ardent desire to see them, that I could not be satisfied before I had beene there, though it were forth and backe ten miles out of my way. Therefore I will first describe them, and after returne to the discourse of the Monastery againe.

My observations of the Bathes of Baden.

CErtainly this is the sweetest place for bathes that ever *The baths of* I saw, by many degrees excelling our English bathes *Hinderhove.* both in quantity and quality. The antiquity of them is such, that (as a certaine learned man told me in the same place) it is thought they were found out before the incarnation of Christ. The place is called Hinderhove, being seated in a low bottome about a bow shot from the high way, and about halfe an English mile westward from the high way, and about halfe an English mile westward from

139

the Citie of Baden. They are much the more commodiously and pleasantly situate by reason of the sweete river Limacus running by them, which divideth them into two parts, the greater and the lesser. For those on this side

[p. 403.]

the river are called the greater, and those beyond it the lesser. The bathes are distinguished asunder by severall houses that are nothing else then Innes serving for the entertainment of strangers. And whereas every Inne hath

Baths named from the signs of the Inns.

his proper signe, the bathes have their names from the same signes. As in one Inne which hath the signe of the Beare, the Bathes in the same place being in number sixe are called the Beare bathes, and so the rest of the bathes have their denomination from their peculiar signes. In another Inne called the Sunne are eight, in a place called the Statehove eleven, at the signe·of the Crowne seven, at the Flower three, at the Oxe sixe, in a place called by the same name that is the generall appellation of all the bathes, viz. Hinderhove, seventeene, in an open court sub dio two publike bathes, whereof one is the greatest of them all ; in which I told seven and thirtie poore people bathing of themselves. For these two serve onely for the plebeian and poorer sort. So that the totall number of them amounteth to threescore. None are admitted to these bathes in the Innes but the richer sort, and such as doe sojourne in the same. For many of the strangers are tabled there for a certain stinted price by the weeke. And some of the thriftier sort onely pay for their lodging, and procure them provision from the Citie. For it is a place of great charge to them that pay for their weekly diet. Although the number of the bathes be so great as I have already spoken : yet the originall fountaines that feede them all are but few, no more then two, which are so hot at the first spring thereof, that a man can hardly endure to touch them with his bare hands, the like whereof I will report hereafter of the bathes of the lower Baden in the Marquisate. Howbeit the water of these bathes

A great concourse of people.

themselves is of a very moderate temperature. Here was a great concurse of people at the time of my being

THE BATHS OF BADEN

there, which was at the Autumne, even the eight and twentieth day of August; as at the same time every yeare many resort thither from Zurich, Basill, Berne, and [p. 404.] most of the Helveticall Cities, and from the Citie of Constance, &c. the strangers that are to be seene in Hinderhove, amounting sometimes to the number of a thousand persons, besides some few that lie abroad in the country for the bathes sake. Many of those people that lay at Hinderhove when I was there, were Gentlemen of great worth that repaired thither from the foresaid Cities partly for infirmities sake, and partly for meere pleasure and recreation. Most of the private bathes are but little, but very delicate and pleasant places, being divided asunder by certaine convenient partitions wherein are contrived divers windowes, to the end that those in the bathes may have recourse to each other, and mutually drinke together. For they reach out their drinking glasses one to another through the windowes. The roomes over head are lodgings for the strangers. Here I have observed the people in the bathes feede together *Strange* upon a table that hath swimmed upon the superficies of *customs of the* the water. Also I have noted another strange thing *bathers.* amongst them that I have not a little wondred at. Men and women bathing themselves together naked from the middle upward in one bathe: whereof some of the women were wives (as I was told) and the men partly bachelers, and partly married men, but not the husbands of the same women. Yet their husbands have bene at that time at Hinderhove, and some of them in the very place standing hard by the bathe in their cloathes, and beholding their wives not onely talking and familiarly discoursing with other men, but also sporting after a very pleasant and merry manner. Yea sometimes they sing merily together but especially that sweet & most amorous song of solus cum solâ ; I meane another mans wife, & another man naked upward (as I have aforesaid) in one bath. Yet all this while the husband may not be jelous though he be at the bathes, and seeth too much occasion

141

[p. 405.] of jealousie ministred unto him. For the verie name of jelousie is odious in this place. But let these Germanes and Helvetians do as they list, and observe these kind of wanton customes as long as they will; for mine owne part were I a married man, and meant to spend some little time here with my wife for solace and recreation sake, truly I should hardly be perswaded to suffer her to bath her selfe naked in one and the selfe same bath with one onely bachelar or married man with her, because if she was faire, and had an attractive countenance, she might perhaps cornifie me. For I might have just cause to feare lest if she went into the water with the effigies of a male lambe characterized upon her belly, the same might within a few howers grow to be an horned ram (according to a merry tale that I have sometimes heard) before she should return again to my company. Here also I saw many passing faire yong Ladies and Gentlewomen naked in the bathes with their wooers and favorites in the same. For at this time of the yeare many woers come thither to solace themselves with their beautifull mistresses. Many of these yong Ladies had the haire of their head very curiously plaited in locks, & they wore certaine pretty garlands upon their heads made of fragrant and odoriferous flowers. A spectacle exceeding amorous. A certaine learned man that I found bathing himselfe in one of the bathes, told me that
Henry Pantaleon's book. Henry Pantaleon that famous Philosopher and Phisition of Basill, (who made his abode two or three yeares in this place) hath written a peculiar booke of the vertue and effect of these bathes. Moreover he affirmed that they are of very soveraigne vertue for the curing of these infirmities, viz. the tertian and quartan ague, the itch, the cholicke and the stone; and it hath one most rare vertue that I never heard of any bathes in all the world. For he told me that they are of admirable efficacie to cure the sterilitie of women, and make those that are barren, very fruitfull bearers of children. A
[p. 406.] matter verified and certainly confirmed by the experience

THE BATHS OF BADEN

the verie name
...these Germe...
...rve these kind...
...for mine ow...
to spend some le...
...recreation al...
...suffer her to lye...
...me bath with so...
...her, because if s...
...rance, she migh...
have just cause t...
with the effigies o...
...bally, the sun...
be an horned m...
...sometimes hear...
...company. Ha...
Ladies and Gentl...
...their wooers ...
time of the yea...
...mselves with th...
...young Ladies h...
...ly plaited in lock...
...upon their head...
owers. A spectac...
ed man that I found...
thes, told me tha...
opher and Phisitia...
or three yeares s...
ooke of the vertue...
...he affirmed th...
...the curing o...
quartan ague, the...
...it hath one mo...
...bathes in all the...
are of admirable...
...and make thos...
...of children. A...
...by the experience

of many women. The water of the bathes is mingled with great store of brimstone and a small quantity of alum, (as Munster affirmeth, from whom I derive these few lines following concerning the vertue of the bathes) *Virtues of the* by meanes whereof it beateth and dryeth up all noysome *baths.* and cold humours. Also it is good for those infirmities which proceede from the cold of the head, as the lethargie, the apoplexie, the diseases of the eares and eyes. It consumeth the fleame, beateth and dryeth up the stomach, helpeth the digestive faculty, openeth the obstructions of the liver and spleene, asswageth the biting and fretting of the guts, appeaseth the paine of the members that proceedeth from cold, and to conclude, it cleanseth the skinne from spots and freckles. But it hurteth those that have a hot and drie complexion, and such as are weakened with the consumption. But old.folkes, of what sexe soever they are, reape no benefit by these bathes. A place that imparteth his vertue after a partiall manner rather to the feminine then masculine kinde. And so finally I end this discourse of the Helveticall bathes of Hinderhove with that elegant Elogium of Poggius the Florentine in praise of the same, even that it is a second Paradise, the seate of the Graces, the bosome of Love, and the Theater of pleasure.

Thus much of the Helveticall bathes of Hinderhove commonly called the bathes of Baden.

I Departed from Hinderhove about foure of the clocke in the afternoone the same Sunday, and about sixe of the clock returned to the foresaid Monastery of Kinings- *Monastery of* felden situate in that part of Switzerland which is called *Kiningsfelden.* Ergovia, being accompanied with my learned associat of the same place, whom I have before mentioned, who very kindly shewed me all the principall and most notable [p. 407.] things of the Monastery. This place doth now belong to the noble Citie of Berna, the Church thereof being translated from Popery and superstitious uses to the true service and worship of God, where every sunday there is

143

a sermon preached by a learned Minister. This Monastery was first founded about the yeare 1408. by a certaine Empresse called Elizabeth who was the daughter of Meinhard Earle of Tyrol and Goricia, and Duke of Carinthia, a woman much famoused amongst the historians for finding out the mines of salt in the Towne of Halles near Gemunden in the higher Austria. Shee was wife even the only wife of Albert the Emperor and King of the Romans, unto whom shee bare (as historians doe record) no lesse then one and twenty children. She imposed the name of Kiningsfelden (which is a Dutch word compounded of two more that doe signifie the Kingsfields) upon the foresaid Monastery. The reason of which appellation was this. Because in the same place her husband Albert above named was slaine betwixt the rivers of Arola and Risus, by his nephew John Duke of Suevia, and afterwards buried in this Monastery. But before I write any more of this Monastery I will relate a very notable history which I have read in the third booke of Munsters Cosmographie, concerning the lamentable death of the said Emperour in this place, hoping that it will be very grateful to any reader whatsoever to reade so memorable a matter as I will now report. The foresaid John being the Emperor's nephew by his eldest sonne Rodolph, was lately come to a Princely estate by the death of his father, who was newly slaine in his chamber. And shortly after he beganne to play the scape-thrift, being much given to prodigall expences. Whereupon his grandfather restrained him from the managing of his estate, assigning the Dukedome of Suevia which was now in his possession, to the administration of some principall Stewards that should have the oversight of his lands and revenewes, till he came to more maturity of yeares. And in the meane time maintained him in his owne Palace in a convenient state answerable to the degree of a young Prince. But John beganne to murmure against his grandfather for that he curbed him of his former liberty, and being impatient of these matters consulted with three Gentlemen more that

The Empress Elizabeth.

Death of Albert Emperor of the Romans.

[p. 408.]

144

['TES

ter. This Mona
1408. by a cert
the daughter
and Duke of G
ngst the histor
e Towne of Ha
ia. Shee was v:
peror and King
(as historians
children. She
ch is a Dutch w
signifie the King
The reason of whi
he same place be
ne betwixt the riv
hn Duke of Suev
ry. But before
I will relate a ve
the third booke
the lamentable de
ing that it will
to reade so men
foresaid John be
nne Rodolph, wi
death of his fath
And shortly af
ing much given to
father restrain
igning the Duke
possession, to th
wards that shou
ewes, till he cam
the meane tim
a convenient sta
Prince. But Joh
her for that he
ing impatient of
lemen more that

were continually conversant with the Emperour (for they were the principall Squiers of his body) how he might be revenged upon his grandfather. The names of these were Rodolphus de Wart, Walterus de Essenbach, and Huldricus de Palma. It hapned upon the eight day of May Anno 1308. within a short space after these Catilines had linked themselves together in this mischievous league of conspiracy, that the Emperour being in a merry humour at table where these foure sate, did put certaine garlands of roses upon his sonnes head that sate at the same table. But these conspirators were so farre from being merry with the rest that they would not as much as eate any thing with them, but still ruminated upon their diabolicall *A diabolical plot.* plot how they might compasse it to massacre the Emperor, which they prosecuted in this manner. The Emperor after he had dined tooke horse to ride towards the river Rhene, where he meant to take boate, and so to passe downe to the City of Rheinfelden. In his journey he was accompanied with these foure only. When they were past a pretty way in their journey, these lewd miscreants having the good Emperour alone by himselfe, Rodolphus said to his confederates how long shall we suffer this carkasse to ride? and so taking the horses bridle by the hand, when as the innocent Emperour rode on securely (as he thought) and familiarly talked unto them accordingly to his wonted manner, Duke John his nephew drew his poinado out of *Murder of the Emperor.* his sheath, and with the same gave the Emperour the first blow upon the necke, wherewith he strooke him downe from his horse. Next came Huldricus de Palma, and with his fawchon clove his head and face asunder, (ô most Cy- [p. 409.] clopical villaine) and the other two stabbed and grievously hackled his body with many wounds. So this was the most tragicall end of this worthy Emperour, that by the historians is much commended for his heroicall vertues, after he had reigned ten yeares, and most valiantly fought twelve severall battels in the field, in all which he got a glorious victory of his enemies. But the Lady Adrastia (I meane the just vengeance of God) pursued these impious blood suckers according to that elegant speech of the Lyrick Poet.

Rarò antecedentem scelestum
Deseruit pede pœna claudo.*

For all foure of them came to most lamentable ends.

Duke John that gave the first blow, after he had lived a most uncouth and solitary life in the desert forrests and woods among the dens of wilde beastes, conveighed himselfe at length into Italy, where being sent by the Pope to the City of Pisa in Hetruria to the Emperor Henry the seventh the successor of the foresaid Emperour Albertus, he was condemned to perpetuall imprisonment in the habit

of an Eremitan Frier. Huldricus de Palma that clove the Emperours head asunder, dyed miserably in a poore house in the City of Basil, his Castell being seised upon by Leopold Duke of Austria, and divided amongst his brothers, with all his other substance. Rodolphus de Wart after he had a long time hid himselfe, was at length

detected with his man. Himselfe being tyed to a horses taile, was after a most ignominious maner drawen to execution, and all his members very cruelly broken with the torment of the wheele: so was his man also. And the last of them Walterus de Essenbach, after he had lived a sheepheards life for the space of five and thirty yeares, at

last dyed very obscurely. This worthy historie I have thought good to prefixe before my ensuing discourse of this Monastery of Kiningsfelden by way of introduction

thereunto; having taken occasion of this historicall narration, partly by meanes of the denomination of this place of Kiningsfelden, and partly for that the Emperors body was buried there by his foresaid wife; Who erected the Monastery for that purpose, and for a perpetuall monument of that most execrable villany committed by those foure cut-throates above named, even in the yeare 1308. before mentioned. And again the next yeare following it was translated therehence to the City of Spira, where it

*Hora. lib. 3. Carmi. Od. 2.

146

TIES

MONASTERY OF KININGSFELDEN

was intombed with a most mournefull solemnity upon the fourth day of September, next to his father Rodolphus Habspurgensis the Emperour, as I will hereafter report in my Observations of Spira. Therefore I will now returne againe to the foresaid Monastery. The abovesaid Empresse assigned this place for the habitation of Monks of the family of St. Bennet, and Nunnes of the order of St. Clara. Who although they lived apart in severall and distinct roomes of the Monastery, yet it is to be conjectured that as fire and flaxe, when they meete together, doe yeeld a flame; so these perhaps might sometimes have some furtive conversation in hugger mugger si non castè, tamen cautè. A thing that hath eftsoones hapned in such Monasteries as are the receptacles of those promiscuous convents of both sexes Monks and Nuns. The bodies of divers royall persons were buried in this Monastery, besides the Emperour Albert whom I have already mentioned. Whereof the principall was the foresaid Empresse Elizabeth foundresse of the house. Here also was buried Agnes her owne daughter by the foresaid Albert, and the wife of Andrew King of Hungarie, who after the death of her husband having renounced the world, and consecrated her selfe wholly to a religious life, spent the remainder of her daies, even eight and forty yeares in the citie of Brooke neare adjoyning to this Monastery, where at last shee was buried as I have already said. Likewise here was buryed that famous Leopold the last of that name Duke of Austria, surnamed gloria or decus militiæ, the glory of the military discipline; who was nephew to the Emperour Albert before mentioned, and fourth sonne of Albert surnamed the wise, who intitled himselfe the first Exarch of Austria.

This Leopold about the yeare 1385. concluded a peace betwixt the house of Austria and the Confederates of Switzerland, with an intent to abolish all manner of contention betwixt them. But shortly after this the hot broiles of wars began more fiercely by reason of certain tumults that rose betwixt the Prefects of the country and

Monks and nuns.

Royal burials in the monastery.

[p. 411.]

Leopold last Duke of Austria.

147

the Citizens of Lucerne: so that many of the confederate
cities rose in armes against the Duke, who both assaulted
and sacked certaine townes that the house of Austria laid
claim unto. Whereupon the adverse armies confronting
each other in the field, the Confederates surprised the
Dukes forces in the yeare 1386. Againe the same yeare
there was a fresh truce concluded betwixt them, which being
shortly after violated, they mustred up their forces once
more on both sides that same yeare, and joyned battell
againe the second time neare to the towne of Sempach
in Switzerland, the Duke having adjoined unto him the
strength of many German Peeres and noble Personages,
who aided him with the best power they were able. The
Confederates understanding that the Duke was approached

Leopold defeated and slain by the Swiss. neare to Sempach aforesaid, met him in a certaine uneven
place to his great disadvantage, where he & the rest of his
Nobles being well horsed, were constrained to alight from
their horses, and abandon them. For they could stand
them in no steed in that place, & so at length they came
to hand strokes, & fought a most vehement skirmish on
both sides. But the Duke & the Nobles being tired out
with the extreme heat of the Sunne, & their long fight,
were forced to give place to their enemies, so that they
retired themselves backe toward their horses, but before
they could come to them, they were so eagerly pursued

[p. 412.] by the Switzers, that they were almost all slaine in that
conflict: Duke Leopold himselfe lost his life; Otto, the
Marquesse of Hochberg, John Earle of Zollern, and many
other Nobles of inferiour degree. After that the bodie of
the Duke and of threescore of his Nobles were brought to
this Monastery, where they were all buried. The monument of the Duke standeth in the bodie of the Church,
being inclosed within an yron grate, where there is written
this Dutch Epitaph following, which my scholasticall companion abovesaid copied out for me, and here I have set
downe the very same words, word for word, that he
delivered me, even these.

IES

of the confede...
who both assemb...
...se of Austria...
armies confront...
...tes surprised...
...ne the same yea...
...them, which be...
...their forces on...
and joyned bated
towne of Sempa...
...ned unto him...
noble Personage...
...y were able. Th...
...e was approch...
...a certaine une...
...& the rest of his
...ed to alight fro...
...they could ste...
...length they ca...
...rent skirmish a...
...es being tired o...
& their long figh...
...mies, so that the...
...horses, but befo...
so eagerly pursu...
...st all slaine in th...
his life; Otto, the
f Zollern, and ma...
...er that the bodie...
...les were brought...
...ried. The moo...
die of the Church,
ere there is writte...
...y scholasticall con...
...d here I have set
or word, that he

In disem grab ligend von unseren hochgeboren hershafft *The Duke's* von Osterych, die Edlen Frauwen und herren. *epitaph.*
Die hernach geschriben stond. Zum erstenfrauw Eliza-beta geborne von Kerndten Kunigs Albrects von Rome gemachel, der of der Hofstat verlor syn leben. Demnach Agnes Iro dochter wylund Kinigin in Ungern. Ferner auch unser gnediger Herr Herzog Lupold der Zu Sem-pach vorlor synleben. 1386.
Hertzog Lupold der Alt, und frauw Catrina syn gemachall geborne von Saphoy. Un frauw Catrina Iro tochter Herzogin von Lessin. Herzog Heinrich und fro Elizabeta syn gemachel geborne von Virnburg.
Herzog Friderich Kunig Friderichs der von Rome.
Fro Elizabeta Herzog in von Luttringen.
Frauw Gutta Grauin von Ottingen Deren gedencken [p. 413.] thund.

The same in English.

In this grave are buried of our most excellent house *The epitaph* of Austria, these Noble Ladies and Lords. *Englished.*
First Lady Elizabeth of Kerndten, wife of Albertus King of the Romanes, which was slaine in his Palace.
Next Agnes their daughter, sometimes Queene of Hungarie.
Item, our gracious Lord Leopold that lost his life at Sempach. 1386.
Duke Leopold the old, & Lady Katharina of Savoy his wife, and Lady Katharina their daughter, Dutchesse of Lessin.
Also Henry and Ladie Elizabeth of Virnburg his wife.
Duke Fredericke sonne of Fredericke King of Rome.
Lady Elizabeth Dutchesse of Lorraine.
Lastly Lady Gutta Countesse of Ottingen, whom forget not in your praiers.
Morover in the Quire of the same Church I saw the Dukes picture made in his armour upon the wall with fourteene of his Peeres painted in armes also on the right

hand of him, and thirteene more on the left hand. Besides they shewed me a certaine long wooden chest in a high gallery, which the foresaid Duke filled up with halters, wherewith he meant to have hanged the noblest Captaines and other worthy persons of the Confederates. I observed a thing in the Cloyster of this Monastery that moved no small commiseration in me : which by reason of the rarenesse of the example I will not let passe unmentioned. *An example of* My companion shewed me a certain old man walking alone *human frailty.* by himselfe, who having beene from his youth till within these late yeares, a learned man of singular gifts, & a most excellent Schollar, was so much altred now in his decrepit [p. 414.] age, that he had not only lost his memory, being unable to remember his owne name, (an accident that I have read hath hapned heretofore to two famous Orators, whereof the one was Messala Corvinus, a noble Gentleman of Rome : the other George Trapezuntius, a learned Orator of Greece, & principall Secretary to one of the later Popes) but also was come to that most miserable state, that he could not discharge the necessaries of nature after that civill and decent manner as other people do, but after a most loathsome & beastly fashion. Truly this man was a most notable example to put every learned man in mind of his humane frailty, and to teach many proud princocke scholars that are puffed up with the opinion of their learning to pull downe the high sailes of their lofty spirits, and to keepe the golden meane in the levell of their thoughts, since God is able to make the learnedest and wisest man in the world not only a child againe in his declining yeares, but also such a kind of odious creature by depriving him of the use of reason, and the light of understanding, as doth equal the unreasonable beastes of the field in a brutish filthinesse.

Thus much of the Monastery of Kiningsfelden.

Brooke. FRom this Monastery I tooke my journey to the city of Brooke, being about foure furlongs beyond it, whither I came about 8 of the clocke in the evening,

something applauding my selfe in a manner, and congratu-
lating my owne good fortune & successe for that experience
which I had gotten the same day by the sight of the citie
of Baden, the Bathes of Hinderhove, & the noble Monastery of Kinings-felden. This daies journey was but small,
no more then sixe English miles.

Of this citie I can say but little, because I came in late,
and went away betime in the morning. Onely I understood that it is all Protestant, consenting with the
Tigurines in religion. Here I found the kindest host
that I had in my whole voyage out of England.

I departed from Brooke about sixe of the clocke in the [p. 415.]
morning the nine & twentieth of August being Munday,
and came about seven of the clocke in the evening to the
Citie of Rheinfelden, this daies journey being twenty *Rheinfelden.*
English miles. I can say very little of this Citie, because
I made my aboad there but a night, and departed therehence betime the next morning, even about sixe of the
clocke; onely one short note I will give of it, and no
more: That the ancient Earledome of Rheinfelden derived
his denomination from this citie, a famous Prince (of whom
I have often read,) being the last Earle thereof, namely
Rodolphus Duke of Suevia, unto whom Pope Gregory the
seventh sent a golden crowne when he warred against the
Emperour Henry the fourth, with this memorable (that I
may not say prophane) inscription.

Petra dedit Petro, Petrus diadema Rodolpho.

I observed that it professed the Popish religion, and that
it is sweetly watered by the Rhene. About the townes
end a little before I entred the Citie, I observed a great *A great*
gallows supported with three great pillars of free stone, *gallows.*
neere unto which there was a wheele that served for the
execution of murderers, the like whereof I have often
seene in France (as I have before mentioned) and many
such in divers other places of Switzerland.

I departed from Rheinfelden about sixe of the clocke
the next morning being Tuesday, and the thirtieth day of

August, and came to Basil, sixe English miles beyond it, about nine of the clocke. In this space I observed a great multitude of verie faire Vineyards planted on both sides of the Rhene.

My Observations of Basil, in Latine Basilea.

Basle.

THis noble citie is situate in that most fertile territorie of Sungovia heretofore called Sequania, bordering upon the confines of Switzerland, which though it standeth not in the province of Helvetia, yet it is reputed one of the Helvetical Cities, both because it confineth upon the frontires of the country, and also for that it was incorporated into the confederation in the yeare 1501, since which time it hath continually maintained her liberty maugre all her enemies, and embraceth that popular government that the other cities doe. Who was the first founder of it I cannot certainly finde. For I have not read it in any author. But I conjecture that it began to be built shortly after the dilapidations and ruines of the *Augusta Rauracorum.* ancient Citie of *Augusta Rauracorum, which was built not farre from this Citie by the same noble Roman Gentleman that was the founder of the Citie of Lyons, Munatius Plancus, whom I have before mentioned. The ruines of which Citie are shewed at this day as notable monuments of the antiquitie and beautie thereof, when it flourished in ancient times. From this Citie Augusta was Basil also heretofore called Augusta Rauracorum. Truly it is very likely that the founders of this Citie of Basil first derived much of the matter for the founding and beautifying of their Citie from the foresaid Augusta. In regard whereof the Citizens of Basil have very lately erected a most beautifull statue of the foresaid Munatius Plancus made of wood in his military ornaments, which I saw placed upon a wooden pillar in the court of their Senate house, and honored with a learned Elogium. Munster proveth out of the thirtieth booke of the histories of Ammianus

* This City or at the least the Rudera thereof now remaining are at this day called Augst.

152

Marcellinus that most learned souldier that served under [p. 417.]
the Emperour Julian the Apostate, that Basil was a
flourishing and famous Citie in the time of those colleague
Emperours Gratian and Valentinian about 382 yeares after
Christes incarnation. As for the name of the Citie the *Etymology of*
authors doe something differ. For some will have it called *Basle.*
Basilea quasi Pasilea, that is, a place of passage, because
there was a common passage from one banke to the other
in boats upon the river Rhene, before the bridge was built
for the use of the Citie. But Munster saith that Ammianus aforesaid draweth the etymologie of it from the
Greeke word βασιλεία which signifieth a kingdome, as
being a royall and kingly Citie fit for the residence of a
Kings court. Surely it is exceeding sweetly situate,
having on one side of the Rhene a pleasant plaine that
yeeldeth great abundance of wine and corne, but especially
corne; on the other side hils, in number three, whereon
one part of the Citie standeth. Also the ayre of this *The wholesome*
Citie is esteemed as sweet and comfortable as in any City *air of Basle.*
of the whole world, as a certaine English Gentleman told
me that sojourned in the University for learning sake at
the time of my being there, who affirmed that it was the
most delectable place for ayre that ever he lived in.
Againe, it is as finely watered as ever I saw Citie, partly
with goodly rivers, and partly with pleasant springs or
fountaines that doe incessantly flow out of delicate conduits. The rivers are these, the Rhene, the Byrsa and
the Wiesa. The Rhene divideth the Citie in the middest,
and maketh two several Cities, the greater and the lesser
Basil: the greater being on the farther side of the Rhene
upon the foresaid hils, which Citie was esteemed heretofore
a part of the territory of the Sequani, and a member of the
French Kings dominion; the lesser on the other side upon
the plaine, which was ever reputed part of Germany. But
at this day both the Cities are accounted within the compasse of the German precincts. But because I now
speake of the division into two parts by meanes of the [p. 418.]
river Rhene running betwixt them, I will mention a thing

153

unto thee (gentle reader) out of my poore experience in travell, that if thou meanest to see these countries thy selfe, thou maiest hereafter observe this particular matter as well as I my selfe have done alreadie. The ancient Germanes and Helvetians observed this rule in former times at the founding of their Cities, that when they laid the foundation of any Citie hard by any famous river, they *An ancient* built one part of it on one banke of the same river, and *custom in* the other on the opposite banke. Which thing I have *building cities.* seene with mine owne eyes in three Helveticall cities, namely, in Zurich situate by the foresaid Limacus, Baden by the same river, and this citie of Basil by the Rhene; and the like I have heard is to be seene in two more Helvetian Cities, namely Lucerne upon the river Ursula, and Solodure upon the Arola. After the same manner also the Citie of Lyons in France is built upon the rivers of Arar and Rhodanus, Paris upon the Sequana, the City of Vicenza in Italy upon the Bacchilio, and Verona upon the Athesis. But the Cities of the other parts of Germany are not built thus, though they stand by goodly rivers; as Heidelberg by the Neccar, Mentz & Colen by the Rhene, Nimmighen by the Wahalis, Confluence by the Mosella and Rhene &c. every one of them standing wholy upon one banke. But to returne againe to the Rhene by this Citie of Basil, these two Cities, the greater and the lesser Basil are united and conjoyned together by a *A mean* woodden bridge made over the river, which bridge is a *bridge.* very base and meane thing, being compacted together of many rough plankes and uneven peeces of timber that hang something loose, so that a stranger being un-acquainted with the way will be afraid to ride over it. Yet by reason that it is of a convenient breadth, both horses and carts do passe securely too and fro that way. [p. 419.] I wondred to see so base a bridge belonging to so faire a Citie. But a learned Gentleman of the University yeelded *A good reason* a good reason to me for the same. For he tolde me that *for the same.* the Citizens are afraid of the Duke of Savoies assaulting of them, who if he should suddenly invade them, the lesser

Citie in the plaine he may perhaps take by force of armes, but they will prevent him from comming to the greater Citie on the hils by taking up the bridge, which they can doe in a moment, by reason that the boords do so loosely hang together; wheras if it were a strong bridge, they could not dissolve it with so great expedition. I will speake something also of the abovenamed Rivers Byrsa and Wiesa. These are much inferiour to the Rhene in greatnesse, but very commodious to the Citie. For the Byrsa doth cary pretie boats wherein are brought many *The River Byrsa.* necessaries to the Citie, as much timber that serveth for the building of their houses, and wood for fuell to make fire in their chimneies. This river springeth out of the famous mountaine Jura, mentioned by Cæsar that divideth the Helvetians ftom the Sequani, distant about one daies journey from the city. The place where it riseth being inhabited by French men, and passing well wooded, which is the reason that the river doth communicate such store of Wood to the Citie. The other river Wiesa springeth *The River Wiesa.* out of a contrary place, out of the blacke wood which is called in Latine nigra Sylva, being a part of that famous wood Hercinia mentioned by Cæsar. This river imparteth the same commodities to the Citie that the Byrsa doth and one more. For it yeeldeth great store of fish, especially trouts. As for the fountaines or publicke conduits of the Citie before mentioned, they are exceeding delectable & pleasant to behold. For whereas there are many market places in the citie, these conduits are erected in every several market place, which doe continually spout out water most pleasantly, as those of the citie of Brixia in Lombardie which I have before spoken of, but these are both fairer & pleasanter then the Brixian conduits; a [p. 420.] commodity that ministreth no small ornament to the citie. For they are in number many, and very curiously built. Each of these two cities is walled about with very ancient *The ancient walls.* and faire walles of a convenient hight, adorned with battlements that doe make a beautifull shew, especially those on the North side of the greater Basil, being built upon the

155

very brinke of the banke of the Rhene. In the wals of both Cities are seven gates, five in the greater Citie, and two in the lesser. Upon the outward wal of the gatehouse of one of these foresaid gates, even the same gate where I entred the greater Citie after I had passed the foresaid bridge, I saw the picture of an exceeding huge Gigantean Switzer, advanced on horse-backe on the right hand of the gate. He is painted in his armour like a martiall Captaine with his banner displaied in his hand, wherein is represented a staffe which is the armes of Basil. He is

A giant Swiss. pourtraied something lesse then those monstrous kinde of Giants that are written of in ancient histories, yet much greater (in my opinion) then the greatest man that is now to be found in the whole world. It is reported by the Citizens that there was heretofore a certaine Switzer of a bignesse correspondent to this picture. But I could finde no man that could tell me the true historicall narration of the matter, though I was very inquisitive of many. The streets of the Citie are very faire, and neatly kept: the private buildings beautifull, many of them being of a goodly height, foure stories high, and for the most part built with timber.

I was at their Councell or Senate house, which is like to be a very sumptuous building when it is once finished. For it was not throughly ended when I was there. Here I saw the statue of Munatius Plancus of whom I have before written.

The Churches of the citie are in number eight, whereof foure are called Parish Churches, and the other foure

The Cathedral Church. Deacons Churches. The Cathedrall Church is dedicated to our Lady, and standeth in the greater City. A building

[p. 421.] of singular magnificence and beauty, the sight whereof and that passing variety of worthy monuments in the same gave me such true content, that I must needs say I preferre it before the fairest Church I saw in Germany, though the Cathedral Churches of Strasbourg, Spires, Wormes, Mentz, and Colen be greater; yet certainly for curiosity of architecture and exceeding decent keeping, the best of

156

these is inferiour to this: only I except a part of the Church of Strasbourg, namely the tower, which I will hereafter describe; for I attribute so much to the same, that I give the superiority unto it not only of all those towers that I saw in my whole voyage, but also of all other towers whatsoever in Christendome, as I have heard very learned and famous travellers report that have seene both that and the fairest towers of Europe. But to returne to this glorious and most elegant Church of Basil the very Queene of all the German Churches that I saw, according *The queen of German churches.* as I have before intitled our Lady Church at Amiens of the French Churches; truly I extoll it so highly that I esteeme it the most beautifull Protestant Church that ever I saw, saving our two in London of Paules and Westminster, which doe very little excell this in beauty (though something in greatnesse) if any thing at all. The body of it is garnished with two rowes of goodly pillars, sixe in a side. Also it is beautified with a very faire paire of Organs that are decked with passing curious wainscot worke, and a very sumptuous Pulpit adorned with a most excellent peece of workemanship of wainscot also. Likewise at the West end of the body there are two very stately rowes of seates made of wainscot with very exquisite workemanship, and most artificiall devices in the same. Over the which are raised three curious borders, in the middle whereof which is advanced to a very convenient heigth, this impresse or inscription is written in golden *Inscription over the seats.* letters upon a blacke ground.

D. S. [p. 422.]
In Honorem
Summi Basiliensis
Magistratus
Veræ religionis assertoris,
Juris justitiæque defensoris,
quo ipsam loco
In Dei conspectu gratabunda
suspicit Ecclesia,

157

CORYAT'S CRUDITIES

Eundem ipsi piâ devotâque
observantiâ,
Summissè consecrare
volvit.

Truly I observed every thing in the body of this Church disposed in such a comely order, and so trimly kept, that it did even tickle my soule with spirituall joy to behold the same, and so I thinke it will every zealous and godly Protestant, in so much that I did even congratulate and applaude the religious industry of the Basilians. And I am perswaded that one godly prayer pronounced in this Church by a penitent and contrite-hearted Christian in the holy Congregation of the citizens, to the omnipotent Jehovah through the only mediation of his sonne Jesus Christ, is of more efficacy, and doth sooner penetrate into the eares of the Lord, then a centurie yea a whole myriad of Ave Maries mumbled out upon beads in that superstitious manner as I have often seene at the glittering Altars of the Popish Churches. The Quire is very decently graced with many faire pillars, and the frontispice thereof marvailously adorned with gilt scutchins and armes of divers royal and Princely Potentates. On the left hand of the body of the Church as you enter into the Quire, I

Tomb of Erasmus. saw the Sepulcher of that thrise-famous Erasmus Roterodamus that Phœnix of Christendome, and well deserving man of the common-weale of learning, who was so

[p. 423.] delighted with the noble City of Basil, that he studied here many yeares together, being a great benefactor to the City as I wil hereafter mention, and at last finished his life in the same. His body lieth interred under a flat stone, neare to the which is erected a beautifull pillar of red marble about three yardes high (according to my estimation) two foot thicke, and an ell broad, at the toppe whereof the effigies of his face is expressed, with this word Terminus (by which impresse I thinke is meant that death is the end of all things) written under it in golden letters: and under the same this epitaph cut in golden letters also.

Christo Servatori S.
Des. Erasmo Roterodamo
viro omnibus modis Maximo, cujus
incomparabilem in omni disciplinarum
genere eruditionem pari conjunctam
prudentiâ posteri & admirabuntur, et
prædicabunt: Bonifacius Amerbachius, Hier. Frobenius, Nic. Episcopius
hæredes, & nuncupati supremæ suæ
voluntatis vindices, Patrono optimo,
non memoriæ (quam immortalem sibi
editis lucubrationibus comparavit, iis
tantisper dum orbis terrarum stabit,
superfuturo, ac eruditis ubique gentium colloquuturo) sed corporis
mortalis, quo reconditum sit, ergô,
hoc saxum posuere. Mortuus est
IIII. Id. Jul. jam septuagenarius.
An. à Christo nato
M.D.xxxvi.

In the North side of the Quire I observed the monu- [p. 424.]
ment of the Empresse Anna, upon the which her image
is made at length with her young sonne Charles hard by
her within an yron grate, and in the wall adjoyning I read
this epitaph.

D. O. M. S.
Annæ Augustæ
Burchardi Comitis Hoven-
burgensis filiæ, Rodolphi
1. Imperatoris Augusti, Comitis
Habspurgensis, &c. Conjugi, &
fœcundæ parenti Austriæ Prin-
cipum, Sereniss. Alberti. 1. Imper. matri,
unâ cum Carolo *filiolo, Anno

*Munster saith in the life of Rodolphus Habspurgensis, that shee
had another sonne buried with her, namely Hartmannus that was
drowned in the river Rhene.

159

1289. 19. Martii hìc sepultæ.
S. P. Q. Basiliensis, quum sacram
hanc ædem nitori suo pristino
restituendam curaret, hono-
ris ergô, circitèr 316. post exequias Annos,
H. M. L. P

The cloisters. At the East end of the Church are two faire Cloisters, wherein I observed a little common-weale of worthy monuments, whereof some are auncient and some new. Certainly I never saw so many epitaphs together in one Church in all my life. For most of those that have beene erected of late yeares, being inserted into the walles of the Cloyster round about, are beautified both with elegant epitaphs, and with pretty little turned pillars of marble, or other faire kinde of stones, garnished with gilt scutchins, armes, and such like curious workes. In one of these Cloysters I saw these three epitaphs together, side by side, in one and the selfe same row, written in certaine convenient stones upon the wall, and under the same as many severall flat tomb-stones, under which the bodies of those famous men are interred that are nominated in the same

The first epitaph in the cloisters. epitaphs : The first of them was this.

[p. 425.]

Dum Jacobum Meierum
hujus inclytæ urbis
Consulem prudentis-
simum, consultissimum
que, pietatis sanæ
cultorem, ac promo-
torem primarium,
omnis honestatis,
quod in ipso fuit
instauratorem dili-
gentissimum, lapis
subjectus contegit.
Anno Salutis M. D. X X X I I. F. F.

The second is this.

D. Io. Oecolampadius
professione Theolo
gus, trium linguarum
peritissimus, author
Evangelicæ doctri-
næ in hac urbe pri
mus, & templi hujus
verus Epus. Ut doc
trinâ, sic vitæ sanc-
timoniâ pollentissi-
mus, sub breve saxum
hoc reconditus jacet.*

*The second
epitaph.*

The third this.

Domino Simoni Grynæo
almæ hujus Academiæ
rectori, & laude, &
memoriâ sempiternâ
ob linguarum Latinæ
Gracæ & Hebraicæ
peritiam, omnisque
phinæ ad miraculum us-
que cognitionem, ob
Theologiæ veræ sci-
entiam & usum digno,
monumentum hoc dicatum est.

*The third
epitaph.*

[p. 426.]

That which is omitted about the yeare of his death, I
will add my selfe. He dyed Anno 1539. In one part of
the other Cloyster I saw these two epitaphs something
neare together, the one of that famous man Pantaleon
written in golden letters in a faire stone, inserted into the
wall directly over his tombe.

I. F. F.

* Here he hath not expressed the yeare of his death, which was 1531.
shortly after Zuinglius was slaine in Switzerland.

CORYAT'S CRUDITIES

Epitaph to Henry Pantaleon.

Trinuno
D. O. M. S.
Henrici Pantaleonis
Basil. Philos. et Medici Epita.
Disce tuam sortem quicunque hæc pelligis ; istâ
    exuviæ recubant Pantaleonis humo.
Scin cujus, quem nec sacræ latuere Camœnæ,
    qui potis in numerum cogere dulce melos.
Clinicus, & rerum naturæ conscius omnis,
    doctus & in fastos didere gesta patrûm.
Testis erit sacris physicis operata juventus,
    regia quâ Rhenus mœnia lambit aquis.
Testis erit generosa armis quam vindice penna
    claravit scriptis Teutonis ora suis
Testis bonos vivax, amplissima jura palati
    queis auxit Comitem Maxmiliana manus.
Longa ævi series, trieteris & hebdomas annûm
    bis quina, adversis intemerata malis.
Lustra novem physice, thalamus dena unus & idem
    vendicat, & senâ bis quoque prole beat.
Sic famæ, sic naturæ sat vixit, & hujus
    pertæsus vitæ cessit in æthceream.
Vixit an. lxxii. M. viii. d. xxii. an. Ch. cIↄ. Iↄ.
    xcv. Martii iii.

The other of that learned Civilian Franciscus Hotomannus, which was erected above his tombe also, and
written in golden letters with a deaths-head, and an houre-
glasse over it.

[p. 427.]

Epitaph to Francis Hotoman.

Trinuno S.
Franciscus Hotomannus
    ex ant. & nob.
Hotomannorum famil. apud Siles.
    German. pop.
Lutetiæ Par. natus,
Pius integerque juris justitiæque
    Antistes,
Jus C. Rom. Scrip. illustr

162

OBSERVATIONS OF BASLE

Valent. Cavar. & Avarici Bitur.
ann. mult. docuit :
De sum. reipub. consultus
sap. respon.
Legation. German.
Sub Car. ix. Franc. Reg.
prosperè gest.
Patriam ob civil. bell.
spont. linqu.
In Germ. ceu patr. alt.
concess.
Principib. ob scient. ac prob.
acceptiss.
Basileæ Rauracorum
pub. damno luctuque
plac. fato funct.
B. A. L X V. M. V. D. X X.
ɵ A. c I ʒ. I ʒ. XC. P. id. Feb.
Io. F. amicique Basileæ p.

Againe under the same I read this written upon a flat
stone that covereth his bones.

Fran. Hotomanni
I. C.
Mortales exuvias
Tantisper asservandas,
dum
Christo jubente
Immortales exurgant,
Amici
Sub hoc saxo
deposuere.
Loco honoris ergô
Ab ædis curatorib.
liberal. concesso.
vix. an. lxiii. Men. v. d. xx.
ob. prid. id Febr.
ann.
c I ʒ. I ʒ. X C.

[p. 428.]

163

CORYAT'S CRUDITIES

Epitaph to Francis Hotoman.

Againe upon the same stone these verses are written.

Gallia progenuit, servat Basilea sepultum,
  Interitus expers nomen ubique viget.
Hunc pietas tumulum, tumulum hunc Astrea tuentur,
  Astrea cultorem suum,
Cultoremque suum pietas post fata tuetur
  Adversa fata huic seculo.
Et si desertas gemebundâ voce queruntur
  Cultore privatas suo :
Quin reditum ad superos infestâ voce minantur,
  Ni talis exemplum viri
Hujus tu inspector tumuli, pietate sequaris,
  Ni nos sequamur posteri.
Hoc ipse è tumulo clamat post fata superstes,
  Hoc ipsè mandat posthumis.

In another part of the same Cloyster I saw these three epitaphs together written in golden letters in the wall, with armes and scutchins over them, directly over the bodies of the persons themselves.

The first of that famous Cœlius Secundus Curio, of whom I have before spoken in my description of Turin.

Epitaph to Cœlius Secundus Curio.

[p. 429.]

Hospes have, & disce
Non Cœlius heic,
Sed Cœlii σῶμα, imò σῆμα
Spiritum Christus habet.
Cætera nomen
veræ pietatis,
humanitatis,
singularis eruditionis,
prudentiæ,
insignisque constantiæ,
quum σῶμα in*
tunc verè erit

* The Word which is here wanting was Hebrew, which (I confesse) I omitted, by reason that I am ignorant of the Language.

164

OBSERVATIONS OF BASLE

)ultrum,
viget.
unc Astrea tuea?

Cœlius Secundus Curio.
hospes si didicisti,
vale
Reliquit æt. su. an. lxvii.
Sal. cIɔ. Iɔ. Lxix.
A. D. viii. K. L. D. C. B.

a tuetur

eruntur

The second of one of his sonnes.

voce minantur

e sequaris,

ta superstes,

Leoni
Curioni Cœlii S. C. F.
Religionis purioris causâ
cum parentib. exuli.
nobili, integro,
sincero
Peregrinationibus,
Captivit. laboribus
attrito.
An. Ch. M. D. C. I. die Octo. vi.
æta. suæ. an. lxv.
extincto
Conjux & liberi
amoris & pie
tatis ergô
H. M. P.

Epitaph to his son.

ter I saw these thre...
...tters in the n...
...ctly over h...

Secundus Curio, i
scription of Tim...

.

The third.

Cœlius Secundus Curio Augustino filio dulciss. sanc-
tissque polyhistori ac fa-
cundo Basil. Scholæ Rhe-
tori. cujus corpus beìc cum
I I I. sororib. lectiss. jacet,
spiritus cum Christo : nomen immortal. lib. scriptis
vivit in terris. socio &
hærede studiorum or-
batus, dum reviviscit po.

The third epitaph.

[p. 430.]

riua
..at.

z,

ew, which (I confess)
nguage.

165

CORYAT'S CRUDITIES

vixit ann. xxiix.

obiit an. Do. cIɔ. Iɔ. lxvii.

die xxiiii.

Oct.

Hujus ad exemplum juvenes florentibus annis
vivere ritè Deo discite, ritè mori.

Many notable
epitaphs. Many other notable epitaphes I saw there, which the shortnesse of my aboade in Basil and the urgent occasions of calling me away therehence would not permit me to write out, as of Hierom Frobenius, and Michael Isingrius, two famous printers of the citie, &c. But what is now wanting, I hope shall be hereafter supplied ; for by Gods grace I will one day see Basil againe.

But one most elegant epitaph I will adde, which is to be found in this citie, and very memorable both for the fame of the person upon whome it was made, and the worthinesse of the Author that composed it. There was given me by a learned man, a student of the Universitie (of whome I was inquisitive for the antiquities of the citie) this excellent epitaph which he told me is extant in a Church of the lesser Basil beyond the Rhene that belonged once to the Carthusian Monkes, made upon the death of that famous Civilian Ludovicus Pontanus a Roman borne, who died of the plague in this citie of Basil, anno 1439. at the time of the generall Councell celebrated here : the author hereof was Æneas Sylvius who was afterward Bishop of Rome (as I have before written) by the name [p. 431.] of Pius Secundus, the learnedest Pope that hath beene these thousand yeares. The Epitaph is this.

[p. 431.]

Epitaph by
Æneas
Sylvius.

Si mille aut totidem rapuisses usque virorum
Pestis, adhuc poteram parcere sæva tibi.
Vivens quo nusquam fuerat præstantior alter,
Extinctum potiùs reddis iniqua lues.
Quem fletis leges, quem fletis jura, sacrique
Nunc Canones : obiit, quem coluistis, herus.
Hic vos ornârat, vestras, ubicunque fuerunt,
Solverat ambages : nunc sine voce jacet.

166

Heu voces, heu verba viri divina, memorque
  Ingenium : quo vis nunc tua multa loco est?
Heu Romane jaces, quo non Romanior ullus
  Antè fuit, quo nec fortè futurus erit.
Te pater, & charus retur modò vivere frater,
  Heu quantos gemitus ille vel ille dabit?
Te Roma atque omnis plorabit Etruria, teque
  Tota petet lachrymis Itala terra piis.
Te nunc Concilium, te nunc ululatibus unum
  Ipsa quoque extinctum queritat Ecclesia.
Heu vanas hominum mentes, heu pectora cœca,
  Cuique dies certum est fata dedisse suos.
Et nos, cùm superi statuent, veniemus ad illos,
  Nemo parùm vixit, cui bona vita fuit.

I was in their theological schoole which is at the south *Theological* corner of the church, unto the which you cannot passe but *school of Basle.* through the Quire. It is a very decent and comely place, but inferiour to our Divinity schoole of Oxford. At the upper end is a seate for the Divinity reader to sitte in : and all the middle from one end to the other is filled up with very convenient seates for the hearers. The walles are decked with Hebrew, Greeke, Latine, and Dutch sentences out of the Scriptures, and with the testimonies of those famous men of our reformed religion that have been heretofore Readers in that place, as of Andreas Carolostadius, &c.

In this schoole I heard Amandus Polanus a Polensdorf, [p. 432.] that famous Divine & learned Writer reade a divinity lecture, but his audience at that time was very small : I observed a certaine forme of teaching at this lecture which *A divinity* I never noted in any place before that time. For he did *lecture.* often repeat every principall sentence of note, a matter very avaylable for the hearers memory : not used by any publike professour of Oxford. The like custome I have heard is observed by the professours of many other Dutch Universities, especially by those of Leyden in Holland. In this roome also it was my good fortune not only to see,

but also to converse with in familiar discourse (to my
great joy & comfort) that admirable ornament of this
Joannes University Joannes Jacobus Grynæus the sonne of the fore-
Jacobus said Simon Grynæus whose Epitaph I have above written.
Grynæus. A man of such speciall marke that he may be well called
a second Oecolampadius, that is, a glittering lampe of
Gods House. For he is a man famoused over most of
the Westerne Universities of Christendome for his learned
lucubrations and most solid workes of Divinity, which are
divulged to the world to the great benefit of Christes
Church. As the Ecclesiasticall history of Eusebius, Ruf-
finus, Socrates, Theodoret he hath illustrated with a learned
Chronographie. Also the workes of Ireneus Bishop of
Lyons, with arguments and observations of divers reading.
An epitome of the Bible containing the arguments of the
bookes and chapters of the olde Testament. A short
interpretation of the psalmes 133. 110. 19. Also he hath
written a commentary upon the Prophets Haggeus,
Hababuc & Malachie: a brief Chronology of the Evan-
His books. gelicall history: A Sciographie of sacred Theologie
according to the three formes of methode, synthesis,
analysis, and definition. Unto the which he hath added
threescore Theses contayning the principall heads of our
religion. Likewise he hath written a synopsis of the
[p. 433.] history of man. And two hundred several Theses disputed in this University. A consolatory booke in the
time of the pestilence. An excellent treatise to the Count
Palatine of Rhene de Ecclesiæ Palingenesia, which I have
often read with great pleasure. All which workes have
bene printed in this Citie. This worthy man continueth
to this day a publike Divinitie reader of this University.
And at that time when I was there did begin to interprete
the Genealogie of Christ out of the first chapter of St.
Mathewes gospell, as he himselfe tolde me. Hee is at this
time betwixt seventy & eighty yeares of age. They
esteeme him in Basil an Imitator of Erasmus his phrase as
Polanus of Cicero. I found him very affable, and full of
learned discourse and singular variety of matter, and so

OBSERVATIONS OF BASLE

facil and plausible in his delivery, that me thinkes that notable verse of Homer in praise of Nestor may be very properly spoken of him.

τοῦ καὶ ἀπὸ γλώσσης μέλιτος γλυκίων ῥέεν αὐδή

Which is thus incomparably well interpreted by Cicero: Cujus ex ore melle dulcior fluebat oratio. He tooke great pleasure in discoursing of our English Universities, and of the learned men of England in former times, as of Veneralis Beda, (whom I have before mentioned in my notes of Paris) and Alcuinus the schoolemaister of Carolus Magnus. And also he highly commended Queene Elizabeth and our present King James.

I observed one thing in the outside of this Cathedrall Church (whereof I have before written) that I never noted in any other, which although the reader perhaps will esteeme but a meane thing and unworthy the mention, yet for the novelty of the matter I will speake of it: it is *Exquisite tiling.* nothing else but the tyle. A matter of rare curiosity. For this Church is so exquisitely tyled, that it maketh a wondrous faire shew a farre off: the tyles being made of many colours, blew, yellow, and red, and wrought by way of checker worke. In a little pretty greene yard or court walled about adjoyning to this Church and neere to the [p. 434.] Rhene I noted the strangest Tree that ever I saw, being *A notable* of the Latines called Tilia, of the Dutchmen Linda, which *tree.* standeth in the middest of the court, and spreadeth his boughes and limmes a great way forth in an equall compasse, at the least thirtie foote broad (in my opinion) every way. The boughes being supported with a great company of long poles to beare them up the more orderly. I heard there is such another tree in the Citie; but I saw it not. The like I saw standing in the high way within a few miles of the Citie of Heidelberg, but it is much inferiour to this. In the outside of the West end of the Church there is erected a goodly Statue of Saint George on horse-back, thrusting his launce into the throate of the Dragon. Likewise I observed at the West end of the Church a very

169

plaine yard, which I therefore mention because in times past they were wont to celebrate notable justes and tornaments in this place about the beginning of Lent, upon that day which we commonly call Shrove-tuesday.

A famous tournament. Amongst the rest there was one famous meeting here (as a certaine learned Gentleman of the University told mee, being also mentioned by Munster in his description of Basil) upon the yeare 1376. at what time one of the Leopolds Duke of Austria, exercised himselfe at the aforesaid game, with many other great Peeres. This tornament is something memorable, because at that time there was raised such a tumult amongst the Citizens, that the Duke was constrained to flie over the Rhene to the lesser Basil with many of his Nobles, whereof some were taken prisoners, as Rodolph Earle of Habspurg, Rodolph Marquesse of Hochberg, &c. But at length the matter was pacified after those Citizens that were the ring-leaders of the sedition, were executed for their malapertnesse.

The University. The Universitie is seated in the greater Citie, beeing first instituted by that learned Pope Pius secundus, who [p. 435.] was first called Æneas Sylvius before his Papacie. It hapned that when he made his abode in this Citie, he was so exceedingly delighted with the situation thereof, that within a short space after, he made it a seminary of learning, endowing it with such priviledges and liberties as Bononia in Italie and other Universities did enjoy. His first grant he confirmed at Mantua in the yeare 1459. and the second yeare of his Popedome. The Colledges are but few, no more then two in number, beeing distinguished by the names of the higher and the lower colledge, both which I visited. The lower was built by Erasmus, which he hath inriched with maintenance. The higher hath no revenewes or very little to maintaine the same; so that the greatest part of Students are tabled in the Citie at their own charge.

A Greek lecture. In a certaine roome of Erasmus Colledge I heard a very learned Greeke lecture read in one of Homers Iliads by Mr. Zuinggerus the publike professour of the Greeke

tongue, who was the sonne of that famous Theodorus
Zuinggerus a great Philosopher of this University.
Surely although the Academie be but small, yet it hath
bred a great multitude of passing learned men within these
threescore yeares of all principall faculties, especially
Divines, and many excellent Philosophers. For besides
those famous men whose monuments and epitaphs I have
before mentioned, many worthy professours of learning
have spent their time in this noble University as in a most
sure harbour and pleasant receptacle of all the Muses. As
Sebastian Munster, Conradus Lycosthenes, Henricus
Glareanus, Hieronymus Gemusæus, Joannes Amer
bachius, and his three learned sonnes, Bonifacius, Bruno,
and Basilius, whereof the two later have most learnedly
illustrated the workes of Saint Hierome; Gulielmus
Gratarolus whome I have before mentioned in my
description of Bergomo; Sebastianus Brandus, Theodorus
Zuingerus, and many other excellent men, whose memory
will ever live in their learned workes.

    Amongst other calamities that this Citie hath in former
times sustained, as the sacking of it by barbarous Attila,
King of the Hunnes, and the burning of it afterward by
the Hungarians in the time of Lewes the fourth Emperour
of that name, there happened two notable earthquakes (as
I both heard of a learned man in the Citie, & also read
in Munsters Cosmographie) that did not a little ruinate
the same. Whereof the first was in the yeare 1346.
The second 1356. at what time most of the principall
buildings of the Citie, both sacred and civill were utterly
shaken, and rooted out of their foundations, the Citizens
by good fortune escaping with their lives by flight out
of the Citie, yet one hundred of them were slaine with the
fall of the houses. Moreover the ruine of the buildings
caused so great a fire by the collision of them together, as
lasted many dayes, and destroyed both man and beast.
A spectacle exceeding tragical. For the repayring of
which ruines many came to Basil from some of the Cities
of Alsatia and Helvetia, and within a short space well

Many worthy professors of learning.

[p. 436.]

Basle sacked by Attila.

Notable earthquakes.

171

repeopled the Citie, and beautified it with many stately houses that they raised up from the foundations. This Citie was heretofore Episcopal, the first Bishop thereof being one Walanus in the yeare 704. who lived in the time of Pipin King of France, the father of Carolus Magnus. And it was for the space of many yeares adorned with the residence of a Bishop whose Palace was in the lesser Basil till the yeare 1365. one Joannes de Wan an Italian, being the last Bishop; a man of that turbulent spirit as utterly overthrew the Bishopricke by his insolent behaviour.

Besides many other notable things that have much *Council of Basle.* enobled this stately Citie, these two are esteemed not the least, namely that famous *Councell that was celebrated and kept here anno 1431. under the Emperour Sigis-[p. 437.] mundus and the Popes Eugenius the fourth, & Felix the fifth: and that notable art of printing, which hath these many yeares much flourished in this Citie, not so much for the excellency of the print (which indeed is no better here then in other Cities) as for the singular industrie and great labours of the Printers of the Citie (that have bene as learned men as most of that faculty *Great printers.* in Christendome) namely Joannes Operinus, the two Frobenii, John the father, and Hierome the sonne, Michael Isingrius, Sebastian Henricpeter, Joannes Hervagius, Nicolaus Episcopius, Joannes Wolphius, &c. Which worthy men have taken as great paines to purge many ancient and learned authors both sacred and prophane from those manifold faults and errours which by the injury of the times were crept into them, as Hercules did in times past in the cleansing of Augeas stable. Of those battels that have beene waged neere to this Citie, I finde two above *Two notable battles.* the rest most memorable: whereof the one was fought by Julius Cæsar against Ariovistus King of the Germanes, even the last battel that was waged with him, at a place called St. Apollinaris, which was one Dutch mile from

* At this Councell it was decreed that the authority of a generall Councell was greater then of the Pope.

OBSERVATIONS OF BASLE

Basil, standing in the same side of the Rhene which was heretofore accounted part of France : The other was waged neere to the Citie upon the seventh of September in the yeare 1444. betwixt the Armeniaci (so called from a certaine Earledome of Aquitanie, the Earle whereof was a great Commander in that Armie) under the conduct of Ludovicus Dolphin of Fance, who was afterward the eleventh King of that name ; and the Helvetians. Which battell is much the more memorable by reason of the unequall number of the fighters. For three thousand of the Helvetians conquered twenty thousand of the French men. But so that all the Helvetians lost their lives in fight, in that manner as we reade the valiant Spartans did at the skirmish of Thermopylæ in Greece, when three hundred of them being conducted by their valiant Captaine [p. 438.] Leonidas, opposing themselves with a few other Grecians against the huge armie of the Persians.

The men of this Citie weare great codpieces and ruffe *Fashions of* bandes as the Tigurines do. Also they weare a strange *the city.* kind of hat, wherein they differ from all other Switzers that I saw in Helvetia. It is made in the forme of a cap, very long crowned, whereof some are made of felt, and some of a kinde of stuffe not unlike to shagge in outward view. It hath no brimmes at all, but a high flappe turned up behind, which reacheth almost to the toppe of the hat, being lesser and lesser towards the toppe. This fashion is so common in the Citie, that not onely all the men generally doe weare it both Citizens and Academicks (in so much that Amandus Pollanus wore the same in the Divinity schoole) but also the women whatsoever, both yong and old. Moreover their women, especially maides doe weare two such plaited rowles of haire over their shoulders wherein are twisted ribbons of divers colours at the endes, as the women of Zurich. I observed many women of this Citie to be as beautifull and faire as any I saw in all my travels : but I will not attribute so much to them as to compare them with our English women, whome I justly preferre, and that without any partialitie of affec-

173

tion, before any women that I saw in my travels, for an elegant and most attractive natural beautie.

Diet of the people.   The diet in their principall Innes is passing good, especially at their Ordinaries. For the variety of meate and that of the better sort, it is so great that I have not observed the like in any place in my whole journey saving at Zurich. But indeed it is something deare, no lesse then eight battes a meale, which are twenty pence of our money. They use to sitte long at supper, even an houre and a halfe at the least, or almost two houres. The first noble

[p. 439.] carowsing that I saw in Germany was at mine Inne in Basil. Where I saw the Germanes drink helter-skelter very sociably, exempting my selfe from their liquid impositions as well as I could. It is their custome whensoever they drink to another, to see their glasse filled up incontinent, (for therein they most commonly drinke) and then they deliver it into the hand of him to whome they drinke,

Drinking habits.   esteeming him a very curteous man that doth pledge the whole, according to the old verse :

    Germanus mihi frater eris si pocula siccas.

But on the contrary side, they deeme that man for a very rusticall and unsociable peasant, utterly unworthy of their company, that will not with reciprocal turnes mutually retaliate a health. And they verifie the olde speech ἢ πίθι ἢ ἄπιθι, that is, eyther drinke or be gon. For though they will not offer any villanie or injury unto him that refuseth to pledge him the whole, (which I have often seene in England to my great griefe) yet they will so little regard him, that they will scarce vouchsafe to converse with him. Truly I have heard Germany much dispraised for drunkennesse before I saw it ; but that vice reigneth no more there (that I could perceive) then in other countries. For I saw no man drunke in any place of Germany, though I was in many goodly Cities, and in much notable company. I would God the imputation of that vice could not be almost as truly cast upon mine owne nation as upon Germany. Besides I observed that they impose not such an inevitable necessity of drinking a whole health, especially those of the greater size, as many of our English gallants doe, a custome (in my opinion) most barbarous, and fitter to bee used amongst the rude Scythians and Gothes then civill Christians: yet so frequently practised in England, that I have often most heartily wished it were clean abolished out of our land, as being no small blemish to so renowned and well governed a Kingdome as England is.

It was my chance to heare very dismall and unhappy *Hugh* newes in this city of my most learned and worthy countri- *Broughton.* man Mr. Hugh Broughton. For there was dispersed a [p. 440.] fame for a little time about the University that he had utterly abandoned his religion, and inserted himselfe into the Jesuitical family at Mentz. But afterward I understood that it was a very false and malicious tale. For when I came to Mentz I heard of all the particulars by a certaine English Priest living amongst the Jesuites, who told me that there hapned a certaine unlucky occasion of acquaintance betwixt Nicholas Serrarius the Coryphæus of the Jesuites of that City and Mr. Broughton, which ministred the original matter of that scandalous rumour in many German Cities: but that he continued as vehement an adversary against the Papisticall religion as ever he was. Thus at length I end my discourse of this renowned City and University of Basil with the remembrance of my famous countriman Mr. Broughton, who for his exquisite skill in the sacred languages of the Hebrew, Chaldean, Syrian, and Greeke hath purchased himselfe a great fame in some of the worthyest Cities and Universities of Germany; the place of his aboade being the noble Citie of Amsterdam in Holland, when I was in the Netherlands.

Thus much of Basil.

I Made my aboade in Basil all Tuesday after nine of the *Travelling* clocke in the morning, all Wednesday being the one *down the* and thirtieth and last of August, and departed therehence *Rhine.* in a barke secundo cursu upon the river Rhene betwixt five and sixe of the clocke in the morning the first day of

175

September being Thursday, and came to the Citie of Strasbourg, which is foure score English miles beyond it, about eleven of the clocke the next morning being Friday, and the second day of September. By the way I passed by two Cities, both seated on the right hand of the Rhene, whereof the one is called Neobourg, the other Brisac.

[p. 441.] Both these are Papistical. The Thursday night it was my chaunce to lie about twenty miles on this side Strasbourg in my boate sub dio upon a wadde of straw, having for my coverled the cold open aire which did not a little punish me : yet I comforted my selfe with the recordation of the old verse,

Dulcia non meruit qui non gustavit amara,

that I did not deserve the sweet junkats of my little experience without some bitter pilles and hard brunts of adverse fortune.

But before I come to the description of Strasbourg I will speake something of the Rhene, because at Basil where I first was imbarqued upon the same, it extendeth it selfe *The source of* in a greater bredth then I could see before. This noble *of the Rhine.* Rhene, being next to the Danubius the fairest river of all Germany, which it disterminateth from France, deriveth his original spring from a certaine Mountaine of the Rheticall Alpes called Adula but a little way distant from the Citie of Curia above mentioned, which yeeldeth two severall fountaines, wherehence rise two rivers that meete together in one about five English miles above the said Curia, whereof one is called the first Rhene, the other the second. Betwixt these two fountaines and the spring of the Rhodanus that I have above spoken of in my description of Lyons, there is interjected no longer space then of three houres journey, the high Mountaine Godard (which is commonly esteemed the highest of all the Alpine Mountaines) deviding them asunder. Virgil calleth this river bicornis : as

*Extremique hominum Morini Rhenusque bicornis,

* Ænei. 8.

because it hath in a manner hornes, and those in number two, whose names are Lecca and Wahalis. In which *Branches of* respect other Poets also as well as he termed it bicornis. *the Rhine.* By these hornes are meant certayne armes as it were or secondary rivers derived out of the same. For indeede in Virgils time it had two cornua only, which about the [p. 442.] entrance of Holland, heretofore called Batavia, doe disgorge themselves partly into the river Mosa, and partly into the westerne Ocean. But within a few yeares after Virgils death it beganne to be called tricornis by the addition of a third river whose name is Isella. Which Drusus the brother of the Emperour Tiberius, at what time he levied armes against the Germanes, conveighed out of the Rhene by the meanes of a large ditch that his Souldiers digged out of the maine land for the same purpose, to the end that he might object the same as an obex or a barre for repulsing the violent invasion of the Batavians, which were the people of the country, against him. Julius Cæsar caused the portraiture of this river (as Tranquillus writeth in his life) to be made in gold, and presented in his triumph of France, as being the only river that devided Germany and France, which he had with such great difficulty made subject to the Romans : the like whereof he did of the famous river Rhodanus, as I have before written in my Observations of Lyons. One most memorable and admirable thing I will report of this river, which I have read in an eloquent Epistle of Angelus Politianus sent to his friend Jacobus, Cardinal of Pavie. A thing that he hath borrowed (as I conjecture) out of the booke of Cornelius Tacitus de Germanorum moribus, which was this. The Rhene had in times past one more strange *A strange* property then any river in the whole world that I could *property.* either heare or reade of in any history whatsoever sacred or prophane, that whensoever any infants were cast into his channell (a thing that hath sometimes hapned) if they were begotten out of lawfull wedlocke, the river as a just revenger of the mothers polluted bedde would presently swallow it up in his swift streame ; but if he found them to be begotten in the honest and chaste couple of marriage, he would gently and quietly conveigh them upon the toppe of the water, and restore them into the trembling handes

[p. 443.] of the wofull mother, yeelding safety unto the silly babe as a most true testimony of the mothers impolluted chastity.

The end of my Observations of Switzerland.

My Observations of some parts of high Germanıe.

The bounds of Germany.

Eing I am now come into Germanie I wil speake something of the boundes of the country, and their names together with their etymologies, that are very elegant. Also I will make some short mention of Alsatia, the name of the territory wherein Strasbourg standeth, and so anon descend to the description of the City it selfe. Germanie is the largest region of all Europe, being divided from France by the river Rhene, from Rhetia and Pannonia by the Danubius, from Sarmatia now called partly Polonia partly Prussia, likewise from Dacia (whereof the greatest part is now called Transylvania) by certaine mountaines. The other parts are bounded with the Ocean. This country had two names heretofore before it was called Germany,

Etymology of Teutonia.

viz. Teutonia and Alemannia. Teutonia some will have to be so called quasi Tuisconia from Tuisco the sonne of the Patriarch Noah by his wife Arezia, who after the generall inundation of the world, having all that vast country that lyeth betwixt the rivers Tanais and the Rhene, assigned unto him by his father for a Kingdome to reigne in, came into these westerne parts of the world shortly after the deluge, and made his residence in some place neare to the Rhene. Others derive it from one Teutanes (which derivation is the better in my opinion, and more answerable to the name of Teutonia) who was the Lord of this country after the death of King Tuisco.

[p. 444.] Likewise the name Alemannia hath foure etymologies.

For some write that it taketh his denomination from Alemannus the surname of Hercules, who (as that ancient Chaldæan authour Berosus writeth) did heretofore reigne in this country. Others say that it commeth from Mannus the sonne of the foresaid Tuisco. But the best and most elegant etymologie of all, is to derive it (as some learned doe) from two German wordes which doe altogether agree with our English, even from All man, as the people called Marcomanni (which are now those of Moravia) had their name from Marck, which signifieth the bound of a country, and the word Man. So that they which deduce the name of Alemannia from All man (as Munster doth) give this reason for it, because the auncient Alemannes were very couragious and valiant men, yea they were All men : as when we in our English idiome doe commend a man for his valour, we sometimes say such a man is all courage, all spirit : so the Aleman quasi All man, he is all valour, every part of him is viril, manly, and couragious, no jot effeminate, which indeede was verified by their fortitude and manly cariage in their warres against the Romans. Though this etymologie be passing good and deserveth (in my opinion) to be most approved above all the rest, yet I perceive that Philip Melancthon, speaking according to the opinion of other writers, affirmeth that the Aleman is so called quasi Allerleyman a Dutch word which signi-fieth a promiscuous multitude, which heretofore conjoyned themselves together to recover their liberty, by reason of the tyrannicall insolencies of the Roman Captaines. Againe I observe in reading of histories the first mention of this word Aleman, in the historie of the Emperour Valerius Probus, who of the Franci and Alemanni slew foure hundred thousand. The third name Germania which is the moderne appellation of the country, hath as elegant an etymologie as Alemannia. For it is called Germania from the Latin word Germânus, which doth sometimes signifie a mans naturall brother both by father and mother, quasi ex eodem germine natus, one that issueth from the same stocke, that is, one that springeth from one

Etymology of Alemannia.

Melancthon's opinion.

Germania.

[p. 445.]

179

and the selfe same mothers belly. The reason of this
etymologie is this : Because the auncient Germans did with
such a brotherly affection share dangers and fortunes of
warre, that those which remained at home by applying
themselves to the affaires of husbandrie, maintayned the
wives and children of them that were gone into the warres
for the common safety of their country : and againe those
that had beene a yeare abroad in warfare, returned home
into their country to exercise tillage, & to nourish the
families of those men that were pressed forth into the wars
in their roome. Now though I doe in this place prefixe
this discourse of the boundes and the auncient names of
this country by way of an introduction to my ensuing
description of the German cities, you must consider that
this particular country on the farther banke of the Rhene
where Basil, Strasbourg, Spira, Wormes, Mentz, &c. doe
stand, was not heretofore in the time of the auncient
Romans, as Julius Cæsar, Drusus, and other valiant
Worthyes that conquered it, called Germanie (for al this
long tract was devided from Germany by the river Rhene
as I have before said about the beginning of this discourse)
but in those times it was ever esteemed for a part of Gallia,
and so was reputed for the space of many hundred yeares
after, till the time of the Emperour Charlemaine and his
successors, and then it beganne to be called Germany as
well as the other parts on the hither side or banke of the
Rhene (which are indeed the true and ancient Germanie)
since which time it hath continually retained the same
name to this day. Having now spoken of the boundes
and names of Germany, I will briefly mention this country
wherein Strasbourg standeth, and so at length after so long
a preamble (which I hope will not be irksome to a judicious
[p. 446.] reader) relate the particulars of the City itselfe. The
Alsace. name of the country is Alsatia (as I have before written)
but commonly called in Dutch Elsass. It is devided into
two parts, the higher and the lower Alsatia : a territory
very populous, frequented with goodly Cities and townes
(whereof these are the chiefest, Strasbourg, Rubeaquum

commonly called Rufach, and Colmaria) inriched with *The garden* precious mines of silver, and is accounted so fertile a plot *of Germany* of ground that some doe not doubt to call it the garden of Germany. Heretofore it was called the lesser France, and that for the space of five hundred yeares. Afterward it was converted to a Landgraviat, and for many yeares acknowledged a Landgrave for the supreme Lord thereof, as the territorie of Hassia doth at this day, and as Thuringia did heretofore.

Thus much of the Bounds and divers Names of Germanie, and of the territorie of Alsatia.

My Observations of Argentina or Argentoratum, commonly called Strasbourg the Metropolitan City of Alsatia.

SInce I came into England I found these verses following in praise of Strasbourg and the famous tower of the Cathedrall Church, in a certaine elegant booke that a Gentleman a kinde friend of mine and my neighbour in *George* my country of Somersetshire, one Mr. George Sidenham *Sidenham's* the sonne and heire of my right Worshipfull friend Sir *verses in* John Sidenham, very lovingly communicated unto me, *praise of* which by reason of the elegancy thereof I have thought *Germany.* expedient to prefixe before my description of this noble City, hoping that they will be very pleasing to the learned Reader.

URbs antiqua jacet (primi coluere Triboces) [p. 447.]
    Argentoratum, ripis contermina Rheni.
Dives opum, & nulli veterum virtute secunda,
Sive fidem spectes, & religionis honorem:
Sive forum, canosque Patres, sanctumque Senatum,
Justitiæque decus: seu limina culta Lycei,
Insignesque viros: seu duro mænia saxo
Condita, & armatas adversa in prælia vires,
Marmoreasque domos, atque ardua tecta domorum.
Hâc templum augustum, cœlataque turris in urbe
Vertice prospiciens alto (mirabile dictu)

181

George Sidenham's verses in praise of Germany.

Surgit, & excelsum caput inter nubila condit.
Tota toreumatibus, pictisque excisa columnis,
Tota patens luci, & leni perflabilis aurâ,
Et cono insignis galeæ, & testudine circum
Quadruplici septa, & nullo violabilis ictu.
Prima solo posuit quondam fundamina duro
Steinbachiâ natus de gente Ervinus, & omne
Ad galeam duxit *opus, & testudine sepsit.
Tempore quo imperii gessit Rodolphus habenas
Habspurgus, Comitum Germanus origine Cæsar.
Nunc illam multis servantque foventque minores
Impensis, magnoque locant in honore, suosque
Majores hâc laude æquant. Nam fulmine tactam
Sæpiùs immensi repararunt sumptibus æris.
Jamque adeò nuper, foribus quâ maxima templi
Stant adyta austrinis, sociâ testudine juncta,
Excelso fabricam posuerunt pariete muri
Intùs ut exactas mortalibus indicet horas,
Et Solis Lunæque vias, noctesque diesque,
Et menses, fastosque in longum digerat ævum.
Mirum opus ingenii, mirandâque arte paratum.

[p. 448.]

Quale laboriferi nescisset radere tornus
Praxitelis, Cous nec depinxisset Apelles,
Nec Polycletæus duxisset in ære caminus.
Quale nec Ætnæis olim Telchines in antris,
Nec rigidus Steropes, nec qui polit arma Tonanti
Mulciber æterna potuisset fingere massa.
Quale nec hoc toto quisquam conspexit in orbe,
Nec facilè aspiciet, seu Gallica regna pererret,
Seu totam Italiam lustret, seu Teutonis orbem
Viribus ingenii superantem climata mundi
Toties invisat, seu Persica rura peragret,
Sive adeat Libyen atque ultima littora Thules.

Strasburg. STrasbourg standeth in the lower Alsatia, and is situate in a very pleasant and delectable plaine about a quarter of an English mile distant from the Rhene, yet well watered

* A fault but something tolerable.

182

with three other rivers, as the Kintzgus, the Illa, and the Bruschus, whereof the last runneth through a part of the City; a place of such passing fatnesse and fertility (as a certaine English Merchant told me called Robert Kingman an Herefordshire man borne, but then commorant in Strasbourg with his whole family when I was there) that for amenity of situation and exceeding plenty of all things that the hart of man can wish for, it doth farre excell all the *Amenity of its situation,* other Cities of the same territorie, though some of them are very faire, as Rubeaquum, Selestadium, Colmaria &c. in so much that when I did throughly contemplate the sweet champaignes, meadowes, lakes, vineyards, and gardens about the same, I said to myselfe that I might very justly call the circumjacent plaine about this City sumen Alsatiæ, that is, the most principall and fruitfull place of all Alsatia, as Flavius Vopiscus an ancient historiographer did heretofore terme the fields of Rosea neare to the City of Bononia, sumen Italiæ. This part of the country with some other bordering places thereof was once inhabited by a kinde of people called *Triboces, before such time as it was called Alsatia, wherehence it was called Tribocum regio. So ancient is this City that it is thought *A very ancient* it may contend with any German City whatsoever for *city.* antiquity, saving those three that I have before mentioned, [p. 449.] namely Trevirs, Zurich, and Solodurum. Nay Munster doth not doubt to affirme (but speaking after other men) that it was built at the same time those Cities were, so that as the City of Trevirs had her denomination from Trebeta the sonne of Ninus King of the Assyrians : so was this city first called Trebesburgum (as the same Munster reporteth) or Tyrasburgum from the very same founder. And afterward by the changing or addition of some letters it was called Strasburgum. Againe there are others that attribute the change of the name from Trebesburgum to Strasburgum (as the foresaid author writeth) to the tyrannie of Attila King of the Hunnes, who after he had demolished this City with many other noble cities of Germany, did

* These are mentioned by Cæsar.

183

with such extreme furie deface the walles thereof, that he opened a free way and passage for all manner of people whatsoever promiscuously to enter the same; which accident gave occasion of the name Strasbourg, that is, a City that yeeldeth a common way for all men to passe through: for Stroze in the high Dutch signifieth a way. Also the same Attila imposed an other name upon it, which it retained but a little while, viz Polyodopolis, which signifieth as much as the former name Strasbourg. For it is composed of three Greeke wordes, πολὺς which signifieth many, ὁδὸς a way, And πόλις a City, that is, a City that a man may many wayes passe through. But the name Argentina was imposed upon it from the Latin word Argentum that signifieth silver, because when the City was subject to the Roman Empire, some Quæstor in the behalfe of the Senate of Rome made his residence and kept his Audit in this City to gather up all the rents and tributes due to the Romans in those parts, as being their gazo phylacium, that is, a place where their checker-chamber was for the safe keeping of the Roman treasure, even as Lyons was heretofore appointed a checker City for the Romans in the Province of France, where they had such another Officer assigned for the same purpose, I have before written in my Observations of that Citie.

[p. 450.]

There are many goodly things in this renowned City that doe much beautifie the same. As the loftinesse of the building, the multitude of their houses, the beauty and spaciousnesse of their streetes and the cleane keeping thereof, the great frequency of people, their strong walles made of hard stone, and adorned with stately battlements, divers towers, strong bulwarkes, faire gates, mighty and deep trenches that are moated round about: and of those walles I observed two severall, being by a convenient space distant asunder, and each of them environed with a deepe ditch. Truly these double walles do much grace the Citie. But the principall things of all which do especially illustrate and garnish Strasbourg are but two, which because they are the most matchlesse and incomparable fabrickes of all

OBSERVATIONS OF STRASBURG

Christendome, no Citie whatsoever in all Europe yeelding the like, I will something particularly discourse thereof. These are the Tower of the Cathedral Church and a Clocke within the Church. But before I speake of eyther of these I wil first make relation of their Church, because that is as it were the maine body, whereof these two are the principall and fayrest members.

The Cathedrall Church is dedicated to our Lady, and commonly called the Minster of Strasbourg. It was first founded about the yeare 508. by Clodoveus the first Christian King of France, who was the founder of the principal church of Zurich also, which is called by the name of Saint Felix and Regula as I have before said. At the entrance of the Church are three dores made of massie brasse, and decked with many historical matters of the old and new Testament, which are very curiously expressed in pretty little images over the same dores. Within the Church, about the west end of the body thereof, there is a faire paire of Organs that were new mending when I was there, and like to be passing beautifull when they are throughly ended. For the Citizens bestowed great charges in gilding of them. I observed one thing in this Church that I never saw in any Church before, even a Well in the South side of the body: the water whereof serveth for divers uses, as to sprinkle the Church to the end to keepe it cleane, also for the baptizing of their Children, &c. But this Church yeeldeth the superiority to the Cathedral church of Basil that I have before so much commended (saving only for the two foresaid matters which I will hereafter describe) for I could not perceive as much as one monument in the whole Church. They have a very religious exercise in this Church. For twise every day in the weeke here is a sermon preached by a learned Divine. The other Churches in the citie are sixe in number.

Having now spoken of the Church, I will next mention those two memorable things that I have already named. But I will first begin with the Tower, in regard it is the fairest of the two. Surely the same is by many degrees

Cathedral Church of Our Lady.

[p. 451.]

A well in the church.

Tower of the church.

185

the exquisitest peece of work for a Tower that ever I saw, as wel for the height, as for the rare curiosity of the architecture; so that neither France, Italy, nor any City in Switzerland or vast Germany, nor of any Province or Island whatsoever within the precincts of the Christian world can shew the like. It was begun in the yeare 1277. at what time Rodolph Earle of Habspurg was Emperour of Germany, and was continually building for the space of eight and twenty yeares together, till it was *The architect.* brought to full perfection. The principall Architect was one Ervinus of Steinbach (as the Author of those excellent Hexameter verses which I have prefixed before this description of Strasbourg doth testifie) who contrived the whole modell of the worke himselfe, and was the chiefe *[p. 452.]* Mason in the performing of this peerelesse Machine, which he raised from the very foundation to the toppe with square stones most artificially and rarely cut. The staires that leade up to the tower, are made windingly, being distinguished with foure severall degrees, and where the thicknesse doth begin to be acuminated in a slender toppe, there are eight degrees more of those winding staires that *The ball.* rise above the first foure. The ball which standeth upon the highest toppe of all, seemeth to those that are beneath upon the ground, no greater then a bushel, yet the circumference thereof is so large that it will well containe five or sixe sufficient and stout men upon the same. The manifold images, pinnacles, & most curious devices carved in stone that are erected round about the compasse of the Tower, are things of such singular beautie, that they are very admirable to behold, and such as will by reason of the rare novelty of the worke, drive a stranger that is but a *Altitude of the* novice into a very extasie of admiration. Also the altitude *tower.* of it is so strange, that from the bottome to the toppe it is saide to containe five hundred seventy foure Geometrical foote; which much exceedeth the famous Italian Towers, as that of Cremona, which is esteemed the loftiest of all Italy, Saint Markes of Venice, which although it be but two hundred eightie foote high, yet the Venetians doe

OBSERVATIONS OF STRASBURG

account it a Tower of notable heigth, as indeed it seemeth to all those that come to Venice by Sea: likewise the slender tower of Vicenza is very high: but they all are much inferiour to this unmatchable tower of Strasbourg. Wherefore to conclude this discourse of this tower, I attribute so much unto it, that I account it one of the principall wonders of Christendome.

The second notable thing is a Clock (as I have already spoken) which standeth at the South side of the Church neere to the dore. A true figure or representation wherof, made according to the forme it selfe as it standeth at this day in the Church I have expressed in this place. Truly it is a fabricke so extraordinarily rare and artificiall that I am confidently perswaded it is the most exquisite piece of worke of that kinde in all Europe. I thinke I should not commit any great errour if I should say in all the world: the bolder I am to affirme it, because I have heard very famous travellers (such as have seene this Clocke and most of the principall things of Christendome) report the same. It was begun to be built in the yeare 1571. in the moneth of June by a most excellent Architect & Mathematician of the Citie of Strasbourg, who was then alive when I was there. His name is Conradus Dasypodius, once the ordinary professour of the Mathematicks in the Universitie of this Citie: A man that for his excellent art may very fitly be called the Archimedes of Strasbourg; and it was ended about three yeares after, even in the yeare 1574. in the same moneth of June about the feast of Saint John Baptist. This work contayneth by my estimation about fifty foote in heigth betwixt the bottome and the top; it is compassed in with three severall rayles, to the end to exclude all persons that none may approach neere it to disfigure any part of it, whereof the two outmost are made of timber, the third of yron about three yardes high. On the left hand of it there is a very ingenious and methodicall observation for the knowing of the eclipses of the Sunne and Moone for thirty two yeares. At the toppe wherof is written in fair Roman letters

The clock.

[p. 453.]

The Archimedes of Strasburg.

TYPI ECLIPSIUM
SOLIS ET LUNÆ
AD ANNOS XXXII.

On the same hand ascendeth a very faire architectonical
Machine made of wainscot with great curiosity, the sides
being adorned with pretty little pillers of marble of divers
colours, in which are three degrees, whereof each con-

Carvings on
the clock.

tayneth a faire Statue carved in wainscot: the first the
Statue of Urania one of the nine Muses, above which her

[p. 454.]

name is written in golden letters, and by the sides these
two words in the like golden letters, Arithmetica &
Geometria. The second the picture of a certain King
with a regall Scepter in his hand. But what King it is I
know not. Above him is written Daniel 2. Cap. The
last is the picture of Nicolaus Copernicus that rare
Astronomer, under whom this is written in faire Roman
letters: Nicolai Copernici vera effigies ex ipsius autographo
depicta. At the very toppe of this rowe or series of
worke is erected a most excellent effigies of a Cocke which
doth passing curiously represent the living shape of that

A counterfeit
cock crow.

vocal creature, and it croweth at certaine houres, yeelding
as shrill and loud a voice as a naturall Cocke, yea and such
a kinde of sound (which maketh it the more admirable)
as counterfeyteth very neere the true voyce of that bird.
The houres are eleven of the clocke in the morning, and
three in the afternoone. It was my chance to heare him
at the third houre in the afternoone, whereat I wondered
as much as I should have done if I had seene that famous
wooden Pigeon of Architus Tarentinus the Philosopher
(so much celebrated by the ancient Historians) flie in the
ayre. On the right hand also of this goodly architecture
there is another row of building correspondent to the foresaid in heigth, but differing from it in forme. For the
principall part thereof consisteth of a paire of winding
staires made of free stone, and most delicately composed.
I could not perceive for what use they serve, so that I
conjecture they are made especially for ornament. Againe

188

OBSERVATIONS OF STRASBURG

in the middle worke betwixt these two notable rowes that
I have now described, is erected that incomparable fabrick *An*
wherein the Clocke standeth. At the lower end whereof, *incomparable*
just about the middle, I observed the greatest astronomicall *fabric.*
globe that ever I saw, which is supported with an artificiall
Pellican wounding his breast with his beake; wherewith
they typically represent Christ, who was wounded for the
salvation and redemption of the worlde: and about the [p. 455.]
middest goeth a compasse of brasse which is sustayned
with very elegant little turned pillers. Opposite unto
which is a very large spheare beautified with many cunning
conveighances and wittie inventions. Directly above that
standeth another orbe which with a needle (this is a
mathematicall terme signifying a certaine instrument about
a clocke) pointeth at foure houres only that are figured at
the foure corners thus: 1. 2. 3. 4. each figure at a severall
corner. At the sides of the orbe two Angels are represented, whereof the one holdeth a mace in his hand, with
which he striketh a brasen serpent every houre, and hard
by the same standeth a deaths head finely resembled; the
other an houre glasse, which he moveth likewise hourely.
Notable objects tending to mortification. Both the lower
endes of this middle engine are very excellently graced
with the portraiture of two huge Lyons carved in marble.
This part of the third fabricke wherein standeth the clocke,
is illustrated with many notable sentences of the holy *Sentences on*
Scripture written in Latin. As, In principio creavit Deus *the tower.*
cœlum et terram. Gene. 1 cap. Omnis caro fœnum,
Pet. 1. cap. 1. Peccati stipendium mors est. Rom. 6. Dei
donum vita æterna per Christum. Rom. 6. Ascendisti in
altum, cepisti captivitatem. Psal. 68. Againe under the
same are written these sentences in a lower degree: Ecce
ego creo cœlos novos et terram novam. Esaiæ 65. Ex-
pergiscimini et lætamini qui habitatis in pulvere. Esa. 26.
Venite benedicti patris mei, possidete regnum vobis paratum. Discedite a me maledicti in ignem æternum. Math.
25. Above these sentences divers goodly armes are
advanced and beautified with fayre Scutchins. Under the

Exquisite devices.

[p. 456.]

same many curious pictures are drawne which present onely histories of the Bible. Again above that orbe which I have already mentioned, there is erected an other orbe or spheare wherein are figured the houres distinguishing Time, and a great company of mathematicall conceits which doe decipher some of the most abstruse & secret mysteries of the noble science of Astronomy. Likewise an other Orbe standeth above this that I last spake of, within the which is expressed the figure of an halfe moone and many glittering starres set forth most gloriously in gold, and againe without are formed foure halfe moones and two full moones. Above the higher part of this Orbe this impresse is written: Quæ est hæc tam illustris, similis auroræ, pulchra ut Luna, pura ut Sol? At the sides of it beneath, this poesie is written, which is thus distributed: Dominus lux mea, on the left hand; & this on the right hand, Quem timebo? Also above the same Orbe I

Seven bells of 'hrass.

observed an other very exquisite device, even seven little pretty bels of brasse (as I conceived it) standing together in one ranke, and another little bell severally by it selfe above the rest. Within the same is contrived a certaine vacant or hollow place wherein stand certaine artificial men so ingeniously made that I have not seene the like. These doe come forth at every quarter of an houre with a very delightfull and pleasant grace, holding small banners in their hands wherewith they strike these foresaid bels, every one in order alternis vicibus, and supply each other with a pretty diligence and decorum in this quarterly function. Under the place where these two men doe strike those foresaid bells, these two sacred Emblemes are written: Ecclesia Christi exulans: And, Serpens antiquus Antichristus. The highest toppe of this fabricke is framed with such surpassing curiositie that it yeeldeth a wonderfull ornament to the whole engine, having many excellent little portraitures and fine devices contrived therein of free stone, and garnished with borders and workes of singular art. Moreover the corners of this middle worke are decked with very beautifull little pillers of ash-coloured marble, whereof there stand two in a place, those above square, those beneath round.   Thus have I something superficially [p. 457.] described unto thee this famous Clocke of Strasbourg, being the Phœnix of al the clocks of Christendom.   For *The Phœnix of all the clocks of Christendom.* it doth as far excel al other Clocks that ever I saw before, as that of the Piazza of St Marks in Venice, which I have already mentioned, that of Middelborough in Zeland which I afterward saw, and all others generally, as farre (I say) as a fayre yong Lady of the age of eighteen yeares that hath beene very elegantly brought up in the trimming of her beauty, doth a homely and course trull of the Countrie, or a rich orient pearle a meane peece of amber.

But I am sorry I have not made that particular relation thereof as that excellent fabricke doth deserve.   For these few observations which I have written of it I gathered in little more than halfe an houre, where I had no mans assistance to instruct me in the principall things that I doubted off, determining then to make a full description of those particulars that I have expressed in the effigies thereof, had I not been barred of opportunity by the Sextin that at that time that I was in the middest of my curious survay of the same, was to shut up the Church dores. Howbeit I wish that that little which I have written of it *A good example.* (if it should happen to be read by any of the wealthy Citizens of London) may bee an encouragement to some wealthy Fraternity to erect the like in Paules Church, or some other notable Church of London for the better ornament of the Metropolitan Citie of our famous Island of great Britaine.   A thing that I heartily wish I may one day see come to passe.   Having therefore now ended this discourse of the Clocke (whereof I wish all English Gentlemen that determine hereafter to see Strasbourg, to take an exact view, as a matter most worthy of their curious observation) I will returne to the relation of some other memorable things of this Citie.

The Armourie of Strasbourg, which it was not my good *The armoury.* fortune to see, was reported unto me by a Gentleman of [p. 458.] the University to be a most worthy and beautifull place,

furnished with such admirable variety of all manner of
munition fit for warre-fare, that no Citie of all Germany
can shew a fairer, saving only Dresden in Saxony where
the Duke keepeth his Court.

Thus much of the Clocke of Strasbourg.

Many of the buildings of Strasbourg are very faire
and of a goodly heigth, foure stories high, especially
their publique houses, as their Councell house, &c. But
Houses of the greater part of their houses are built with timber.
Strasburg. This thing I especially observed in the houses of Strasbourg, which I noted else where in divers other cities of
Germany both before I came thither and afterward, as in
Basil, Mentz, Heidelberg, Spira, &c. that both the endes
of their houses doe rise with battlements, and a great many
of these houses of Strasbourg I saw built in that manner
that not only the endes, but also the sides are garnished with battlements, a forme of building much
affected by the Germans, and indeede it giveth no small
grace and ornament to the house. Here also I observed
one of the fairest shambles that I saw in all my travels.
In the front of one of the citizens houses I saw fifteene
of the first Roman Emperours very galantly painted.
The There is in this City a University, but a very obscure
University. and meane thing, nothing answerable to the majesty of so
beautifull a City. For it hath but one Colledge, which I
visited, being both for building and maintenance one of
the poorest Colledges that ever I saw, in so much that I
cannot report any memorable thing of it, only it hath a
prety Cloister belonging unto it.
Women's I observed that some of the women of this City do use
fashions. that fashion of plaiting their haire in two long locks hang-
[p. 459.] ing downe over their shoulders, as before in Zurich and
Basil. But it is not a quarter so much used here as in
Basil. As for those strange kinde of caps that the women
promiscuously with the men doe weare in Basil (as I have
before said) none of them are used here, but most of the
women, especially their Matrons doe weare very broad

192

A true figure of the famous Clock of Strasbourg

caps made of cloth, and furred, and many of them blacke velvet caps of as great a bredth.

The battels that have been fought in former times neare *Famous* Strasbourg have not a little famoused the citie. For here *battles.* fought the Emperour Julian the Apostata about the yeare 360. with the Allemanne forces, at what time eight of the Allemanne Kings having united their power together, con veighed their armies over the Rhene, and incountred the Emperour in this place, but with very unfortunate successe. For the Romans got the victory of the Allemannes, and tooke their corpulent King Chondomarius prisoner in battell. Againe about the space of twenty yeares after that overthrow, the Emperor Gratian slew no lesse than thirty thousand Alemannes neare this City. Also the Emperour Philip that succeeded Henry the sixth, made warre against Strasbourg about the yeare 1200. and at last surprized the same by force of armes.

It was first converted to Christianity in the time of the *Strasburg* Emperour Nero by the preaching of St. Maternus one of *converted to* the Disciples of St. Peter the Apostle, who was assisted in *Christianity.* that holy worke by his two companions Valerius and Eucharius. But not long after that it renounced the Christian religion, till the Bishops of the City of Mets reconciled them again unto Christ, in regard whereof the City continued a long time under the Diocesse of the Bishop of Mets. But at last Dagobert King of France created one Amandus a holy man of Aquitanie, Bishop of Strasbourg about the yeare 630. and instituted a goodly Bishoprick in the City, being then a member of the King- dome of France (as I have before said) which he endowed with most ample rents and revenewes. Ever since which [p. 460.] time the City hath had a Bishop of her owne, the seate of the present Bishop being the antient towne of Taberna commonly called Zabernia in Alsatia; where the Bishops of Strasbourg have these many yeares made their residence.

The governement of Strasbourg hath beene often *Government of* changed. For it was first subject to the Lords of the City *Strasburg.* of Trevirs; after that to the Roman Empire, to whom it

was tributarie for the space of five hundred yeares till the
time of the inclination thereof : this City being the seate
of residence for the Roman Lieutenant that was first con
stituted here by Julius Cæsar himselfe, and commonly
called Comes Argentoratensis, who resided here with a
garrizon of Souldiers for the defence of the City against
the Germans, having the administration of al that tract of
Alsatia under the people of Rome, yet his authority was
subject to a superior Roman Gentleman that was resident
in Mentz, who was commonly called Dux Moguntinus.
Thirdly to the French men, especially in the time of their
King Dagobert. But in processe of time it came into
the hands of the German Emperors, from whose jurisdiction being afterward in a manner exempted, it doth at this
day enjoy full libertie, a golden peace, and tranquilitie of
estate, being governed after a most excellent aristocraticall
forme of common-weale, the particulars whereof I cannot
as yet report unto thee, because I spent so little time in
the City, no more than one whole day, that I was not able
to informe my selfe so fully in their government as I wished
to have done.

The religion   The religion of the City is the same that the reformed
of Strasburg. Churches of Germanie doe embrace, which it hath ever
most constantly professed unto this day since the maine
reformation begunne in Germanie shortly after Martin
Luthers oppugning of the venall indulgences in the
Universitie of Wittemberg.   The principall instaurators
[p. 461.] of the Evangelical doctrine in the city were those valiant
champions of Jesus Christ Martin Bucer, Wolfangus Fabricius Capito, and Gaspar Hedio.   Whereof the two last
died in this City, and were here buried.   But the present
religion professed among them is not altogether conform-
able unto ours in England.   For they embrace the
Lutheran doctrine, wherein they differ something from
our Church of England, as in the omni-presence of Christ,
the consubstantiation, &c.

Besides many other learned men of great note, five most
worthy ornaments of learning hath this famous citie bred,

194

with remembrance of whom I will end my description of Strasbourg. These five were Joannes Sturmius, Joannes Sleidanus, Jacobus Micyllus, Joannes Guinterius, and Joannes Piscator : which have much ennobled this City by their rare learning, The first partly by his honorable Ambassages undertaken for the common-weale of Strasbourg to divers forraine States, having spent nine yeares amongst them : and partly by his excellent works, being as sweet a Ciceronian as any University of Christendome did yeeld. The second by his manifold learned bookes, especially by that historie worthy of immortall praise digested into six and twenty bookes (commonly called his Commentaries) which he wrote concerning the state of religion in Germanie, and those memorable accidents that hapned in the Empire after the Coronation of Carolus Quintus : both these men died in Strasbourg, and doe there lie buryed. The third hath written many excellent workes of great learning, which have purchased him immortality of fame. The fourth is Joannes Guinterius borne in the towne of Andernach situate by the Rhene, who hath consecrated his name to posteritie as well as the rest by his learned writings. He was a notable Physition, and learned Greeke reader in the University of this City : he also died in this City, and was here buried, The fifth and last Joannes Piscator (who when I was in Germanie was alive, and flourished with great fame of learning in the citie of Herborne, where he was publike reader of Divinity) hath as much famoused this noble Citie with his learned lucubrations as any of the foresaid writers, being such solid workes of Divinitie as have exceedingly profited those members of Christs Church which doe embrace the reformed religion.

Five most worthy ornaments of learning.

A notable Physician.

[p. 462.]

Thus much of Strasbourg.

I Remained in Strasbourg all Friday after eleven of the clocke in the morning, and departed therehence the Saturday following being the third day of September, about eleven of the clocke in the morning. A little beyond the

A rude bridge over the Rhine. townes end of Strasbourg I passed a wooden bridge made over the Rhene that was a thousand four score and sixe paces long. For I paced it. The longest bridge that ever I passed. But it is nothing faire. For the boordes and plankes are verie rudely compacted together. At one end thereof there is erected a little house, where a certaine officer of the city dwelleth, that remayneth continually there at the receipt of custome to receive money of every stranger that passeth that way for the maintenance of the bridge; the common pay being something lesse then our English farthing.

About sixe of the clocke in the afternoone I came to a Protestant towne called Litenawe, where I lay that night. This towne is about sixteen English miles distant from Strasbourg.

English and German miles. But because I will from henceforth cease to use that often repetition of this word English in the computation of the German miles, I will exclude that word hereafter, and put downe mile only: whereby I understand the English mile, as much as if I did expresse the word. For I am desirous to reduce the computation of the long Dutch miles to our English account. My reason is, [p. 463.] because as I have already cast up the generall summe of all the miles betwixt the place where I was borne in Somerset-shire and the Citie of Venice, and that according to our English miles: so likewise I determine after I come to the end of Germanie, or arrive at London, to cast up the number of al the miles betwixt Venice and my country according to our ordinarie miles of England. But because a man cannot altogether so precisely and exactly reduce the German miles to our English, as to say the space between two such Cities or townes containeth just so many English miles, neither more nor lesse: I doe therefore aime and give the nearest conjecture that I can by tracing of their *Helvetian, Middle German and Netherland miles.* ground. For this is my generall rule, to reduce an Helvetian mile which is the longest of all the German miles, to five English, being in some places of Switzerland as much as sixe of our miles: every mile betwixt the Cities

oden bridge and
)ur score and the
st bridge that eve
t the boordes and
:ther. At one end
, where a certain
th continually the
ey of every streere
ince of the bridge
e then our English

:rnoone I came to :
cre I lay that night
. miles distant fro

:h cease to use the
1 .n the computation
:ar word hereaster,
r I understand the
expresse the word
:-::tion of the long
:. Mr reason is
:-::il summe of all
: ::::e in Somerset
:-: according to me
:-: after I come to
:-::n, to cast up the
:: and my country
::-: But because
(: :::::ly reduce the
:: :- space between
(:: so many English
(:-::fore anne and
(: :r tracing of their
(:. to reduce all
::: all the German
:::: of Switzerland
::::::wixt the Cities

OBSERVATIONS OF LOWER BADEN

of Strasbourg and Mentz to foure English, those in that
space being called the middle German miles, which are
afterward almost as great in all that space betwixt the said
Citie of Mentz and Colen. And finally those of the
Netherlands which beginne at the City of Colen, and are
commonly esteemed the least miles of Germanie, to three
English.

I departed from the foresaid Litenawe a little after seven   *Lower Baden.*
of the clock in the morning the next day being Sunday,
and came to the City of Baden the Metropolis of the
Marquisate of Baden, about foure of the clocke in the
afternoone. This dayes journey was sixteene miles. I
found almost as great difficulty in finding out this Baden
so famous for her bathes, as I did when I went to the
bathes of Hinderhove neare the higher Baden, as I have
before mentioned. For by the way I had this mischance,
that whereas I passed all the way betwixt these two places
in woods and vast deserts, glancing sometimes by meere
chance upon some poore hamlet, I found the waies to be   *Intricate*
so exceeding intricate, that after I had wandered almost   *wayes.*
three miles about the wood alone by my selfe, at length   [p. 464.]
to my great discontent I returned to a village where
I had beene about two houres before. So that I was for
the time in a kind of irremeable labyrinth, not knowing
how to extricate my selfe out of it, till at the last an honest
clowne that dwelt thereabout in the country, brought me
into the right way, and gave me such certaine directions,
that after that time I missed my way no more betwixt that
and Baden.

About a mile and halfe on this side Baden I observed a
solitarie Monasterie situate in a wood : being desirous to
see it I went to the place, and craved to enter into it, but I
could not by any meanes obtayne accesse into the house :
but one of the Friers (for here dwell five Franciscans of   *A hospitable*
the Mendicant familie) to the end to give me some kinde   *Friar.*
of recompence and amends for my repulse, like a very
good fellow bestowed upon me a profound draught of good
Rhenish wine, which gave great refection to my barking

197

stomache. A courtesie that I neither craved nor expected. Also he told me that their fraternity was much infested by the Lutheran faction of the country. As I departed there-hence towards Baden I met one of the foresaid five riding homeward, who immediately returned againe, and having overtaken me he discovered his griefe unto me after a very pensive and disconsolate manner. For he told me that he had lost his Breviarium, and asked me whether I had found any such booke. This Breviarium is a certaine kinde of Popish booke containing prayers to their Saints and other holy meditations, which Priests and Friers doe as frequently use as we Protestants doe the Bible. The first of them that I saw was in Venice. At last the Frier after very diligent seeking having found his precious jewell, returned home once more, and when he met me, told me with a chearefull countenance and mery heart that he had found that for the which he had before so much dejected his spirits.

A Breviary lost and found.

One notable accident happened unto me in my way a little before I came to this Monastery and the citie of Baden, of which I will here make mention before I write any thing of Baden. It was my chance to meete two clownes commonly called Boores, who because they went in ragged cloathes, strooke no small terrour into mee; and by so much the more I was afraid of them, by how much the more I found them armed with weapons, my selfe being altogether unarmed, having no weapon at all about me but onely a knife. Whereupon fearing least they would eyther have cut my throate, or have robbed me of my gold that was quilted in my jerkin, or have stripped me of my clothes, which they would have found but a poore bootie. For my clothes being but a threed-bare fustian case were so meane (my cloake onely excepted) that the Boores could not have made an ordinary supper with the money for which they should have sold them; fearing (I say) some ensuing danger, I undertooke such a politike and subtile action as I never did before in all my life. For a little before I mette them, I put off my hat very curteously unto them, holding it a pretty while in my

[p. 465.]

Ragged Boors.

198

OBSERVATIONS OF LOWER BADEN

hand, and very humbly (like a Mendicant Frier) begged *A begging insinuation.* some money of them (as I have something declared in the front of my booke) in a language that they did but poorely understand, even the Latin, expressing my minde unto them by such gestures and signes, that they well knew what I craved of them : and so by this begging insinuation I both preserved my selfe secure & free from the violence of the clownes, and withall obtained that of them which I neither wanted or expected. For they gave me so much of their tinne money called fennies (as poore as they were) as paid for halfe my supper that night at Baden, even foure pence halfe-peny.

My Observations of Baden. [p. 466.]

THis Citie is called the lower Baden in respect of the *Lower Baden.* higher Baden of Switzerland that I have already described : both which are about 140 miles distant asunder. It is but little, being seated on the side of a hill, well walled, and hath no more then two Churches, whereof one is within the walles, adjoyning to their Market place, being dedicated to Saint Peter and Paul, and was built by their first Marquesse, as a learned man of the Citie told me. The other standeth without the walles. The Citie is invironed round about with hills greatly replenished with wood. It is the capitall Citie of the countrie where it standeth, which taketh her denomination from this citie, being called the Marquisat of Baden. For there is a Marquesse of this citie, and of the whole territorie *The Marquess* belonging to the Marquisat, who is a soveraigne Prince *of Baden.* of great power and authority. Sometime he keepeth his Court in this citie, as in the winter time ; the Palace of his residence beeing a very sumptuous and Princely building. But all the Sommer time he is most commonly resident partly at the towne of Turlowe a principall member of his Dominion and Principality, whereof I will hereafter make relation ; and partly at his stately Castell of Milberg which is about foure miles distant from the foresaid Turlowe. Also in former times their Prince was wont

199

to keepe his Court in a certaine ancient Castell of great strength that I saw eastward standing upon the side of a hill, and distant some halfe mile from the citie. A place of great antiquity.

The Marquis-
ate created
A.D. 1153.

The Marquisate of this Citie and the circumjacent territorie was first instituted by the Emperour Barbarossa about the yeare of our Lord 1153. who created one Hermannus an Italian Nobleman of the citie of Verona, and a kinsman of his, the first Marquesse. A higher dignity then his predecessours of that country enjoyed, who intituled themselves no more then Earles of Baden. The said Hermannus inlarged this princely title by the addition of another Marquisate, namely that of Hochberg in Brisgoia, not farre from the citie of Friburg, both which Marquisates he attained unto by the marriage of a certaine German Countesse whose name was Judith. Since which time all the succeeding Princes of Baden have ever stiled themselves Marquesses of Baden & Hochberg, to the present Prince Frederick now living. This Prince is a Protestant, but of the Lutheran religion. A man that granteth full liberty of conscience to those his subjects that wil not be reclaimed from the Popish religion; so that he suffereth Masses, and such other Papistical ceremonies in this citie of Baden (which I understood to be wholy Popish) without any such restraint as other German Princes doe use, especially the Count Palatine of Rhene & the Lansgrave of Cassia, who (as I have heard) do not permit any exercise of the Romish Religion in any part of their Dominions.

[p. 467.]

A tolerant
Lutheran.

But having thus far digressed from my discourse of Baden, upon the occasion of mentioning the first institution of the Marquisate & the religion of the present Prince, I will now returne to the description of the city. There is one thing that maketh this citie very famous, namely the Bathes, which are of great antiquity. For authors doe write that they were found out in the time of Marcus Antoninus surnamed Philosophus the seventeenth Emperour of Rome, about the yeare of our Lord 160. who was

Baths of great
antiquity.

Castell of great
... the side of ...
... citie. A pla...

...umjacent ten...
Barbarossa abou...
...one Hermannu...
... and a kinsma...
... ignity then hi...
...intituled then...
The said Herma...
...tion of anothe...
... in Brisgoia, an...
...is Marquesates ...
...certaine German
Since which time
have ever stiled
Hochberg, to the
This Prince is a...
... A man that
...is subjects that
...tion; so that he
...cial ceremonies in
...tood to be wholy
as other German
Palatine of Rhene
...ave heard) do not
...tion in any part of

...my discourse of
the first institution
present Prince, |
the city. There
famous, namely
For authors doe
time of Marcus
enteenth Emper-
...d 160. who was

so delighted with the bathes of this place that he built the
citie for their sakes. Truly they are very admirable for
two respects. First for the heate. Secondly for the multitude. As for the heate it is so extreme that I beleeve they
are the hottest of all Christendome, especially at their
fountaines, whereof I myself had some experience. For
I did put my hand to one of the springs, which was so hot [p. 468.]
that I could hardly endure to handle the water, being of
that force that it would scald my fingers very grievously if *Scalding hot*
I had suffered it to runne upon them till I had but told *water.*
twenty. Yea the heate is so vehement, that it is reported
it will seeth egges, and make them as ready to be eaten
as if they were boyled in water over the fire. Also if one
should cast any kinde of bird or pigge into the water at the
original spring, where it is much hotter then in the bathes
themselves that are derived from the same, it will scalde
off the feathers from the one, and the haire from the other.
Likewise the multitude of them is marvailous, which I
will report, though many incredulous persons will (I
beleeve) applie the old proverbe unto me, that travellers
may lie by authority. The number of them I heard doth
amount to three hundred severall bathes at the least.
Which I did much the more wonder at because when I
was at the bathes of Hinderhove by the Helvetical Baden,
I saw so great a company there, even sixty (which I
esteemed a marvailous number in comparison of the few-
nesse of our English bathes at the City of Bathe in my
country of Somersetshire, where wee have no more then
five) that I thought there were not so many particular
bathes so neare together in any one towne of Europe.
But in this lower Baden the number of them is so exceed- *Three*
ingly multiplied, that it will seeme almost incredible to *hundred baths*
many men that have ever contained themselves within *at Baden.*
the limits of their owne native soyle, and never saw the
wonders of forraine regions. For whereas the bathes of
the lower Baden are distinguished by severall Innes, in
number thirteene, but after an unequall manner, so that
some Innes have more and some lesse: that Inne wherein

[p. 469.]

The virtues
of the baths.

I lay, which was at the signe of the golden Lyon, contained more bathes then all these foresaid threescore of Hinderhove. For in the same Inne were no lesse then threescore & five severall Bathes, as a learned man told me that laie in a house adjoyning to my Inne. All these bathes are devided asunder by a great many roomes of the house, and covered over head; the space that is limited for each bath being square and very narrow, so that in one and the selfe same roome I observed foure or five distinct bathes. All these bathes are of an equall heate, none hotter or colder then an other. Also I heard that they are most frequented in the Sommer time, contrary to our English bathes & those at Hinderhove, which are used only at the spring and autume. The water of the bathes is mingled with matter of three severall kindes, brimstone, salt, and alume, as Munster writeth: unto whome I am beholding for this short ensuing discourse of the vertue of these bathes, as I was before in the description of the bathes of Hinderhove. Those that have tried them have found the vertue of them to be very soveraigne for the curing of divers diseases, as the asthma, which is an infirmity that proceedeth from the difficulty of the breath, the moistnesse of the eyes, the crampe, the coldnesse of the stomacke, the paine of the liver and the spleene proceeding from cold; also it helpeth the dropsie, the griping of the bowels, the stone, the sterility of women: It appeaseth the paine of a womans wombe, keepeth off the white menstruous matter, asswageth the swelling of the thighes, cureth the itch and blisters or whelkes rising in any part of the body; and to be short, it is said to be of greater efficacie for curing of the gowte then any other bathes whatsoever either of Germany or any other country of Christendome.

I saw one thing in this citie that I did not in any other place of Germany. For that morning that I went therhence, I saw a muster of a band of gallant soldiers in the Market place.

Thus much of Baden in the Marquisate, commonly
called lower Baden.

202

I Departed from Baden about eight of the clocke in the [p. 470.]
morning of the fifth day of September being munday,
and came to the towne of Turlowe eighteene miles beyond
it, about sixe of the clocke in the afternoone. The things
that I observed betwixt these two places are these. After
I was passed a few miles beyond Baden, I survayed an
exceeding pleasant and fruitfull country full of corne *Ample corn*
fieldes, whereof some are so ample, especially one that I *fields.*
noted above the rest, that it contayneth at the least sixe
times as much in compasse (according to my estimation)
as the best corne field of that famous mannour of Martock
in Somersetshire neere to the parish of Odcombe where I
was borne. Also that country is passing even and plaine,
and wonderfully replenished with wood. The townes
betwixt any cities I finde to be very frequent and faire,
having gates, and some of them walls. One towne I
passed betwixt Baden and Turlowe, called Etlingen, that *Ettlingen.*
is very memorable for the antiquity thereof. For according to a faire inscription lately written in the towne wall
neere to one of their gates, it appeareth that it was built
about MCX yeares before Christs incarnation. It much
grieved me that a certaine occasion called me away so
suddenly that it deprived me of the opportunity to write
it out, otherwise I had ranked that with these memorables
of Germany. In this towne was that famous Historiographer Francis Irenicus borne, who hath written twelve
bookes of the German Cities. I observed also marvailous *Marvellous*
abundance of fruits in the Marquisate of Baden, especially *abundance of*
of peares, insomuch that the very hedges in the high-way *fruits.*
neere to any towne or village have great store of peare
trees growing in them. Likewise I noted a wonderful
great company of frogges in most places of this territory,
especially in their Lakes. So that a man can hardly walke
by any lake but he shall see great abundance of frogs leape
into the water out of the bankes wherein they shrowd
themselves. I observed also likewise in most places not
only of this territory but also in most of the other parts [p. 471.]
of high Germany neare to any Towne or Village, an extra-

203

Great quantity of vegetables. ordinary great quantity of cabbages, coleworts, turnips, and radishes, which are sowen in their open fields, where are to be seene hundreds of acres sowen in one of their fields. I never saw the like either in France or Italie. For their store is so great that I am perswaded they have a hundred times more of these commodities than we in England, though equall and indifferent quantity of ground be opposed to each other. Moreover I perceived that because God hath so plentifully blessed them with these commodities, that they are not such niggards of them as to watch them in the field, to the end to preserve them from strangers, but rather they give free leave to any passengers to trespasse them, by going boldly into their ground, and taking a convenient quantity of these things for their owne use. For their turnips and radishes are so toothsome and pleasing to the palate, that I have often seene many a poore traveller with a farthing loafe in his hand (for bread is so cheape in many places of Germany, especially in some of the higher parts, that a man may buy a convenient loafe for two of their little tin coynes called fennies that value but little more then an English farthing) goe into their common fields, and take so many turnips and radishes out of a plot, that he hath made an indifferent meale to satisfie nature, & asswage hunger for one poore farthing ; though his meale in an Inne or victualling house might perhaps cost him twenty times as much how thrifty soever he were.

I could see no Snaile in all Germanie but red, like those that I saw a little on this side the Alpes in Savoy, as I have before written. In every part of the country I espied *Hemp beaters.* great store of hemp which the women do beate out of the strannes with certayne pretty instruments made of wood [p. 472.] (such as I have before mentioned in my description of the Grisons country) not decorticating it, or as we call it in Somersetshire scaling it with their fingers, with that extreme labour and difficulty as our English women doe. I never saw country so well wooded (Lombardie only excepted) as all this territory betwixt Baden and Turlowe, the Martian Forrest otherwise called Nigra Silva, so spoken of in many authors, spreading it self over the country, through part whereof I have travelled. Also I attribute very much to all the other parts of Germanie that I travelled through for singular plenty of wood.

My Observations of Turlowe.

THey are so strict in Turlowe for the admittance of *Turlowe.* strangers into the towne, the gates being continually guarded with Halberdiers appointed for the same purpose, that a stranger can very hardly obtaine the favour to come into the towne. So that before I could enter within the gates, I was constrained to send certaine testimonies that I had about me to the Prefect of the Princes Court, whom I found afterward to be a very courteous and affable Gentle man, and one that used me very graciously.

This is a very prety towne, though but little, situate in a most fruitfull playne, having on the North-east-side a certaine hill that is planted round about as full with vine-yards as can be. Upon the top of this hill standeth a very *The Tower of* high and eminent tower which in some places of Germanie *Turlowe.* is to be seene at the least forty miles off as I thinke. From this tower hath the towne his name, being called in Latin Turlacum from the Latin word turris, which signifieth a tower. The Emperor Rodolph that was Earle of Habs-purg before his inauguration to the Empire, conquered this [p. 473.] tower together with the towne, at what time he made warre upon the Marquesse of Baden. This towne was added to the Marquisate by the Emperour Frederick the second, who out of his imperial bounty bestowed the same upon the Prince for the better inlarging of his territory. The towne is well walled, adorned with faire gates, and with *A fair town.* one streete amongst the rest that yeeldeth a beautifull shew, even the same wherein the Princes Palace standeth, the houses being of a goodly heigth. The religion of the towne is Lutheran according to that of their Prince, the principall Pastor being intitled the Superintendent of Tur-lowe. Also the towne is beautified with a goodly schoole which yeeldeth a notable Seminarie of learning. For therein are read most of the liberall sciences. The Princes house is a very magnificent and beautifull Palace, but it was not my good hap to survay the inward beauty thereof. For no strangers can be permitted to enter into any of the German Princes Palaces without great difficulty, whereof I had experience againe afterward at Heidelberg at the Court of the Count Palatine of Rhene. The Prince of Baden was not resident in Turlowe when I was there, but at his stately Castell of Milberg five miles from it, where with certaine German Earles and divers other noblemen of the country, he solaced himselfe at hunting of Deere. I saw the Castell a farre off, which seemed to be a building of great strength and magnificence.

Thus much of Turlowe.

I Departed from Turlowe the sixth day of September being Tuesday about eleven of the clocke in the morning, and came to a solitary house standing in the middle way betwixt Turlowe and Heidelberg, about seven of the clocke in the evening, where I lay that night. This house was fourteene miles beyond Turlowe. After I had travelled a quarter of a mile beyond Turlowe, I observed a matter that made me wonder. For I saw almost a thousand haymakers dispersed abroade in severall great meadowes about the towne. The like I observed all that day in my journey forward. At the first sight of this I imagined that it was their only hay-harvest, and that they had not mowed their meadowes at all before that time : but after more mature consideration of the matter, when as I called to my remembrance the late hay-harvest that I saw in Switzerland about thirteene dayes before, I conceived that it was their second harvest. For the fertilitie of their meadowes is such that they mow them twise in a Sommer. The like whereof I have noted in sundry places of England : but in Germanie it is much more common then with us, in so much that I thinke they use it a hundred to one more then we in England.

206

ES

f learning. In
es. The Prince
ull Palace, but i
d beauty thereof
er into any of the
difficulty, whereof
Heidelberg at th
The Prince if
:n I was there, but
:es from it, when
rs other noblemen
hunting of Deere.
ed to be a building

we

:::r of September
clocke in the morn-
:::::g in the middle
, about seven of the
::::::. This house
:::::- I had travelled
:: ::served a matter
::: a thousand fap-
:-: meadowes about
|- :.:r in my journey
|-:::ed that it was
|.::-not mowed their
|.::er more mature
|-:.:d to my remem-
| Switzerland about
|:: was their second
|::::res is such that
|::a like whereof I
|.. but in Germanie
|:n so much that I
more then we in

OBSERVATIONS OF HEIDELBERG

I departed from the foresaid solitary house the seventh
day of September being Wednesday about sixe of the
clocke in the morning, and came to the noble City of
Heidelberg twelve miles beyond it about noone, being
almost wet to the skinne with a vehement shower of raine.

My Observations of Heidelberg.

Julius Cæsar Scaliger hath written these verses upon
Heidelberg.

NObilis Imperio Franconia dextra potenti
    Belligero nulli Marte secunda viget.
Cum victis ab se pepulit vectigal Alanis,
    Libera Germano nomine Franca fuit.
Nec contenta suis angustis finibus (illi
    Quæ par virtuti terra futura foret?)
Egreditur: superat. Germani ô pectus honoris.
    Victoris victos nomina ferre sat est.
Non aliunde venis, Francusve est Hectoris ullus.
    Quid petis à victo stemmata? tota tua es.

Scaliger's
verses upon
Heidelberg.

[p. 475.]

The territorie wherein this City standeth is called the
lower County Palatine, or the lower Palatinate (whereof
Heidelberg is the Metropolitan City) a very fertill soile,
especially the plaine part thereof that yeeldeth abundance
of all necessaries for the sustenance of man, as store of
wheate of the finest sort, barlie, coleworts, cabbages,
turnips, and radishes, such as I have before spoken of in
the Marquisate of Baden. This Plaine is fairely beautified
with goodly meadowes and pastures also which do feede
plenty of fat bullocks, and sheepe. Likewise the hilly
part is plentifully furnished with vineyardes and chest-nut
trees, & much frequented with Deere, Goates, and Kids.
Neare the City great store of Hearnes doe nestle themselves in the woods upon the hils. This short discourse
of the commodities of .the territorie I thought good to
prefixe before my description of the City by way of an
introduction to the ensuing Treatise. Therefore now I
will relate the particular matters of the City it selfe. And

Heidelberg
the Metro-
politan city of
the lower
Palatinate.

207

The etymology of Heidelberg. I will derive my beginning from the etymologie of the name. Some derive this word Heidelberg from Heydelber which doth signifie black-berries, such as doe grow upon brambles, because in former times there were more of them growing about this City then in any other part of the country. Some from Heydelbeern, that is, myrtle trees, which doe yet grow plentifully upon the hilles about the City. Of this opinion is that learned Paulus Melissus, who calleth Heidelberg urbem myrtileti. Againe there are others that draw the name from the Dutch word Heyden, that signifieth a Nation, because this place was ever wel inhabited with people by reason of the opportunity of the seate. Moreover there are some that affirme it is called Heidelberg quasi Adelberg, that is, a noble

[p. 476.] City, in regard of the nobility, the elegancie, and sweetnesse of the situation thereof. Wherefore seeing there is so great diversity of opinions amongst the learned about the derivation of the name, I will not dispute the matter which is best or worst, but referre it to be discussed by the learned censure of the judicious reader. Truly the situation thereof is very delectable and pleasant. For it standeth in convalli inter fauces montium, that is, in a narrow valley which is on both sides beset with hils, and those very commodious. For they are planted with many fruitfull vineyards. Also it is most pleasantly watered

The river Neckar. with the famous river Neccarus, otherwise called Nicrus, that runneth by the north side of the City. And it is of so great note, that they commonly esteeme it the third river of Germany next to the Danubius and the Rhene. It riseth in Suevia even in the black Forrest which is called in Latin Nigra Sylva about the space of foure houres journey from the fountaine of Danubius, and at length exonerateth it selfe into the Rhene, being before multiplied with some other rivers, as the Cocharus and the Iaxus, which doe infuse themselves into the Neccar not farre from the towne of Wimpina in Suevia abovesaid. I observed a goodly wooden bridge built over the Neccar, the fairest certainly that I saw in Germany, but not the longest,

etymologie of the
'erg from Heydel-
such as doe gov
s there were ma-
in any other pa
ern, that is, ay
on the hilles abou
d Paulus Melissus
eti. Againe that
t the Dutch wor
ause this place ra
ason of the oppo-
re some that affirm,
'3, that is, a noble
egancie, and swee-
efore seeing there is
st the learned abou
dispute the matte
to be discussed by
reader. Truly the
d pleasant. For th
them, that is, in t
beset with his wal
planted with many
pleasantly watered
wise called Nicra
City. And it is of
deeme it the third
lus and the Rhene
most which is called
le of foure houses
lus, and at length
y before multipli
lus and the Imus,
ccar not farre from
said. I observed
Neccar, the fairest
not the longest,

supported with sixe huge stony pillars strongly rammed into the water, and very fairely covered over head with an arched roof of timber-worke. At the farther end whereof there standeth a faire tower on the banke of the Neccar which doth very much beautifie the bridge. This river is very commodious to the City of Heidelberg in two respects. First for that being navigable it carieth a kind *Boats on the* of rude boate called of the Latines ratis (such as I have *Neckar.* seene in divers other places of Germany, and also in France, used upon their greater rivers for carrying of hay, timber, wood, &c.) which is most commonly laden partly with timber for building, and partly with wood for fire that commeth out of the Forrest called Ottonica a part of the [p. 477.] Hercynia not farre from the city of Heidelberg; and by this Neccar the said commodities are brought first to Heidelberg for the furnishing of the City, and from that to the Rhene, wherewith it mingleth it selfe a little on this side Spira, and therehence to all the westerne Cities and townes situate on both sides of the Rhene as farre as the towne of Bing. Secondly, because it ministreth great abundance of good fishes to the City, especially the delicate barbils.

The City is strongly walled, and hath foure faire gates *The City.* in the walles, and one very goodly streete above the rest both for breadth and length. For it is at the least an English mile long: and garnished with many beautifull houses, whereof some have their fronts fairely painted, which doe yeeld an excellent shew. Also it hath sixe Churches. Namely that of the holy Ghost: St. Peters: The Church in the Princes Palace: the French Church: a Church in the suburbes: And the Predicatorie church which belonged once to the Dominican Friers. But the Church of the holy Ghost which adjoyneth to their great market place, is the fairest of all, being beautified with two singular ornaments above the other Churches that doe greatly grace the same: the one the Palatine Librarie, the other the monuments of their Princes. The Palatine *The Palatine* Librarie is kept by that most excellent and generall Schollar *Library.*

CORYAT'S CRUDITIES

Mr. Janus Gruterus the Princes Bibliothecarie, of whom
I have reason to make a kind and thankeful mention,
because I received great favours of him in Heidelberg.
For he entertained me very courteously in his house,
shewed me the Librarie, and made meanes for my admis-
sion into the Princes Court. Well hath this man deserved
of the common-weale of good letters, because he hath
much benefited and illustrated it by his elegant workes,
as his Animadversions upon all the workes of Seneca the
Philosopher, and his Fax artium, which though it be

[p. 478.] nothing but the compiling together of other mens workes,
yet the singular industrie that he hath shewed in it together
with his fine methode, doth deserve no small praise. A

*A scholarly
librarian.* man that for his exquisite learning hath beene received into
the friendship of some of the greatest Schollars of
Christendome, especially of Justus Lipsius, betwixt whom
divers elegant Epistles have passed that are published to
the world. I observed him to be a very sweet and
eloquent discourser. For he speaketh a most elegant and
true Ciceronian phrase which is graced with a facill &
expedite deliverie. In so much that I dare parallell him
in a manner for the excellency of his Latin tongue with
Mr. Grynæus of Basil whom I have before so much
extolled. But I will cease to praise my friend Mr.
Gruterus, because his owne worth doth more truly commend him then I shall ever be able to doe with my
inelegant stile, and so I will returne to that famous Palatine Librarie. It is built over the roofe of the body of
the Church. A place most beautifull, and divided into
two very large and stately roomes that are singular well
furnished with store of bookes of all faculties. Here are

*Ancient
manuscripts.* so many auncient manuscripts, especially of the Greeke
and Latin Fathers of the Church, as no Librarie of all
Christendome, no not the Vatican of Rome nor Cardinall
Bessarions of Venice can compare with it. Besides there
is a great multitude of manuscripts of many other sorts,
in so much that Mr. Gruterus told he could shew in this
Librarie at the least a hundred more manuscripts then

thecarie, of whom
ankeful mention,
m in Heidelberg
sly in his house,
nes for my admi-
this man deserved
, because he hath
us elegant workes,
rkes of Seneca the
hich though it be
other mens workes,
hewed in it togethe
10 small praise. A
beene received into
ea'est Schollars of
sius, betwixt whom
at are published to
a very sweet and
a most elegant and
zed with a facill be
l dare parallell him
Latin tongue with
.e before so much
e my friend Mr.
th more truly con-
e to doe with my
o that famous Pala-
fe of the body of
and divided into
t are singular well
aculties. Here are
llr of the Greeke
no Librarie of all
tome nor Cardinall
it. Besides there
many other sorts,
could shew in this
manuscripts then

OBSERVATIONS OF HEIDELBERG

Mr. James the publique Bibliothecarie of Oxford could in his famous Universitie Librarie. For what bookes that Librarie hath or hath not he knoweth by Mr. James his Index or Catalogue that was printed in Oxford. Amongst other bookes that he shewed me one was a faire large parchment booke written by the great grandfather of Fredericke the fourth that was the Count Palatine when I was there. Truly the beauty of this Librarie is such both for the notable magnificence of the building, and [p. 479.] the admirable variety of bookes of all sciences and languages, that I beleeve none of those notable Libraries *Notable* in ancient times so celebrated by many worthy historians, *Libraries.* neither that of the royall Ptolomies of Alexandria, burnt by Julius Cæsar, not that of King Eumenes at Pergamum in Greece, nor Augustus his Palatine in Rome, nor Trajans Ulpian, nor that of Serenus Sammonicus, which he left to the Emperor Gordianus the yonger, nor any other whatsoever in the whole world before the time of the invention of printing, could compare with this Palatine. Also I attribute so much unto it that I give it the precedence above all the noble Libraries I saw in my travels, which were especially amongst the Jesuits in Lyons, Spira, and Mentz. Howbeit Mr. Gruterus will pardon me I hope if I preferre one Librarie of my owne nation before the Palatine, even that of our renowned University of Oxford, whereof the foresaid Mr. James is a keeper. For indeede I beleeve it containeth a few more books (though not many) then this of Heidelberg. There hapned one disaster unto me when I was in this Librarie. For shortly *A disaster.* after I came within it, and had survayed but a few of the principall bookes, it chanced that two yong Princes of Anhalt which are descended from the most ancient Princely family of all Germanie, came suddenly into the roome upon me, being usherd by their golden-chained Gentlemen. Whereupon I was constrained to withdraw my selfe speedily out of the Librarie, all the attendance being given unto the Princes: by which sinister accident I lost the opportunity of seeing those memorable antiquities and

211

rarities which Mr. Gruterus intended to have communicated unto me, and so consequently I my selfe the same to my country. Let this therefore suffice for the Palatine Librarie.

The second ornament of this Church of the Holy Ghost is the Chappel wherein the monuments of their Princes are contained. This standeth at the East end of the Church, being a most elegant roome, and is inclosed on one side with certaine yron dores made lattise-wise, and for the most part locked, that I could not procure the meanes to see them, my learned friend Maister Gruterus being busie with the foresaid young Princes. Therefore

for these monuments I must trust my eares (the worst witnesses) rather then my eyes. There I heard were buried these Princes, Rupertus Senior Duke of Bavaria, Count Palatine of Rhene, and King of the Romanes, the founder of the Church of the holy Ghost; and his wife Elizabeth, who dyed about the yeare 1410. also two Counts Palatine Rodolphus & Ludovicus under one altar, whereof the first died anno 1209. and the other 1319. againe Frederick that died in the yeare 1476. also Wolphangus Count Palatine of Rhene that died in the yeare 1558. All these lye within the said Chappell with other Princes and Princesses. But the Epitaphes which I thinke are elegant to grace the memory of so great persons, I could not obtaine. Notwithstanding what is wanting of those Epitaphes within the Chappell, shall be a little supplyed with one most excellent Epitaph that I found in the body of the Church written upon the monument of Philip Count Palatine of Rhene, one of their worthiest Princes, who was very famous in his life time for many memorable acts, especially for freeing the noble citie Vienna from the siege of the Turkes. Seeing I was frustrated of the other Princes Epitaphes in the Chappell which I hoped to have brought with me into England, being very unwilling to leese this also which I saw was worthy the carrying over the Sea, I apprehended it with my pen while the Preacher was in his pulpit : for I doubted

have communi-
selfe the same
for the Palatine

the Holy Ghost
of their Princes
last end of the
...d is inclosed on
lattise-wise, and
not procure the
Maister Gruterus
...: Therefore
cares (the worst
...re I heard were
Duke of Bavaria,
...e Romanes, the
...os ; and his wife
...t 1410. also two
... under one altar,
... the other 1314
... 1216. also Wal-
... ...d in the yeare
... ...ll with other
... which I thinke
... great persons, I
... is wanting of
... ...ll be a little
...ph that I found in
the monument of
... their worthiest
... time for many
... the noble citie
... Seeing I was
... in the Chappell
... into England,
... which I saw was
... ...ended it with
... for I doubted

least if I had differred it till the end of the sermon, the
dores might have bene sodainly shut, & so I should have
bin defeated of the opportunity.   The monument it selfe *Monument to*
is in that side of the Church where the pulpit standeth, *Count Philip.*
being inserted into one of the main pillers of the church,
and invironed round about with a pretty inclosure or rayle [p. 481.]
made of yron worke.   There is represented his Statue at
length carved in milke-white Alabaster with his glittering
Armour gilted, holding a short Pole-axe in his right hand,
and a sword in his left; that part of the monument where
his Statue standeth, is wonderfull curiously wrought with
very exquisite workes in stone, wherein are represented
many pretty histories.   At the toppe are erected his armes
and scutchin.   Under the which, betwixt his armes and
the higher part of his Statue, his Epitaphe is written in
touchstone.   It seemeth a double Epitaph.   For one is
Latin, and the other Dutch.   The Latin after these tedious
preambles I do now at length present unto thee.

Cætera qui circum lustras monumenta viator,   *The epitaph.*
    Hæc quoque non longa est perlege pauca mora.
Si ducis audita est forsan tibi fama Philippi,
    Clara Palatinæ quem tulit Aula domus:
Qui modò Pannoniam defendit ab hoste Viennam,
    Et solvit trepidos obsidione viros ;
Tunc cum Threicii vastarent omnia Turcæ,
    Et tremerent subito Norica regna metu.
Mox etiam implevit magnum virtutibus orbem,
    Utilis hinc armis, utilis indè togâ.
Illius hâc tegitur corpus venerabile terrâ,
    Hic animam, hîc vitam reddidit ille Deo.
Quò te si pietas, si quid movet inclyta virtus,
    Junctaque cum summâ nobilitate fides:
Huic opta ut cineres placidâ cum pace quiescant,
    Condita nec tellus durior ossa premat.
Nam pius ad cœli sublatus spiritus arces,
    Cum Christo vivit tempus in omne suo.
        Decessit 4. Non. Julii
        Anno Dom. M. D. Xlviii.

CORYAT'S CRUDITIES

Ætatis suæ Xliii. cujus P. F. Memoriæ Dux
Otto Henricus Comes Palatinus
Frater amantissimus M. H. F. C.
Anno Dom. M. D. L.

Thus much concerning the Church of the Holy Ghost.

BEsides this foresaid Church, there are two things more which doe very notably adorne and beautifie this stately Citie, the first the most gorgious Palace of the Prince, which is commonly called in Dutch Das curfur stelich Sloss. The second, the famous University. The Princes Palace I will first speake of. It is exceeding difficult for a stranger to enter into one of the Germane Princes Courts (as I have before said in my description of Turlowe) except he hath some friend living in the same, which I found verified by mine owne experience at the Count Palatines Court. For I could not possibly be admitted without some speciall and extraordinary favour, which was this. Master Gruterus understanding by my owne report that I was acquainted with our noble Ambassadour Sir Henry Wotton then resident with the Signiorie of Venice, the fame of whose excellent learning and generose qualities hath greatly spread itselfe in Heidelberg (for there hath he beene heretofore, and Honorably entertained at the Princes Court) counselled me to goe to a learned Doctor of the Civill Lawe dwelling in the Citie, whose name was Master Lingelsemius, heretofore Tutor to Fredericke the fourth, who was then the Count Palatine when I was in Heidelberg, (and therfore the better able to procure his friend accesse to the Court) and a familiar acquaintance of Sir Henry Wotton. Whereupon I repaired to his house, insinuating my selfe partly with a token from Master Gruterus, and partly by the meanes of Sir Henry Wottons name, which was so acceptable unto him, that he entertained me after a very debonaire and courteous maner, and sent one of his men with mee to the Prefect of the Princes Court, who gave me admittance into the Palace;

The Princes Palace.

Master Lingelsemius Doctor of Civil Law.

214

I noted the situation thereof to be very pleasant. For it *Palace of* is seated at the South side of the Citie upon the side of *Heidelberg.* an eminent hill, having as sweete an ayre as any Palace whatsoever in all Germanie. At the foote of the same hill on the left hand, there is a very faire building, which serveth for the Chancerie house of the Palatinate, wherein matters of controversie are handled; and from thence there is a very tedious & difficult ascent by a steepe stonie way to the Palace it selfe. I learned at the Court that there was heretofore an other Palace besides this, situated upon the very top of the same hill, which hapned to be utterly destroyed in the yeare 1537. as it appeareth by certaine elegant Elegiacal verses that worthy Jacobus Micyllus of the Citie of Strasburg, wrote to his learned friend Joachimus Camerarius about the yeare and day of the ruine thereof, by a certaine memorable yet rufull accident; for the fire of heaven it selfe consumed it. The *The Palace* Telum trisulcum Jovis (I meane the lightning) striking *destroyed by* casually a heape of Gunpowder that was kept in a certaine *lightning* *A.D.* 1537. roome of the Palace, which no sooner tooke fire, but immediately in the very twinckling of an eye it burnt up the whole building, and scattered the stones (a most lamentable spectacle to behold) farre asunder, some downe to the present Palace where the Prince now dwelleth, and some to the Citie, to the great detriment of both places. The ruines of the same palace are yet shewed (as I heard) upon the top of the hill. But now I will returne againe to the Princes palace where he keepeth his residence; every thing that I saw there did yeeld matter of speciall marke and magnificence. The father of Fredericke the fourth, and Prince Fredericke himselfe have beene great builders. His father built all the part of the Palace on the left hand of the first Court, which is beautified with a very stately frontispice, and distinguished with great varietie of not-able workmanship. But Prince Fredericke hath built an [p. 484.] other part of the Palace which doth farre excell that; even all that gorgeous building at the entrance, which by reason of the most admirable and rare sumptuousnesse of the

215

Architecture, being built all with square stone, and garnished with goodly statues, doth adde infinite grace to that part of the Palace. Both the Fronts of the Palace whereof I now speake, as well that without looking towards the Citie, as the other within towards the Court, doe present workmanship of great state, as I have already said. But there is great difference betwixt them. For the inward front is much more glorious and resplendent then the other. The principall ornament that graceth it, is the multitude of faire statues (which the outward Front wanteth) very loftily advanced towards the fairest part of the Court, whereof there are foure distinct degrees or Series made one above another. The same statues are carved in a singular faire milk-white stone, which seemeth as beautifull as the fairest Alabaster, and formed in a very large proportion, expressing all the parts of a mans body, and done with that artificiall curiositie, that I beleeve were those famous statuaries Polycletus and Praxiteles alive againe, they would praise the same, and confesse they were not able to amend them. For they imitate the true naturall countenance and living shape of those heroicall and Princely Peeres, whom they represent. Most of them

are the statues of the famous Palatine Princes to the last of them Fredericke the fourth. Also Emperours, Kings and Queenes are there pourtrayed. This Front is raysed to a very great height, and decked with marveilous curious devices at the top, all which ornaments concurring together doe exhibit to the eyes of the spectator a shew most incomparable. Truely for my owne part I was so exceedingly delighted with the sight of this rare frontispice, that I must needes confesse I attribute more unto it, not out

of any partiall humour or overweening phantasie, but according to the upright sinceritie of an impartiall opinion, then to the Front of any Palace whatsoever I saw in France, Italy or Germanie. Yea, I will not doubt to derogate so much from the Fronts of the French Kings palaces which I saw both in Paris and Fountaine Beleau;

of the Duke of Venice, of that exquisite building before mentioned which belongeth to one of the sixe Companies or Fraternities of Venice, adjoyning to St. Roches Church, where I heard that heavenly musicke; so much I say doe I derogate from the fronts of al these Palaces, that the fairest of them doth vale bonnet (in my opinion) to this royall inward front of the Count Palatines Palace. The lower part of the same front doth containe one of those sixe Churches whereof I have before made mention, viz. The Courtly Church, where the Prince & his family of the *The Court* Court heareth divine service and sermons, and the higher *Church.* part many gorgeous roomes for the Princes use: wherein many noble Peeres of Germanie and France solaced them-selves when I was at the Court, the number of whom was so great that I heard there were then resident at the court forty worthy personages of great note out of both Nations, besides their followers, Gentlemen that ruffled it very gallantly. But to conclude my narration of this part of the Palace, certainly it is so regall a structure that I conjecture it cost at the least forty thousand pounds sterling. This Prince hath newly built a very stately long porch also at the entrance of the Palace, which was not throughly finished when I was there.

There is a notable thing to be seene in this Palace, the sight whereof it was not my hap to enjoy, because I heard nothing of it before I went out of the Palace: a matter of great antiquity. Namely certaine ancient stony pillars, *Five pillars* in number five, which the Emperor Carolus Magnus above *brought from* eight hundred and fifty yeares since brought from the City *Italy.* of Ravenna in Italie, and placed them afterward in his [p. 486.] Palace of Ingelheim a place of high Germany within a few miles of the City of Mentz, where he was borne, and oftentimes kept his Court. The same pillars were of late yeares removed from the said Ingelheim to Heidelberg by the Prince Philip of whom I have before made mention in my discourse of the Church of the holy Ghost, who erected them in this Palace whereof I now speake, and are there shewed for a principall ancient monument to this day.

217

But some of the Gentlemen of the Princes family did sufficiently recompence my losse of the sight of these ancient pillars by shewing me a certayne peece of worke *The great tun* that did much more please my eies then the sight of those *of Heidelberg.* pillars could have done. For it is the most remarkable and famous thing of that kinde that I saw in my whole journey, yea so memorable a matter, that I thinke there was never the like fabrick (for that which they shewed me was nothing else than a strange kinde of fabrick) in all the world, and I doubt whether posterity will ever frame so monstrously strange a thing : it was nothing but a vessel full of wine. Which the Gentlemen of the Court shewed me after they had first conveighed me into divers wine cellars, where I saw a wondrous company of extraordinary great vessels, the greatest part whereof was replenished with Rhenish wine, the totall number contayning one hundred and thirty particulars. But the maine vessel above all the rest, that superlative moles unto which I now bend my speech, was shewed me last of all standing alone by it selfe in a wonderfull vast roome. I must needes say I was suddenly strooken with no small admiration upon the first sight thereof. For it is such a stupendious masse (to give it the same epitheton that I have done before to the beauty of St. Marks streete in Venice) that I am perswaded it will affect the gravest and constantest *One of the* man in the world with wonder. Had this fabrick beene *wonders of the* extant in those ancient times when the Colossus of Rhodes, *world.* the Labyrinths of Ægypt and Creta, the Temple of Diana [p. 487.] at Ephesus, the hanging gardens of Semiramis, the Tombe of Mausolus, and the rest of those decantated miracles did flourish in their principall glory, I thinke Herodotus and Diodorus Siculus would have celebrated this rare worke with their learned stile as well as the rest, and have consecrated the memory thereof to immortality as a very memorable miracle. For indeede it is a kinde of monstrous miracle, and that of the greatest sise for a vessell that this age doth yeeld in any place whatsoever (as I am verily perswaded) under the cope of heaven, Pardon me

I pray thee (gentle Reader) if I am something tedious in discoursing of this huge vessel. For as it was the strangest spectacle that I saw in my travels: so I hope it will not be unpleasant unto thee to reade a ful description of all the particular circumstances thereof: and for thy better satisfaction I have inserted a true figure thereof in this place (though but in a small forme) according to a certaine patterne that I brought with me from the City of Franckford, where I saw the first type thereof sold. Also I have added an imaginary kinde of representation of my selfe upon the toppe of the same, in that manner as I stood there with a cup of Rhenish wine in my hand. The roome where it standeth is wonderfull vast (as I said before) and capacious, even almost as bigge as the fairest hall I have seene in England, and it containeth no other thing but the same vessell. It was begunne in the yeare 1589. and ended 1591. one Michael Warner of the City of Landavia being the principall maker of the worke. It containeth a hundred and two and thirty fuders, three omes, and as many firtles. These are peculiar names for certain German measures. Which I will reduce to our English computation. Every fuder countervaileth our tunne, that is, foure hogsheads, and is worth in Heidel berg fifteene pound sterling. So then those hundred two and thirty fuders are worth nineteene hundred and fourescore poundes of our English money, The ome is a measure whereof six do make a fuder, the three being worth seven pounds ten shillings. The firtle is a measure that countervaileth six of our pottles: every pottle in Heidelberg is worth twelve pence sterling. So the three firtles containing eighteene pottles, are worth eighteene shillings. The totall summe that the wine is worth which this vessell containeth, doth amount to nineteene hundred fourescore and eight pounds and eight odde shillings. This strange newes perhaps will seeme utterly incredible to thee at the first: but I would have thee beleeve it. For nothing is more true. Moreover thou must consider that this vessel is not compacted of boords as other barrels

The tun three years in building.

[p. 488.]

The wine contained in the tun is worth £1988. 8s.

219

are, but of solid great beames, in number a hundred and twelve, whereof every one is seven and twenty foot long. *The tun's* Also each end is sixteene foote high, and the belly *dimensions.* eighteene. It is hooped with wonderous huge hoopes of yron (the number whereof is sixe and twenty) which doe containe eleven thousand pound weight. It is supported on each side with ten marvailous great pillars made of timber, and beautified at both the ends and the toppe with the images of Lyons, which are the Princes armes, two Lyons at each end, a faire scutchin being affixed to every image. The wages that was paid to the workeman for *Its cost.* his labour, (the Prince finding all necessary matter for his worke, and allowing him his dyet) came to two thousand three hundred and fourescore Florens of Brabant, each Floren being two shillings of our money, which summe amounteth to eleven score and eighteene pounds sterling. When the Cellerer draweth wine out of the vessel, he ascendeth two severall degrees of wooden staires made in the forme of a ladder which containe seven and twenty steps or rungs as we call them in Somersetshire, and so goeth up to the toppe. About the middle whereof there [p. 489.] is a bung-hole or a venting orifice into the which he con- veigheth a pretty instrument of some foote and halfe long, made in the forme of a spout, wherewith he draweth up the wine, and so poureth it after a pretty manner into the glasse or &c. out of the same instrument. I my selfe had experience of this matter. For a Gentleman of the Court accompanied me to the toppe together with one of the Cellerers, and exhilarated me with two sound draughts of *The wine.* Rhenish wine. For that is the wine that it containeth. But I advise thee gentle Reader whatsoever thou art that intendest to travell into Germany, and perhaps to see Heidelberg, and also this vessell before thou commest out of the City; I advise thee (I say) if thou dost happen to ascend to the toppe thereof to the end to tast of the wine, that in any case thou dost drinke moderately, and not so much as the sociable Germans will persuade thee unto. For if thou shouldest chance to over-swill thy selfe with

OBSERVATIONS OF HEIDELBERG

wine, peradventure such a giddinesse wil benumme thy braine, that thou wilt scarce finde the direct way downe from the steepe ladder without a very dangerous precipitation. Having now so copiously described unto thee the vessell, I have thought good to adde unto this my poore description, certaine Latin verses made by a learned German in praise of the vessell, which I have selected out of the coppy that I bought at Franckford, being printed at the Universitie of Leyden in Holland by one Henry Hœstenius Anno 1608. and dedicated to a certaine Noble man called Hippolytus Lord President of the Princes Chancerie Court.

The verses are these.

OTia dum vario partiri quemque labore,
    Exercere suas experiorque vices.
Nauta rates, enses miles, rus curvus arator,
    Piscator tractat retia, pastor oves.
Me quoque dum studium novitatis dulce tenebat,
    Nescio quod rari verso laboris opus.
Vas immane, ingens, quod fortè jacere videbam,
    Vas majus nostro robore pondus erat.
Diogenis tanti præ pondere Vasis habebat
    Dolioli parvi parva figura nihil.
Nec qui projectis turbabat montibus æquor
    Hoc versare Cyclops sustinuisset onus.
Nec, qui ducebant, potuissent ducere plures
    Trojanum, Trojæ flebile robur, equum.
Voluendo tanto desperabundus abibam,
    Par oneri nec enim, nec satis unus eram.
Quis mihi conanti tantum superare laborem
    Attulerit sociam certus amicus opem?
Vos Oratores, quos has Fredericus in oras
    Misit in auxilium pacis, adeste, precor.
Forsan erit, nostrâ per vos hac mole levatâ,
    Nonnihil hoc vestrum quo relevetur onus.
Ergo jugum mecum superate quod indicat arcem,
    Quâ vas artifices hoc statuere manus.

Verses in praise of the tun.

[p. 490.]

221

Nec dubia est, facilis nos semita ducet euntes,
    Omnibus est signis & via nota suis.
Est locus excultis genialis & utilis hortis,
    Collibus apricis, pampineisque jugis.
Quâ Nicer excelsas Pater alluit inclytus arces,
    Et prono Rhenum spumifer amne subit.
Quâ myrtillorum montem probat esse Melissus,
    Qui Myrtilleti nomen in astra tulit.
Hìc specimen natura loci, geniusque locavit,
    Copiæ & hìc cornu fertile, dixit, habe.
Ubertas rerum nullis feliciùs arvis,
    Hic Bacchi, hìc Cereris copia tanta venit.
Horrea distendant ut fruges sæpè, coloni
    Respondet votis tam benè cultus ager.
Sæpè per autumnum superantia munera Bacchi,
    Condere ritè suas copia nescit opes.
Quin sua sæpè nocet lascivis copia Faunis,
    Quo nimìs occœcat prodigus usus opûm.

[p. 491.]

Et dubitamus adhuc dare pectora grata datori
    Nostra Deo, tantis cœlitùs aucta bonis?
Sed designatis ne collibus altiùs istis,
    Terminus hic positus, progrediamur, erit.
Collibus Heroes prisci his habitasse feruntur,
    Servat adhuc sedes signa decusque Patrum.
Sed præter veterum monumenta augusta Parentum
    Nil prius Aonidum vertice collis habet.
Dum licuit cultos hos olìm intravimus hortos,
    Et posthac tempus visere forsan erit.
Nunc age, fas magni Vas instar visere montis,
    Divinâ structum Palladis arte cadum.
Vel Cuppam, vel quo te molem nomine dicam,
    Seu monstrum, salvâ te pietate, vocem.
Authorem primam si Pallada vasis habemus,
    (Nam rerum artificem tot posuere Deam.)
Invideat Bacchus, fiatque injuria Divæ,
    Cum Baccho quid enim mascula Pallas habet?
Vitisator Dux acer ades; tibi nostra parentet,
    Te Musa authorem Dux Casimire canit.

222

OBSERVATIONS OF HEIDELBERG

[p. 492.]

Pro charo Princeps dum sceptra Nepote gerebas,
    Pace Palatinam multiplicante domum.
Inter, quæ domus alta colit, decora alta Parentum,
    Qui tantæ, optabas, conderet artis opus.
Nobilis author, adest, urbs quem Landavia misit,
    Fine potita suo gloria ponit opus.
Ponit opus, decus acre Ducum, non quale priorum,
    Ætas vel vidit, nulla vel ausa manus.
Non, mihi si præstent mirandam Dædalus artem
    Ipse, Syracusius vel faber ille suam :
Immanem molem satìs hanc describere possem,
    Antè suo voluam pondus onusque loco.
Clara Rhodos jactet miraclum immane Colossum,
    Et Laurentiacum Bœtica terra suum,
Et Batavi currum, qui prævolat ocyor Euro,
    Quodque fide majus nullo agitatur equo.
Quisque suum jactet : par huic tamen esse negamus
    Dolium, onus, molem, pondus, & artis opus.
Laude opus hoc dignum est : oculos cum cætera pascant,
    Spectaclum ventres hoc satiare potest.

Verses in praise of the tun.

Thus finally I shut up the description of this strange Vessell with a certaine admirable thing that I heard reported of it in Frankford, after my departure from Heidelberg, that the same being full of Wine was once drunke out in the space of eight dayes, at the time of a certain noble meeting of Princely Gallants at the Court.

Seeing I am now writing of the memorables of the Princes Palace, I will make mention of the Prince him selfe that is the Lord of the Palace, and of his Princely titles or Electorall dignitie. But first of his titles. Thus he is most commonly stiled : Serenissimus Princeps, &c. Elector, Comes Palatinus ad Rhenum, Sacri Romani Imperii Archidapifer, & Bavariæ Dux. He is the chiefe Elector Prince of the Empire above the other secular Princes, which are the Duke of Saronie, and the Marquesse of Brandenburg, having the superioritie of them in these two respects. First in that he giveth his suffrage in

The Prince's titles.

223

the election of the Emperour before them. Secondly, because he taketh prioritie of place above them at any imperiall Diet. For he sitteth on the right hand of the Emperour, being the next man to the King of Bohemia. *Archidapifer.* The reason why he is intitled Archidapifer (which word doth signifie the principall Sewer to the Emperour) is because he is chiefe Sewer to the Emperour, and attendeth him at Table the first meale that hee maketh after his Election, according to an ancient custome that hath beene continually observed at the Emperours election any time these six hundred yeares and a little more, by the first institution of Otho the third Germane Emperor of that name. As for his title of Palatinus added to Comes, the *Etymology of* opinions of the learned doe much differ about the etymo-*Palatine.* logie of the word; for some say it is derived from the [p. 493.] word Palas which was heretofore the name of a Country called Capellatium, inhabited in former times by the ancient Intuergi, a people that dwelt in that part of the Palatinate where Heidelberg now standeth. Of this opinion is Gaspar Peucerus and learned Beatus Rhenanus. Whereof the later citeth a place out of Ammianus Marcellinus for the better confirmation of the matter. Others draw the word Palatinus from Palatium, because the Count Palatine is an eminent Peere of the Emperours Palace : for indeede Counts Palatine were heretofore the Prefects of Palaces, especially in the Courts of Emperours, where they bare the like authoritie to him that was in times past Major Domus in the French Kings Court. Againe, there are some that affirme it hath his name from a certaine Castle situate in the middle of the Rhene, called Pfaltz, which word signifieth in the high Dutch a Palace. It was my chance to passe by this foresaid Castle in my journey by water upon the Rhene betwixt the Cities of Mentz and Colen, as I will hereafter report. From the same word Pfaltz this Prince is most commonly the Pfaltsgrave of Rhene; but that etymologie, which I approve above the rest, is the derivation of Palatinus from Palas the Name of the Countrey : for it maketh more for the dignitie and

them. Secondly,
ove them at any
right hand of the
King of Bohemia.
...ter (which word
the Emperour) is
our, and attendeth
maketh after his
ne that hath beene
s election any time
more, by the first
e Emperor of that
...ded to Comes, the
...r about the etymo-
derived from the
name of a Country
...ner times by the
in that part of the
standeth. Of this
d Beatus Rhenanus.
Ammianus Marcel-
the matter. Others
, because the Court
...rours Palace: for
...: the Prefects of
...perours, where they
in times past Major
Againe, there are
m a certaine Castle
...alled Pfaltz, which
Palace. It was my
: in my journey by
...ties of Mentz and
...om the same word
the Pfaltzgrave of
approve above the
...m Palas the Name
...r the dignitie and

is at this day shewed in the Palace
Heidelberg

OBSERVATIONS OF HEIDELBERG

honour of the Prince, to derive his name from that then from any other thing, because it argueth the greater antiquity of his title. For Ammianus Marcellinus that calleth the tract about Heidelberg, Palas, lived for more then a thousand & two hundred yeares since, even in the time of the Emperor Julian the Apostata. Moreover the addition of these words (Ad Rhenum) to Comes Palatinus groweth herehence, because the greater part of his territorie doth lye by the river Rhene. As for the originall of this renowned stocke of the Casimires (for that is the *Family name* gentilitiall name of the Count Palatines familie) it is *of the Prince* derived from Arnolphus surnamed Malus the eldest sonne *Palatine.* of the Emperor Arnolphus by his first wife Agnes. So [p. 494.] that it is above seven hundred yeares old. Likewise the Electoral dignity of this Princely familie is of good antiquity. For it beganne about the yeare 1003. At what time the hereditarie succession of the Empire was converted to an election; Henry the Count Palatine being the first Elector of this familie, who with other Princes Spiritual and Temporal elected Henry the second surnamed * Sanctus (the first of all the German Emperors that was chosen by the Suffrages of the Elector Princes) into the Empire in the yeare abovesaid; but now I will speake a little of him that was Count Palatine of Rhene at the time of my being in Heidelberg, namely Fredericke the *Frederick IV* fourth of that name, who died as I understand this last *Count* Sommer. He was a man of most heroicall and Princely *Palatine.* parts. He matched in the Princely house of Orange. For he marryed the noble Lady Ludovica daughter to William that worthy Prince of Orange that was slaine at the Towne of Delph in Holland, and sister to that renowned Prince Maurice generall Commander of the

* Hee was so called for his most rare continencie, because though he had a most faire Lady to his wife called Cunegunda, and did continually lie in the same Bed with her: Yet both of them with a mutuall consent abstained from carnall copulation and preserved their virginity till their death. The like example I thinke is not to bee found at this Day in Christendome.

Armies of the united Provinces: hee was much addicted
to learning, and accounted a great Mecœnas and patron
of the Muses. And (which is the principall thing of all)
hee was a singular Nutritius and foster-father of the
Church. For hee professed the same reformed Religion
that wee doe in England, and hath utterly rooted Poperie
out of his Dominion, which first began to be suppressed in
the Palatinate by Fredericke the second of that name
Count Palatine of Rhene, in the yeare 1546. Besides hee
deserveth great praise for one most princely vertue, even

His royal hospitality. his royall hospitalitie; for he hath the fame to be the most
magnificent House-keeper of all the Germane Princes, the
Duke of Saxonie (though his superiour in largenesse of
Dominion and opulencie of estate) the Marquesse of
Brandenburge, the Duke of Brunswicke, and all the other

[p. 495.] Soveraigne Princes of Germanie, being inferiour unto him
in this most laudable exercise of Hospitalitie; who was
sometimes so passing bountifull, that I have heard there
have beene a hundred severall Tables in his Palace filled
at one meale with ghests, and very bountifully furnished
with meate. It was my chance when I came to the Citie
of Colen, to see his Effigies very curiously made, answerable to the life, according to the originall patterne whereof
I have procured another Figure to be made, as truely
correspondent to the first, as my Carver could by imitation
attaine unto, and have placed it here for the better ornament
of this discourse of the Count Palatine. Likewise I have
added six Latine verses, which I found subscribed to his
Effigies in the foresaid Citie of Colen, with mention of
which I wil end this treatise of the titles attributed to the
Count Palatine of Rhene, and the narration of Prince
Fredericke the fourth.

[p. 496.] Thus much of the Pfaltzgraves Palace, his Electorall
dignitie, titles, and Princely hospitalitie.

[p. 497.]
University of Heidelberg. WHereas I said before that there are two things which
doe notably beautifie this Citie, besides the Church
of the Holy Ghost, namely the Princes Palace, and the Uni-

versitie; having ended my description of the former two, I will now make relation of the Universitie, being verie sorie that I cannot discourse so largely thereof as I would. For that little time that I spent in Heidelberg (which was no more then one whole day) I bestowed in seeing the Palatine Library, the principall Church, and the Princes Court. So that I omitted to see any of their Colledges, and therefore unable to satisfie thy expectation of those things which perhaps thou wilt most require at my hands. Only I can tell thee the founder of the Universitie was Rupertus the elder, whom I have before mentioned, Count Palatine of Rhene, and King of the Romanes, the same that founded the Church of the holy Ghost. This laud- *University* able worke he began in the yeare 1346. The Colledges *founded A.D.* are but three in number, whereof that which is called the *1346.* Colledge of Wisedome is the fairest, in which their theologicall exercises are handled. The second is the Casimirian Colledge, wherein are exercises of all the liberall sciences. The third is called the Bursa, wherein all faculties are professed also: although this Universitie be but little, yet it hath partly bred, and partly entertained many singular men of rare learning that have both eternized their owne names, and greatly graced this Universitie with the excellent fruits of their studies that they have communicated to the world. For here lived and died famous Rodolphus Agricola that most learned Frisian of the noble Citie of Groninga. The Elogium *Erasmus's* of whose excellent learning written by Erasmus (as I finde *elogy on* it in his Chiliades, even in the first Chiliad in the nine *Rodolphus* and thirtieth adage of the fourth Centurie) because it is *Agricola.* very memorable, and doth greatly illustrate the glorie of this rare man, I will here expresse, whose words are these. Hoc equidem adagium eò libentiùs refero, quod mihi refricat novatque memoriam paritèr ac desiderium Rodol- [p. 498.] phi Agricolæ Frisii, quem ego virum totius tùm Germaniæ, tùm Italiæ publico summoque honore nomino : illius, quæ genuerit: hujus, quæ literis optimis instituerit. Nihil enim unquam hic Cisalpinus orbis produxit omnibus literariis dotibus absolutius: absit invidia dicto. Nulla erat honesta disciplina, in quâ vir ille non poterat cum summis artificibus contendere. Inter Græcos Græcissimus, inter Latinos Latinissimus. In carmine Maronem alterum dixisses: In oratione Politianum quendam lepore referebat, majestate superabat. Oratio vel extemporalis adeò pura, adeó Germana, ut non Frisium quempiam, sed urbis Romanæ vernaculum loqui contenderes. Eloquentiæ tam absolutæ parem adjunxerat eruditionem. Philosophiæ mysteria omnia penetraverat. Nulla pars musices quam non exactissimè calleret. Extremo vitæ tempore ad literas Hebraicas ac Scripturam divinam totum animum appulerat. Atque hæc conantem fatorum invidia virum terris eripuit nondum annos natum quadraginta, sicut accipio. Thus much Erasmus of Rodolphus Agricola, whose testimonie consisting of so many sweete words I was the more willing to alledge, because it is an introduction to a most elegant *Agricola's* Epitaph written upon the said Agricola by that famous *epitaph.* and learned Venetian Gentleman Hermolaus Barbarus Patriarch of Aquileia; which Epitaph (as it is extant upon the monument of him in one of the lesser Churches of Heidelberg) was communicated unto me by a learned Gentleman of the Universitie, (and mentioned also by Erasmus himselfe in the same adage whence I have derived the premisses) who told me that Agricola was buried there Anno 1485 in the habite of a Franciscan Frier, according as I have sometimes observed secular men buried in Italy.

The Epitaph is this.

Invida clauserunt hoc marmore fata Rodolphum
Agricolam, Frisii spemque decusque soli:
[p. 499.] Scilicet hoc uno meruit Germania laudis
Quidquid habet Latium, Græcia quicquid habet.

Having now insisted upon the praise of worthy Rodolpus *Other learned* Agricola in regard he was buried in this renowned city, I *men.* wil briefly name some other learned men of this noble

University, & so finally end this discourse of Heidelberg. Here lived Joannes Dalburgius counseller to Ludovicus Count Palatine of Rhene, and afterward Bishop of Wormes, a man of singular learning. Here also professed that admirable Hebrician Conradus Pellicanus, who read the Hebrew lecture; and Sebastian Munster his *Sebastian Munster.* successor in the same lecture which he read there five years, as he himselfe doth write. Likewise he wrote some part of his Cosmographie in this Universitie, as Mr. Gruterus told me: here Joannes Virdungus that notable Mathematician professed the Mathematicke disciplines. Here Gulielmus Xylander borne in the renowned citie of Augusta, and famoused over all Christendome for his excellent learning, especially in the studie of humanitie, read Philosophie and Astrologie for the space of many yeares; and also did at last shut up his vitall daies in this citie. Here that Phœnix and miracle of her sexe Olympia *Olympia Fulvia Morata.* Fulvia Morata an Italian Gentlewoman borne, spent a good part of her time in sacred meditations, and most sweete exercises of learning, after she had abandoned the vanities of the Duke of Ferraraes Court in Italy, and the popish religion; who by her incessant study profited so much in the Greeke and Latine tongues, that she hath immortalized her fame by her most elegant writings, and added some grace to Heidelberg even by leaving of her precious bones there. Here Victorinus Strigelius publikely professed after he had before bene a professor in the two Universities of Jene and Leipzicke. Here Joannes Willingus a singular Divine and preacher of the Court florished. Here preached that worthy man Gaspar Olevian: here those rare divines, three shining lamps of Christs Church, Emanuel *Three shining lamps of the church.* Tremellius a Jew borne as I have before written in my note *[p. 500.]* of Venice; Zacharius Ursinus, and Petrus Boquinus read with no lesse profit then praise the publike lectures of divinity. Whereof the first hath infinitely profited the Church by his excellent translation of all the old Testament out of Hebrew into Latine with his learned copartner Francis Junius, and their sound scholaies upon the same.

The other two have like most valiant champions of Christ,
especially Ursinus, fought the Lords battell against the
enemies of Gods true religion, partly with their eloquent
tongues, and partly with their elegant quilles.   The one
of them, I meane that holy Ursinus, having besides many
other most learned tracts of divinity, written so incomparably learned a Catechisme, and so profitable unto Gods
Church, that I thinke there was never any booke of the
like subject since the time of the Apostles worthy to be
paralleled with it ;   the other, besides many excellent
theologicall tracts that he hath written, hath most manfully
defended the old and ancient Christianisme against the new
and counterfaited Jesuitisme.   Here also lived Paulus
Melissus that excellent Poet and worthy Knight Palatine.
Here Bartholomew Kicherman that notable artist professed
Logicke and Philosophy.   Here finally flourished those
Four famous
men. foure famous men at that time that I was in Heidelberg ;
David Pareus publike professor of Divinity, Dionysius
Gothofredus an excellent civill Lawyer, Doctor Lingelsemius and Janus Gruterus whom I have before mentioned,
such as greatly gratified me in the citie.   All these from
the first to the last have bene so excellent and learned
writers that they have gotten themselves such a celebrity
of name, as will never be extinguished while the fabricke
of the world do last.

Thus much of Heidelberg.

[p. 501.] I Departed from Heidelberg the eight day of September
being Thursday about nine of the clocke in the morn
ing, and came to the City of Spira which is twelve miles
beyond it, about five of the clock in the afternoone.
A great wood. Betwixt these two Cities I passed through a great wood,
which by reason of the manifold turnings and windings of
the way like a company of voluminous Meanders, did so
exceedingly perplexe me, that I got out of the same with
no small difficulty.   About three miles before I came to
Spira I was ferried over the Rhene in a boate.

230

My Observations of Spira commonly called Spier.

THis City hath had two names, Spira and Nemetum; *Spires.*
whereof Spira was the ancientest: which Peucer
affirmeth to have been imposed upon the City from the
Greeke word σπεῖρα, which amongst many other signi-
fications signifieth also a Prætorian cohort. Because
whereas Constantius Chlorus the father of Constantine
the great was esteemed either the first founder or the
inlarger thereof, (in which I have read he buried his
mother Claudia the daughter of Flavius Claudius the
Emperour, and the predecessour of the Emperour Aurelianus) he placed a Prætorian cohort in this City for the
defence both of the same place and of the territorie about
it. Therefore seeing it doth manifestly appeare (saith *Founding of*
Peucer) that Constantius made his Rendevous about these *Spires.*
places neare adjoyning to Spira, the conjecture is neither
absurd nor aliene from the historicall truth, that Spira had
her denomination from certain Grecian cohorts. But in
process of time this name Spira was converted to Nemetum from certaine people called Nemetes, who inhabited
that territorie where the City now standeth, which name it
retained for the space of many yeares till the yeare after
Christs incarnation 1080. at what time it recovred her old
name againe, by reason that a certaine Bishop whose name [p. 502.]
was Rudiger (as Munster relateth the history) did include
a certaine Village called Spira neare adjoyning to the said *Spires also*
Nemetum (which indeede was the true remnant of the *called*
ancient Spira built in the time of the foresaid Constantius) *Nemetum.*
within the walles of the City. And by this meanes the
old but not the first name Nemetum (received from the
foresaid people Nemetes) was extinct: and the other name
of Spira (the true ancient appellation first attributed unto
it at the time of her originall foundation) rose againe.
Since which time it hath continually retained the same
name to this day, but with an addition of the name of the

people Nemetes. For it is commonly called Spira Neme-
túm. Againe Munster differing from the opinion of
learned Peucer draweth the name of Spira from a certaine
river so called, that issueth out of certaine hils not farre
from the City. Which river (saith he) gave the name to
the ancient village, and hath since communicated the same
unto the City it selfe, because it runneth at this day
through the City. But I preferring the opinion of Peucer
had rather derive it from the Greeke word σπεῖρα signifying a band of Souldiers (which me thinks is the more
elegant derivation) then from the river Spira.

Situation of Spires.

The situation of it is very pleasant. For it standeth in
a fertill plaine, being watered partly by the foresaid river
Spira that runneth through it, and partly by the noble
Rhene, which indeede washeth not the walles thereof as it
doth Basil, Mentz, and Colen, and many other Cities and
Townes, but is remote from it about the space of one
furlong. The compasse of it is something larger then
that of Heidelberg, and is invironed with goodly walles
that are exceedingly beautified both with battlements, and
with very lofty *towers being of such a heigth that they
equal the towers of many of our English Churches, the
like whereof I have not seene in any place in my whole

[p. 503.]

journey, saving only one in Padua called Antenors tower
whereof I have before spoken. Also many of these
towers have peculiar gate-houses belonging to them, which
doe greatly garnish the City, and make it very conspicuous

Its streets and buildings.

a farre off. The streets are many, and very faire as well
for breadth as length; especially the great streete that
leadeth to the Cathedrall Church, which is on both sides
five and thirty paces broade; for I paced it: and decked
with many sumptuous buildings that yeeld the farre fairer
shew, because some of the principallest have their fronts
very curiously painted. Also that exquisite forme of
building their houses (whereof I have made mention before
in my description of Strasbourg) by garnishing both the

* These towers and their walles were built by one of their Bishops
called Rudiger, of whom I have already spoken.

232

d Spira Neme-
he opinion of
from a certaine
e hils not farre
ve the name to
dcated the same
:th at this day
inion of Peucer
rd στειρα signi-
aks is the more
pira.

or it standeth in
ne foresaid river
iy by the noble
lles thereof as t
other Cities and
he space of one
ing larger then
ch goodly walls
battlements, and
heigth that they
h Churches, the
ice in my whole
. Antenors tower
many of these
g to them, which
very conspicuous
rery faire as well
reat streete that
is on both sides
l it: and decked
d the fare fairer
rave their fronts
uisite forme of
e mention before
ishing both the
e of their Bishops

Fridericus 4. D. G. Sacr: Rom: Imperij Septemuir.

Comes Pal: Rheni, Dux Bauaria, Princ: Germania.

Imperij Proceres armíq; opibusq; superbos
Suspicis? Heroum forha facta placent?
FRIDRICVM aduerte:huic facies & Martia Virtus,
Iustitia, & pura huic cum pietate fides.
Sceptra quibus magni moderatur magna leonis?
Emporibusq; facit cedere prisca suis.

Gu: Hol: sculp:

OB

endes with ℔
acuminated ℔
adorne ther :
Heidelberg ꜰꜱ
lower Germꜰꜱ
   The Churꜱ
whereof foure ꜱ
Churches, foure
and one of Jesuꜱꜱ
to our Lady, ꜱ
man Robert Tꜱ
Bavaricus, ꜱꜰꜱꜱ
ꜱs a white roꜱꜱ
structure that ꜱꜱꜱ
by reason of ꜱꜱꜱ
thereof, whꜱꜱ
present a prꜱꜱ ꜱ
This Church wꜱs
Emperour Conrꜱꜱ
upon the twelfꜱꜱ
first fundamentꜱꜱ
reason that Goꜱ :
could accompꜱꜱꜱ ꜱ
the third in hꜱs ꜱ
Empire, to ꜱꜱꜱꜱ ꜱ
accordingly perfꜱꜱ
   I observeꜱ ꜱꜱꜱ
Persons buriꜱꜱ ꜱꜱ
other whatsoever :
bodies of eighꜱ (
besides many oꜱꜱ
Emperors I willꜱ ꜱ
The first was C.
Emperor, and ꜱꜱ
conia, who was ꜱ
said. Here wꜱs
yeares, his body
Utricht in the ꜱ

endes with battlements, which are by little and little acuminated till they rise to a sharpe toppe, doth especially adorne their buildings. Which fashion I observed in Heidelberg also, and in most Cities both of higher and lower Germanie.

The Churches of the City are in number sixteene, *Churches of* whereof foure are Collegiat, foure that are called Parish *Spires.* Churches, foure of Mendicant Friers, three of Nunnes, and one of Jesuits. Their Cathedrall Church is dedicated to our Lady, (which our eloquent but Apostate country-man Robert Turner in a Tract intitled Triumphus Bavaricus, affirmeth to be as great a grace to this City as a white tooth to an Æthiopian) a very magnificent structure that yeeldeth a most gorgeous shew a farre off by reason of the foure lofty turrets built at the corners thereof, which to those that come towards the City do present a pretty kinde of forme not unlike to a cradle. This Church was founded about the yeare 1030. by the Emperour Conrade the second surnamed Salicus. Who upon the twelfth day of Julie the same yeare placed the first fundamentall stone with his owne handes. But by reason that God called him out of the world before he could accomplish his worke, he injoyned his sonne Henry the third in his death-bedde, who succeeded him in the [p. 504.] Empire, to finish the building that he beganne, which was accordingly performed by his said sonne.

I observed more monuments of Emperors and royall *Many royal* Persons buried in the Quire of this Church then in any *monuments.* other whatsoever in my whole voyage. For here lie the bodies of eight German Emperors and two Empresses, besides many other worthy wights of both sexes. The Emperors I will reckon by degrees in order as they reigned. The first was Conradus Salicus the sixteenth German Emperor, and the first of the imperiall familie of Fran-conia, who was founder of the Church as I have already said. Here was he buried after he had reigned fifteene yeares, his body being translated hither from the City of Utricht in the Netherlands, where he died in the yeare

Henry III.
seventeenth
German
Emperor.

1039. Also his wife Gisela the daughter of Lotharius King of France was buried in the same place about five yeares after. The second was Henry the third the seventeenth German Emperor surnamed the Blacke, the foresaid Conradus his sonne by his wife Gisela, who died in the yeare 1056. of his age forty, of his Empire seventeene, being choaked with a morsell of bread. There was he interred the fifth day of November which was the same day that he was borne. Their monuments I saw in the middle of the Quire, being not built with that royall magnificence as the Tombes of great Potentates are in this ambitious age. There were some other royall Peeres of the same stocke or familie buried there also : but every one hath not his severall epitaph. For this one short epitaph serveth for them all.

Filius hìc, pater hìc, avus hìc, proavus jacet istìc,
Hìc Proavi conjux, hìc Henrici senioris.

Henry IV.
eighteenth
German
Emperor
[p. 505.]

By Proavi conjux is meant the Empresse Gisela, by Henrici senioris the Empresse Bertha. The third was Henry the fourth, the eighteenth Germane Emperour surnamed the elder, the former Henry his sonne by the Empresse Agnes the daughter of the Duke of Aquitanie : this is that heroicall and martiall Emperour that fought sixtie two battels in the field, in most whereof hee got the victorie : hee died in Liege upon the seventh day of August, in the fiftie and six yeare of his age after he had reigned fortie nine yeares, and in the yeare of our Lord 1106. his body was brought to Spira, five yeares after his death (during al which time it was kept above ground in the foresaid Citie of Liege, and deprived of the honour of buriall by the Popes commandment) where he was interred neere to his wife Bertha the daughter of Otto an Italian Marquesse ; shee was buried there about nineteene yeares before, in the yeare 1087. her body being translated thither from the Citie of Mentz. The fourth was Henry the fifth, the nineteenth Germane Emperour, surnamed the yonger, the foresaid Henry the fourths sonne by his

Henry V.
nineteenth
German
Emperor.

234

wife Bertha: his body was brought thither from Utricht, where he died the tenth day of August 1125. after hee had reigned nineteene yeares. The fifth is Philip borne in *Philip of* the Citie of Bamberg, once Duke of Suevia, the foure and *Bamberg.* twentieth German Emperour, and the fifth sonne of that famous and victorious Emperour Fredericke Barbarossa by his wife Beatrix: hee was slaine by Otto Palatine of Whittelbach in his Chamber in Bamberg, when his Physition did let him bloud upon the tenth day of July in the yeare 1208. after he had reigned ten yeares. His body was first buried in the Cathedrall Church of Bamberg neere the Emperour Henry surnamed the Holy, and afterward by the Emperour Fredericke the second brought to Spira. His monument is graced with no other Epitaph, but this short inscription:

Philippus Bambergensis.

The sixth, Rodolphus Habspurgensis the two and thirtieth *Rodolph of* German Emperor, who died in a towne called Germers- *Hapsburg.* heim seated upon a banke of the Rhene, the eighteenth day of August in the year 1291. of his age seventie and [p. 506.] three, of his Empire nineteene: from the same hee was brought to Spira shortly after his death, and buried here with the rest. The seventh Adolphus Nassousensis the *Adolf of* successor of the foresaid Rodolphus, who after hee had *Nassau.* reigned eighteene yeares, was slaine neare this Citie upon the sixth day of July in the yeare 1298. by Albertus Austriacus afterward Emperour and the sonne òf the Emperour Rodolphus Habspurgensis. For they fought a Duell, that is, a single combat in a field hard by Spira, where Albert suddenly invaded Adolphus as soone as hee was dismounted from his horse; for as Adolphus was rising up to take horse againe, Albert prevented him, and with his sword did cut his throate. The eight and last Emperour is the foresaid Albert, of whom I will make no more mention in this place, but that hee was buried here. Because in my discourse of the Monasterie of Kiningsfelden in Switzerland I have written a large history

235

of his most lamentable end, and of the translating of his body to this place.

Besides the Monuments of all those renowned persons intombed in the Quire, I also saw in the same place a memorable inscription in Latine verses concerning the persons themselves, which because I was barred of the opportunitie to write them out before I departed out of the place, by good fortune I procured the same of a learned man of the Citie, who recited them to me perfectly by heart, even these.

Epitaph of the Emperors.

Famosi Reges, clari Comitesque Ducesque,
　　Et Reginarum nobilis usque phalanx :
Hoc in magnifico (dum stabunt secula) templo
　　Vestrarum laudum fama perennis erit.
Quippè domo nostrâ, cui munera magna dedistis,
　　Haud frustrâ placuit corpora vestra tegi.
Sperastis precibus animas quandoque levari,
　　Hic facilem ad superos spes erat esse viam.

[p. 507.]

Vivite fælices æternâ laude sepulti,
　　Quoram animas cœlum, corpora terra tenet.

In the body of the Church I saw many things very worthy the observation. But two of them are more memorable then the rest. Therefore I will name them *Relics of Saint* first. These were matters concerning Saint Bernard *Bernard.* Abbot of Claraval in Burgundy. The one his salutation to the Virgine Mary The other a coppy of a certaine Epistle that he wrote to the Bishop of Spira &c. His salutation to the Virgin Mary is a most notable matter, which I was the more willing to observe, because I had both read, and often heard of it before I came thither. The history is this. When Saint Bernard came at a certaine time to the this Citie of Spira, he went to the Cathedrall Church to serve God, and as soone as he came within the first dore at the west end of the Church, he kneeled very devoutly upon his knees, and zealously elevating both his hands he saluted the image of the Virgin Mary (which is shewed to this day at one corner of the

236

anslating of his

nowned persons
he same place a
concerning the
is barred of the
departed out of
same of a learned
me perfectly by

iucesque,
lanx :
::la) templo
ais erit.
iagna dedistis,
stra tegi.
que levari,
: ese viam.

. terra tenet.

:::nr things req
them are more
I will name then
∴ Saint Bernard
ine his salutation
::∵ of a certaine
Spira &c. His
:∵ notable matter,
e, because I had
e I came thither.
:nard came at a
he went to the
soone as he came
the Church, he
and zealously
e of the Virgin
e corner of the

outside of the Quire on the right hand thereof as you
enter into the Church from the west dore) with these three
salutations, which for the better confirmation of the
memory of the matter to posterity were shortly after
written in three severall places of the Church where he
kneeled, being the space of thirty five foote distant
asunder. The first was this, written in capitall letters in
the same manner as I present it to thee.

O
CLEMENS
MARIA.

Which wordes are cut in brasen letters within a round
peece of blew marble. But the word Maria is written
otherwise then the rest. For it is contrived in that manner
that the 5. letters of her name are severally made in the
5. leaves of a rose, which are very curiously represented
in the same peece of marble. In the middle stone where
he kneeled the second time, is written his second salutation.

O
DULCIS
MARIA.

In the third his last salutation.

O
PIA
MARIA.

It is reported that the image did utter a voyce at that time
to Saint Bernard very like to a living and articulate voice
of a man, by way of thanking & commending him for his
devotion. But what the speech was I could not reade
in any authentick author (though I know Robert Turner
whome I have mentioned a little before, writeth in his
Triumphus Bavaricus, that the image made this answere :
Gratus ades nobis Bernarde,) nor heare from the report of
any learned man. Yet I was very inquisitive for the

Saint Bernard's three salutations.

[p. 508.]

A speaking image.

237

matter in Spira amongst the learned of all sorts both Protestants and Papists, no man being able to tell me. But the answere that Saint Bernard made to the image I meane to conceale till some other edition of my booke after my future travels, (if God shall mercifully prolong my life to accomplish some other outlandish voyage) and that for certaine reasons of no meane importance which I will not discover to the world.

The other memorable thing of Saint Bernard that I saw in the body of this Church, was a coppy of a certaine Epistle that he wrote to the Bishop of Spira, the Clergie, and the people of the citie, to the end to exhort them to joine their helpe and assistance unto those heroicall Princes that did in his daies undertake that famous voyage under the conduct of Godfrie Duke of Bouloigne to conquer the holy land, and eject the barbarous Saracens and Paynims that had possessed the same. Howbeit in this Epistle he maketh no mention at al of the foresaid Godfrie. I finde that St. Bernard lived about forty six yeares after he wrote this Epistle. For whereas it is very likely that he wrote it about the time of the Councell of Clermont in France which was assembled by Pope Urban the second, of purpose to animate the Christian Princes to undertake that honourable expedition for the expugning of the holy land; that Councell was holden anno 1094. and St. Bernard died 1140. about the end of the raigne of the Emperour Lotharius the second. Surely the sight of the epistle did much comfort my heart, and in a manner refocillate my spirits. It is written in a very ancient peece of Parchment (which seemeth to be very neere five hundred yeares old, as being written either in the time of St. Bernard himselfe, which is almost so long since, or very shortly after) and hanged upon one of the pillars on the right hand of the Church. First of all this in red letters: Hæc est epistola quam beatus Bernardus tempore illo ad passagium ad hortandum misit Domino Episcopo Spirensi, Clero, et populo universo. Next followeth Saint Bernards owne superscription which

[p. 509.]
Saint Bernard's epistle.

238

all sorts both
)le to tell me.
to the image I
of my booke
cifully prolong
sh voyage) and
ortance which I

rnard that I saw
)r of a certaine
ira, the Clergie,
exhort them to
heroicall Princes
us voyage under
ae to conquer the
ens and Paynims
in this Epistle he
Godfrie. I finde
ares after he wrote
:ely that he wrote
:rmont in France
:e second, of pur-
:o undertake that
:of the holy land;
:S. Bernard died
:t the Emperour
of the epistle did
:er refocillate my
:naace of Parth-
:e hundred yeares
:of St. Bernard
or very shortly
pillars on the
all this in red
Bernardus tem-
misit Domino
universo. Next
scription which

was this. Domino et patri *karissimo venerabili Epis
copo Spirensi, et universo, Clero, et populo, Bernardus
Clarevallensis vocatus Abbas in spiritu fortitudinis abun
dare : then followeth the epistle itselfe in the latine tongue,
which because I cannot communicate to my country for a
meere novelty (for it hath bene commonly printed in all
the editions of Saint Bernards workes, being in number
the three hundreth two and twentieth epistle) I will not [p. 510.]
set downe in Latin, supposing that many learned men will
censure it for a superfluous labour, seeing it hath bene
these many hundred yeares so common in the world. Yet
since it was my hap to finde it out as I walked alone in the
Cathedrall Church of Spira whereof I now write, being
indeede a most excellent treatise in respect of the worthinesse both of the argument and the author ; I thought it
not impertinent to translate it according to my meane skil
into our vulgar tongue (which I never heard to be done
before by any man whatsoever :) submitting my simple
translation to the favorable censure of the curteous
reader.

The Epistle I say itselfe is this.

 Am to treate with you about a businesse of Christ, *Saint*
in whom is all our salvation. This I speake that *Bernard's*
the authority of the Lord may excuse the unworthi- *epistle*
nesse of the person of the speaker, and that the considera- *Englished.*
tion of selfe-utility may excuse it also. I wis I am but a
meane man, yet I doe not meanely desire you all in the
bowels of Jesus Christ. Now then there is that occasion
of my writing unto you that I dare presume to salute the
whole community of you with my letters. More gladly
would I doe it by word of mouth, if as I want not will, so
also I had opportunity to performe it. Lo †now (my
brethren) is the acceptable time, lo now is the day of plentifull salvation. For the earth hath moved and trembled,

* Thus was this word written even with the letter k at the beginning,
according to that olde and obsolete manner.

† 2. Cor. 6. cap. 2. ve.

Saint
Bernard's
epistle
Englished.

[p. 511.]

because the God of heaven hath begunne to lay waste his owne land. His I say, wherein he hath bene seene to teach the word of his Father, and man with men to converse for the space of thirtie yeares and more. His certainly, since he hath illustrated it with so many miracles, and dedicated it with his owne bloud, in which the first flowers of resurrection budded, and now our sinnes requiring it, the adversaries of the Crosse have sacrilegiously made head, wasting in the face of the sword the land of promise. For now it is well neare come to passe, if there be no bodie to resist, that they will rush into the very Citie of the living God, overthrow the very shops of our redemption, and pollute those holy places which were purpled with the bloud of the Lambe immaculate. Yea they yawne with sacrilegious mouthes (out alas) to enter the very sanctuary of Christian religion, and they endeavour to invade and tread under feete that very bed wherein our life for our sakes hath slept in death. What doe ye valiant men? what doe ye that are the servants of the Crosse? what, wil ye give that which is holy unto dogs, †& pearls unto swine? how many sinners having there confessed their sinnes with teares have obtained pardon, after that the uncleannesse of the Pagans hath bene banished out of the Citie by the swords of our forefathers? the malicious man sees this, and envies at it, gnasheth his teeth, and pines away. He stirreth up the vessels of his iniquity, intending not to leave as much as any print or step of so great devotion, at the least if he can seise upon (which God forbid) those ‡Holyes of Holyes. And that would be to all ages a most disconsolate griefe, because the losse is irrecoverable, but especially unto this most impious generation it would breed an infinite confusion, and shame everlasting. But what thinke we brethren? what, is the hand of the Lord §shortned or become weake to save, in that he calles his little wormes to preserve and restore unto him his inheritance? what, is he not able to send more then twelve legions of Angels, or but say the word, and

† Matth. 7. cap. 6. ve.   ‡ Sancta Sanctorum.   § Esay 57, cap. ve. 2.

OBSERVATIONS OF SPIRES

lay waste his
seene to teach
o converse for
certainly, since
, and dedicated
owers of resur-
quiring it, the
sly made head,
promise. For
: be no bodie to
tie of the living
'edemption, and
urpled with the
hey yawne with
ie very sanctuary
ir to invade and
, our life for our
ve valiant men?
ie Crosse? what,
† & pearls unto
e confessed their
⁀, after that the
⁀ished out of the
⁀ the malicious
⁀ teeth, and pulls
⁀ iniquity, intead-
⁀ step of so great
⁀on (which God
⁀at would be to
⁀se the losse is
; most impious
⁀sion, and shame
⁀en? what, is the
⁀eake to save, in
⁀nd restore unto
⁀ to send more
⁀ the word, and
⁀ 57, cap. re. 1.

your land shall be delivered? verily it is in his power to *Saint Bernard's epistle Englished.* do it when he list. But I tell you the Lord God doth trie you. He lookes backe upon the sonnes of men if there be any that understands, and enquires for ‖ her, and [p. 512.] bemoanes her case. For the Lord hath pitie on his people, and doth provide a wholesome remedie for those that are grievously fallen. Consider how great cunning he doth use to save you, and be amazed at it. Behold the depth of his pietie, and be of good cheere O ye sinners. He will not your death, but that ye may be converted and live. For he seekes an occasion not against you, but for you. For what is it but a studied occasion of salvation & picked out only by God himselfe, that the omnipotent doth vouchsafe to quit from their bondage murderers, robbers, adulterers, perjured men, and those that are vassals to other crimes, as if they were a nation that had wrought righteousnesse? Doe *not distrust ô ye sinners, the Lord is debonaire. If he meant to punish you, he would not only not crave your service, but would not entertaine it being offered by you. I say againe, weigh the riches of the goodnesse of the most high God, observe the counsell of his mercy, he either makes himselfe to have want, or seemes as though he had, while he covets to relieve your necessities. He will be held a debtor that he may give wages unto those that serve in his warfare, even indulgence of sinnes, and everlasting glory. Blessed may I call the generation whom so plentifull a time of indulgence layes hold upon, whom that pleasing yeare to the Lord and truly Jubilie doth finde alive. For this blessing is dispersed over all the world, and to the ensigne of life all men flie together with a kinde of contention. Therefore for as much as your territorie is fruitfull of † valiant men, and knowen to be full of such as are in the

‖ The Citie of Jerusalem.   * Joel 2.
† In the Latin coppy of Saint Bernards Epistle I find these wordes. Quia ergò fœcunda vitiorum terra vestra, &c. wherein I observe a fault. For I am perswaded that that word vitiorum should be virorum. Otherwise there can be no sense in it. The consideration whereof hath induced me to translate it accordingly.

C. C. II   241   Q

Saint Bernard's epistle Englished. prime of their youth (as your praise is spread all over, and the fame of your prowesse hath filled the whole world) be yee also couragiously girt, and in zeale of the Christian name betake yourselves to happy armes. Let former not warfare but malice cease, wherewith yee are wont mutually to destroy one another, that yee might be mutually consumed. What direfull wilfulnesse stirreth up wretches, that [p. 513.] neighbours should pierce that body whose soule perhaps is in case to perish. But he shall not escape to boast of it, and a sword hath pierced him to the very soule when he doth but onely rejoyce at the fall of his enemie. To expose ones selfe to such a danger, were a token of madnesse, not of prowesse. Neyther might it be ascribed to hardinesse, but rather to folly. Now thou hast couragious soldier, thou hast warlicke man where thou maiest skirmish without danger, where it is both a glory to conquer, and to die a gaine. If thou art a wise and thriving Merchant, if a purchaser of this world, I bring thee tydings of a great fayre, see thou slippe it not. Take the signe of the crosse, and thou shalt obtaine indulgence of all thy sinnes whereof thou shalt make a confession with a contrite heart. The matter it self if it be bought, is had for little or nothing. If it bee taken upon a devout shoulder, without doubt it is worth the Kingdome of God. Well therefore have they done that have already taken the heavenly cognisance, and others may doe well to lay hold on that which may availe to their salvation. Touching the rest I advise you (my brethren) yet not I, but also Gods *Apostle with me, that credite is not to be given to every spirit. We have heard and rejoice how the spirit of God boileth in you : but it is altogether necessary that a due temperature of knowledge be not wanting. The Jewes are not to be persecuted, nor to be slaine, no not so much as to bee banished from you. Aske yourselves the holy Scriptures. I know what is read in the § Psalme prophesied of the Jewes. God shewes me (quoth the Church) concerning my enemies, that thou kill them

* 1 John 4.   § 50.

not, least at any time my people prove forgetful. They *Saint* are certaine living marks pointing out unto us the Lords *Bernard's* passion. For this cause they have beene dispersed into all *Englished.* Countreys, that while they sustaine the just punishment of so great a crime, they may be witnesses of our redemption. Whereupon the Church speaking in the same psalm addeth [p. 514.] this, Disperse them in thy vertue, and put them downe O Lord my protector: which hath accordingly come to passe. For they are dispersed, they are put downe, they sustaine hard captivity under Christian Princes. Notwithstanding about the evening they shall be converted, & there will be a respect had of them in time. Finally, when the multitude of the Gentiles shall enter in, then all Israel (saith the † Apostle) shall be saved. But in the meane time whosoever dieth, remaineth in death. I say not that wheresoever they ‡ are not, we grieve that Christian usurers doe worse Judaize, at the least if they ought to be fitly called Christians, and not rather baptized Jewes. If the Jewes are altogether confounded, how then shall their salvation or conversion promised in the end, prosper? Surely the very Gentiles themselves (if their conversion were likewise to be expected) were rather to be forborne then *smitten with the sword. But now since they first began to offer violence unto us, it behoveth those that doe not carry the swordes in vaine, to repulse force with force. Yet it is a part of Christian piety as to conquer the proud, so also to spare subjects, especially those whose the lawe is by promise, those from whome the Fathers were decended, and from whom Christ sprang according to the flesh, which is blessed for ever. Howbeit it were to be required of them, according to the tenor of the Apostolicall mandate, that they should altogether exempt al those free from the exaction of usurie that shall take on them the badge of the crosse. Also it is necessary (my most beloved brethren) that if any man perhaps

† Rom. 11.   ‡ The Jewes.

* In most of the Latine copies it is expetendi. But it is false. For it must be petendi.

243

Saint
Bernard's
epistle
Englished.

[p. 515.]

desirous to be cheefe amongst you, would by his forward-
nesse forestall the government of the armie, yee give no
† eare at all unto him : and if he make as though he were
sent from us, it is not true.   Or if he sheweth letters sent
as from us, ye may say they are altogether false, that I may
not call them furtive.   Ye ought to choose warlike men,
and Chieftains expert in those affaires, and to take order
that the armie of the Lord may march together, that It
may every where have strength, and may not sustaine
violence from any whatsoever.   For there was a certaine
man in the first voiage before Jerusalem was taken, called
Peter, of whome ye also (unlesse I am deceived) have often
heard mention.   He marching alone with his soldiers,
exposed the people that believed him, to so great dangers,
that either none of them or very few escaped, that perished
not either with hunger or the sword.   Therefore it is
altogether to be feared that if yee shall doe the like, the
like may happen unto you also.   Which God turne from
you that is blessed for ever.   Amen.

Having now ended those two things that I said before
were the most memorable of all in the body of this Church,
I will digresse to some other matter, and will first make
A sumptuous
pulpit. mention of a certain pulpit that standeth on the left hand
of the body of this Church, as you come into it from the
street.   I suppose that some hyper-criticall carpers will
taxe me of vanity for adding such triviall things to my
Observations, as descriptions of Pulpits.   But I crave
pardon of them although I describe this pulpit of Spira.
For it was so glorious and resplendent an architecture, that
I was unwilling to let it passe unmentioned, being the
fairest thing of that nature that I saw in my travels, saving
one onely pulpit before mentioned in my discourse of the
City of Amiens.   Which notwithstanding in some respects
is inferiour to this whereof I now speake.   The roofe or
covering of this sumptuous pulpit is made but of wainscot,
but so wonderfull gorgeously gilt, and adorned with

† The ordinary Latine text is false.   For instead of audeat it must be
audiatur.

244

sundry colours, that it yeeldeth a shew most beautifull : in certaine square peeces of this roofe I read these sacred poesies. The first this. *Hodiè si vocem ejus audierîtis, nolite obdurare corda vestra. In the lower square this. Beati qui audiunt verbum Domini & custodiunt illud. A little under this †Prædica verbum, insta opportunè, importunè, argue, obsecra, increpa in omni patientia & doctrina. The other part of the pulpit is exceeding sumptuous also, being made of white free-stone, which is so faire that it may compare with some kinde of alabaster, and garnished with curious images, works, and borders most richly gilt, and decked with many sentences taken out of the holy Scriptures. In the inside of the dore where the preacher ascendeth the pulpit, this is written in golden letters. ‡Ascendo ad patrem meum & patrem vestrum. Also these sentences are written in the outside of the pulpit about the compasse as the Preacher doth ascend. §Quomodo prædicabunt nisi mittantur? sicut scriptum est. Quàm preciosi pedes Evangelizantium pacem, Evangelizantium bona? Next this. *Euntes in mundum universum prædicate Evangelium omni creaturæ. Againe this. †Dominus dabit verbum Evangelizantibus virtute multâ. Then this. ‡Clama, ne cesses, quasi tuba exalta vocem tuam, & annuncia populo meo scelera eorum. All these sentences are written in one row. Under these in the lower part of that curious stony compasse this is written. §In novissimo autem die magno stabat Jesus & clamabat, dicens, Si quis sitit, veniat ad me & bibat. Likewise there are set forth in the outside of this exquisite workemanship the images of the foure Doctors of the Latin Church. St. Augustine and St. Ambrose in their Episcopall habites, St. Hierome in his Cardinals weedes. St. Gregorie with his triple crowne. Our Lady with Christ in her armes. St. Stephen Pope, and two Bishops more whose names are not expressed.

*Psal. 94. †2 Tim. 4. cap. ‡John 20. v. 17.
§Rom. 10. 15. *Mar. 16. 15.
†Psal. 67. 12. ‡Esa. 58. ver. 1. §John 7. 37.

Inscriptions on the roof of the pulpit.

[p. 516.]

Inscriptions on the outside of the pulpit.

245

The seven works of mercy.

Also the seven workes of mercy are after an historicall manner very artificially represented in stone. Under the first this is written in golden letters. Esurientes pascere. Under the second. Potum dare sitientibus. Under the third. Operire nudos. Under the fourth. Captivos redimere. Under the fifth. Ægrotos invisere. Under the sixth. Hospitio peregrinos suscipere. Under the

[p. 517.]

seventh. Mortuos sepelire. Also the base of this pulpit is very sumptuous, on both sides whereof there are inserted peeces of touch-stone. In one side this is written. Eberhardus Dei gratiâ Episcopus Spirensis & Præpositus Weissenburgensis, Imperialis Cameræ Judex, &c. Cathedram hanc in honorem Dei omnipotentis & ornamentum celeberrimæ hujus basilicæ novâ hâc formâ construi & erigi fecit Anno Salutis humanæ. M.D.X.C.V. nihil aliud optans quàm ut posteritas ex hoc loco verbum Dei piè & Catholicè erudita, fusis ad Deum precibus, semper sui grato animo meminisse velit. On the other side of the base this also is written in another peece of touch-stone. Reverendissimus Princeps & Dominus Restaurator hujus Cathedræ Eberhardus â Dienheim electus fuit in Episcopum Anno Domino M. D. Lxxxi. ætatis suæ xxxix. Et in Judicem Cameræ solito juramento receptus ultima Aprilis cum xxvii. ejusdem antè solenni equitatu in urbem Spirensem esset ingressus Anno Salutis Humanæ M. D. Lxxxiiii. obiit Anno ætatis suæ, *&c. Episcopatus, &c.

Monument to a Bishop.

On the left hand of the bodie of the Church there is a passing sumptuous monument of one of the Bishops of Spira, whose image is made at length with a representation of his Episcopall habits, and many curious workes and histories are excellently cut in stone. Also it is adorned with many sentences of Scripture. At the very top of all this is written. Si charitatem non habuero, nihil sum: and under that: Repleti sunt omnes spiritu sancto, where the effigies of a dove is carved. Above the effigies of Christ this in golden letters. Mihi autem absit gloriari nisi in cruce Domini nostri Jesu Christi. Gal. 6. under that

* The yeare is not expressed in the original.

246

:r an historicall
ie. Under the
irientes pascere.
us. Under the
irth. Captivos
ivisere. Under
re. Under the
ise of this pulpit
there are inserted
, written. Eber-
s & Præpositus
dex, &c. Cathe-
is & ornamentum
à construi & erigi
...hil aliud optans
)e: pie & Catholicè
it sui grato animo
' the base this also
-e Reverendissi-
: cujus Cathedræ
Episcopum Anno
Et in Judicem
:--a Aprilis cum
:.:em Spirensem
.\. D. Lxxxiii
-s, &c.
'.e Church there is
-: the Bishops of
-. a representation
:-.s works and
.::o it is abroad
.:e very top of all
.:er., nihil sum:
:-:u sancto, where
.e the effigies of
-m absit gloriari
.:! 6. under that
sal.

againe. Vigilate, quia nescitis diem neque horam. Matth.
25. under that, his Epitaph in golden letters, which is this.
Reverendissimo Principi ac Domino Domino Marquardo
ab Hattstein Episcopo Spirensi & Præposito Weissenbur-
gensi Cæsareæ Majestatis Consiliario, ac Imperialis Cameræ
Judici pro laudatissimæ memoriæ, dum vixit, pietate, doctrinâ, authoritate, rerum experientiâ, consiliis, & singulari [p. 518.]
prudentiâ conspicuo & celeberrimo, nec non de Ecclesiâ
Spirensi multis modis optimè merito, monumentum hoc
pietatis & nunquam apud posteritatem intermorituræ
recordationis ergò poni fecerunt ejus heredes. Obiit
autem ætatis suæ 51. Episcopatus 21. Judicatus 21. 7.
Decembris. Anno Domini 1581. cujus anima requiescat
in pace. Amen. under that is written this sentence. In
principio creavit Deus cœlum & terram. Gen. 1. under
which sentence the historie of the creation of the world
is very curiously expressed in stone.

Opposite unto this there is erected on the right hand of *Another*
the Church a faire monument of another Bishop of Spira, *monument.*
whose image is made at length also as that of the former,
with his episcopall habits, and under the same this Epitaph
is written. Reverendo atque illustri Domino D. Georgio
Episcopo Spirensi ac Com. Palat. Rheni Ducique Bavariæ
admirandâ clementiâ, prudentiâ, & pietate undique conspicuo, ac demum flagranti Anglico sudore immaturâ
morte defuncto, pius in Episcopatu Successor Philippus
â Flersheim hoc monumentum instituit. Obiit autem
Anno Salutis 1529. die 28. Septembris, qui æternâ luce
fruatur.

There is adjoyning to the South side of this Church a *A goodly*
goodly cloister, in the which I observed an exceeding *cloister.*
multitude of ancient monuments wherewith the cloyster
is beautified round about, but the time would not give
me leave to write them out. For I made my aboad in
this city but one whole day. This cloyster invironeth a
very pleasant greene quadrangular Court, in the midst
whereof there is the most memorable thing of that kinde
that I saw in my travels, even a representation of the

mount Olivet. This is (in my opinion) one of the most exquisite works in all Europe, built in a round forme, and raised to the height of some forty foote by my estimation. It is supported with six goodly pillars of free stone, within the which is described the history of Christs praying upon the Mount Olivet, for there he is represented prostrate upon his knees, and elevating his hands when he prayed to his Father. Also three of his disciples are pourtraied sleeping in as many several places apart. The whole fabricke within those pillars consisteth of many notable devices. There are two very artificiall rayles of stone contrived in the maine worke, and within the same there stand the pourtraitures of ten souldiers having as many severall and distinct weapons in their hands. In another place are pourtraied five soldiers more standing together, and concluding how they may take Jesus. Also Judas comming to kisse his master with a treacherous kisse is excellently presented. About the top of the Mount where there standeth an Angell with a crosse in his hand, the figures of olives are very cunningly expressed. Likewise round about the rocke (for the lower part of this structure is made in the form of a rock) they are so artificially made, that they yeeld a most delectable shew. Within the rocke is a little Chappell having windowes made in the maine rocke to conveigh in the light. Here every Friday is Masse said. The outside of the building is inclosed with a faire inclosure of stone worke. Upon the which, round about the same, is made a faire compasse or rayle of yron, such as we call in Latine Cancelli, of some two yardes high that incompasseth the whole worke. Also the tops of those barres are headed like the forkes of arrowes, to the end that no man shall come within the place. There is but one onely dore that leadeth to this Mount Olivet and the Chappell within the same. To conclude, such is the strange curiositie of this worke, that it driveth all the beholders into admiration, and is a thing of such fame that few strangers come to the Citie but see it before they goe forth againe.

[p. 519.]

Representation of Mount Olivet.

248

ne of the most
round forme,
by my estima-
rs of free stone,
Christs praying
epresented pro-
hands when he
us disciples are
ces apart. The
sisteth of many
tuticiall rayles of
within the same
ldiers having as
their hands. In
rs more standing
take Jesus. Also
i treacherous kisse
p of the Mount
∴se in his hand,
expressed. Like-
ower part of this
) they are so arti-
delectable shew.
∴ing windows
∴ the light. Here
∴ of the building
∴ worke. Upon
∴ a faire compasse
Cancelli, of size
∴e worke. Also
∴ the forkes of
∴me within the
∴ leadeth to this
∴ the same. To
∴ this worke, that
∴ and is a thing
∴ Citie but see

Who was the first Bishop of this Citie I cannot finde. *Bishopric of Spires.* But I have read that there was a Bishopricke instituted in the same before 348 yeares after Christ. From which time [p. 520.] till the reigne of Dagobert King of France, it was exceedingly eclipsed and deceased. But the same King well repaired it againe, and created Athanasius that was one of his Chaplaines, Bishop of Spira about the yeare 610. since which time there have bene many famous Bishops, whereof those of later yeares have bene stiled with the titles of Princes: he that was Bishop when I was there, was called Eberhardus Adinheim, who was about the age of threescore yeares when I was in the Citie: one that alwaies resideth at a Palace he hath in the countrie, as the rest of his predecessors have done these many yeares.

Thus much of the Cathedrall Church and the Bishopricke.

I Was in the Colledge of the Jesuites who used me verie *College of the Jesuits.* kindly. But one especially above all the rest, whose name was Jonas Keinperger the chiefe of the Jesuiticall family, who shewed me their librarie, where I saw a notable company of goodly bookes, But in one of them I observed a matter that argued the injurious and naughty dealing of the Jesuits. For whereas amongst the rest of their bookes they had Munsters Cosmography, I looked into it to informe my selfe something of the antiquities of the Citie, and by chance turning over some leaves, I found notable places expunged by these criticall Aristarches, and demanded of them why they did deface any part of so famous an authors workes. They answered me that Munster was an heretike and an apostate, affirming that after he had renounced his Monkish religion, he maintained many heretical points in his writings. Wherefore because there were certaine matters in his Cosmography that made against the faith of the Catholike Church of Rome, they would not suffer them to remaine in the booke. How these men and others of divers Papisticall orders have dealt with the Fathers of the Church also, and

[p. 521.]

divers godly authors of great antiquitie by their wicked falsifications, putting out those things that have made against them, and supplying the same with some commentitiall forgeries of their owne braines, it doth evidently appeare to the world by the Index expurgatorius printed at Geneva and Strasbourg. I found one of those Jesuites so skilfull in some of our English histories, that he discoursed unto me of certaine ancient matters of old Brittaine, especially of our Kings of Northumberland. In their Library they keepe the picture of their Bishop Eberhardus above named, because he hath shewed himselfe a

Church of the Jesuits.

great benefactor unto them. Father Jonas shewed me their Church also. Which though it be not very great, yet it is exceeding glorious and beautifull, being garnished with a great multitude of faire pictures and images. Their table above the high Altar is a passing sumptuous thing. But I could not perceive the inward glory thereof, because it is most commonly shut, and never opened but upon speciall daies. At the upper end of the Church there are certaine seates made onely for Earles, Countesses, and other great persons to sit in, who do eftsoones repayre to their Masses, as Father Jonas told me. And by the sides of their walles in the inside of the Church, they have lately made five very curious seates of wainscot, three on one side, & two on another, for the Priest to sit in, to the end to heare the confessions of offenders. All this Church was built within these few yeares, not at their owne cost, but meerely by the benevolence and liberality of well disposed benefactors that have bountifully contributed to the building thereof. Of the Fraternitie of these Jesuites there are onely twentie.

Ancient temples.

I heard that there were certaine temples of idolatrie heretofore in this city erected by the Ethnicks, before it was converted to Christianity, & those in number three; which is also confirmed by Munster, whereof one was dedicated to Diana, which was nere to the place where the Cathedrall Church now standeth. An other to Mercury in a place where there was afterward a Monastery

OBSERVATIONS OF SPIRES

y their wicked
nat have made
ith some com-
t doth evidently
torius printed at
f those Jesuites
ies, that he dis-
matters of old
iumberland. In
eir Bishop Eber-
iewed himselfe :
onas shewed me
t not very great,
, being garnished
nd images. Their
sumptuous thing,
y thereof, because
pened but upon
: Church there are
. Countesses, and
::::es repayre to
And by the sides
::::h, they have
::::sot, three on
:: to sit in, to the
All this Church
:. their owne cost,
::y of well dis-
[:::ibuted to the
[:: these Jesuits
[
:.:s of idolatrie
::::ks, before it
(:::ber three;
'::::of one was
'::: place where
(::her to Mer-
:; a Monastery

of Benedictine Monkes. And the third to Venus, upon [p. 522.]
a hill at the west end of the city, where I observed the
Church of Saint Guido; but at last Dagobert King of
France demolished them all, so that now there are not to
be seene vel Vestigia quidem, as much as the least ruines
thereof; but only the places where they stood.

Attila King of the Hunnes after he marched out of *Spires sacked*
Hungary and Austria with his huge Armie to conquer *by Attila.*
Germany, greatly wasted this city of Spira, ransacking
it after a most cruell and mercilesse manner with fire and
sword, as he did other of the German cities that I have
already described, and others also that I shall hereafter
describe.

This City doth not embrace that unity of religion that *Protestant and*
the cities of Strasbourg, Basil, and the other reformed *Papist*
cities of Switzerland, but is distracted into a double *religions.*
religion, Protestant and Papisticall; the Protestant pro-
fessing the Lutheran Doctrine, beeing the predominant
part, though the Cathedrall Church belongeth to the
Papistes in regard their Bishop is a Papist. For a learned
preacher of the city one Nicolaus Frisius that used me
very curteously, told me that most of the principall
families professe the reformed religion. But there is a
kind of murmuring betwixt both parts, though it be so
concealed that it breaketh not out into any open jarres,
full liberty of conscience & exercise of religion being
permitted to each faction without any contradiction.

Now it were fitte to speake something of the governement of this noble city, and to mention their principall
Magistrates, their affaires in justice, and such other
memorable pointes of policy, as the description of so
worthy a City doth require. But seeing I made so shorte
aboade there, I hope thou wilt be satisfied with the
premisses. Only I can say that it is an imperiall city.
Therfore let this suffice for Spira.

Thus much of Spira.

[I departed

251

[p. 523.]

Worms.

I Departed from Spira about eight of the clocke in the morning the tenth day of September being saturday, after I had made my aboade there all friday, and came to the beautifull city of Wormes about sixe of the clock in the afternoone. This daies journey was seventeen miles. Betwixt Spira and Franckendall twelve, and from that to Wormes five. I observed that all the tract betwixt these two cities doth yeeld a most fertile & pleasant soyle that bringeth forth abundance of all manner of commodities, as corne, grapes, fruites, all manner of rootes, and what not?

Frankenthal.

I observed that in Franckendal which I never saw in any city or towne before, and I have not heard of the like to be seene in any city of Christendome saving only in the city of Nancy the Metropolitan of Lorraine. For all the houses of the towne are newly built, having bene raised from the foundations within fifty yeares, as I heard in Spira. Before which time Franckendall was the name of a Monastery onely and not of a Towne. Part of the Monastery being defaced, the whole Church remayneth to this day, being the onely Church of the Towne, and a very goodly building, which a man may see a farre off from every quarter of the country. This Monastery was built in the time of the Emperour Henry the fift about the yeare 1119. by a certaine rich Gentleman of the city of Wormes called Eckenbertus Kemerer, who converted his whole estate into money, and bestowed the same upon the building of this Monastery, which he devided into two parts, & distinguished it by the names of the greater and the lesser Monastery. For the greater served for Monkes, whereof he himselfe having abandoned the world, was the first Abbot; and the other for Nunnes, whereof his wife Richlindus was the first Abbesse. But now this Monastery is alienated from Popish uses, the Church being possessed by the Protestants of the towne that

[p. 524.]

professe the same religion that we doe in England, where they hear Gods word truly preached, & receive the Sacraments duely administred. I observed one faire street in

this towne
For all the :
before) ::
goodly ::
cannot sp::
at all there, :
Wormes.

THere in
middest :
Wormes, ::
journey ::
into a ::
from the ::
wherewith I ::
that I might as
times before in
controulement.
and so returned
and jovially tow.
neere at hand.
for so are the :
with a halbert in
very violently m
in the frontispice
me with eyes q
Almanne wordes
insolently with :
using manner at :
was in deadly fe
for the wormes
gallant City of
make any ::
weapon then a
out of Italy.
yet I gathered
cause of his

this towne which is much graced with the new buildings. For all the buildings of the towne being new (as I said before) they yeeld the much fayrer shew. Also I saw a goodly market place in the towne. More then this I cannot speake of Franckendall because I made no aboade at all there, but only glanced through it in my way to Wormes.

Thus much of Franckendall.

THere hapned unto me a certaine disaster about the *A disaster.* middest of my journey betwixt Franckendall and Wormes, the like whereof I did not sustaine in my whole journey out of England. Which was this. I stept aside into a vineyard in the open field that was but a litle distant from the high waie, to the end to taste of their grapes wherewith I might something asswage my thirst: hoping that I might as freely have done it there, as I did often times before in many places of Lombardie without any controulement. There I pulled two little clusters of them, and so returned into my way againe travelling securely and jovially towards Wormes, whose lofty Towers I saw neere at hand. But there came a German Boore upon me *An angry* (for so are the clownes of the country commonly called) *boor.* with a halbert in his hand, & in a great fury pulled off very violently my hat from my head (as I have expressed in the frontispice of my booke) looked very fiercely upon me with eyes sparkling fire in a manner, and with his Almanne wordes which I understood not, swaggered most insolently with me, holding up his halbert in that threatning manner at me, that I continually expected a blow, and was in deadly feare lest he would have made me a prey for the wormes before I should ever put my foote in the gallant City of Wormes. For it was in vaine for me to [p. 525.] make any violent resistance, because I had no more weapon then a weake staffe, that I brought with me out of Italy. Although I understood not his speeches, yet I gathered by his angry gestures that the onely cause of his quarrel was for that he saw me come

253

forth of a vineyard (which belike was his maisters) with a bunch of grapes in my hand. All this while that he threatned me with these menacing termes I stood before him almost as mute as a Seriphian frogge, or an Acanthian grashopper, scarce opening my mouth once unto him, because I thought that as I did not understand him, so likewise on the other side he did not understand me. At length with my tongue I began to reencounter him, tooke heart a grace, and so discharged a whole volley of Greeke and Latin shot upon him, supposing that it would bee an occasion to pacifie him somewhat if he did but onely thereby conceive that I had a little learning. But the implacable Clowne

> *Non magis incepto vultum sermone movetur
> Quâm si dura silex, aut stet Marpessia cautes.

And was so farre from being mitigated with my strange Rhetoricke, that he was rather much the more exasperated against me. In the end after many bickerings had passed *Friends in need.* betwixt us, three or foure good fellowes that came from Wormes, glaunced by, and inquired of me what the quarrell was. I being not able to speake Dutch asked them whether any of the company could speake Latin. Then immediately one replyed unto me that he could. Whereupon I discovered unto him the whole circumstance of the matter, and desired him to appease the rage of that inexorable and unpleasant peasant, that he might restore my hat againe to me. Then he like a very sociable companion interposed himselfe betwixt us as a mediator. But first he told me that I had committed a penal trespasse in presuming to gather grapes in a vineyard without leave, [p. 526.] affirming that the Germanes are so exceeding sparing of their grapes, that they are wont to fine any of their owne countreymen that they catch in their vineyards without leave, either with purse or body; much more a stranger. Notwithstanding he promised to do his endevour to get my hat againe, because this should be a warning for me,

* Ænei. 6.

and for that he conceived that opinion of me that I was a good fellow. And so at last with much adoe this controversie was compounded betwixt the cullian and my selfe, my hat being restored unto me for a small price of redemption, which was twelve of their little coynes called fennies, which countervaile twenty pence of our English money. But I would counsel thee gentle reader whatsoever thou art that meanest to travell into Germany, to beware by my example of going into any of their vineyardes without leave. For if thou shalt happen to be apprehended in ipso facto (as I was) by some rustical and barbarous Corydon of the country, thou mayest perhaps pay a farre deerer price for thy grapes then I did, even thy dearest blood.

Counsel to travellers.

My Observations of Wormacia Otherwise called civitas Vangionum, but most commonly Wormes.

THe situation of this famous city did as much delight me as of any city whatsoever I saw in Germany. For it is situate in a most pleasant plaine that doth very plentifully yeeld great store of all manner of commodities serving as well for pleasure as profit. For I saw goodly store of corne, especially wheate growing in the fertile and spacious fieldes about the city. Also they have great plenty of faire vineyards, yea such exuberancie of all things I observed in the whole compasse about the city, that I think there is nothing wanting unto them that the heart of man can desire. Besides it is much the more opportunely seated by reason of the noble river Rhene that runneth neere unto it, yet not so neere that it watereth the walles thereof, as it doth Mentz, but is so farre distant from it as from the City of Spira, that is, about the space of one furlong. I heard a thing in this city that I did not a little wonder at, that the territory round about the same is so exceedingly frequented with people, that there are no lesse then two hundred several townes & villages within the space of foure Dutch miles of the city, which doe make sixteene of our English. Withall he added this, that it hath bene often observed that some people of

Situation of Worms.

[p. 527.]

A populous country.

each of these two hundred Townes and Villages have repayred to the city to market, and returned backe againe the same night to their owne houses. A matter that seemed so strange unto me, that I have neither read nor heard of the like to be observed in so small a plotte of ground.

Founding of Worms.

This City is esteemed of great antiquity. For some authors doe write that it was a colonie of the Trevirians, and that it beganne to be built within a few yeares after the City of Trevirs situate by the Mosella was founded by that Babylonian Prince Trebeta the sonne of King Ninus. The people that did first inhabite it were called Vangiones, which was the name not only of the inhabitants of the City, but also of all such as dwelt round about in divers places of the country a pretty way remote from the City. From these Vangiones the City tooke her denomination of Civitas Vangionum, which name it retaineth to this day. Also it was in former times called Berberomagum as learned Peucer doth write. Which name he saith is mentioned by Ptolomæus in his Geographie. From which word the present name Wormacia (for at this day it hath two Latin names, viz. Civitas Vangionum and

[p. 528.]

Wormacia) taketh his denomination. For they make this etymologie of it, Wormacia quasi Bormacia. As for the moderne Dutch word Wormes it is derived by contraction of the letters from the Latin word Wormacia.

Buildings of the city.

The buildings of this City are very faire, both sacred and civill, and many of their streetes doe yeeld a beautifull shew both for length, breadth, and the stately houses on both sides. Their walles are strong and ancient, and beautified with faire gate-houses. Their Churches likewise, because the City standeth in a plaine, doe present a most delectable and gorgeous sight to those that approach towards the City from any quarter whatsoever, either west,

Cathedral Church of S. Peter.

north, or south; especially their Cathedral Church dedicated to St. Peter, which being adorned with foure most eminent towers of a very magnificent structure, do exhibite to the eies of the beholder a forme like to a cradle. The

256

like whereof I have before reported of the foure towers of the Cathedrall Church of Spira. This Church of St. Peter I visited, but observed no such memorable monuments therein as our Lady Church of Spira yeelded to me, and therefore I will passe it over with a word commending it for a building of notable magnificence, and (as I conjecture) of great antiquity, though I must confesse I know not the historie of the foundation of it. Because none of the learned men of the City, amongst whom I was very inquisitive for the matter, could certifie me thereof. But that which is wanting in the description of the Cathedrall Church, shall be a little supplied with the mention of the Bishops stately Palace adjoyning thereunto, although I *The Bishop's* cannot write halfe so much of the same as I would have *Palace.* done if I could have obtained accesse into the inner roomes, which I found to be a matter of great difficulty, because the Bishop whose name was Gulielmus (more then that they could not tell me) was resident in the country at his Palace of Ladenburgum when I was in Wormes. So that what I now write of the Palace is only of the frontispice [p. 529.] thereof, a matter of surpassing beauty; and that which I will report of this front is a thing so notably memorable, that as I saw not the like before, and doe doubt whether I shall ever see the like againe hereafter in any place of Christendome in my future travels: so I hope it will be very pleasant to the learned reader to reade so rare a matter as I will now present unto him. Even the sacred Prophecies of those twelve famous Prophetesses called the *The Sibylls'* Sibyllæ, who although they were Pagans borne, and lived *prophecies.* and died amongst the Gentils, yet Almighty God did infuse into them that ἔνθεος furor, that divine spirit of prophecie, that they pronounced many excellent Oracles of the Saviour of the world Jesus Christ, whereof some are such as doe in some sort agree with the predictions of Gods owne Prophets of his holy city Hierusalem. These prophecies are written upon the front of the Bishops wall (as I have already said) which hath beene lately so beautifully repaired, that it is at this day the most sumptuous front of any Bishops Palace that ever I saw. Each of these prophecies hath the picture of the authour thereof made above it with her name annexed to the same, and a notation of the yeare is added to some of them but not to all, wherein they flourished before Christs incarnation.

The first is Sibylla Delphica under whom this is written. Vixit ante adventum Christi 1525. And againe under the same picture this prophecie is written in faire Roman letters.

The first prophecy. 1. Nascetur Propheta absque coitu ex Virgine, eum cognosces proprium Dominum tuum, ipse verus erit Dei filius.

The second is Sibylla Samia. Vixit Anno ante adventum Christi 1365. Her prophecie is,

The second prophecy. 2. Ecce veniet dives & nascetur de pauperculâ, & bestiæ terræ adorabunt eum, clamabunt, & dicent: Laudate eum in atriis cœlorum.

[p. 530.] The third Sibylla Erythræa. Vixit ante adventum Christi Anno 1289. Her prophecie is,

The third prophecy. 3. In ultimâ ætate humiliabitur Proles divina, jacebit in fœno agnus, & puellari offâ educabitur.

The fourth Sibylla Phrygia. Vixit ante adventum Christi 1215. Her prophecie is,

The fourth prophecy. 4. Ex Olympo Excelsus veniet, & firmabit concilium in cælo, & annunciabitur Virgo in valibus desertorum.

The fifth Sibylla Cumana. Vixit ante adventum Christi 550. Her prophecie is,

The fifth prophecy. 5. Magnus ab integro seclorum nascitur ordo,
Jam redit & Virgo, redeunt Saturnia regna,
Jam nova progenies cœlo demittitur alto.
Tu modò nascenti puero, quod ferrea *Pu
Desinet, ac toto surget gens aurea mundo.
Casta fave Lucina, tuus jam regnat Apollo.

The sixth Sibylla Hellespontia. Vixit Anno ante adventum Christi 544. Her prophecie is,

The sixth prophecy. 6. De excelso cælorum habitaculo prospexit humiles

* I found it thus in the original, by which what they mean I know not.

suos, & nascetur in diebus novissimis de Virgine Hebræâ cum cunabulis terræ.

The seventh Sibylla Tiburtina. Vixit ante adventum Christi 92. Her prophecie is,

7. Nascetur Christus in Bethleem, annunciabitur in Nazareth regnante Thauro pacifico fundatore quietis. O fœlix illa mater cujus ubera lactabunt illum. *The seventh prophecy.*

The eighth Sibylla Cimerica. Vixit ante adventum Christi 332. Her prophecie is,

8. In primâ facie Virginis ascendet puella, facie pulchrâ, capillis prolixa, sedens super sedem stratam, puerum nutriens, dans ei ad comedendum & bibendum, jus proprium lac de cœlo missum. *The eighth prophecy.*

The ninth Sibylla Agrippa. Vixit ante adventum Christi, &c. † Her prophecie is,

9. En invisibile verbum palpabitur, germinabit ut radix, siccabitur ut folium, non apparebit venustas ejus, circundabitur alvus maternâ & florebit Deus lætitiâ sempiterna, & ab hominibus conculcabitur. *The ninth prophecy.* [p. 531.]

The tenth Sibylla Libyca. Her prophecie is,

10. Ecce veniet dies, & illuminabit Dominus densa tenebrarum & solvetur nexus Synagogæ, & recinent labia hominum, & videbunt regem viventium, & tenebit illum in gremio virgo Domina gentium, & regnabit in miseri cordiâ, & uterus matris ejus erit statera cunctorum. *The tenth prophecy.*

The eleventh Sibylla Europæa. Her prophecie is,

11. Venit ille, & transibit colles & latices Olympi, regnabit in paupertate, & dominabitur in silentio, & egredietur de utero Virginis. *The eleventh prophecy.*

The twelfth Sibylla Perfica. Her prophecie is,

12. Ecce bestia conculcaberis, & gignetur Dominus in orbem terrarum, & gremium Virginis erit ısalus gentium, & pedes ejus in valetudine hominum, invisibile verbum palpabitur. *The twelfth prophecy.*

Above these pictures are written many elegant distiches in divers severall places, two verses in a place, which seeme

† The notation of her time is omitted, and so of all the rest following.

to have beene newly written. I had a great desire to write them out. But the time would not give me leave. For that day that I wrote these Sibylline prophecies, I spent but six hours in Wormes, by reason that a certain urgent occasion called me away from the City even about noone, which deprived me of the opportunity to write those verses. Otherwise I had set them downe in this place.

Bishopric of Worms.

I will now give a little glance at the Bishopricke of Wormes, seeing this discourse of the Bishops Palace doth give me occasion to make some relation thereof. For many yeares since this was an Archbishopricke, but by whom it was first founded it is a matter altogether uncertaine. For some write (as Munster saith) that it was instituted by Clodoveus the first Christian king of France, about the yeare of our Lord 500. others againe doe report

[p. 532.]

that it began many yeares before. Which the said Munster proveth to be true. For he affirmeth that one Victor Archbishop of Wormes was at the generall Counsell holden at Colen in the yeare 348. with many other Bishops that were assembled thither from all the famous Christian countries of Europe for the deposing of Euphrates Archbishop of Colen, because he was with such pertinacy addicted to the Arrian heresie, that he would not be reconciled to the unity of the Church. The Archbishop of this Citie was in ancient times a man of so great power and

Richest prelate of Germany.

eminent authority, that he was absolutely the richest Prelate of all Germany. For he was Lord over all those large territories which the Count Palatine of Rhene, the Landgrave of Hassia, and the Archbishop of Mentz doe possesse. Also he had no lesse then sixteene Bishops under him that were subject to his jurisdiction as his Suffragans. The first Archbishop was the foresaid Victor, from whose time the Archbishoprick flourished till the time of Pipin King of France, who deposed one Guerilio from his Archiepiscopall dignity by reason of a certaine lewd fact that he had committed, and translated the Archbishopricke from Wormes to Mentz, which hath ever since retained it to this day. Also the said Archbishop

great desire to
give me leave.
phecies, I spent
a certain urgent
:n about noone,
to write those
in this place.
Bishopricke of
hops Palace doth
)n thereof. For
hopricke, but by
altogether uncer-
:::) that it was
a king of France,
againe doe report
ch the said Mun-
th that one Victor
generall Counsell
any other Bishops
famous Christian
Euphrates Arch-
:n such pertinacy
:::d not be recon-
::hbishop of this
great power and
::ly the richest
:: over all those
:: of Rhene, the
:n of Mentz doe
sixteene Bishops
:::::tion as his
:e foresaid Victor,
:::::ed till the
:::d one Guerilio
::n of a certaine
:::ed the Arch-
::th hath ever
::d Archbishop-

ricke of Wormes was from thenceforth converted to a Bishopricke, one Wernharius that immediately succeeded the foresaid Guerilio, being chosen the first Bishop thereof in the time of Carolus Magnus. From which time the Citie of Wormes hath bene ever graced with a Bishop by a continuall and orderly succession of them till this present Bishop Gulielmus, whom I have before mentioned.

Thus much of the Archbishopricke and Bishop of Wormes.

THe Prætorium or Senate house of the Citie that adjoineth to the market place is a very sumptuous building, the front whereof is beautified with many faire pictures. But the fairest of all is of Fridericke the third of that name Emperour, who is very gloriously painted in gold, sitting in his throne with his Imperiall crowne upon his head, and his Scepter in his hand, and under him this is written. *The Senate House.* [p. 533.]

Fridericus 3. Imper. Aug.
1593.

Under that this.

Renovata est hæc basilica 1592.

Againe under that I read this distich written in golden letters.

Astra Deo nil majus habent, nil Cæsare terra,
Si terram Cæsar, si regit astra Deus.

Also under that I read this inscription in a long line, above the which two souldiers were painted in their armour, leaning downe a little. And at one end of the front another souldier in his complete armour, displaying an ancient, and at the other end is painted a Queene with a crowne upon her head. This inscription (I say) did I reade there in that long line.

Libertatem quam majores peperere dignè studeat fovere posteritas. Turpe enim esset parta non posse tueri.

261

Quamobrem Vangiones quondam cum Julio conflictati jam tibi Cæsar perpetuâ fide cohærent.

Statues of four German Emperors. Next unto this in another part of the same front are erected the statues of foure German Emperors that were benefactors to the citie, very sumptuously gilted for the better ornament of the prætorium, with their imperiall Diadems upon their heads, each carrying a sword in one hand, and a globe in another. They are represented onely to the girdle : The first Carolus Quintus, the second Ferdicandus Primus Cæsar, the third Maximilianus Secundus, the fourth Rodolphus Secundus. And under them is written in golden letters Anno 1581. Georgio Euchario Mosbach & Joanne Kigele Reipub. Ædilibus, basilica hæc est ædificata. Againe under that I read this inscription written in golden letters. Austriacæ familiæ heroibus vindicibus libertatis patriæ ultra C C L annos amissæ [p. 534.] vetustæ Vangionum Wormaciæ S P Q. beneficiorum memor locavit. Anno 1581. Also in the same ranke of that part of the front this impresse following is written in the like golden letters upon a ground of Azure, neere to the portraiture of a greene Dragon supporting a coate of armes, wherein is figured a key ; which dragon with *Arms of* the rest is the armes of this Citie of Wormes. Draco *Worms.* clavem tenens industriâ vastas solitudines excoli, fide & constantiâ ad decus perveniri demonstrat. Hæc majores Vangionum urbis suæ arma esse voluerunt. Also another part of this Prætorium is beautified with sundry notable historicall descriptions of the ancient Romanes. Under one whereof I read this following.

Ancient Romans. Sexti Tarquinii regii filii libidine factum est, ut Romæ exactis regibus consulare imperium jurejurando constitueretur, isque honos primò Lucio Junio Bruto sceleris vindici decerneretur. Next this.

Patrii amoris vim ex animo potiùs ejicere, liberosque securi ferire quàm libertatem civium perfidiâ imminui nobili exemplo.

L I Br. docuit ·

' conflictati jam

'ront are erected
.hat were bene-
:d for the better
periall Diadems
.n one hand, and
'ed onely to the
:ond Ferdinandus
, Secundus, the
r them is written
..chario Mosbach
basilica hæc est
this inscription
:.:.::: herorbus
L annos amissæ
Q beneficiorum
·'·e same ranke of
...owing is written
: of Azure, neere
|:.:.::ng a coate
|:.:. dragon with
|'::.::as. Draco
|-:: excoli, fide &
|.. Hæc majores
|:.. Also another
|': sundry notable
|.:.::as. Under

|... est, ut Romæ
|:.:·:..:o consti-
|.:.:: Beate sceleris

|:.:.., liberosque
|:.::.: imminui

Then againe this.   Horatium Coclitem contra omnes
hostium copias tenuit in ponte solum sine ullâ spe salutis
suæ patriæ salus.   Also this.   Pro imperii gloriâ atque
dignitate magnum animum suscipiendum Mutius ad necem
Porsennæ impulsus, docet.   Last of all this.   Ut Clœlia
Virgo, ita omnes suo casu aut confirmare patriæ salutem,
aut periculum morari debent.

Under the Senate house there is a faire walke supported
with stately pillars that doe make a pretie arch at the top.
Also the roofe of the walke is finely painted, wherein are
made the pictures of all the Emperours.   A sight very
beautifull.

The government of this Citie hath bene divers accord- *Government of*
ing to the change of times, and it hath acknowledged many *the city.*
Lords.   It was first subject to the Trevirians, as being a
colonie of the Citie of Trevirs, to whom they payed a [p. 535.]
yearely tribute.   Next, to the Romanes, where one of their
Prefects resided with a garrison of souldiers for the defence
of the citie against the Germans on the other side of the
Rhene.   Their first Prefect was appointed by Julius Cæsar,
who in the like manner assigned more Prefects with garrisons for other cities & townes, as I shall hereafter declare
in the description of them, the authoritie of each being
so limited, that he was subject to a superiour Governor
who was the Prefect of Mentz, or rather the Duke of
Mentz commonly called Dux Moguntinus, as I have
before written in my observations of Strasbourg.   Thus
for the space of 500 years this Citie sustained the yoke of
a servile subjection under the Romane Emperours, even
till the time of that flagellum Dei Attila King of the *Worms sacked*
Hunnes, who breaking with a great armie out of the *by Attila.*
country of the Sicambrians which are now those of
Gelderland, destroyed this Citie together with all the
other famous cities that were situate on that banke
of the Rhene, which was in those daies esteemed a great
part of the French Kingdome.   From the time of that
miserable ruine and depopulation, the Citie was ever alienated from the Romanes.   Againe within fewe years after

that desolation, the inhabitants of the territory thereabout
reedified the City, adorning it with walles, Churches, and
goodly buildings.   And within few yeares after these
reparations it came into the hands of the French kings,
who governed it a long time; and were so delighted with
the sweetnesse of the situation, and the opportunity of
the place, that some of them kept their Court there, as I
will hereafter mention.   But at length by the fatal revolu-
tion of time it descended to the sway of the Germane
Emperours, whereof some have graced it partly with the
residence of their Court in this Citie, partly by the
solemnization of great marriages, and partly by the celebration of generall councels and other famous meetings,

[p 536.]

as I will by and by more particularly declare.   So that at
this day it flourisheth in a most opulent estate, and
enjoyeth great peace under their sacred clientele and
protection.

So delicate a place is this City of Wormes (for indeed
I attribute much to it by reason of the admirable amenitie

French Kings
resided at
Worms.

of the situation thereof) that some of the French Kings
did eftsoones keepe their royall residence here when it was
subject to their dominion, as I have before written.   For
we reade that Pipin King of France kept his Court here in
the yeare 764. when he condemned Tassilo King of
Bavaria of treason.   Also in the yeare 769. the said King
Pipins sonne Charles (who was afterward that most
renowned and victorious Emperour of Germanie surnamed
the Great, from the greatnesse of his valiant exploites) was
in this city crowned King of France.   Againe in the yeare
770. Prince Adolphus that was the Generall Captaine of
King Charles forces, marched from this city with his armie
towards the Saxons, and in the yeare 779. brought with
him some of the Princes of Saxonie to this City as hostages
to King Charles.   In the yeare 783. Charles being now
inaugurated into the Empire, solemnized a royall marriage
in Wormes with the Lady Fastrada, who was his fourth
wife, and the daughter of the Earle of Franconia.   In the
yeare 790. the same Charles the Great kept his imperiall

Court for the space of a whole yeare in this City, but by
reason that his Palace was casually burnt and utterly consumed with fire, he removed his Court therehence to his
Palace of Ingelheim where he was borne, not farre from
the City of Mentz. Moreover there have bene five
famous Councels kept in this City. Whereof the first *The Councils*
was celebrated by Ludovicus Pius the Emperour and sonne *of Worms.*
of the foresaid Charles the Great in the yeare 829. The
second by Ludovicus the second who was the sonne of the
foresaid Emperor in the yeare 868. in thè moneth of May,
having assembled together a great multitude of Princes
and Bishops against the errors of the Grecians. The third [p. 537.]
by Henry the third and Pope Leo the ninth about the
time of Christs nativity (which we commonly call Christ-
masse) in the yeare 1051. The fourth by that worthy
Emperour of sacred memorie Henry the fourth in the
yeare 1076. which Councell is much the more famoused
for that by the consent of all the German Bishops which
he then assembled together, saving those of Saxonie, he
deposed Pope Hildebrand otherwise called Gregorie the
seventh. The same Emperour at divers other times much
frequented this City, because in the middest of all his bitter
persecutions and conflicts which he suffered by meanes of
the Romish Clergie, he found Wormes a most secure
refuge and shelter for him ; the Citizens being so lovingly
inclined to succour him in his afflictions that they never
forsooke him, but exposed both their bodies and goods
for his safety to the very utmost of their power, which
thing hath purchased them no small praise. The fifth and *Fifth and last*
last Councell by the Emperour Henry the fifth in the *Council.*
yeare 1122. the Bishop of Ostia being sent thither with
two Cardinals in the behalfe of the Pope, at what time that
great controversie was composed betwixt the secular
Princes and the Ecclesiasticall Prelates about the bestowing of Bishopricks and spirituall preferments. As for
great marriages celebrated in this City, I have read of one
very famous marriage kept here besides that before men- *Famous*
tioned of Charles the Great, which I am the more willing *marriages.*

265

to mention because the woman here married was borne in my owne country of England. For here in the yeare 1235. or thereabout, the Emperour Fredericke the second, solemnized a most pompous marriage with the Lady Isabella the daughter of King John of England. This Lady was his third wife. Amongst many other things that historians have written of this City one memorable matter is of one of our English Kings, even King Richard, [p. 538.] for whose memorie sake I will make some mention of him; after that William King of the Romans was slaine by the Frisians there was a great jarre betwixt the Elector Princes about the election of a new Emperour. For some of them stoode for Alphonsus King of Castella, others *King Richard of England.* for Richard King of England. In this Dissension the chiefest Princes which were of the predominant faction, namely the two Archbishops of Mentz and Colen, and Ludovicus Count Palatine of Rhene, chose the foresaid King Richard. Whereupon shortly after this election he travelled into Germany, and after many solicitations and great promises of favour he was honourably entertained in this City of Wormes in the yeare 1258. in the moneth of Julie. But before he was admitted within the gates of the City, the Wormacians drew him to this composition, that he should presently disburse ten thousand markes of silver for the necessity of the City: which being performed according to their demand, they afterward did homage unto him. After which time King Richard returned into England, and about two yeares after, even in the yeare 1260. came backe againe to Wormes, where he was a prety while resident in the City, during the time of whose residence there he compounded certaine controversies both betwixt the city of Wormes & the towne of Oppenheim, and also betwixt Wormes it selfe and some Noblemen of the same City. Moreover the same King *Diet of Worms.* celebrated a famous Diet in this City of Wormes about nine yeares after that, even in the yeare 1269. and concluded a publique peace in the whole City, abolishing all manner of tolles and taxes both by land and water. All

ied was borne
re in the yeare
cke the second,
vith the Lady
:ngland. This
iy other things
one memorable
n King Richard,
me mention of
mans was slaine
wixt the Elector
:our. For some
Castella, others
; Dissension the
ominant faction,
and Colen, and
:\ose the foresaid
r this election he
solicitations and
rably entertained
5 in the moneth
within the gates
tnis composition,
usand markes of
:..: being per-
:. afterward did
King Richard
:.:es after, even
Wormes, where
during the time
certaine contro-
& the towne of
selfe and some
the same King
Wormes about
1.:5, and con-
.: :listing all
:.:d water. All

these memorable histories tending to the illustration of this renowned city of Wormes, I have thought good to insert into these my observations, as I have found them in Munsters Cosmographie, unto whom they were sent from the Senate of the same City (as he himselfe affirmeth) by way of an epitome of the Wormacian Annals, for the better garnishing of his Cosmographicall volume.   [p. 539.]

What famous persons of great marke have bene buried in this city I know not, because I surveyed not the monumentes, but surely I heard of no more then one great man, who was a Prince of great renowne in his daies.   Namely one Conradus Duke of Franconia, surnamed the Wise, *Conrad the Wise.* who was the sonne in lawe of the Emperour Otho Magnus, whose daughter Ludgarda he married.   This Conradus was slaine with an arrow in that famous battel that the foresaid Emperor fought with the Hungarians upon the fourth day of August anno 955. neere to the city of Augusta, from which place his body was afterward brought hither to Wormes, and here interred.   But it was not my hap to see the monument it selfe.

One principall thing that I observed in my observations of Basil, Strasbourg, and Heidelberg, namely the writing of a short index of such famous professours of learning as have lived or died therein, I have omitted in these two last *An omission.* cities of Spira and Wormes.   Because I have neither read nor heard of any excellent men that they ever bred.   Onely Wormes was once adorned with one singular scholer whome I will not let passe without mention, and yet but briefly name him, because I have already spoken of him in my observations of Heidelberg.   This was Joannes Dalburgius a very rare man in the age wherein he lived, & a great Mecœnas and fosterer of learned men : who after he had enjoyed the Episcopall dignity foure yeares, died in the yeare 1503. in his Palace of Ladenburgum. More then him I cannot name in this city of Wormes.

It remayneth now that I speake a little of the religion *The religion of* of this city, according to that course that I have hitherto *Worms.* observed in every German city saving Basil.   Therfore I

267

[p. 540.] will briefly touch this, and so make an end of this history of Wormes. The religion is mixed as that of Spira. For it is partly Protestant of the Lutheran religion, and partly Papisticall. Unto the Papistes belongeth the Cathedrall Church as that of Spira, because the Bishop of this City is a Papist. But the Protestant faction is both the greater in number, and the stronger in power. For almost all the better families of the City are Protestant.

Thus much of Wormes.

Oppenheim.

I Departed from Wormes about halfe an hower after twelve of the clocke the eleventh of September being Sunday, and came to Oppenheim a pretty faire towne in the lower County Palatine, which is about twelve miles beyond Wormes, about sixe of the clocke in the evening. I observed a very fruitfull soyle in all that space of ground betwixt Wormes and Oppenheim bearing notable commodities, as corne, vineyardes, &c. This Towne belongeth to the Pfaltzgrave of Rhene, and professeth the same religion that he doth. Here died Rupertus King of the Romanes who was afterward buried at Heidelberg, as I have before mentioned in my notes of that City. The inhabitants of this towne do attribute very much to the situation of it. For they affirme that it is situate in the

Oppenheim compared with Jerusalem.

same manner as holy Jerusalem was : Because it standeth upon the side of a hill. For so we may reade that a part of Jerusalem stood, even the same part which is called Sion, which (as Historians do write) was built upon the very side of a hill, the toppe whereof was adorned with King Davids Palace. Also the inhabitants of the City of Bergomo in Italy (whereof I have before written) may as well compare the situation of their City with that of Jerusalem, as these men of Oppenheim. For that standeth as pleasantly upon the side of a hill as this doth. Truly the sight of them both is so pleasant that the Citizens may justly boast of it. They have one pretty Church in

[p. 541.] Oppenheim called Saint Catharines which is seene afarre off.

I departed from Oppenheim the twelfth day of September being munday about sixe of the clocke in the morning, and came to the city of Mentz about tenne of the clocke in the morning, which was tenne miles beyond it. It was my hap in this journey betwixt Oppenheim and Mentz to have such a notable companion as I never had before in all my life. For he was both learned and *A learned* unlearned. Learned because being but a wood-cleaver *wood-cleaver.* (for he told me that he was the Jesuits wood-cleaver of Mentz) he was able to speake Latine. A matter as rare in one of that sordid facultie as to see a white Crowe or a blacke Swanne. Againe he was unlearned, because the Latin which he did speake was such incongruall and disjoynted stuffe, such antipriscianisticall eloquence, that I thinke were grave Cato alive (who for his constant severity was called ἀγέλαστος, because he never or very seldome laughed) he should have more cause to laugh if he should heare this fellow deliver his minde in Latin, then when he saw an Asse eate thistles.

My Observations of Moguntia otherwise called Moguntiacum, but commonly Mentz.

THe situation of this City is pleasant, yet not com- *Situation of* parable to that of Strasbourg, Spira, and Wormes. *Mayence.* For each of these standeth in a pleasant plaine. But this is inclosed on the south and east sides with a hill, which me thinkes doth something eclipse the beauty of the city. Yet these hilles are very commodious to Mentz. For they are most plentifully planted with faire vineyardes. All the north side is washed with the river Rhene which runneth hard by the walles thereof. I observed that this city is built in a longer forme then any other German [p. 542.] citie that I saw, saving Heidelberg, the breadth of it being not very great. Yet this length doth yeeld a passing faire shew to those that approach towards the city from any quarter either by land or water, saving onely from the south. Because the hilles on that side doe interclude the sight of the city. The streetes are many, and some very

269

The ancient city.

faire, being adorned with many goodly buildings of great antiquity, whereof divers I observed foure stories high; also their walles are very strong and ancient, & beautified with five gates. But the olde Mentz that flourished in the time of Julius Cæsar, stood not so neere the Rhene as this doth; but higher upon the hill, as it doth manifestly appeare by those ancient rudera that I perceived in divers places of the same hill. Which being afterward destroyed by Attila King of the Hunnes, the founders of this second city thinking this to be a more opportune place for the building of their City then that upon the hill, have now built it hard by the Rhene, as I have already said. I finde some difference amongst the historians about the first founder of this City. For some write that it was built by Prince Trebeta the founder of Trevirs and Strasbourg.

Derivation of the name.

Others ascribe the first foundation to one Moguntius a Trojan, from whom they say it hath the denomination of Moguntia. And others againe do affirme that the name Moguntia is derived from Moganus a river running neere to it, which is otherwise called Mœnus that runneth by the city of Franckford. For at this City the Mœnus and the Rhene do meete and make a confluent, as at Lyons the Arar and the Rhodanus, at the Citie of Confluence (whereof I shall heereafter speake) the Mosella and the Rhene. How this appellation of Moguntia degenerated in processe of time to this moderne name of Mentz I do not know. But the like abbreviation I perceive hath hapned to other German Cities. For the old name of

[p. 543.]

Aquisgranum that noble City of Province is now come to Aach, Turegum (of whom I have before written) the Metropolitan of Switzerland to Zurich, Rubeachum a famous City of Alsatia to Rusach, Wormacia to Wormes, and so Moguntia to Mentz.

The Cathedral Church.

The churches of the city are tenne, whereof the Cathedrall is a building very sumptuous, and adorned with a tower of a very eminent heigth, but inferiour to other German churches that I saw before, especially those two of Basil and Strasbourg. This church is dedicated to Saint

270

Martin, and was first founded about the yeare 1011. by one Willigisus the foure and thirtieth Bishop of Mentz that was privie Counseller to the Emperour Otho the second, and the first elector of the Empire of all the Moguntine Archbishops. Of whom it is written that he had the picture of a wheele painted in his refectory with this inscription *The origin of the Arms of Mayence.*

Willigise memineris quid sis, et quid olìm fueris.

Since which time the wheele hath ever beene the armes of the Archbishoprick of Mentz, and confirmed by the Emperour Henry the second surnamed the Holy. This foresaid Cathedrall church was onely begun by that Bishop Willigisus, but not finished by him. For the third Bishop that succeeded him, one Bardo Abbot of Fulda was the man that brought that noble worke to perfection. I observed a thing both in this church, & in most of the other German churches, as also in many of the civill buildings of their cities, that I could never perceive in any of mine owne country of England, or France, Savoy, or Italy : that in the outside of the roofe of their buildings, even in the middest of the tiling they have a great company of open places like windowes contrived in both sides of *Open windowes.* the roofe, to what use it served I could not devise. For if it be made for light sake, it seemeth in my opinion something needlesse, because the other windowes of the same edifice do minister sufficient light. Therefore I thinke it served for some other use, which unto me is altogether unknowne. Many goodly monuments this [p. 544.] church contayneth both ancient and moderne, but especially of their Bishops. Whereof one I observed to be more beautifull then the rest, which is erected on the north side of the body of the Church, and inserted into one of the maine pillers. This is of their last Archbishop. His *An Archbishop's monument.* statue is erected at length in his episcopall ornaments, most curiously carved in alabaster with a miter on his head exceeding richly beset with pearles and precious stones fairely represented in the same. Also it is garnished

with many pillars of costly marble, and sundry golden
scutchins. At the top of all two Angels are pourtrayed
sitting, and holding a peece of parchment in their right
hands, wherein this is written,

Memento homo quòd cinis es.

And in their left handes lilies. Above them is represented
an other Angel sounding of a Trumpet. Beneath, about
the base of the monument, this Epitaph is written upon a
faire peece of touchstone.

D. O. M.

R^{mo} et Illmo Dño Dño Wolphango de nobili et vetustâ
Camerariorum de Wormaciâ dictorum â Dalburg familiâ :
Archiepiscopo et Principi Electori Moguntino prudentiâ,
eloquentiâ, et justitiâ singulari, de totâ Ecclesiâ et repub.
benè merito, anno Dñi 1592. magno omnium desiderio et
consensu electo, in regimine annis 19. moderato et pacifico ; anno denique 1601. die Aprili 5°. piè placidèque
defuncto, et hìc publico omnium luctu recondito Joannes
Suicardus Successor Prædecessori meritissimo F. C. Anno.
1606.

Also on the South side of the Church, a little within the
entrance, I saw another more sumptuous monument then
this before mentioned, of a certayne Bishop of Wormes,
who was also Warden and Deane of this Cathedrall Church
of Mentz. I take this monument to be nothing else then
a cenotaphium, that is, a Sepulchre void of a body, being
erected only for honour sake, according to the custome of
the ancient Romans. For it appeareth by the epitaph
subscribed that the body was buryed at Wormes. It is
raised to an exceeding heigth, even thirty foote high by
my estimation, garnished with goodly pillars of great
value, partly of changeable-coloured marble and partly of
touch-stone ; and adorned with great store of Scutchins
and Armes, curious golden borders, and workes. About
the middle is made the effigies of him at length in his
Episcopall ornaments with his Crosier, and his hands that
are covered with his episcopall red gloves, are elevated to

A cenotaph.

[p. 545.]

272

sundry golden
are pourtrayed
(in their right

the image of Christ erected opposite unto it upon a faire Crosse of touch-stone. Under the same this epitaph is written in golden letters upon a faire ground of touch- stone.

The Bishop's epitaph.

.s.

m is represented
Beneath, about
s written upon a

> Georgius Dei gratiâ Episcopus Wormacien.
> ex nobili familiâ â Sconenburg ortus, hujus
> Metropolitanæ Ecclesiæ Præpositus, ac priùs
> Annis xviii. Decanus, tandem verò Cæ-
> saris Rodolphi II. vices in Conventu De-
> putatorum Imperii gerens obiit Spiræ,
> sepultus autem Wormaciæ in Ecclesiâ
> Cathedrali. In pace quiescit Princeps de
> Repub. Christianâ ac presertìm Ecclesiâ
> cui prudentiâ singulari, studio & labore
> indefesso, laudeque eximiâ præfuit atque pro-
> fuit, optimè meritus. Anno M. D. lxxxxv.
> die xi. Mensis Augusti.

nobili et vetusti
D..burg familiæ:
runtino prudentiâ,
E..esiâ et repub
mnium desiderio et
moderato et pru-
.. .. placideque
recondito Joannes
t:ssmo F C. Anno.

Opposite unto this rich monument there is a marvailous curious Altar adorned with great variety of marble, and exquisite images gilted and carved in Alabaster. Amongst the rest I noted one thing very attentively, even a great Whale swallowing up the Prophet Jonas. A device pass- ing finely contrived. Many other goodly monuments I saw there of their Prelats and others decked with Epitaphs, which the shortnesse of time would not give me leave to write out. Besides I observed two faire Pulpits in the body of the church. Whereof one was very sumptuoùs, the toppe being wonderfull curiously decked with many excellent works richly gilted, yet al made in wainscòt: besides I noted certaine pretty little images of alabaster very artificially expressèd in the same toppe. As of the three principal christian vertues. Faith, Hope, and Charity. Also the foure Cardinall morall vertues, Justice, Fortitude, Prudencè, and Temperance. There are written these two sentences out of Saint Paul.

Jonah and the whale.

[p. 546.]

a little within the
[..s monument that
Bishop of Wormes,
Cathedrall Church
..thing else the
.. of a body, being
..to the custome of
.. by the epitaph
at Wormes. It is
..ry foote high by
.. pillars of great
..le and partly of
store of Scutchins
.. workes. About
.. at length in his
..d his hands that
.., are elevated to

Stella a stellâ differt in claritate : sic resurrectio mor- tuorum. 1. Cor. 15. ca. also above that this is written in

golden letters.   Prædica verbum, insta opportunè, impor-
tune, argue, obsecra, increpa, in omni patientiâ et doctrinâ.
2. Tim. 4.

Conversion of
Mayence.

This City was converted to Christianity in the time of
Saint Paul the Apostle as soone as any city of all Germany.
For eyther Crescens which was one of Saint Pauls scholars
whome he mentioneth in the second Ep. to Tim. 4. cap. 10.
ver. or Crescentius who was also his Scholer, was the first
Apostle of this city, and (as they say) the first Bishop.
After whom there was a succession of many holy and godly

An Englisman
first
Archbishop of
Mayence.

Bishops.   But their first Archbishop was mine owne
countryman (as I have both often read, & also heard from
that learned Jesuite Nicolas Serrarius of Mentz) whome
I will therefore honoris causâ, mention.   Even Bonifacius
an Englishman, one of the rarest and worthiest men that
ever possessed the Sea of Mentz, and therefore much
celebrated amongst the learned Germanes for his divine
learning and holy conversation of life.   His name was
first Winifride, and was a Benedictine Monke (as Serrarius
told me) before he came to Mentz.   He was the seventeenth Bishop of this City, and came over in the time of
Pipin King of France, about the yeare 776.   At what time
the Archbishoprick of Wormes being extinct in the time of
their Archbishop Gervilio, was translated hither, as I have
before reported in my observations of that City.   This

[p. 547.]

Boniface was in â manner the second Apostle of Germany,
and much reformed divers Churches in many parts of that
Country, as in Thuringia and elsewhere (as I have reade in
the workes of learned Melanthon) greatly taxing the
Priestes for adultery, and inflicting the punishments of a
whole yeares imprisonment upon the offendours.   He was
Archbishop of this City five and thirty yeares, and the
founder of that most famous Abbey of Fulda in Buchonia,
which remaineth yet to this day, and is esteemed one of
the most magnificent Monasteries of all Christendome;
in the which at last he himselfe was buried, after he had
suffered martyrdome in his old age amongst the Frisians
for the free preaching of the Gospell.   So that his monu-

274

OBSERVATIONS OF MAYENCE

ıtiá et doctrinâ.

in the time of
of all Germany.
ıt Pauls scholers
Tim. 4. cap. 10.
ıler, was the first
the first Bishop
r holy and godly
was mine owne
& also heard from
if Mentz) whome
Even Bonifacius
worthiest men that
:d therefore much
unes for his divine
t. His name was
Monke (as Serrarius
He was the seven-
... in the time of
... At what time
... in the time of
... other, as I have
... that City. This
... ple of Germany,
... ther parts of that
... as I have reade it
... sorely taxing the
... punishments of i
... dours. He was
... yeares, and the
... Fulda in Buchovia,
... esteemed one of
... all Christendome;
... ... after he had
... st the Frisians
... that his monu-

ment is shewed in that Abbey to this day.   Besides many
other worthy Archbishops that flourished in this City after
my countryman Bonifacius, Rabanus Maurus that was once
Abbot of the foresaid Abbey of Fulda, is much celebrated
by authors, being the fifth Archbishop after Bonifacius,
whome I therefore name because he was the disciple of
an other most famous and learned countryman of mine
owne, Venerabilis Beda.   I have before mentioned who
was the first elector Archbishop of this city, namely
Willigisus.   Ever since which time the Archbishop of this *The
city hath beene a soveraigne Prince of most eminent Archbishop of
authority.   For besides his great Signiory and large terri- Mayence a
tory that he hath to maintaine his principalitie, he is the sovereign
cheef Elector Prince of the sacred Roman Empire next to Prince.*
the King of Bohemia above al the rest.   Also he is intituled
Chancellor of Germany for the more addition of dignity.
Moreover his spirituall jurisdiction extended it selfe so
farre that he hath these 12 Bishopricks subject to his sea,
namely that of Curia in Rhetia, Constance in Suevia, Strasbourg in Alsatia, Spira, Wormes, Wirceburgum Franconia,
Augusta in Vindelicia, Aistet in Bavaria, Padeborna in
Westphalia ; in Saxony these 3. Hildiheim, Halberstat, &
Verda.   The name of him that was the present Archbishop [p. 548.]
of Mentz when I was there was Joannes Suicardus, who
then kept his residence at a palace he had in the countrie.
I observed his Palace in the Citie to be a building of great
magnificence standing about the farther end of the west
part of Mentz, and built hard by the Rhene, which to
those that come to the Citie eyther by water, or by the
North side of the land doth present a very faire shew,
and much beautifie that part of the Citie.   Also there is
another goodly building adjoyning next to it, which is the
Chancery house of the Citie.
   The antiquities of this Citie both sacred and civill are *Antiquities of
more then in any City whatsoever in all Germany.   In so Mayence.*
much that the foresaid Jesuite Serrarius hath lately written
a very elegant booke of the Moguntine antiquities which
he shewed me ; having dedicated it to the present Arch-

275

bishop Joannes Suicardus. But it was my chance to see but one of them, which of all the civill is esteemed the most remarkable in the whole Citie. And indeed a thing very worthy the observation both for the worthinesse of the founder, the nobility of the worke, and the mention of it in ancient authors. In that I came to the sight of it I do thankfully acknowledge my selfe beholding to the foresaid Jesuite, who very kindly procured me the meanes to see

A stone Colossus.

it. This is nothing else then a stonie Colossus erected in a vineyard upon the top of a certaine hill on the South side of the Citie, (where in former times a part of the ancient Citie stood) neere to a Monastery dedicated to St. James, in which there is a convent of St. Bennets Monks at this day. The vineyard is invironed round about with a wall of a convenient height, to the end to preserve the monument that none may come to it without leave. And there is but one way to it by a dore that is alwaies locked. The author of this was Drusus Nero the sonne in law of Augustus Cæsar by his fourth and last wife

[p. 549.]

Livia Drusilla, and the brother of the Emperour Tiberius. This monument did he erect just about the time of Christs incarnation, when he waged warre with the Germanes in this place (as both Cornelius Tacitus and Suetonius do make mention) leaving it unto posterity as a memorial of his name, that he had once skirmished there with the Germanes, and conquered them in battell. The thing it selfe is a very huge and massie moles of stones rammed together, and made something in the forme of an akorne. For which cause it is called in the Germane tongue Cichelstein which signifieth an akorne. Howbeit the lower part of it differeth something from the fashion of an akorne. But the higher part resembled it as neere as can be. For all the lower part from that part of the foundation which appeareth above the ground to almost the middle, is made square, whereas the lower part of an akorne is round; and from corner to corner I take it to be almost fortie foote. All the higher part ascendeth lesser and lesser towards the top, yet after such a round manner, that it doth very

276

artificially resemble an akorne. One very strange thing I *A strange* observed in this masse, that whereas I and another Gentle- *sound.* man that went with me to see it, stroke the stones of the worke at the farther corners, he at one corner, and I at another, with little stones that we tooke up for the same purpose; the noise of the stroake would easily be heard from one corner to another which were about fiftie foote asunder, though we strooke the stones of the moles as soft as could be possible. A matter much to be wondered at except either the foundation be hollow, or some part of the same square masse. A Gentleman of good quality told me that when Albertus Marquesse of Brandenburg did of late yeares oppugne this Citie with great hostilitie, he did set a worke certaine masons to pull it downe, as being *A hard task.* a prophane Pagan monument. But they found such extreme difficulty in pulling the stones asunder, though they laboured most painfully with their mattocks and other [p. 550.] instruments, that after they had done a little they ceased from their worke. For they found it almost as difficult to pull it downe as to build it up, by reason that the stones are with such admirable hardnesse compacted together. Yet that which they did to the upper part of it, hath much disfigured and blemished the grace of the monument.

Besides many other things that have greatly graced this city, and made it famous over all Christendome, as the Archiepiscopal dignity, the antiquity of the foundation, the noble monuments, the sumptuousnesse of their build-ings publike and private, the frequency of people inhabiting the same, and the opportunity of the situation, that most incomparably excellent art of printing which was first *Art of* invented in this city, is not to bee esteemed the least, nay *printing first* rather it deserveth to bee ranked in an equal dignity with *invented in* the worthiest matter of the whole city, if not to bee *Mayence.* preferred before it. For in this City of Mentz was the divine art (to give it an epitheton more then ordinary by reason of the excellency of the invention) of printing first devised by a Gentleman or rather a Knight of this city one Joannes Cuttenbergius in the yeare of our Lord one

277

thousand foure hundred and forty, even in that very yeare
that Fredericke the third was inaugurated into the Empire;
and in the time of their Archbishop Theodoricus who was
the sixty seventh after Crescens the first Apostle of the
City. Well might that ancient Poet write those verses in
praise of this noble art that Kirchnerus hath cited in his
oration of Germany; which I have inserted into my
observations;

> O Germania muneris repertrix,
> Quo non utilius dedit vetustas,
> Libros scribere, quæ doces, premendo.

For surely if we rightly consider it, we shall finde it to
be one of the most rare and admirable inventions that ever
was since the first foundation of the world was laid. For

[p. 551.] what I pray can be devised in rerum naturâ more strange
then that one man should be able by his Characters composed of tinne, brasse, & *stibium to write more lines
in one day then the swiftest Scrivener in the world can
do in a whole yeare? according to that old verse

> Imprimit una dies quantum vix scribitur anno.

A matter that may seeme incredible to the understanding
of many men, yet most certainely verified by experience.

Virtues of By vertue of this arte are communicated to the publike
printing. viewe of the Worlde the monuments of all learned authors
that are set abroach out of the sacred treasurie of antiquity,
and being now freed from that Cimmerian darknesse
wherein they lurked for the space of many hundred yeares,
and where they did cum tineis ac blattis rixari, to the great
prejudice of the common weale of learning, but especially
of Gods Church, are divulged to the common light, and
that to the infinite utility of all lovers of the Muses and
professours of learning. By this arte all the liberall
sciences are now brought to full ripenesse and perfection.
Had not this art bene invented by the divine providence of

*This is a kind of white stone found in silver mines which they
use in printing.

God, it was to be feared lest the true studies of all disciplines both divine & humane would have suffered a kind of shipwrack, and have bene halfe extinct before this age wherein we breathe. I would to God we would thankefully use this great benefite of our gracious God (as a learned author saith) not to the obscuration but the illustration of Gods glory, not to dis-joine but rather to conjoine the members of Christes militant Church here on earth.

Within a short space after this singular invention of printing ensued the institution of a University in this *University of Mayence.* city, in the time of the Archbishop Theodoricus, under whom printing began. I think this University was never great. Surely what it was in former times I know not, but at the time of my being there it consisted principally of one Colledge, which was that of the Jesuites, a building *[p. 552.]* that was lately founded within these few yeares, and endowed with convenient maintenance by the munificence of the Archbishops, whereof Joannes Suicardus who was Bishop when I was there, (as I have before said) hath bin a notable benefactor to it. This Colledge is a convenient faire house, but much inferiour to the majestie of divers Colledges in our famous Universities of Oxford and Cambridge, to whome I attribute so much for the statelinesse of their building, that I preferre some of them by many degrees before any Colledges that I saw in my travells. It was my hap to visite this Colledge, where Nicolaus Serrarius the Antesignanus of all the Jesuiticall familie used me more kindely and familiarly then I thinke he doth every Protestant that commeth to him. For besides other courtesies he shewed me their Library, which is a *The Library.* passing faire place, and furnished with great variety of excellent bookes, especially Theologicall. I will give this Serrarius his due ; for Virtus etiam in hoste micat : certainly he is a man of that excellent learning, that hee deserveth great praise. Also he is reported to be so rare a linguist, that I heard he speaketh at least six languages. I would to God hee would cease to write so virulently

279

against our Protestants, especially poore Martin Luther, whom he hath most bitterly exagitated in that invective booke intituled de Lutheri magistro, by magistro meaning the Devill.

Besides these two things last mentioned, the art of printing and their Universitie, this City is much celebrated by historiographers for three other matters. First the fighting of many famous battels neare to this City. Secondly for certaine notable bridges built here over the Rhene. Thirdly for the death of great personages in the same City. The principall battels fought there were waged by the Romans: as by Drusus Nero whom I have before mentioned, who skirmished in this place with the Germans. But this was not the place where he brake his legge by falling from his horse, as some doe write. For that mischance he had at the towne of Bing (as I will hereafter mention) which is situate about some ten miles beneath Mentz upon the left banke of the Rhene. Also Aurelianus the sixe & thirtieth Roman Emperor fought a great battell here with the Franci,* when he was but a yong man, before he was chosen into the Empire, and in that skirmish got a glorious victorie by slaying at the least thirty thousand of them. Likewise the Emperour Otho surnamed the Great, brought a great armie hither against his rebellious sonne Ludolphus (whom I shall hereafter mention againe) intending to have incountred him in battell, but it hapned otherwise. For Ludolphus not daring to skirmish with his father, contained himself within the walles of the City, where after he had beene besieged for the space of nine weekes, there was a truce concluded betwixt his father and himselfe. The bridges that were built here were two, very famous for their founders. For the first was built by Julian the Apostat the three and fortieth Emperour of Rome, and is mentioned by Ammianus Marcellinus the historiographer, which he caused to be made after he had conquered the Alemannes about Strasbourg, as I have before mentioned. After that battell

Great battles fought near Mayence.

[p. 553.]

Famous bridges.

* These were Germans, and the inhabitants of Franconia.

280

Martin Luther, that invective gistro meaning ed, the art of much celebrated ters. First the : to this City. It here over the ersonages in the ght there were ro whom I have is place with the here he brake his : the write. For i Bing (as I will s' some ten miles the Rhene. Also Emperor fought a ie was but a yong ---, and in that i--- at the least i Emperour Otho --- hither against I shall hereafter ------red him at '. Ludolphus not (--- himself within (--- beene besieged (--- --- concluded ------ that were ------ ders. For ------ the three and ------ by Ammi- --- he caused to ------- about After that battell :: Franconia.

he came thus farre down with his armie from Alsatia, and made this bridge for the better conveighing of his Souldiers over the Rhene, to the end to skirmish with the Germans on the other side of the water : the other bridge was built by the Emperour Charlemaine in the year 813. he bestowed marvailous cost on this bridge, though it were made but of timber. For the workemen were ten whole yeares building of it; who compacted it together with such admirable strength, that it was thought it would have lasted for ever. But in the yeare of our Lord 823. even in the moneth of May, it hapned by a very dismall chance to be utterly consumed with fire, the raging furie whereof [p. 554.] wasted that in the space of three houres, which ten yeares labour with infinite cost did scarce joyne together. As for great persons that ended their lives in this City I have read of foure especially of eminent marke. The first was that famous Roman Emperor Alexander Severus, *The Roman* who by the meanes of one Maximinus a Thracian Captaine *Emperor* that succeeded him afterward in the Empire, was here most *Severus.* cruelly slaine by a company of seditious souldiers that he appointed for the same purpose, even after he had lived nine and twenty yeares, three monethes and seven daies. His death was the more memorable because the historians write that he died the very same day that Alexander the Great did, which was the eight and twentieth of Julie, being the day of his nativity also. The second was that vertuous Lady Mammea mother to the foresaid Emperour, and Aunt to that vicious Emperour Heliogabalus, who was slaine here at the same time with her sonne. The third an Empresse, whose name was Fastrada, the fourth wife of the Emperour Charlemaine, of whom I have made mention before in my Observations of Wormes. In this City shee was buried in the year 792. in the Church of St. Albanus. Also in the same Church is shewed the monument of Ludolphus Duke of Suevia, the eldest sonnè of the Emperour Otho surnamed the Great, by his first wife Edith an English Lady. This Ludolphus died a naturall death in Lombardie after he had gotten the victory

281

of King Berengarius the third of that name, being sent against him by his father Otho. But his body was afterward brought to this City of Mentz by the meanes of his brother William Bishop thereof. Ludovicus Pius the first Emperour of that name, and the sonne of the Emperor Charlemaine, died in this City in the threescore and fourth yeare of his age, after he had reigned seven and twenty yeares: but his body was afterward buried in the City of Mentz neare his mother Hildegardis. Likewise many of Gods Saints and holy Martyrs of the Church have beene crowned in this City with the crowne of martyrdome. But the chiefest of all was the foresaid Albanus, who being a Grecian borne was expelled out of his native City Philippi of Greece (unto the inhabitants whereof St. Paul wrote his Epistle) by certaine Heretiques of his country in the yeare 425. and shortly after arrived at this City of Mentz, together with one of his countrymen called Theonestus, where at length he suffered death for the Gospels sake, and was buried in a part of the city, where there was a Church erected afterward to the honour of his name. In which the body of the foresaid Empresse Fastrada doth lie interred.

One thing that is very memorable I will not omit in the discourse of this famous City of Mentz, that it gave the first vitall light to that learned and Rhetoricall Shee-Pope Joane, where after shee had sate two yeares in the Popedome, immediately after Leo the fourth, she died in child-birth. For it is most certaine that shee was borne in this place, being confirmed by the authority of many learned and ancient authours, though Onuphrius Panuinius an Augustinian Frier of Verona, and some of the Patriarches of the Jesuiticall societie have of late yeares gone about to prove the contrary.

Julius Cæsar having conquered all the Cities on this side of the Rhene which was in his time called Gallicum littus, the shore of Gallia, &c. planted garrisons in each of them as I have already said, for the better fortification of the place, and to keepe the bordering people living in

[p. 555.]
Saints and martyrs.

Pope Joan.

Julius Cæsar's conquest of Gallicum littus.

282

me, being sent
body was after-
e meanes of his
us Pius the first
of the Emperor
score and fourth
ven and twenty
d in the City of
Likewise many
he Church have
wne of many-
reasid Altars,
out of his native
tants whereof St.
Heretiques of his
ster arrived at this
x his countrymen
suffered death for
a part of the city,
ward to the honour
foresaid Empresse

I will not omit in
Mentz, that it gave
Rhetoricall Shee-
two yeares in the
fourth, she died
at shee was borne
rity of many
Onuphrius Panv-
and some of the
are of late yeares

Cities on this
called Gallicum
risons in each
er fortification
people living in

the same territorie in awe and subjection of the Romans. For which cause he assigned Lieutenants called in Latin Prœfecti, to all the principall Cities and Townes that he had conquered. But him that he appointed Governour of this City he placed in a more eminent degree of dignity then the rest. For he intitled him Dux Moguntinus, as I have before written in my Observations both of Stras- [p. 556.] bourg and Wormes. So that all the other inferiour Pre- fects were altogether subject to his becke. And of those Prefects there were ten severall persons that resided in as *Roman* many distinct places for the defence of the country. *prefects.* Whereof the chiefest was commorant at Strasbourg, as I have before said. The second at a place called Seltz. The third at Zabern in Alsatia where the Bishop of Stras- bourg doth commonly keepe his residence. The fourth at Altrip not farre from Spira. The fifth at Wissenburg. The sixth at Wormes. The seventh at Bing. The eight at Boppard. The ninth at Confluence. The tenth and last at Andernach. The authority of all these inferiour Lieutenants was confined within those limits, that they had not the power to attempt any matter of moment without the leave of the Moguntine Marshall or Lieutenant whom they acknowledged for their Generall Captaine. Also every one of them had a complet legion assigned him for the defence of the place, which how much it containeth I have before mentioned in my notes of Lyons. Two principall Marshals or Lieutenants of the Romans *Two eminent* that made their residence in this city I will briefly mention, *Roman* because they were men of great eminency, and much *lieutenants.* celebrated by the ancient Roman historiographers. The first was Flavius Vespasianus, the same that was afterward Emperour, and the successor of Vitellius. Here he resided in the time of the Emperour Claudius as I take it. The second was Rufus Virginius, a man much mentioned by Cornelius Tacitus. This Virginius is the same that with Julius Vindex Captaine of the Roman legions in France, and Sergius Galba (afterward Emperour) of those in Spaine made an insurrection against the Emperour Nero,

283

[p. 557.]

the newes whereof drove him to that pittifull exigent that he was faine to cut his owne throate. But how long this City was swayed by a Roman Marshall after the time of Julius Cæsar, truly I do not certainly know, howbeit I conjecture that it was subject to the Romans as long as the other Cities in the same banke of the Rhene, as Strasbourg, Wormes, &c. even till the time of the Hunnicall King Attila, which being then expugned by his hostile sword, and consumed to dust and ashes by his incendiarie souldiers, it was afterward most sumptuously reedified by Dagobert King of France, remaining for the space of many yeares under the dominion of the French Kings, till at last having shaken off the yoke of forraine Lords, it was wholly subject to their Archbishop, who is at this day the soveraigne Prince and Lord of Mentz, which City doth professe the same religion that he himselfe doth, which is that of the Church of Rome.

Thus much of Mentz.

I Was imbarked at Mentz the thirteenth of September being Munday, about seven of the clocke in the morn ing, and passed downe the goodly river Mœnus, which at Mentz doth mingle it selfe with the Rhene till I came to a towne within foure miles of Frankford where I arrived, and from thence performed the rest of my journey by land, and came to the Citie of Frankford which is sixteene miles from Mentz, about five of the clocke in the afternoone. But before I begin to write any thing of Franckford, I will make some further mention of the river Mœnus, and of such things as I observed betwixt Mentz *River Maine.* and Franckford. This Mœnus which heretofore was otherwise called Mogonus, is a very faire navigable river, in some places almost as broad as the Rhene at Mentz. It is commonly esteemed the fourth river of Germany, and is in the catalogue of the Germane rivers ranked next to the Neccar that runneth by Heidelberg. It riseth in the countrie of Voitlandia which confineth upon Saxonie, even a little beyond the Citie of Bamberga, and so rowling

284

ifull exigent that
ut how long this
after the time of
know, howbeit I
ans as long as the
:ne, as Strasbourg
: Hunnicall King
his hostile sword
y his incendiarie
ptuously reedified
g for the space of
: French Kings, till
lorraine Lords, it
, who is at this day
itz, which City doth
selfe doth, which is

centh of September
woke in the morn
: Mœnus, which at
Rhene till I came
Frankford where I
rest of my journey
Frankford which is
the clocke in the
the any thing of
ention of the river
ed betwixt Mentz
retofore was other-
vigable river, in
at Mentz. It is
Germany, and is
nked next to the
It riseth in the
Saxonie, even
and so rowling

along with a great company of crooked windings (not much *[p. 558.]* unlike to the noble Asiaticke river Mæander so celebrated by the ancient Poets for his often turnings) through the territory of Franconia, and entertaining these three rivers more, the Pegnetius at Norimberg, the Tuberus at Roten-burg a Citie of the foresaid Franconia, and the Mimlingus (all which doe issue out of the forrest Ottonica that I have before named in my discourse of Heidelberg ;) at last it joyneth with the Rhene, right opposite to the city of Mentz as I have already said. I have read foure Greeke *Melancthon's* verses of Philip Melancthon with a translation of the same *verses on the River Maine.* into as many Latine, which he once made in a very con-ceited and wittie veine upon the five letters of the name of the river Mœnus, which according to a pretty kind of hieroglyphicall manner he hath so finely contrived, that the five letters (but as they are the elements of the Greeke alphabet, not as Latine characters) doe express the full number of the daies of the yeare. I have therefore thought good to mention those verses in this place, since this present discourse of the Mœnus doth minister this occasion unto me : because I thinke they will be very acceptable to the learned reader. The learned reader I say, but not to the unlearned. For indeed he must have both learning and a good capacity that shall rightly conceive the meaning of them. Truly the elegancy of them in my poore judgement is such, that for mine owne part I will boldly say they do expresse the most ingenious conceit that ever I read in my life. In so much that the first time I saw them, I did even hugge them with a great applause. Whatsoever thou art that dost applaud elegancies, judici-ously reade these verses, and then I thinke thou wilt say they are worthy to be placed in the very front of thy index of elegant conceits. Without any longer preambles I present unto thee the verses themselves, even these.

Ε'ξωχα τῶν ἄλλων τὰς φοίβου Φράγκε πορείας
μάνθανε, οὐρανίους καὶ θεοῦ ἔργα φορὰς.
Ο῀ττι ἔτους συνόλου ἕλκει πόσα ἤματα κύκλος,   *[p. 559.]*
τοῦ ποπάμου φράζει τοὔνομα ὑμαδεπου.

285

The Latine translation is this.

Discite præcipuè solis motumque viasque,
  Vos quibus est patrium Francica terra solum.
Namque dies totus quot traxerit ambitus anni,
  Id fluvii vestri vox benè nota sonat.

Solving of the conceit. Now the whole pith and marrow of the conceit doth consist in the resolving of the five letters of the word *Menus. For if thou apply every letter of it as one of the Greeke Alphabet unto those numerall figures that the same Greeke letters do expresse, then thou shalt presently apprehend the conceit, and must needs praise it for a passing witty invention.   Therefore thou must thus resolve the letters:

M	40
E	5
N	50
O	70
Σ	200

The totall number doth make up the exact summe of all
the daies in the yeare, even
365.

Now I will returne againe to my liquid journey betwixt Mentz and Franckford upon the river Mœnus.   The *Sundry travellers.* barke wherein I was carried contained a strange miscellany of people of sundry nations at that time, whose languages [p. 560.] were (I thinke) a quarter as much confounded as theirs were in ancient times at that famous confusion of Babel.   For in this barke there were some few of every principall nation of Christendome travelling towards Frankford Mart that began the day before.   Amongst the rest, one of them was borne in the country of Lithuania that adjoyneth to a part of Poland, a passing sweet scholler, and a traveller that had lately lived in the University of Monachium commonly called Mynichin in Bavaria, a man that yeelded

* Though the word be Mœnus with œ dipthong ; yet here he doth write it Menus, eliding the dipthong.   For otherwise the conceit will not hold.

286

singular delight unto me by his variable discourse seasoned with much polite learning. On both sides of the Mœnus I observed a very fat soile, and two sumptuous palaces. *Sumptuous palaces.* Whereof one that I saw on the right hand, situate alone by it selfe in a very spacious and pleasant meadow, was the most Princely and royall building that I saw in Germany, saving the Pfaltzgraves of Rhene in the citie of Heidel berg. For this was a seat well beseeming an Emperours Court; and the situation so sweet and delectable that it seemed to me to stand in a second garden of Eden. This one place doth sufficiently confirme the truth of Kirchners elegant agnomination in his Oration of the praise of Germany, that the Mœne will yeeld as great amenity as the Po of Italy, or any other forraine river. The name of the place is Kelsterbach. Heretofore the Landgrave of *Kelsterbach.* Hassia was Lord of it. But I understood that he hath sold it within these few yeares to a certaine Germane Prince. The other Palace stood in a certaine towne on the left hand of the Mœnus about foure miles on this side Franckford, and belongeth to the Archbishop of Mentz; but that is much inferiour to this. A little on this side the townes end of Franckford I observed a most rufull *A rueful sight.* spectacle that strooke a certaine horrour into me, and so I think did into the hearts of most other relenting travellers that passed that way: the bodies of sixteene men hanging upon a great stonie gallowes hard by the high way side, supported with many great stony pillars.

My Observations of Franckford. [p. 561.]

Julius Cæsar Scaliger hath written these verses upon
Franckford.

MUlta laboratis debet Franckfordia sulcis: *Scaliger's*
Multa racemiferis vinea culta jugis. *verses on*
Quid referam, quanta & quæ convexere metalla? *Frankfort.*
Quæ Mars bellipotens, quæ petit alma Ceres?
Hùc Italus patriis miratur partibus orbem,
Advectum hùc stupuit Gallica magna suum.

287

CORYAT'S CRUDITIES

Hic Oriens, hic terra nobis comperta sub astris
Agnoscit Genii semina plena sui.
Nec tamen in brutis sola hæc commercia rebus:
Hic animi æternæ sed cumulantur opes.
Quod si res paucas operosa est dicere merces:
Non magis est, cunctas res operosa dare?

This City is commonly called Franckfort am Mayn,
that is, Franckford situate by the river Mœnus. For they
give that addition to the name to the end to make a difference betwixt this Citie, and another of the same name in
the dominion of the Marquesse of Brandenburg, situate
by the river Odera that is famous for her Universitie.

Territory and situation of Frankfort. The Territory wherein it standeth is called Franconia aliâs
Francia Orientalis, situate in the very meditullium or heart
of all Germany, at the farthest edge whereof Franckford
standeth. The situation of it is pleasant. For it is seated
in a spacious plaine that yeeldeth notable abundance, yea
a very Cornucopia of all necessary commodities. The
Citie was first called Helenopolis from Queene Helena an
English woman borne, and the mother of Constantine the
Great. But in processe of time the denomination was
changed from Helenopolis to the present name Franco-
[p. 562.] furtum, which is derived from Francus the name of a
Prince who was the sonne of Marcomirus King of the
country of Franconia, wherein (as I have already said)
Franckford standeth. It is distinguished by the river
City divided into two parts. Mœnus into two parts, the greater and the lesser. The
lesser is called Saxenhausen, that is, the houses of the
Saxons. Againe, these two are joined together by a very
faire bridge built all with stone, and supported with a
dozen goodly stony pillers each couple making a faire
arch. Though the city be divided into two parts, yet the
government is all one, and they are governed by one
Senate. The walles that do inviron the citie, are built
with such admirable strength, beeing compacted all of
hard stone, and beautified with a great company of towers,
strong bulwarks, and faire gatehouses, that they yeeld a

ib astris

cia rebus:
opes.
nerces:
dare?

cfort am Mayn,
œnus. For they
to make a diffe-
the same name in
adenburg, situate
r her Universitie
led Franconia also
...illium or heart
...ereof Franckford
ra. For it is seated
able abundance, yea
commodities. The
Queene Helena in
...: Constantine the
...omination was
...ent name Franc-
L...s the name of a
L...us King of the
...ve already said,
...ed by the river
...: the lesser. The
...le houses of the
...ether by a very
supported with a
...e making a faire
two parts, yet the
governed by one
...s citie, are built
compacted all of
...many of towers,
...at they yeeld a

most singular grace to the city. Also the same walles are inclosed with deepe trenches and moates. The principall Church of the city, which was built by Pipin King of France (as Munster affirmeth) who dedicated it to the honour of our Saviour, though it bee now called Saint Bartholmewes Church, doth present a goodly shew a farre off. Yet the inward matter of the Church is but ordinarie, and differeth but little from other colledge Churches of Germany.

There are two things which make this citie famous over all Europe. The one the election of the King of the Romanes, the other the two noble fayres kept heere twise a yeare, which are called the Martes of Franckford. As for the election, Charles the fourth Emperour of that name established a decree for the perpetuall choosing of the King of the Romanes in this citie about the yeare 1350. which he confirmed with his golden seale of armes. Before which time the place of the election was uncertaine. For it was sometimes at Mentz, sometimes at Hagenaw, sometimes also at Franckford, and elsewhere, according to the discretion of the Elector Princes. By the King of the Romanes I meane him that either in the life of the Emperour which is in possession of the Empire, or shortly after his death, is chosen for his successor by the Elector Princes; which title the chosen Prince doth retaine till he be afterward confirmed and crowned by the Pope. And after his coronation that title being abolished, he is stiled Emperour Augustus. The first institution of this custome is attributed to Otho the third German Emperour of that name, who being in the city of Rome about the yeare of our Lord 1000. after he had punished those two famous rebels, Pope John the eighteenth, and Crescentius Consull of the City, ordained it for a perpetuall decree by the consent of Pope Gregory the fifth, that hee which should be successour in the Empire, should be intituled King of the Romanes untill by his coronation hee were throughly inaugurated into the Empire.

The first that was chosen King of the Romanes was

Election of the Emperor of the Romans.

[p. 563.]

Henry II. the first Roman Emperor chosen at Frankfort.

Henry the second surnamed Sanctus. This constitution of Charles the fourth hath remained inviolable ever since his time for the space of two hundred and fifty yeares. For there was never King of the Romanes chosen in any place since his death but onely in Franckford. Munster maketh mention of a certaine custome observed in this City, as a lawe at the time of the Electors dissention about the election of the King of the Romanes; which is this: when the Elector Princes cannot agree, one of the competitors that are named Kings of the Romanes, is to lie in armes neere the city of Franckford with an army of men for the space of halfe a moneth, to the end to skirmish with his competitor; and if he getteth the victory in battel, or by other peaceable meanes doth grow to a composition with his adversarie, then hee is admitted within the gates of the citie, and saluted King of the Romanes, not else. Experience of this hath bene made betwixt Henry Landgrave of Thuringia and Conrade the sonne of Frederick the second.

[p. 564.]
The fairs of Frankfort.

And also betwixt Ludovicus the Bavarian, and Frederick of Austria. As for the Fayre it is esteemed, and so indeed is the richest meeting of any place of Christendome, which continueth 14 daies together, and is kept in the moneth of March for the Spring, and in September for the Autumne. This Autumnall Mart it was my chance to see. Where I met my thrise-honourable countryman the Earle of Essex, after he had travelled in divers places of France, Switzerland, and some parts of high Germany. The riches I observed at this Mart were most infinite, especially in one place called Under Den Roemer, where the Goldsmithes kept their shoppes, which made the most

Goldsmiths' work.

glorious shew that ever I saw in my life, especially some of the Citie of Norimberg. This place is divided into divers other roomes that have a great many partitions assigned unto Mercers and such like artificers, for the exposing of their wares. The wealth that I sawe here was incredible, so great that it was unpossible for a man to conceive it in his minde that hath not first seene it with

his constitution
.lable ever since
.nd fifty yeares.
:s chosen in any
:ford. Munster
observed in this
ectors dissention
the Romanes;
es cannot agree,
·d Kings of the
city of Franck-
space of halfe a
ith his compet-
.attel, or by other
.position with his
n the gates of the
not else. Expen-
.enry Landgrave of
·derick the second
.rian, and Frederick
..·.·.t, and so indeed
..·.·:tendome, which
.·.·. in the moneth
...·mber for the
[·.·:s my chance to
.·.·. countryman that
[·.·. divers places of
.·.· high Germans
(·.·.·.·.·. most intimate,
.·.·. Roemer, where
.·.·.·:h made the most
.·.·., especially since
.·.·. is divided into
.·.· many partitions
.·.·:hcers, for the
.·.·:t I sawe here
.·.·:ble for a man
.·.·:t seene it with

his bodily eies. The goodliest shew of ware that I sawe
in all Franckford saving that of the Goldsmithes, was made
by an Englishman one Thomas Sackfield a Dorsetshire-
man, once a servant of my father, who went out of England
but in a meane estate, but after he had spent a few yeares
at the Duke of Brunswicks Court, hee so inriched himselfe
of late, that his glittering shewe of ware in Franckford did
farre excell all the Dutchmen, French, Italians, or whom-
soever else. This place is much frequented during the
whole time of the Mart with many eminent and princely
persons. There I saw the Earle of Sconenberg one of the
most potent Earles of all Germany. For his yearly
revenues are (as I heard) about forty thousand pound
sterling. Also I sawe many other Earles and some Pfaltzgraves: the number of whome is much multiplied (I
understand) in Germany. The reason whereof is because
if any Landgrave, Pfaltzgrave, or Earle, hath any sonnes,
all of them more or lesse do share in dignity. For all the
Landgraves sons if he hath ten or twenty, are Landgraves
as well as himselfe. The like doth happen to the Pfaltzgraves, Earles &c. But although their dignity be equall,
yet their estates are very unequall. For it falleth out very
often that the eldest brother hath almost al, and many
of the younger brothers but small meanes of maintenance.
After this I went to the Bookesellers streete where I
saw such infinite abundance of bookes, that I greatly
admired it. For this street farre excelleth Paules Churchyard in London, Saint James streete in Paris, the Merceria
of Venice, and all whatsoever else that I sawe in my travels.
In so much that it seemeth to be a very epitome of all the
principall Libraries of Europe. Neither is that streete
famous for selling bookes onely, and that of all manner of
artes and disciplines whatsoever, but also for printing of
them. For this city hath so flourished within these fewe
yeares in the art of printing, that it is not inferiour in
that respect to any city in Christendome, no not to Basil
it selfe which I have before so much commended for the
excellency of that art. Likewise I visited divers Cloysters

*A goodly
shew by an
Englishman*

*Many
noblemen in
Germany.*

[p. 565.]

*Street of the
booksellers.*

full of wares and notable commodities, especially the Cloyster of Saint Bartholmewes Church; where amongst other things I saw a world of excellent pictures, inventions of singular curiosity, whereof most were religious, and such as tended to mortification. Moreover I saw their
The Exchange. Exchange neere to the place before mentioned called Under Den Roemer. This is nothing like to ours in London, the Rialto of Venice, or that which I saw afterward at Middleborough in Zealand. For it is nothing but a part of the streete, under the open ayre. Here I observed a frequent concurse of wealthy Merchants from all the famousest regions of Christendome. I noted a thing in this fayre that I never did before in any place. Every
[p. 566.] man selleth his ware in his owne house, except forreners and those that hire shoppes in the Burse. So that there
A strange custom. is no common place either in the streetes or in any open yard or field (as I observed at the Fayre of Bergomo in Italie and in all other places) but only within the compasse of their owne private houses. Which maketh the Fayre seeme but little, though indeed it be very great. I have read that this City was once deprived of their Fayre by the Emperour Charles the fourth, about some two hundred and fifty yeares since, who for a certaine grudge that he bare to the Franckfordians by reason that they entertayned his adversary Gunterus Earle of Schwartzenburg within the City, and proclaimed him King of the Romanes, tooke away the Fayre from Franckford, and removed it to Mentz; but being afterward reconciled to the City, he restored it againe to them.

I observed no monuments of any note in this City. Though in St. Bartholmewes Church (as a learned man told me after I was gone from Franckford) I might have seene the monument of the foresaid Earle Gunterus, who was competitor with the said Charles the fourth for the Empire, and afterward King of the Romans. For he died in this City being poysoned by a physition, after he had reigned sixe moneths, and was finally buried in the said Church. Here also died Ludovicus surnamed Germanicus for that

292

he was King of Germanie, the third sonne of the Emperour Ludovicus Pius by his first wife Irmengardis, in the yeare of his age threescore and ten, of the Lord 876. But he was not buried here. For his body was afterward carryed by his sonne Ludovicus the third to a place in the territorie of the Wormacians called Laureacum. I went to the Monasterie of the Dominican Friers because I heard that there were certaine monuments and curious rarities to be *Unsociable friars.* seene amongst them, but they were so unsociable and precise, that they would not affoord accesse to any strangers at the time of the Mart.

The religion of this City is both Protestant and Papisti- *[p. 567.]* call; the Protestants professe Luthers doctrine. The principall Church which is dedicated to St. Barthelmew belongeth to the Papists, most of the other to the Protestants, saving the Churches of Monasteries.

I received a speciall kindnesse in this City of an English *Mr. Thomas* Gentleman, with the commemoration of whose name I *Row.* will finish my Observations of Franckford, even Mr. Thomas Row the eldest sonne of Sir Henry Row, that was Lord Maior of London about two yeares since. Truly this Gentleman did me such a singular courtesie there, that he hath perpetually obliged me unto him all the dayes of my life.

Thus much of Franckford.

Having spent two whole daies in Franckford, Wednesday and Thursday, I departed therehence the sixteenth day of September being Friday, about ten of the clocke in the morning, and travelled by land to Mentz whither I came by sixe of the clocke in the afternoone. This journey was sixteene miles. I remained that night in Mentz. And whereas I meant to have gone the next morning to Ingelheim Court sixteene miles from Mentz *Ingelheim* to have seene the place where the Emperour Charles the *Court.* Great was borne, and that magnificent Palace which he built there, wherein he sometimes kept his Imperiall Court, and which is yet shewed to this day; certayne Gentlemen

293

of Colen craved my company in a boate downe the Rhene towards Colen. Whereupon I committed my selfe to the water the same morning being Saturday and the seven teenth of September, about eight of the clocke, and came to the City of Boppard, which is thirty miles beyond it, about eight of the clocke in the evening.

[p. 568.]   My Observations betwixt Mentz and Boppard.

SHortly after I had passed beyond Mentz, when I beganne to observe divers strong Townes and Castles situate hard by the Rhene, and more upon the left banke in that part of Germanie, which was in the time of the Roman Empire reckoned a member of Gallia, then upon *A serious* the opposite shore; I entred into a serious kinde of *examination.* examination of my selfe, how it came to passe that one banke of the Rhene was exceedingly planted with townes and fortresses, and the other very slenderly. And to the end I might be the better resolved in the matter, I asked a learned Gentleman in my boate that was a Senator of Colen, what was the reason that the left banke of the Rhene was more frequently inhabited then the other. Who answered me in that manner as gave me no full satisfaction. At last, after I had ruminated long upon the matter, I called to my remembrance the warres that Julius Cæsar waged with the ancient Germans, and did quickly satisfie my owne selfe without any further inquisition. For I conjectured that many of these Townes and Castels were built by the Romans, at what time they fortified that tract of the Rhene with presidiarie souldiers for the better defence of their Provinces against the violent excursions of the Germans, that bordered neare unto them upon the adverse banke. Neither was my conjecture vaine. For this is most true, and confirmed by the irrefragable authority of many ancient and authenticke historio- graphers, that many of these places were built by the *Many cities* Romans themselves, shortly after Cæsar had conquered *on the left* Gallia. This is the reason that there are so many magni- *bank of the* ficent and ancient Cities on the left banke of that long *Rhine.*

294

tract betwixt Basil and Colen. Namely Strasbourg, Spira, Wormes, Mentz, Bing, Boppard, Confluence, and Bonna. But on the other side I saw no City or Towne of any [p. 569.] note, but only Brisac a little from Basil, and yet that was but a meane thing in comparison of some of these. The like whereof I have heard is to be observed in one of the bankes of the Danubius betwixt the place of the rising thereof and Hungarie. In which banke there are many stately Cities built, as Patavia, Ratisbona, and divers others. But on the opposite banke there are no ancient Cities or Citadels to be seene. The reason is, because the Romans durst not raise any on that side for feare of the sudden invasion of the Germans that dwelt neare at hand.

I observed many custome Townes betwixt Mentz and *Custom towns.* Colen, which are in number eleven. They belong to divers Princes Spirituall and Temporall, who receive a great yearlie revenue by them. All passengers whatsoever they are, noble or ignoble, must arrive in each of these places, and stay a while till the boatemen hath paid custome for his passage. To the passenger it is no charge at all, but only to the master of the boate. If any should dare in a resolute and wilfull humour to passe by any of these places, and not pay the stinted summe of money, the Publicans that sit at the receipt of custome, will presently discharge (as I heard) a peece of Ordinance at them, and make them an example to all after-commers. Richard one of our English Kings did once very graciously abolish all these tolles and taxations by water, to the great benefit of the Germans and al other passengers, when he kept his Court in the City of Wormes, after he was elected King of the Romans by the Elector Princes, as I have before mentioned in my Observations of that City. Which thing purchased him the great love and good will of the people for that little time that he lived in Germanie.

The first of these townes where we arrived was Bing, *Bingen.* a place of great antiquitie, in Latine Bingium, that belongeth to the Archbishop of Mentz, and professeth the Popish religion. At this towne there is a river called Naha [p. 570]

295

that infuseth it selfe into the Rhene, where they both do make a confluent. This is one of the garrison townes that I have before mentioned, that were subject to the Marshall of Mentz, where there lay a company of presidiarie souldiers with a Roman Prefect, by the appointment of Julius Cæsar, for the defence of that limit against the Germanes. There are three things that have much famoused this towne. The first the death of Drusus Nero, whom I have before mentioned. The second the Nunne Hildegardis that once lived there. The third a tower standing in the Rhene, whereof anon I wil write a notable

Death of Drusus Nero. historie. About the death of Drusus the historians do much differ. For some report that he was slaine by the Germanes, sitting upon his horse. Others, that he perished by a fall from his horse. Which of these histories is truest both of the place and manner of his death, seeing I finde difference amongst the historiographers, I will not certainly affirme, but leave it to the judgement of the learned that are more expert in the Romane histories then my selfe. But surely for mine owne parte I am drawn by certain conjectures to beleeve that he died at this towne. Amongst other reasons this is one : because there is a certaine fountaine shewed to this day neare to this towne (as Munster writeth) that is called Druselbrun, that is, the fountaine of Drusus, as having his denomination from the foresaid Drusus that died here. As for the

S. Hildegard. Nunne Hildegardis, she lived here about the yeare of our Lord 1180, as Gesner writeth, and was of the order of St. Bennet, even in the time of St. Bernard Abbot of Claravallis ; betwixt whom there was great friendship, as it appeareth by their mutuall Epistles that they wrote to each other, which are yet extant in the works of St. Bernard. Truly there are very admirable matters written of this woman by the historians. For it is reported that she was often rapt in the middest of her sleepe with

[p. 571.] certaine enthusiasmes, that is, divine inspirations, whereby she learned the Latine tongue after a most miraculous manner without any teacher. A thing that will seeme

296

re they both do
garrison townes
e subject to the
company of pre-
by the appoint-
that limit against
that have much
1 of Drusus Nero,
econd the Nune
he third a tower
nil write a notable
the historians do
was slaine by the
rs, that he perished
these histories is
i h s death, seeing
graphers, I will not
judgement of the
mine histories then
parte I am drawn
it he died at this
: because there
day neare to this
: Druselorus, that
his denominates
here. As for the
reare of our
the order of S.
Abbot of Clar-
friendship, as if
they wrote to
works of S.
matters written
is reported that
her sleepe with
tions, whereby
ost miraculous
will seeme

unto many readers a meere paradoxe, but certainly for my owne part I beleeve it to be true. For I receive it from the authority of a very grave writer Sebastian Munster. Besides she was esteemed a great prophetesse in that age. And she wrote many treatises both in prose and verse : as the life of St. Rupertus the Confessor ; the life of St. Disibodus Bishop : 135 severall Epistles, besides many other things that are mentioned by Gesner in the catalogue of her works. But the third thing that is reported of this towne is a thing passing memorable and very worthy the observation. Such a wondrous and rare accident as I never read or heard of the like before. Therefore I will relate it in this place out of Munster for one of the most notable examples of Gods justice that ever was extant in the whole world since the first creation thereof. It hapned in the yeare 914 that there was an exceeding famine in Germany, at what time Otho surnamed the Great was Emperor, and one Hatto once Abbot of Fulda was Archbishop of Mentz, *Archbishop* of the Bishops after Crescens or Crescentius the two and *Hatto.* thirtieth, of the Archbishops after St. Bonifacius the thirteenth. This Hatto in the time of this great famine before mentioned, when he saw the poore people of the country exceedingly oppressed with famine, assembled a great company of them together into a barne, and like a most accursed & mercilesse caitiffe burnt up those poore innocent soules, that were so farre from doubting any such matter, that they rather hoped to have received some comfort and reliefe at his hands. The reason that moved the Prelate to commit that execrable impiety, was because he thought that the famine would the sooner cease, if those unprofitable beggars that consumed more bread then they were worthy to eate, were dispatched out of the world. For he said that these poore folkes were like to [p. 572.] mice, that were good for nothing but to devoure corne. But Almighty God the just revenger of the poore folks quarrel did not long suffer this hainous tyranny, this most detestable fact unpunished. For he mustred up an army of mice against the Archbishop, and sent them to persecute

His miserable end. him as his furious Alastors, so that they afflicted him both day and night, and would not suffer him to take his rest in any place. Whereupon the Prelate thinking that he should be secure from the injury of mice if he were in a certaine tower that standeth in the Rhene neere to the towne, betooke himself unto the said tower as to a safe refuge and sanctuary from his enemies, and locked himselfe in. But the innumerable troupes of mice continually chaced him very eagerly, and swumme unto him upon the top of the water to execute the just judgement of God, and so at last he was most miserably devoured by those silly creatures; who pursued him with such bitter hostility, that it is recorded they scraped & gnawed off his very name from the walles and tapestry wherein it was written, after they had so cruelly devoured his bodie. Wherefore the tower in which he was eaten up by the mice is shewed to this day for a perpetuall monument to al succeeding ages of the barbarous and inhumane tyranny of that impious prelate, being situate in a little greene Iland in the middest of the Rhene neere to this towne of Bing, and is commonly called in the Germane tongue the Mowse turn.

After I was a little past Bing, even about the west end of the towne, I observed that upon the sides of the Rhene, which I did not perceive before in any other part of Germany. For both sides of the river were inclosed with steepe rocky mountaines that ranne on a great way *A multitude of castles on the hills.* in length as farre as the towne of Bonna, which is a little on this side Colen, even for the space of fiftie miles at the least, upon the tops of which mountaines I saw an exceeding multitude of Towers, Castels, and Citadels on both [p. 573.] sides, which belong unto those Princes in whose territories they stand, being built for the better fortification of those frontier parts of their Princedomes. Some of them seeme to be of that antiquitie that I am perswaded they were built by the ancient Romans, especially those of that shore which was heretofore esteemed a part of Gallia. Also I perceived that these mountaines doe hemme in the Rhene in a farre straighter compasse, then before I came thither,

298

OBSERVATIONS OF BACHARACH

even almost by halfe. For it is in divers places so narrow betwixt the rocks that a man may easily cast over a stone from one banke to the other, as a certaine Germane told me that passed in the same boate with me. But afterward when I came to Bonna, I observed that those hils did desinere in planiciem, which plaine did continue from thenceforth till I came to the farthest bound of my journey upon the Rhene in the Netherlands. None of these rocks could I perceive in that whole tract betwix Basil and Strasbourg, saving one upon the which the towne of Brisac is situate on the right hand of the Rhene; but a pleasant plaine on both sides which I heard extended it selfe as farre as Mentz, and from Mentz likewise the plaine continueth even to the towns end of Bing, and then (as I have said) beginne those steepe rockie mountaines.

There is a very strange custome observed amongst the *A hard custom.* Germanes as they passe in their boates betwixt Mentz and Colen, and so likewise betwixt Colen and the lower parts of the Netherlands. Every man whatsoever he be poore or rich, shall labour hard when it commeth to his turne, except he doth either by friendship or some small summe of money redeeme his labour. For their custome is that the passengers must exercise themselves with oares and rowing alternis vicibus, a couple together. So that the master of the boate (who me thinks in honestie ought either to doe it himselfe, or to procure some others to do it for him) never roweth but when his turne commeth. This [p. 574.] exercise both for recreation and health sake I confesse is very convenient for man. But to be tied unto it by way of a strict necessity when one payeth well for his passage, was a thing that did not a little distaste my humour.

The next custome Towne that we arrived at is called Bacchara, which is in the dominion of the Pfaltzgrave of Rhene, and situate on the same left banke of the Rhene; a place as famous in Germanie for her generose wines *Wines of* growen upon the hill of Furstenberg neare unto it, as the *Furstenberg.* valley Tellina is in the Grisons country, Falernus in Campania, or Chios in Greece. It seemeth by the name to be a towne of great antiquity, and to have beene built in the time of Gentilisme.   For some make the etymologie of the name to be quasi Bacchi ara, the Altar of Bacchus. Because that drunken God Bacchus had Altars erected unto him in this place in time of the Pagan idolatrie.   Others derive it from Bacchus only, which by a Rhetorical figure called metonymia doth signifie wine.   The reason of this derivation is because this towne doth yeeld most excellent wine as I have already said.   The religion of the towne is Protestant.

Caub.   The third telonium is called Cuve which belongeth to the Pfaltzgrave also.   This Towne is situate on the opposite banke, and is very memorable for one thing, which is a certaine Castell (whereof I have before made mention in my Observations of Heidelberg) situate in the middle of the Rhene called Pfaltz, which signifieth a Palace, wherehence commeth the word Pfaltzgrave (otherwise commonly called Palsgrave) one of the most eminent and Princely titles of the Count Palatine of Rhene.   This towne professeth the Protestant religion also.

Ober Wesel.   A little beyond Cuve we passed by the elegant little City of higher Wesel, in Latin Wesalia superior, but commonly called Ober Wesel for distinction sake betwixt that and the lower Wesel in Cleveland.   This towne is

[p. 575.]   situate on the left banke of the Rhene, and belongeth to the Archbishop of Trevirs the third spiritual Elector of the Empire, who hath had the dominion of Wesel these many yeares, even since the time of Henry the seventh Emperour of that name, by whom it was morgaged to the Archbishopricke of Trevirs, for a certaine summe of money, and never since redeemed.   It is strongly walled and beautified with many faire Towers built on the walles. The religion of it is Popish.   Much is this towne spoken

A child martyr.   off for the martyrdome of a yong child in the same called Wernerus, of the age of seven yeares, in the yeare 1287. For it is written that the same Wernerus was in the same yeare upon the thirteenth day of May most cruelly

300

beene built in
the etymologie
tar of Bacchus,
ars erected unto
olatrie. Others
Rhetorical figure
le reason of this
d most excellent
a of the towne is

uch belongeth to
, situate on the
e for one thing,
have before made
e berg) situate in
:, which signifieth
word Pfaltzgrave
one of the most
unt Palatine of
rotestant religion

the elegant little
superior, but
n sake betwixt
This towne is
and belongeth to
ritual Elector of
of Wesel these
very the seventh
engaged to the
re summe of
strongly walled
on the walles.
his towne spoken
the same called
yeare 1287,
was in the same
most cruelly

martyred by the barbarous Jewes, in this manner : They tied him to a certaine wooden pillar in a low vault under the ground, and whipped him so bitterly, that the poore innocent child died with it. After they had thus handled him they conveighed away his corps, and buried it under a certaine hedge where brambles and thornes grew, but being afterward casually found out by some of the townesfolke of Wesel, it was therehence translated to a place called Bavaricum, where they built a church to almighty God in memory of that punie Martyr, & it is called by the name of Wernerus Church at this day. As for the wooden pillar whereunto they tyed him when they scourged him to death, it was afterward removed to an hospitall Church of Wesel neare to the Rhene, where they erected it at the toppe of the high Altar, and is there shewed to this day for a monument of that Jewish cruelty. In this towne was borne that famous Divine *Joannes de Wasalia, mentioned by Matthias Illyricus in his tract intitled Catalogus testium Veritatis, qui ante Lutheri tempora Antichristo reclamarunt. For this Joannes in the middest of the darknesse of Poperie gave a little glimpse of light in Christs Church, though it was greatly obscured and suppressed by the iniquity of the times wherein he lived.

When we were passed Wesel we came to another [p. 576.] custome Towne situate on the same banke of the Rhene, which was the fourth. The name of it is St. Gewere, a *St. Goar.* Protestant towne, and it standeth in that territory whose inhabitants were in former times called †Catti, a very warlike people much mentioned by Cornelius Tacitus and other writers of the Roman histories; but now it hath the name of Hassia, which is a Landgraviat subject to the

* But I will not confidently affirme that hee was borne in this towne. But either in this or the Lower Wesel in Cleve-land I know he was borne.

† From this word commeth Cattinelnbogen the ancient name of a Towne in Hassia wherhence the Landgrave deriveth one of his Princely titles.

301

renowned Prince Maurice the present Landgrave of the Country. To him doth this custome towne belong. It hath the denomination of St. Gewere from a certaine holy man called Goarus (for the Latin name of the towne is Sanctus Goarus) that came hither out of Aquitanie in the time of the Emperour Mauricius, and lived in this place a holy and religious life.

A cataract on the Rhine.

Here I observed a very violent source of the torrent of the Rhene, which commeth to passe by meanes of a swift cataract, that is, a fall of water from some uneven part of the streame. Also I heard that there is a deep gulfe, rapidus vortex in this place, which with a most incessant greedines swalloweth down the water by meanes of the manifold anfracts and intricate windings thereof, which continuall drinking up of the water is said to be the naturall cause of the great violence of the streame that appeareth more there then in other places. It is often observed that this place in the time of a raging tempest is so dangerous that no boates dare passe that way, or if any should by force of the storme be driven in against their willes, the passengers doe very hardly escape with their lives. This foresaid towne of St. Gewere doth not want the meanes to make it something memorable as well as the rest of the Rhenish townes, though in quantity it be inferiour unto all those that I have already named. For there is one thing in it that doth make it much spoken off, whereof I will report a merry and short historie. A little

[P. 577.]

within the towne gate there hangeth an yron collar fastened in the wall with one linke, which is made fit to be put upon a mans neck without any manner of hurt to the party that weareth it, and they use first to conveigh it over the head, and so to the necke. This collar doth every stranger and

A merry custom for strangers at St. Goar.

freshman the first time that he passeth that way (according to an ancient custome observed amongst them) put upon his necke (at the least as the Gentlemen told me that went in my boate) which hee must weare so long standing till he hath redeemed himselfe with a competent measure of wine. And at the drinking of it there is as much jovialty

302

ndgrave of the
rne belong. It
i a certaine holy
of the towne is
Aquitanie in the
red in this place

e of the torrent
by meanes of i
om some uneven
t there is a deep
tich with a most
: water by meanes
windings thereof,
rater is said to be
of the streame that
ſ.... It is ofta
· a raging tempest
use that way, or if
ven in against ther
: essate with ther
::re doth not wast
L...ble as well as
b. in quantity it is
L...ly named. For
l. ...ch spoken of,
(...isorie. A little
l...... collar fastened
ſ. ::: to be put upon
·. to the party that
': it over the head,
'rery stranger and
::t way (according
:. them) put upon
:.ld me that went
·: standing till
.:·::t measure of
.. :.uch jovially

and merriment as heart can conceive for the incorporating
of a fresh novice into the fraternity of boone companions.
And from thenceforth he is free from all such manner of
exactions as long as he liveth.   That this is true I know
by mine owne experience.   For I was contented for
novelty sake to be their prisoner a litle while by wearing
of the foresaid collar.   This custome doth carry some
kinde of affinity with certaine sociable ceremonies that wee
have in a place of England which are performed by that
most reverend Lord Ball of Bagshot in Hamptshire, who
doth with many and indeed more solemne rites invest his
Brothers of his unhallowed Chappell of Basingstone (as
all our men of the westerne parts of England do know by
deare experience to the smart of their purses) then these
merry Burgomaisters of Saint Gewere use to doe.   In this
towne was I like to separate my selfe from my Moguntine
company.   For as soone as I heard that the towne did *St. Goar*
belong to the Landgrave of Hassia, the very name of that *belongs to the*
worthy Prince (whome for his admirable wisedome they *Landgrave of*
do not undeservedly stile with the title of the Solomon *Hesse.*
of Germany) did strike into mee such a longing desire
to see his Court at Cassel, that I was with great difficulty
withdrawne by the perswasions of my company from going
thither.   For he is a Prince of such rare and miraculous
gifts of learning (the same whereof when I was in Germany [p. 578.]
did doctorum volitare per ora virorum, and exceedingly
resounded farre and neare in the eares of all learned men)
that next to my dread Soveraigne King, and his gracious
son Prince Henry, the most unparalleled father and sonne
of all the Christian world, I do most honour and reverence
the memory of this learned and religious Prince.   For his
religion together with the same that is generally professed
over his whole dominion, is altogether consonant to ours
in England.   And his learning is so rare (beeing confirmed *A learned*
by the testimonies of thousands of the learneder sort) *Prince.*
that he speaketh six or seven languages most elegantly,
& his affection to Englishmen is so great, that no stranger
of any part of Christendome can bee more welcome to him

303

then an **Englishman**. Although I say I was strooken with such a longing desire to see the Court of this most famous Prince (whome I have here obitèr glaunced at with this exorbitant digression from my maine matter upon the occasion of arriving in a towne of his dominion) yet the opportunity of my German associats recalled me, and so after much Mercuriall and Joviall conversation in this Towne of Saint Gewere, we returned againe to our boate, and proceeded forward in our journey. A little beyond the west end of this town I observed a very beautiful and stately Castel, the fayrest of all that I sawe that day, situate upon a lofty hill which belongeth to the foresayd Land-grave also as well as the towne. At length about eight

Boppard.

of the clocke at night we arrived at the towne of Boppard, as I have before said, and there reposed our selves till the next morning. This city of Boppard is situate upon the left banke of the Rhene, and was our fifth custome towne. This city is very ancient, for it was built in the time of Julius Cæsar, or (as I thinke) before. But this is certainly true, that it was in that time extant. For here lay an

[p. 579.]

other Roman Prefect with a garrison of souldiers, one of the tenne subject to the Moguntine Marshall, as I have before said. The name of it in those daies was Bodobigra. As for this present name of Boppard, in Latin Boppardia, some write that it is so called quasi Bonport, which word signifieth a good or commodious haven Towne. I have read that it was once oppugned, and after the siege of a

Boppard captured by King Richard of England.

few daies taken by Richard one of our English Kings, because it made resistance against him when he came into Germanie after he was elected King of the Romanes. For in those daies it was an imperiall Citie, in regard whereof King Richard challenged it, & so it remained till the time of Henry the seventh, who morgaged it to the Archbishop of Trevirs for a summe of money, at the same time that he did upper Wesel. Ever since which time it hath bene subject to the dominion of the Archbishop of Trevirs, and professeth the same religion that he doth, which is that of the Church of Rome. I am sorry that I can speake no

304

more of this city, as of the monuments and antiquities thereof (for some I heard are there to be seene) which it was not possible for me to survay, because I came there late in the evening, and departed early the next day beeing Sunday and the eighteenth of September, about sixe of the clocke in the morning. The next Telonium that wee came unto was Lanstein the seventh in number, which is *Lahnstein.* in the dominion of the Archbishop of Mentz, and of the Popish religion. This standeth in the left banke of the Rhene also. From thence we came to the Citie of Confluentia commonly called Cobolentz, on the left hand of the Rhene, which belongeth to the Archbishop of Trevirs; and hath her denomination from the Latin word confluere, which signifieth to runne together, because in that place there is a confluent of two noble rivers, the Rhene and the Mosella. The later of them is called Obrinca by Ptole- *River Moselle.* mæus Alexandrinus. It riseth out of the country of Lingones in France, commonly called Langres, and runneth *[p. 580.]* by the Cities of Mentz and Trevirs, and washeth a great part of the Country that was heretofore called Austrasia, but now Lotharingia, from the Emperour Lotharius the first, who changed the name thereof, commonly Lorraine. I observed a fayre wooden bridge over this river at Confluence supported with thirteene arches. This City is not *Coblenz an* inferiour in antiquity to any other of these Rhenish Cities *ancient city.* or townes that I have named since I came from Mentz. For it flourished in the daies of Julius Cæsar, in whose time it was planted with a garrison of soldiers in the behalfe of the Romanes, and governed by one of the foresaid tenne Roman Prefects that were subject to the high Marshall of Mentz. I observed that this city is invironed with strong walles, fayrly adorned with pretty little Turrets, that do yeeld a very delicate shew. In this City was holden an Imperial Diet about the yeare of our Lord 1137. where most of the greatest Princes of Germany were assembled to choose Conrade the third that was Duke of Suevia, Emperour. The religion of it is Papisticall. Also there was shewed mee a very faire Monastery upon a hill neere the City, which is inhabited by a convent of Carthusian Monkes. Likewise on the other side of the river right opposite to the City, I saw a very strong and *Castle of* impregnable Castell called Hermenstein, situate upon a *Hammerstein.* very eminent rocke. It belongeth to the Archbishop of Trevirs also, and is esteemed the strongest and greatest Castell of all Germany beyond all comparison. I heard that it is exceeding plentifully furnished with all manner of warlike munition, and continually kept by two hundred presidiary souldiers, which do most vigilantly gard it night and day, and are so carefull of it, that they will not give a stranger leave to come within it, though hee would give a great summe of money to see it. The eighth custome Towne is called Engers, which is subject to the Archbishop [p. 581.] of Trevirs. The ninth Andernach situate upon the left side of the Rhene, a very ancient towne in the Diocesse *Andernach.* of the Archbishop of Colen. For here resided another of the Roman Prefects in the time of Julius Cæsar, and was the place where the last of the tenne garrisons lay that were subject to the authority of the Moguntine Marshall. It was in former times called Antennacum. For so doth Ammianus Marcellinus that ancient Historiographer call it. For many hundred yeares agoe it suffered great dilapidations. But in the yeare 1120. it was very fairely re-edified by a certaine Archbishop of Colen who bestowed very great cost upon it. For besides the inward ornaments of the towne hee beautified it with strong walles, & built many fayre Towers in them, which do greatly grace the towne. An ornament that I much observed in these Rhenish Cities and townes betwixt Mentz and Colen. In this towne was that worthy man Joannes Guinterius borne, once publike professour of the Greeke tongue in the University of Strasbourg, as I have before mentioned in my discourse of that City. Neere this towne were *Two great* fought two very great battels in the moneth of October *battels.* anno 876, betwixt the Emperour Charles the second surnamed the Bald, and Lewes the second sonne of the elder brother, surnamed Germanicus, in which battel his Nephew

306

by a convent of
ther side of the
very strong and
situate upon a
e Archbishop of
rest and greatest
^arison. I heard
. with all manner
t by two hundred
intly gard it night
tey will not give 1
i hee would give 1
ie eighth custome
t to the Archbishop
uate upon the left
ne in the Diocesse
ere resided anothe
: Iulius Cæsar, and
tenne garrisons by
x Moguntine Ma-
Antennacum. For
: ancient Histori-
^es agoe it suffered
::10. it was very
:::p of Colen who
^ares the inward
::th strong walls,
:: do greatly grace
^ observed in these
^^ntz and Colen.
^arres Guinterius
' Greeke tongue in
^ before mentioned
^ this towne were
^^eth of October
^^ the second sur-
^^re of the elder
^^ his Nephew

won the honour of the field to his great glory, and did put the Emperour his Uncle to flight. The second was betwixt that victorious German Emperour Otho surnamed the Great, and Ebarhardus Duke of Franconia, wherein the Duke was slaine; and Gislebertus Duke of Lorraine, who married the Lady Gerbirga the Emperours eldest sister, and was confederated with the said Eberhardus, was drowned in the river Rhene but a little from the place where the battell was fought. Here the Emperour partly slue and partly tooke prisoners all those Earles and great Lordes that held with his enemies. This hapned about the yeare of our Lord 950. The tenth is called Lintz, *[p. 582.]* situate on the right banke of the Rhene, and in the Diocesse of the Archbishop of Colen, whose religion it *Linz.* professeth. This towne is famous for the residence of the Emperour Frederick the third, who did sometimes keepe his imperiall Court here, and at last died in this towne of a surfet by eating too many mellons, upon the nineteenth day of August in the yeare of our Lord 1493, and of his age seventy eight, after hee had swayed the Empire fifty three yeares, 4 moneths, & 4 daies. He lived 3 yeares longer then Augustus Cæsar, & reigned 3 yeares lesse. But his body doth not lie here; for it was translated from this place where it lay for the space of 20 yeares, to Vienna in Austria, in the yeare 1315, and the seventh day of November, where his bones have bene kept ever since in a most magnificent Mausoleum. From Lintz we went to an obscure towne in the Diocesse of Colen, called Uber- *Oberwinter.* winter that standeth in the left banke of the Rhene, and came thither about sixe of the clocke in the evening, where wee remained all that night. This daies journey betwixt the Citie of Boppard and Uberwinter contained some thirty miles. In this place we solaced our selves after our tedious labour of rowing as merily as we could. One merry conceit amongst the rest that I heard in this good *A merry* company I will here relate. One of my Moguntine *conceit.* associats that was a merry Gentleman, and one that had lately bene a student in the Universitie of Altorph neere

307

CORYAT'S CRUDITIES

the City of Norimberg, told me as we sate together at supper, that a certain Bishop had two kind of wines in his cellar, a better and a worse, that were called by two distinct names, the better Noli me tangere, the worse Utcunque. And that a certaine merry conceited fellow that sate at the Bishops table, having dranke once or twise of the utcunque, so much disliked it that he would drink no more of it. Therefore he spake to one of the Bishops servants that waited at table, to give him a draught of the

[p. 583.] Noli me tangere, & withal pronounced unto him, in the presence of the Bishop these two merry Latin verses ex tempore.

> Si das Utcunque, dæmon vos tollat utrunque :
> Ibis ad astra poli, si fers Me tangere noli.

With this and such other pleasant conceits we recreated our selves that night at Uberwinter, and the next morning being munday and the nineteenth of September, we tooke boate againe about three of the clocke, and came to Colen which was eighteene miles beyond it, about tenne of the same morning : our whole journey betwixt Mentz and Colen was about seventy eight miles. I observed in a great many places, on both sides of the Rhene, more gallowes and wheeles betwixt Mentz and Colen, then ever I saw in so short a space in all my life, especially within few miles of Colen, by reason that the rusticall Corydons of the country, which are commonly called the Boores and

Free-booters. the Free-booters (a name that is given unto the lewd murdering villaines of the country that live by robbing and spoyling of travellers, beeing called Free booters, because they have their booties and prey from passengers free, paying nothing for them except they are taken) do commit many notorious robberies neere the Rhene, who are such cruell and bloody horseleaches (the very Hyenæ & Lycanthropi of Germany) that they seldome robbe any man but forthwith they cut his throat. And some of them doe afterward escape, by reason of the woodes neere at hand in which they shelter themselves free from danger.

308

ate together at
nd of wines in
e called by two
zere, the worse
conceited fellow
ke once or twice
he would drink
te of the Bishops
a draught of the
unto him, in the
I Latin verses et

' utrunque:
zere noli.

xce ts we recreated
? the next morning
:ptember, we tooke
and came to Colen
about tenne of the
twixt Mentz and
I observed in a
the Rhene, more
'-d Colen, then eve
t.
'· especially within
(·-::all Corydons
-:: the Boores and
'-· unto the land
'-· live by robbing
'-·? Free booters,
-·r from passengers
-·· are taken) do
-· the Rhene, who
·: (the very Hyene
l-:me robbe any
· And some of
·-· woodes neere
:-: from danger.

Yet others are sometimes taken, and most cruelly excarni- *Their*
ficated and tortured upon these wheeles, in that manner *punishment.*
that I have before mentioned in some of my observations
of France. For I sawe the bones of many of them lie
upon the wheele, a dolefull spectacle for any relenting
Christian to beholde. And upon those gallowes in divers
places I sawe murderers hang, partly in chaines, and
partly without chaines. A punishment too good for these
Cyclopicall Anthropophagi, these Caniball man-eaters. I [p. 584.]
have heard that the Free-booters doe make themselves so
strong, that they are not to be taken by the country. For
I observed a towne about twenty miles on this side Colen,
called Remagan, situate neere the Rhene, which about *Remagen*
some ten yeares since was miserably ransacked by these *sacked by*
Free-booters, who banded themselves together in so great *freebooters.*
a troope as consisted of almost three thousand persons.
The towne it selfe they defaced not, but only tooke away
their goods, to the utter undoing and impoverishment of
the inhabitants. The like they did to a goodly Palace
hard by it called the Præpositura, by reason that it
belongeth to an Ecclesiasticall Præpositus, a man of great
authority, that doth sometimes make his residence in that
place. Within a few miles on this side Colen we arrived
at the fayre towne of Bonna situate on the left bank of the *Bonn.*
Rhene, a place of great antiquity. For it was built either
a little before the incarnation of Christ, or in the time of
Christ. That it is ancient it appeareth by the testimony
of that famous Geographer Claudius Ptolemæus of Alexandria, who lived about 140 yeares after Christ, in the
time of the Emperour Marcus Aurelius Antonius surnamed Philosophus. This towne is the eleventh and the
last Telonium of all those betwixt Mentz & Colen. It
belongeth to the Archbishop of Colen, and professeth the
same religion that he doth, which is that of the church
of Rome. Here the Archbishop hath a Palace situated *Archbishop's*
hard by the Rhene, a most magnificent and princely build- *Palace.*
ing, but much inferiour to divers Palaces both of our King
James, and of many Noblemen of England. Which I

309

therefore adde because one of my company that advised me to behold it well, told mee it was a Palace of so great magnificence, that he thought all my country of England could not yeeld the like. But surely his opinion was very false and erroneous. For besides many other English Palaces that do surpasse that of the Archbishop of Colen, there is one in mine owne country of Somersetshire, even the magnificent house of my most worthy and right Worshipful neighbour and Mecœnas Sir Edward Philippes now maister of the Rolles (whome I name honoris causâ) in the towne of Montacute, so stately adorned with the statues of the nine Worthies, that may bee at the least equally ranked with this of Bonna, if not something preferred before it. At this towne the stiepe Rhenish Mountaines, which did on both sides inclose the Rhene like to naturall walles or Bulwarkes betwixt the towne of Bing (as I have before said) and Bonna for the space of more then fifty miles, do desinere in planiciem, which plain continued till I came to the farther bound of my journey upon the Rhene in the Netherlands, as I have before said also. Bonna with Colen and many other goodly Townes in that tract was once most grievously spoyled by the Normans in the time of the Emperour Lotharius the second.

It hapned that this nineteenth day of September when I came to Colen, was according to the computation of the Church of these parts of Christendome the feast of St. Michael the Archangel, which was ten dayes sooner there then with us in England. Upon which day there were many religious ceremonies celebrated in the City of Colen, and great shewes of Saints reliques. Amongst other things I observed a very frequent concurse of people at a little Chappel situate on the left side of the Rhene about a mile on this side Colen, in which they report the body of St. Maternus was buried, who was one of the Disciples of St. Peter the Apostle, and the first converter both of the City of Colen, and of divers other Cities and Townes in the Provinces thereabout from Gentilisme to Christianity.

[p. 585.]

Sir Edward Philipps, Master of the Rolls.

S. Maternus.

310

But at this day there is only the shrine of him shewed in the foresaid Chappell in which his body was once intombed. That shrine they worshipped very religiously with many holy ceremonies upon that day of St. Michael. [p. 586.] But now it is only an empty monument void of any thing. For his bones were afterward carried to the City of Trevirs (as I heard divers report in Colen) where they are kept to this day together with many ancient reliques of other Saints which that City doth more abundantly yeeld (as many have told me in divers places) then any City of all Christendome saving Rome.

The end of my Observations of some parts of high Germanie.

The Beginning of my Observations of the Netherlands.

My Observations of Colonia Agrippina commonly called Colen.

Julius Cæsar Scaliger hath written these verses upon Colen.

Maxima cognati Regina Colonia Rheni,
Hoc te etiam titulo Musa superba canit.
Romani statuunt, habitat Germania, terra est
Belgica, ter fœlix nil tibi Diva deest.

He ancient Ubii that are mentioned by Cæsar and Tacitus, having abandoned their owne native country, which was neare to the river Albis in Saxonie, by reason of their continuall broiles and conflicts with the Suevians, came into this territory where Colen now standeth, and [p. 587.] are said to be the first original founders thereof, many yeares before the incarnation of Christ, from whom the City derived the denomination of Ubiopolis before it was called Colonia. But I cannot finde in any authour

Scaliger's
verses on
Cologne.

Founders of
Cologne.

311

either the designation of the certaine yeare of the foundation, whereby a man might gather how long before the comming of Christ it was first founded, or mention of any principall men of that nation of the Ubii that might be properly intitled the founders thereof.   After it was founded by these Ubii, it hapned that Julius Cæsar having conquered it together with many other Rhenish Cities before mentioned, on the left side of the river, built a wooden bridge over the Rhene, to serve for the conveighing of his armie into the other side of the river, that he might fight with the Germans : and from thenceforth it was under the subjection of the Romans for many yeares.   Not long after the time of Julius Cæsar it was so exceedingly amplified and inlarged by the Romans, that it farre surpassed all the Cities whatsoever in all the *Cologne greatly enlarged by the Romans.* bordering Provinces.   But to whom the glory of this amplification is to be ascribed, the authours doe something differ.   For the Colonians themselves thinke (as it appeareth by a memorable inscription written upon their Prætorium which I will hereafter mention) that Marcus Vipsanius * Agrippa sonne in law of Augustus Cæsar (for he married his daughter Julia the widow of his worthy nephew Marcellus, who was sonne to his sister Octavia) founded it about sixteene yeares before the incarnation of Christ.   Others attribute it to Agrippina the wife of renowned Germanicus Cæsar, and daughter of the foresaid Marcus Vipsanius Agrippa by his wife Julia ; which certainly in my opinion is the more probable of the two, because it is confirmed by the testimony of a very authenticke and irrefragable authour, Cornelius Tacitus, who lived shortly after the time of Agrippina, even in the daies of [p. 588.] the Emperour Tiberius.   For he writeth that the Lady Agrippina to the end shee might shew her power to the bordering nations of her country, commanded that a colonie of old souldiers (which we commonly call trained souldiers) should be planted in the towne of the Ubians,

* This is that Agrippa of whom Virgil speaketh in his eighth Ænei.
Parte aliâ ventis & diis Agrippa secundis arduus, &c.

312

of the founda-
long before the
mention of any
ii that might be
After it was
ius Cæsar having
Rhenish Cities
he river, built a
rve for the con-
ide of the river,
and from thence
Romans for man
lius Cæsar it was
the Roman,
tsoe er n all th
gl ry f th-
ur oe some

m poo ther

ster Octavu
carnation of
the wife of

a; which
the two

who imposed a double name upon it, both that of Colonia,
because it was amplified by a colonie of Roman souldiers,
and that of Agrippina from her owne name, because shee
was borne in that towne. From that time it was inhabited
by the Romans for the space of foure hundred yeares, till
the time of Marcomirus King of France, who chaced them
out of the City. After that the Emperour Otho surnamed the Great, tooke it away from the Frenchmen, and
made it tributarie to the Roman Empire, under whose
sacred protection it hath ever since remained for the space
of more then six hundred years to this day.

The situation of Colen is very delectable. For it *Situation of*
standeth in a pleasant and fruitfull plaine hard by the *Cologne.*
Rhene, which washeth the walls thereof, as it doth Basil
and Mentz. The compasse of it is so great, that I heard
it credibly reported a man can hardly goe round about
it under the space of foure houres, which if it be true, it
containeth in circuit at the least eight of our English
miles. The buildings of the City both publique and
private are very faire, and many of their private houses
I observed to be of a notable heigth, even foure stories
high, whereof some are built altogether with stone, and
some with timber. As for the walles of the City they *City walls.*
are built in that manner that they yeeld great beauty to
the same. For they are compacted of very strong and
hard stone, and raised to a stately heigth, and distinguished
with a great company of turrets which doe specially garnish the citie. Besides whereas the wall extendeth it
selfe in a great length upon the very banke of the Rhene,
it presenteth a farre of a passing beautifull shew unto
them that approch towards the City upon the river, either [p. 589.]
from the East or West. Their streets and market places *Streets and*
are many and very spacious, especially two market places *market places.*
that I tooke exact notice of above the rest, whereof the
one in which they ordinarily sell their necessaries and keepe
their markets, is a hundred threescore and sixteen paces
long, and threescore and three broade. The other where
their Merchants doe meete twise a day which they call

in Latin forum fœnarium, because they use to sell hay in the same, is the fairest that I saw in my whole voyage, saving that of St. Marks street in Venice. For it is two hundred and fourescore paces long, and fourescore and foure broade. For indeede I meated them both. And this last market place is marvailously graced with many sumptuous and stately buildings both at the sides and the endes. Surely the beauty of this market place is such by reason of so many magnificent houses including it, that I thinke if a clowne that never saw any faire shewes in his life should suddenly arrive there, he would be halfe amazed with the majestie of the place. The number of their Churches is more (if that be true that many reported unto me) then in any City I saw in my journey, though I have written of two hundred in Venice. Nay I thinke no city in Christendome doth yeeld so many saving Rome, but I speake with a restriction, if that be true which they reported. For they say their city can yeeld a Church for every day in the yeare: that is, in the total number, three hundred threescore and five. But in this summe they reckon all their little chappels belonging to Nunnes and to all other religious convents whatsoever. Yet I beleeve they can hardly make up the full number of three hundred threescore and five. For Munster that maketh a catalogue of their Churches, reckoneth no more of them then there are weekes in the yeare, even two and fifty, which abridgeth their number by three hundred and fifteen. But indeede he excludeth out of his account all their little chappels, whereof I understand there is a great multitude in the city, all which they adde unto the rest to make up their number of three hundred threescore and five.

Their Cathedrall Church which is dedicated to St. Peter, is a goodly building, but it is great pittie that it is so imperfect. For it is but halfe ended. Doubtlesse it would be a very glorious & beautifull worke if it had been throughly finished, especially for the outward workmanship, which is excellently adorned at the east end with

Cologne has many churches.

[p. 590.]

Cathedral Church of S. Peter.

314

many lofty pillars and pinnacles that doe wonderfully garnish that part. Amongst many other worthy monuments that are contained in this Church, one is that which is the most famous of all Europe, whose fame hath resounded to the farthest confines of all Christendome. For what is he of any meane learning or understanding that hath not at some time or other in his life heard of the three Kings of Colen? Therefore because it is so remarkable a monument, and so much visited by all strangers that come to the Citie, I visited it as well as the rest, and observed it after a more strict and curious manner then every stranger doth. For I wrote out the whole history of them, and have made as particular a discription of the monument as I could possibly doe. Therefore both the description of the sepulcher wherein the bones of the Kings lie, and the history I present unto thee for a noveltie. For certainly I for mine owne part never read it in print before I came thither. Neither have I heard of any man that hath seene it publikely printed but in the same place, which is the reason that moveth me to beleeve that this will be a novelty to every reader that hath not seene the same there as I have done. Blame me not if I am something tedious. For this being the most renowned monument of Christendome may not be briefly past over with a few words. Though I know that most of our learned Protestants will take this history for a meere figment, neither am I for mine owne part likewise perswaded but that there are some vaine and frivolous things contained in it, which cannot be justified by the most learned Papists of Christendome: in so much that whereas I often observed for that little time that I was in the Citie, many devout oraizons made at the monument, I said to my selfe that their praiers unto the kings were in vaine, & did but beate the aire, whether the bones of the Magi were there or no. Howbeit seeing there are some few things amongst the rest that are not altogether unworthy the noting, I hope it will not be offensive unto any learned & zealous Protestant that I have here inserted this history

The three Kings of Cologne.

Their monument the most renowned in Christendom.

[p. 591.]

315

of the three Kings, which I thinke was never before so amply communicated to my country. This famous sepulcher standeth at the East end of the Church in a faire Chappel that containeth nothing but the same Monument, unto the inner part of which Chappell there is no accesse all the day but betwixt sixe and eight of the clocke in the morning, because the dore of it is alwaies locked, saving at that time. The fabricke it selfe by reason of the glorious and most resplendent ornaments about it, is so rich that I never saw the like, neither doe I thinke that in all the westerne parts of the world there is the like to be

The shrine. seene. The shrine that containeth the bones of these Saints is within the Chappel (as I have already said) and is elevated some two yards above the ground, being inclosed round about with a double grate of yron barres of some foure yards high, contrived in the forme of a lattise window, and fairely painted with red in the outside towards the Church. Also in the same part of the lattise that looketh towards the Church, there is represented a great multitude of golden starres, in token that a starre conducted them to Christ. The matter whereof the shrine is composed wherein their sacred bones are shrowded, is pure bright shining brasse, wherein are two rowes of pretty religious images, made in brasse also, and it is garnished with many exquisite devices contrived in checker worke with faire colours that doe much adorne

[p. 592.] the monument. Besides there is wonderfull abundance of precious Stones of different kinds and great worth, inserted into two severall degrees of the monument, whereof many are fully as big as my thumbe. For the tombe is divided into two parts, the higher and the lower. At the

West end of West end or front of it which looketh towards the Church, *the tomb.* there are many glittering and rich ornaments, which are not so openly exposed that every body may come to handle them. For there is a partition betwixt them and that part of the Church where people use to stand to behold them. Some of the principall riches doe consist partly in an image of our Lady, & partly in certaine cups

316

or goblets that hang at the front. The image of our Lady who is represented bearing Christ in her armes, is very costly. For it is said that it is made of pure silver, and double gilted. The goblets in number ten, which are hanged directly before the image upon a brasen rod some two yards long, are said to be made of massie gold, one whereof the Emperour Charles the fifth bestowed upon the monument. For a testimony whereof there is hanged up a square plate of gold, wherein the blacke spread-eagle which is the Emperours armes, is engraved, and this inscription following is written. Invictissimus *Inscriptions on* atque potentissimus Carolus V. Imper. & Hispaniarum *the tomb.* rex Augustissimus, Deo omnipotenti, beatæ Mariæ, S S tribus Regibus die 3 Januarii, Anno Domini. 1554. præclarum munus dono obtulit. Likewise unto another of these tenne there is fixed another square plate of gold, wherein this inscription is written. Beatæ Virgini Mariæ sanctissimæ, & tribus Regibus Reverendus & illustris Princeps & Dominus D. Joannes Gebhardus ex Comitibus à Mansfelt electus & confirmatus Archipræsul Agrippinus, sacri Romani Imperii per Italiam Archicancellarius, Princeps Elector, Westphaliæ & Angariæ Dux, Lega- *Image of Our* tusque natus, dono dicavit. Also, before our Ladies *Lady.* image there hangeth a marvellous rich crosse of massie gold adorned with a great multitude of precious stones, [p. 593.] & under her image there are many rich stones of divers kinds. Moreover before her image there stand foure candelsticks wherein there do alwaies burne foure waxen tapers. Two of these candelsticks are exceeding faire and much costlier then the rest. Againe the top of the frontispice of the monument is beautified partly with the images of the three Kings formed in silver, and richly gilted, who are most curiously counterfaited, bearing their gifts in their hands, gold, myrrhe, and frankencense; and partly with the like image of our Lady standing in the very middest with Christ in her armes. One *Images of the* of the Kings is presented like a blacke Moore with a *three Kings.* golden crowne upon his head. The other two uncovered.

317

In the outward edge of the front these verses are written.

Corpora Sanctorum loculus tenet iste Magorum,
Indeque sublatùm nihil est alibive locatum.
Sunt juncti Felix, Nabor & Gregorius istis.

In the middle of this outward edge there is presented a faire scutchin and armes under the which this is written.

Renovatum ære Q. R. D. Joannis
Walschartz Tungri S. T. D.
Hujus Ecclesiæ Canonici, Anno 1597. ora pro eo.

History of the monument. All this that I have hitherto written since I first made mention of the monument, containeth nothing but a description thereof. Now followeth the history which is altogether as memorable as the monument it selfe. It was within these few yeares printed at Colen, and is pasted upon three severall tables which hang apart in as many distinct places without the Chappel. It is divided into nine particular sections. Also each section hath its marginall notes, which because they are so many that the margent of the Page cannot conveniently containe them, I have (contrary to the common custome) subscribed the quotations belonging to each section, directly under the section it selfe.

[p. 594.]

The title of the history is this.

Brevis historia Magorum ex sacris literis & probatis
Ecclesiæ scriptoribus collecta.

The historie it selfe is this following.

First section. 1ª **M**Agi, qui primi omnium ex gentibus Christi Salvatoris infantiam in Bethleem ᵇdecimotertio post nativitatem die adorarunt, ᶜtres numero fuerunt. Ac si ᵈEpiphanio credimus, ex Abraham originem duxerunt, ex filiis ejus quos ex ᵉCethurâ ancillâ suscepit, descendentes. Cui non repugnat quòd ᶠOrigines et ᵍChrysostomus ad ʰBalaam Prophetam Gentilem, Magorum

lese verses are

Magorum,
tum.
stis.

re is presented a
this is written.

originem referunt. Nam & ipse, sicut etiam ⁱRegina Saba, ex ejusdem Cethuræ filiis duxit originem.

The quotations of this first section are these.

ᵃ Math. 2. ᵇAmmonius Alexandrinus in Harmoniâ Evangelicâ. Alcuinus de divinis officiis. cap. de Epi phania. Anselmus in 2. Math. Nicephorus lib. 1. Ecclesiasticæ historiæ. cap. 13. ᶜLeo serm. 1, 3, 4, 5, 6, 7, 8. de Epiphaniâ. August. serm. 1. de Epiphaniâ, & Rupertus in 2. Math. ᵈIn compendio doctrinæ Christianæ. ᵉGenes. 25. ᶠHomilia 13. in Numer. ᵍHomilia ex variis in Math. locis. Petrus de Natalibus lib. 2. Cata. Sanct. 4 cap. 48. cap. ʰNumer. 24. ⁱ3 Reg. 10.

)⁻. ora pro eo
since I first mak
:h nothing but
history which

:olen, and is pasted
¿ apart in as many
I· is divided into
:tion hath its ma-
so many that the
containe them,
¬e) subscribed the
directly under the

2 Nomina eorum, ætas, & vultus cujusmodi, fuerint, *Second section.* & quæ quisque munera obtulerit, sicut ex majorum traditione acceperat, his verbis describit Venerabilis ᵃBeda. Primus, inquit, dicitur fuisse Melchior, senex barbâ prolixâ & capillis, aurum obtulit regi Domino. Secundus nomine Gaspar, juvenis imberbis, rubicundus, thure quasi Deo oblatione dignâ Deum honorabat. Tertius fuscus, integrè barbatus, Balthasar nomine, per myrrham filium hominis moriturum professus est. Quod autem unus [p. 595.] eorum niger & Æthiops depingi soleat, ut in multis iisque antiquis apud nos picturis apparet, ex eo profectum videtur, tùm quôd Beda tertium fuscum fuisse perhibit, tum quod ex Psalmo 72, die Regum in Ecclesiâ decantatur, Coram illo procident Æthiopes.

& proba s

The quotation of this section is short, only this.

Venerabilis B. in Collectaneis.

ecimotertio post
fuerunt. Ac s

3 Non obscuri eos loci aut ordinis, sed Principes viros *Third section.* atquè etiam Reges fuisse, quod Christi gloriam maximè illustrat, pium est credere. Id enim veteris legis ᵃfiguræ, quæ in Solomone antecessit, & Prophetarum, maximè ᵇDavidis & ᶜEsaiæ, vaticiniis consentaneum est. Quorum ille inquit. Reges Tharsis & insulæ munera

offerent, Reges Arabum & Saba dona adducent. Posterior vero: & abulabunt gentes in lumine tuo, & Reges in splendore ortus tui. Quæ de Magorum vocatione oblationeque ab Ecclesiâ & ^d sanctis Patribus intelliguntur. Item ^e Herodis ac totius urbis Hierosolymitanæ ad eorum adventum trepidatio, munera item preciosa, quæ ex thesauris suis deprompsisse referuntur, Majorum denique traditio scriptis, ^f sermonibus cantionibus, hymnis, & picturis ut vulgaribus sic antiquis prodita, confirmant. Nec quidquam ad rem facit quod Evangelista non appellavit Reges, sed Magos. Id enim ^g consultò factum est, quod Christi gloria nostraque religio Magorum sive Sapientum testimonio potiùs quàm Regum potentiâ constabilienda videretur.

The quotations of the third section.

^a 3 Reg. 10. ^b Psal. 72. ^c Esaiæ 60. ^d Chrysost. homil. 1. ex variis in Matth. locis. Leo sermone de Epiphaniâ. ^e Matth. 2. cap. 3. ver. ^f Tertullianus lib. 3. contra Judæos cap. 9. Isidorus de passione Dominica cap. 15. Anselmus & Theophylactus in 2. cap. Math. Vide Cicer. de Divinatione. Plinius lib. 3. naturalis historiæ. cap. 1. Adam Sasbont homil. de Epiphaniâ. Franciscus Suarez in 3. par. D. Thomæ tomo 2. ^g Melchior Canus lib. 11. Locorum Theologicorum, cap. 5. Hector Pintus in 1. cap. Danielis. Cæsar Baronius lib. 1. Annalium.

[P. 596.]

Fourth section.

4 Ad professionem eorum quod attinet, tametsi non desint qui ¹ Magorum nomine maleficos ac magicis artibus instructos accipiant: potior tamen illorum sententia nobis esse debet qui ² Sapientes astrologos fuisse arbitrantur, qui arte mathematicâ (ut ³ Cyprianus loquitur) vim & discursum noverant planetarum, & elementorum naturam, & astrorum ministeria certis experimentis observabant. Undè convenientèr admodùm, divina ⁴ Sapientia quæ disponit omnia suavitèr, Stellæ potissimùm indicio illos tanquam astrorum peritos ad se pertraxit, accedente tum

320

adducent. Po-
ne tuo, & Reges
corum vocatione
bus intelliguntur.
mitanæ ad eorum
osa, quæ ex the-
Majorum denique
is, hymnis, & pe-
nfirmant. Ne

gratiæ divinæ lumine, tum hominum ex Scripturis demon-
stratione. Nam de loco [5] ubi Christus nasceretur, â
Scribis, ex [6] Michea instructi sunt & Stellam illam Messiæ
ortum significare, ex [7] Balaam Prophetiâ per Majorum
traditionem acceperunt.

The quotations of the fourth.

[1] Justinus dialogo contra Tryphonem. Origines lib.
1. contra Celsum, & homilia 13. in Numeros. Chrysos-
tomus homilia 1 & 14 ex variis in Matth. locis. Augusti.
sermone 2 de Epiphaniâ. [2] Chrisost. homilia 2 operis
imperfecti. Leo sermone 4 de Epiphaniâ. Hieronymus
in 2 cap. Daniel, & 47 Esaiæ. Anselmus & Rupertus in
2 Matth. [3] sermo de stellâ & Magis. [4] Sapientiæ 8.
[5] Matth. 2. [6] Micheæ 5. [7] Numeri 24. Origines
homilia 13 in Numeros & lib. 1 contra Celsum. Leo
sermone 4 de Epiphaniâ.

d c ction.

Chrysost. hom.

5 Ex Arabiâ Fœlice venisse, quod [1] Justinus Martyr, *Fifth section.*
[2] Tertullianus, [3] Cyprianus, & [4] Epiphanius memoriæ prodiderunt, verisimile videtur. Tum quod Arabia respectu
Judeæ ad Orientem, Tacito [5] teste, sita; tum [6] quòd
auri, [7] thuris, & myrrhæ ferax sit: demùm quod hæc
opinio consentiat cum Esaiæ [8] vaticinio: Omnes de Saba
(quæ, teste in eum locum, & libro quæstionum in Gene-
sim D. Hieronymo, Arabia est) venient, aurum & thus
deferentes. Cum illo item [9] Davidico. Reges Arabum
et Saba dona adducent. Et rursus. Dabitur ei de auro
Arabiæ.

M th Vide Cicer

Melchior Cano

s lib. 1. Ann-

The quotations of the fifth

[p. 597.]

tam
agità

torum natoram,
tis observabat
ria quæ dé-

[1] Justinus Martyr dialogo contra Tryphonem. [2] Tertullianus lib. contra Judæos cap. 9 et lib. 3 contra Mar-
cionitas cap. 13. [3] Sermone de Stellâ et Magis. [4] Compendio doctrinæ Christianæ. [5] lib. 5 historiarum.
[6] Psal. 71. [7] Tertullianus Apologetico cap. 30, 42.
Plinius lib. 2 naturalis historiæ, cap. 14. [8] cap. 60.
[9] Psal. 71.

Sixth section. 6 Porrò ¹ auri, thuris, et myrrhæ munera Christo obtu-
lerunt, quod his rebus Arabia imprimis abundaret et
superbiret. Deindè quòd ² Regina Saba, quam ex gente
et familiâ Magorum fuisse proditum est, similia dona,
aurum, inquam, et aromata, quibus gemmas preciosas
addidit, Solomoni Regi, in typum Christi donaverat.
Adde quod, quæ Cethuræ filiis munera dedisse Abraham
in 25 Geneseos commemoratur, ea ex Hebræorum tradi-
tionibus ³ Epiphanius refert, vestes, aurum, thus, &
myrrham fuisse. Postremo non tam gentis suæ morem
& exempla majorum, verumetiam mysticam rationem
secuti, hoc quod cordibus credunt, muneribus ⁴ protestan-
tur; Thus deo, myrrham homini, aurùm offerunt regi,
& his se instruunt donis, ut adoraturi unum, tria se semel
credidisse demonstrent, auro honorantes personam regiam,
myrrha humanam, thure divinam.

The quotations of the sixth.

¹ Math. 2. ² 3 Reg. 10 cap. ³ Compendio Doctrinæ
Christianæ. ⁴ Leo sermone 2 de Epiphaniâ.

Seventh section. 7 Post Christi ascensionem, â ¹ D. Thoma Apostolo in
fide Christi pleniùs instructi, ad hoc baptizati, imô ² Pas-
tores etiam et Doctores sive Episcopi in populo suo
ordinati sunt, magnamque Gentilium turbam ad Christianæ religionis cultum adduxerunt, atque ita ut primitias
frugum copiosa messis consequitur: sic Magos primitias
credentium ex Gentibus, innumerabilium fides populorum,
tanquam uberrima seges est subsecuta, impletumque
vaticinium ³ Davidis, qui postquam prædixerat, Reges
Arabum et Saba dona subjungit, Et adorabunt
eum omnes Reges, et omnes gentes servient ei. Item
[p. 598.] ⁴ Omnes gentes quascunque fecisti, venient et adorabunt
coram te Domine, et glorificabunt nomen tuum.

The quotations of the seventh.

¹ Chrysost. homilia. 2 operis imperfecti. antiquum
Calendarium citatum ab Henrico Pinto, dialogorum

322

ES

era Christo obtu-
nis abundaret et
2, quam ex gente
est, similia dona
gemmas preciosa
x̄..
-hristi donavere.
dedisse Abraha
Hebræorum traf-
urum, thus, &
ge tis suæ more
vsticam rationa
enb s¹ protesta
trum offerunt reg
um tria se sens
personam regias,

parte secunda cap. 21. Petrus de Natalibus in Catalogo
Sanctorum lib. 26. cap. 48. ² Chrysost. homiliæ 6 in
Matthæum, & homilia 17 ex variis in Matth. locis. ³ psal.
71. ⁴ psal. 85.

8 Postquam in senectute bonâ ex hâc vitâ decesserunt, *Eighth section.*
corpora eorum primò Helenæ Augustæ studio Constanti-
nopolin allata, deinde Mediolanum ab Eustorgio ejus
urbis Episcopo traducta, ¹ tandem anno post Christum
natum 1164 una cum corporibus SS. Fœlicis ² & Naboris
Martyrum in hanc urbem Reinoldo Archiepiscopo trans-
lata, hoc loco deposita fuerunt. Ut verò tribus Magis
pari numero consociarentur & Martyres, duplicareturque
funiculus triplex Sanctorum, divinitùs accidit operâ Bru-
nonis Archiepiscopi, ut duobus illis Martyribus accederet
tertius, Gregorius Spoletanus presbyter, sub Dioclesiano
& Maximiano passus. Ex quo tempore Colonia Aggrip-
pina non minus celebris esse cœpit istis trium Regum
aliorumque sanctorum reliquiis, quâm Hierosolyma
Stephano, Roma Petro & Paulo, aut Hispania Jacobo,
Gallia denique Martino & Hilario.

The quotations of the eight.

¹ Gulielmus Neubrigensis lib. 2 rerum Anglicarum
cap. 8. Crantzius lib. 6. rerum Saxonicarum cap. 24.
Petrus de Natalibus Catalogo Sanctorum lib. 2. cap. 48.
& lib. 4 cap. 45. Sigonius libro 140. de regno Italiæ.
² Ambrosius epistola. 85.

9 ¹ Agnoscamus in Magis adoratoribus Christi voca- *Ninth section.*
tionis nostræ fideique primitias, & quem illi infantem
venerati sunt in cunabulis, nos omnipotentem adoremus
in cœlis. Offendebant illi infantem parvulum modicis
& vilibis pannis involutum, videbant reclinatum duro in
præsepio, aut sinu matris pauperculæ exceptum, & tamen [p. 599.]
nihil his omnibus rebus offensi viri barbari, veræque
pietatis & fidei rudes adhuc & ignari, ² procidentes adora-
verunt. ³ Imitemur saltèm Barbaros nos qui cælorum

(marginal notes: pead Doctrin / Apostol , imò ¹ P / antiqua)

323

CORYAT'S CRUDITIES

cives sumus. Et qui Christi majestatem, potentiam, factaque admiranda, & Christianæ fidei mysteria cognovimus, fidem nostram illorum exemplo confirmemus. Itaque cum in Ecclesiâ Catholicâ, quæ verè [4] Bethleem, seu domus panis est, idem Christi corpus externis speciebus tanquam fasciis obvolutum ponitur, consecratur, offertur, sumitur, aut quovis modo nobis representatur: excitemur animo, horrescamusque & quam decet ad tanta mysteria, & animi pietatem & reverentiam corporis afferamus. Nihil nos conturbet cogitationem fluctus, nec sensuum fallax judicium, nihil hæreticorum fabulationes moveant: sed Dei verbum certos faciat. [5] Quoniam ergò ille dixit Hoc est corpus meum: nullâ teneamur ambiguitate, sed credamus, & oculis intellectus id perspiciamus, ac postrati veneremur.

Oratio Ecclesiæ.

Versus. Reges Tharsis & Insulæ munera offerunt,⎫ Psal. 72
Respon. Reges Arabum & Saba dona adducent. ⎭

The quotations of the ninth.

[1] Leo serm. 2 de Epiphaniâ. [2] Matth. 2. [3] Chrisost. homilia 24 in 1 ad Corinth. homil. 6 ad populum Antiochenum. [4] Gregorius Magnus homilia 8 in Evangelia. [5] Chrysost. homilia 83 in Matthæum.

Also this following in the same Table.

Deus illuminator omnium gentium, da populis tuis perpetuâ pace gaudere, & illud lumen splendidum infunde cordibus nostris, quod trium Magorum mentibus aspirasti.

Againe.

Lætetur Ecclesia tua Deus Beatorum Martyrum tuorum Fœlicis, Naboris, & Gregorii confisa suffragiis,

324

atque eorum precibus gloriosis & devota permaneat, &
secura persistat.

Per Christum Dominum nostrum. Amen.

Coloniæ exeudebat Joannes Durekius,

Anno 1596.

Because this history is something memorable, though [p. 600.]
indeed at the latter end there bee some false doctrine
touching the reall presence of Christ in the sacrament,
as being a thing compiled by the Jesuiticall Rabbines of
this city, as I do conjecture: I have thought good to
adde my naked translation of the same, as I have done
before of Saint Bernards epistle to the Bishop of Spira,
because every man that will reade this, cannot (I am
sure) understand it in the Latin. Therefore, that he
might not be deprived of so notable a matter as this is,
I have done my endevour to translate this historie into
English, desiring thee, whatsoever thou art (gentle
reader) to pardon me, if I have not so exactly done it as
thou wouldest require at my bandes. For as I told thee
in my epistle to thy selfe, which I have prefixed before
my booke, I neither professe my selfe a schollar, nor
acknowledge my selfe worthy to be ranked amongst
scholars, but onely wish to be accounted a friende and
lover of the Muses.

A History of the Magi gathered out of the holy
Scriptures, and approved Writers of the Church.

THe Magi, which first of all the Gentiles adored the *First section*
infancy of our Saviour Christ in Bethleem the thir- *Englished.*
teenth day after his nativity, were three in number. And
(if we beleeve Epiphanius) they derived their pedigree from
Abraham, descending from his sonnes which he begot
upon his handmaide Cethura. Neither is it any thing
repugnant unto this, that Origen and Chrysostome do
referre the pedigree of the Magi to Balaam an heathen
Prophet. For both he and the Queene of Saba drew

[p. 601.] the originall of their stocke from the same sonnes of Cethura.

Second section Englished. 2. What their names, age, and countenance were, and what gifts each of them offered, venerable Beda (according as he had received it by the tradition of his forefathers) expresseth the matter in these wordes.

The first, quoth he, is said to be Melchior, an olde man with a long beard and haire. He offered Golde to the King our Lord.

The second, whose name was Gaspar, a beardlesse young man and ruddie, honoured God with Frankensence, as being an oblation beseeming God.

The third, called Balthasar, being tawny and fully bearded, by Myrrhe signified that the Sonne of man should die. But in that one of them is wont to be painted black, and as an Æthiopian, (as it appeareth by many & those very ancient pictures amongst us) hereupon it seemeth to be grounded, both that Beda affirmeth that the third was tawnie, as also that in the 72 Psalme it is sung in the Church upon the Kinges day, The Æthiopians shall fall downe before him.

Third section Englished. 3. That they were not of any obscure place or degree, but princes, yea kings, which doth greatly illustrate the glory of Christ, it is a part of piety to beleeve. For it is agreeable both to the figure of the old law which went before in Solomon, & to the prophecies of the Prophets, especially of David and Esay; whereof the one saith, The Kings of Tarsis and of the Iles shall bring presents, the Kings of the Arabians and of Saba shall bring gifts. The other saith : And nations shall walke in thy light, and Kinges in the brightnesse of thy rising up. Which thinges are understood by the Church and the Holy Fathers, of the calling and oblation of the Magi. This also is confirmed by the feare of Herod, and of the whole City of Jerusalem at the time of their comming : by those precious giftes which they are said to have opened out
[p. 602.] of their treasures, and by the tradition of our forefathers, by writings, speeches, songes, hymnes, and pictures as

common, so very ancient. Neither doth this make at all
to the matter, that the Evangelist hath not called them
Kings, but Magi. For that was done to great purpose, in
regard that Christes glory and our religion seemed to bee
established rather by the testimony of Magi or Wisemen,
then by the power of Kings.

4. As concerning their profession, albeit there are some *Fourth section*
that by the name of Magi doe understand wicked persons, *Englished.*
and those that practise magicke artes : yet the opinion of
them ought to prevaile more with us that thinke they
were wise Astrologers, who by the Mathematicke art (as
Cyprian speaketh) knew the force and course of the
Planets, and by certaine rules of experience observed the
nature of the Elements, and the offices of the Starres.
Wherehence it came very conveniently to passe that the
divine Wisedome, which doth sweetly dispose all things,
drew them unto it especially by the token of a starre, as
being men skilfull in the arte of Astronomy : whereunto
was added both the light of the Divine grace, and also a
demonstration of men out of the holy Scriptures. For
they were instructed by the Scribes out of the Prophet
Micheas concerning the place where Christ should be
borne, and they received it as a certaine tradition of their
forefathers out of the Prophecy of Balaam, that the same
starre did signifie the birth of the Messias.

5. That they came out of Arabia Fœlix (as Justin *Fifth section*
Martyr, Tertullian, Cyprian, and Epiphanius have written) *Englished.*
it seemeth very probable. Both because Arabia, in respect
of Judea, is situate towards the East (according to the
testimony of Tacitus) and also because it yeeldeth plenty
of gold, frankencense, and myrrhe. Finally for that this
opinion doth agree with the Prophecie of Esay. All they
of Saba (which is Arabia, as Hierom doth witnesse upon
the place, and in the booke of his Questions upon Genesis) [p. 603.]
shall come, and bring gold and frankencence. And with
that of the Prophet David. The Kinges of the Arabians
and of Saba shall bring gifts. And againe, unto him shall
they give of the gold of Arabia.

Sixth section Englished.

6. Moreover they presented unto Christ the gifts of golde, frankencence, and myrrhe, because Arabia abounded in these things especially, and gloryed therein. Also the Queene of Saba, whome authors do write to have bene of the stocke and familie of these Magi, bestowed the like giftes, namely golde and spices (unto which shee added precious stones) upon King Solomon as being a figure and type of Christe. Againe those giftes which Abraham in the 37. of Genesis is said to have given to the sonnes of Cethura, Epiphanius writeth (according to the tradition of the Hebrewes) to have bene garments, golde, and myrrhe. Lastly, they did it not so much to follow the manner of their nation and the examples of their forefathers, but also for a mysticall reason sake. For this that they beleeve with their hearts, they protest with their giftes; they offer frankencence to God, myrrhe to a man, and gold to a King. And they provide themselves such giftes, that when they worship one, they declare to the world that they beleeve at one time in three distinct persons; seeing they honour the Kingly person with golde, the humane with myrrhe, and the divine with frankencence.

Seventh section Englished.

7. After Christes ascension they were more fully instructed by St. Thomas the Apostle in the faith of Christ, and also baptized, yea (which is more,) they were ordained Pastors and Doctors, or Bishops of the people amongst whome they lived, and brought a great company of Gentiles to the worship of Christian religion; and even as a plentifull harvest doth follow the first fruits: so the faith of an inumerable multitude of people, as it were most abundant corne, followed the Magi that were the first fruites of the beleevers of the Gentiles; and thus the prophecie of David is fulfilled, who after he had prophecied, The Kings of the Arabians and of Saba shall bring giftes, by and by hee addeth, And all Kings shall worship him, and all nations shall serve him. Also, all nations which thou hast made, shall come and worship before thee O Lord, and shall glorifie thy name.

[p. 604.]

OBSERVATIONS OF COLOGNE

8. After that in their old age they had departed out of this life, their bodies being brought first to Constantinople by the meanes of the Empresse Helena, then to Milan by Eustorgius, Bishop of that Citie, at last in the yeare after the incarnation of Christ 1164. being translated therhence to this city in the time of Reinolds Archbishop thereof, together with the bodies of the holy Martyrs Saint Felix and Nabor, they were reposed in this place. But to the end that the Martyrs might by an even number be accompanied with the three Magi, and that a triple corde of Saintes might bee double-twisted together, it hapned even by the providence of the Almighty, that by the meanes of Bruno Archbishop of this City, a third Martyr should bee added to the former two, to wit Gregory a Priest of Spoletum, that suffered martyrdome under the persecution of Dioclesian and Maximinian. Since which time Colen began to be no lesse famous for the reliques of these three Kings & of other Saints, than Jerusalem was for Stephen, Rome for Peter and Paul, or Spaine for James, or France for Martine and Hilarie.

9. Let us acknowledge in the Magi that were the worshippers of Christ, the first fruits of our calling, & faith, & let us adore him being omnipotent in the heavens, whom they worshipped being an infant in his cradle. They found him wrapped with little base clowtes, they saw him lying in a hard manger, or lulled in the lappe of his poore mother; yet those Barbarians that were as yet utterly ignorant of true piety and faith, being nothing offended with these things, fell downe and worshipped him. Let us then, that are citizens of the Kingdome of [p. 605.] Heaven imitate these Barbarians at the least: & whereas we have knowne the majestie of Christ, his power, admirable actes, and the mysteries of Christian faith, let us confirme our faith by their example. Therefore seeing that in the Catholike Church, which is the true Bethleem or the house of bread, the same body of Christ being wrapped with outward signes as it were with swathing

329

bandes, is placed, consecrated, offered, taken, or any other way represented unto us: let us be stirred up in minde, and tremble, & bring with us both piety of minde, and reverence of body, as it beseemeth those that participate so great mysteries. Let neither the waves of our thoughts, nor the deceitfull judgement of our senses a jote trouble us, neither let the tales of Heretikes any thing move us. But let the word of God assure us in this point. Since then he himselfe hath said, This is my Body; let us be touched with no manner of doubt, but beleeve and perceive the same with the eies of our understanding, and upon our bended knees devoutly worship it.

The prayer of the Church.

The Verse.   The Kings of Tarsis, and of the
  Iles shall bring presents.

Psal. 72.

The Ans.   The Kings of the Arabians and
  of Saba shall bring gifts.

There hapned a thing unto me presently after I had written out these memorable matters of the three Kings and the three Martyrs, that yeelded unto me a kind of recompence for my long labour of writing. For one of *A kind Canon.* the Canons of the Church that stoode neare unto me when I had almost ended my writing, supposing that I was a stranger, and observing that I loved antiquities, invited me [p. 606.] with a kinde of courteous and civill importunity to his house, though we never saw each other before, and entertained me with much variety of good cheare.

Thus much concerning the Monument of the three Kings.

IN one little Chappell of the same Church, this is written over the Tombe-stone of one of their Suffragans.

Laurentius Fabricius Urdingensis S.T.D. Episcopus Cyren. Suffraganeus Coloniensis, obiit xxii. Julii anno CIƆ. IƆ. C. R. I. P.

OBSERVATIONS OF COLOGNE

Neere unto this there is a very faire monument of *Other monuments.* Alabaster erected to the honor of one of their Arch bishops, where I reade this brief Epitaph.

Walramus Dux Juliacensis Archiepiscopus
Coloniensis.

In another little chappell are two ancient monuments of two Bishops more, whereof the one is of Fredericus Comes de Sorverden Archiepiscopus Coloniensis, and St. Reinoldus Archiepiscopus Coloniensis, qui 3 Reges a Medio lano Coloniam attulit.

In the one side of the Church without the Quire lyeth the bodie of the Earle Arnspurgensis, who bestowed his Earledome upon the Archbishoprick of Colen.

Upon one of the yron gates that belongeth to the Chappell where the Archbishop Reinoldus lyeth, there is a table hanged up with a little yron chaine, wherein this religious and holy stuffe forsooth is written, which I have thought good to set downe in this place for a notable *An example of Papist superstition.* example of the grosse superstition and vanity of the Papists in this citie of Colen.

De indulgentiis promerendis in celebratione missæ, quæ [p. 607.] decantatur quotidiè in capellâ Beatæ Mariæ Virginis, Metropolitanæ Ecclesiæ Coloniensi concessis. Anno Domini. 1454.

Sub Archiepiscopo Theodorico.

Omnibus & singulis Christi fidelibus, contritis & confessis, qui hujus missæ celebrationi & decantationi præsentes fuerint, & flexis poplitibus devotè Pater noster cum Ave Mariâ tribus vicibus legerint, de omnipotentis Dei misericordiâ & Beatorum Petri & Pauli Apostolorum ejus meritis et authoritate confisi, quadraginta dierum indulgentias de injunctis iis pœnitentiis miserecorditèr in Domino relaxamus.

Oratio de beatâ Mariâ Virgine contra pestem.

Obsecro te clementissime Deus, qui vitæ ac mortis ordinariam habes potestatem, per intercessionem genitricis Virginis Mariæ, pestilentiæ plagam miseratus a nobis averte: ut in tuâ viventes pietate, fonte vitæ perennis, corde, voce, atque omni operatione laudemus per Christum Dominum nostrum. Amen.

I observed a faire monument erected over an yron dore at the entrance of the east end of the quire, very richly gilted with many curious borders. And in the middle of the same I read this ensuing Epitaph written in golden letters.

Epitaph of Archbishop Adolphus.

> Quis sit sarcophago quæris spectator in isto?
> Hac plebeius humo non requiescit homo.
> Hic Archipræsul Princepsque elector Adolphus,
> Schawenburgiacum stemma decusque cubat.
> Imperii vigor & clarissima gloria sacri,
> Agrippinensis mitra verenda soli:
> Religionis amans & propugnator avitæ,
> Deliciæ populi, nobilitatis amor.
> In terram dignus nunquam fuit ille reverti,
> Si non undè satus quisque recedat homo.
> Terra suam refovet terram ceu sedula mater,
> Ad cœlestem anima est dia reversa patrem.
> Tantisper dum reddatur tibi spiritus ipse,
> Corpus humo natum triste recumbis humo.
> Christus enim corpus terræ revocabit ab alvo,
> Spiritui & reddet cui fuit ante datum.
> In spe coelestis recubas hîc divite vitæ
> O pater, ô placidâ pace potire pater.
> Pace potire Pater toto memorabilis ævo,
> Virtutum specimen pace potire pater.

[p. 608.]

Afterward I entred into the Quire it selfe: Where I observed three faire monuments of their Archbishops, whereof the first is of the foresaid Adolphus, whose epitaph I have already written. He is buried on the left side of *His sepulchre.* the quire. His sepulchre is a very sumptuous peece of Worke. For there his statue is made at length in alabaster, being represented leaning upon one of his armes together with his episcopall roabes. All that part of the monument both above and beneath the statue, is richly decked with

332

faire workes and borders, images and pillars which consist partly of alabaster, and partly of touchstone. About the foote of the monument this epitaph is written.

Reverendissimo Domino D. Adolpho Archiepo.
ac Principi Electori Coloniensi, S. Rom. Impii
per Italiam Archicancellario, legatoque
nato, Westphaliæ & Angariæ Duci, &c. ex
illustri familiâ Comitum â Schawenburg oriundo, electo die xxiiii.
Januarii Anno M. D. Xlvii. qui piè & pru-
dentèr Archiepiscopatui præfuit annis
ix menses ii. dies xxv. tandemque
ultimum diem in Domino clausit. anno
M. D. lvi. die xx. Septembris.

Right opposite unto this monument is the second, being *The second* erected on the right hand. This also is a very sumptuous *monument.* peece of workemanship. For it is advanced to a goodly heigth and garnished with his image contrived at length in alabaster in his magnificall roabes. Likewise the [p. 609.] workes, pillars, and images being composed all of alabaster, are correspondent to those of the opposite monument as much as may be.

The epitaph is this.

Reverendissimo Domino D. Antonio electo ac con-
firmato Principi Electori Coloniensi, S. S. Imperii
Per Italiam Archcancellario, Legatoque nato,
Westphaliæ & Angariæ Duci, ex illustri fami
liâ Comitum â Schawenburg oriundo, electo
Anno M D. lvi. die xxvi. Octobris, qui fratri succedens
in Domino obdormivit. An. M.D. lviii die xviii Junii, atque
preventus morte, fratri justum monumentum
erigere non potuit uti cœperat. Reverendissimus
Dominus D. Gebhardus electus Archiepiscopus Princeps
Elector Coloniensis Dominis & affinibus suis
charissimis pietatis ergô posuit. An. 1501.

The third is of one of their Princes called Gulielmus de

333

Genepe. An ancient thing, his image being made in Alabaster upon the tombe. But no Epitaph saving a few words in prose written about the foure corners of the monument.

Having now ended my discourse of the notable monuments of the Cathedrall Church, I will speake next of the *Bishopric of* Bishopricke before I proceed any further, as being an *Cologne.* adjunct to the Church. The first Apostle of the Ubians was S. Maternus, as I have before written, who was the first Bishop of this Citie of Colen. But who was their first Archbishop I cannot find. It appeareth that it was a very ancient Archbishopricke, because Euphrates that was deposed for his Arrianisme at the Councell holden at Colen in the yeare 348. (as I have before written) was in those daies stiled with the title of an Archbishop. Yet Munster writeth that the Archbishopricke began a long time after, about the Yeare 755. in the time of Charles the Great; being translated hither from the City of Utricht, which was about that time grievously wasted by the Danes & [p. 610.] Normanes. The titles of the Archbishop do appeare by those Epitaphes that I have before written. Therefore it is superfluous to make any more mention of them. *Duchy of* Onely I will add a briefe note of his title of the Dutchie *Westphalia.* of Westphalia and Angrivaria. This title is of good antiquity. For the Archbishop that lived in the time of the Emperour Frediricke Barbarossa, by certaine meanes attained to the Dutchie of Westphalia about some 400 yeares since, which dignity the Elector Prince hath ever since enjoyed to this day. Of the three spirituall Elector Princes this Archbishop is the middle, being next to the Moguntine, and before the Trevirian. His diocesse did in former times extend it selfe very farre. For five other great Bishopricks were subject to his jurisdiction, namely that of Munster in Westphalia, Utricht, and of Liege in the Netherlands, of Minda and Osnaburg in Saxonie. The present Archbishop doth most commonly make his residence at a Palace he hath in the country, and very seldome in the Citie. His religion together with that of Colen and

334

all the other townes in his territory, is Romish. Yet I
have read of two worthy Archbishops of this sea that *Two*
were so much addicted to the reformed religion, that they *Archbishops of*
meant to have rooted Popery out of their dominions, and *the Reformed*
in steed thereof to have planted the true religion of Christ. *Religion.*
But their religious and godly endevors did not take effect.
The first of these was Hermannus Comes a Weda, who
having sent for Philip Melanthon and Martin Bucer in the
yeare 1543 to employ their ministery in reforming the
Churches of his Electorate, was shortly after deposed,
and dispossessed of his Archbishopricke both by the Pope
and the Emperour, the foresaid Adolphus, whose Epitaph
I have before written, being substituted in his roome.
The second was Gebhardus Truccessius, unto whom the
like disaster hapned, to the hindering of his godly designe-
ment, as to the first. Here will I obitèr give a little glance
at a matter which is a kind of appendix unto this discourse [p. 611.]
of the Bishopricke of Colen. After I had something
survayed that long tract betwixt the Cities of Basil and
Colen, whereof some part I had travelled by land, and
had otherwise passed by another part upon the Rhene; and
withall had observed so many goodly Cities endowed with
Bishopricks on that left side of the river, no lesse then *Bishoprics on*
sixe, namely Basil (for that was once a Bishopricke though *the left bank of*
it be not now) Strasbourg, Spira, Wormes, Mentz, & *the Rhine only.*
Colen; and could not heare of any on the adverse side of
the Rhene: by and by I entered into a serious consideration
how it came to passe that there were planted so many
Bishopricks on one side of the river, & none at all on the
other. But at last I searched out the cause which was this.
For that the Cities on the left side being subject first to
the Romanes, and afterward to the Frenchmen, were by
them sooner converted to Christianity, then the Germane
Cities on the right side. For Gallia being converted by
S. Denis (as I have before written) one of the disciples of
S. Paul, gave occasion of the speedier conversion of these
Cities also, in regard they were subject to the kingdome
of France after the time of the Romanes.

After this I visited three other Churches, which next to the Cathedrall are accounted both the famousest and ancientest of all Colen. These are S. Ursulaes, the Macchabees, and S. Gereons. But first I went to S. Ursulaes, because she was my countrywoman. For shee was a Brittane borne, the name of England being unknowne in her time. Here I will take occasion to relate some short history of her, by way of an introduction to my discourse of the monuments of the Church. There was in Brittaine a most Christian King called Dionet, who was the father of this Lady Ursula, the fame of whose vertues extended it selfe so farre that a certaine King (his name I can not mention) hearing of the same, resolved to marry her to his onely sonne, who sent Ambassadors to her father with strict commandement that they should not returne without her. But the king was much afflicted to consider that his daughter being brought up in the faith of Christ, should be married to an Infidell. And therefore was unwilling to give his consent to the marriage. Howbeit by a certaine revelation from God, he was required to grant the king his request, but with this condition, that his sonne should be baptized, and that he should give unto his daughter eleven thousand Virgins, to the end that she might convert them to the Christian religion; which being granted, and she having converted them all to the faith, a little after sailed into France with a prosperous wind, and from thence to Colen, where she with her husband and all her company of Virgins suffred martyrdome for the faith of Christ, in the yeare 238. being all put to the mercilesse dint of the sword by certaine Barbarians, and heathenish Moores that did at that time inhabite this Citie of Colen. The bones of them being afterward gathered together were brought unto this place, and laid in this Church which is dedicated to S. Ursula the principall Captaine of the whole company. Since which time they have been very religiously kept in the same place. Many yeares after which, this Lady Ursula with the rest of the eleven thousand Virgins was canonized by the Church of Rome for a Saint: the sixe

History of S. Ursula.

[p. 612.]

Martyrdom of S. Ursula.

and twentieth d.
memory, as it app
amongst us. Hav
d this Lady Ursu
articular —
I now speake. :::
any monuments.
any sepulchres o
amongst the rest I
ith her image erec
and about with a
are. Also this tog
like infixed into it
ith crownes upon
les of the monume
:i Moores at the c
all of S. Ursula i
the top of the hig
gold, but they are
and Ursulaes head.
I which have certa
the bones of these v
tes, partly in the C
the Church of S. U
them, being direct:
as soone as I ex
t of the church w
the sides of the san
great heaps toge-
tils, all which are
sewing. But in t
are greater multitu
so they are divided
hat their skuls w:
hm. Likewise m
ers places. A: c
ane made in the
air skuls onely, t
c.c n

and twentieth day of October being consecrated to their
memory, as it appeareth by our ordinary Calendars printed
amongst us. Having now made some historical narration
of this Lady Ursula, I will descend to the relation of some
particular matters that I observed in this Church whereof *Church of S.*
I now speake, dedicated unto her. Here I saw a great *Ursula.*
many monuments. For here I told five & thirtie great
stony sepulchres of great height, breadth, & length.
Amongst the rest I saw the tombe of S. Ursula herselfe
with her image erected at one end of it, and it is inclosed
round about with a grate of yron which none of the rest [p. 613.]
have. Also this together with all the rest hath a candle-
sticke infixed into it; and the pictures of many Queenes
with crownes upon their heads are represented upon the
sides of the monuments. Belike they were slaine here by
the Moores at the same time that S. Ursula was. The
skull of S. Ursula with two more is placed in the quire
at the top of the high altar, being put in a case or covering
of gold, but they are never shewed but upon speciall daies.
Saint Ursulaes head is placed in the middest of the three :
all which have certaine yron latteises made before them.
The bones of these virginall Martyrs are kept in severall *Bones of the*
places, partly in the Church of the Macchabees, and partly *martyrs.*
in the Church of S. Ursula. But here is the greatest part
of them, being distributed into divers places of the Church.
For as soone as I entred it, I observed them first in that
part of the church which is without the body, where on
three sides of the same part of the Church, their bones lie
in great heaps together. Under them are placed their
skuls, all which are covered over with a sleight kind of
covering. But in the bodie of the Church I observed a
farre greater multitude of these mortifying objects. There
also they are divided into three parts that inclose the bodie.
And their skuls with the like coverings are laid under
them. Likewise many images of them are erected in
divers places. At one end of the Church there is a certaine
frame made in the forme of a cupboord that containeth
their skuls onely, that are covered with coverings like to

the rest before mentioned, which I saw through a frame of glasse that is placed before them. Againe all the upper parte of the quire round about are filled up with their bones, the skuls being placed under them, whereof most have blacke taffata cases that are distinguished with little spangels, which yeeld a shew like twinkling starres in the firmament. At the west end of the Church I saw a cer-

[p. 614.]

taine secrete roome with an yron dore and strong barres to it, wherein are kept many religious and ancient reliques, which are shewed but upon some speciall festivall dayes.

Superstition of the Papists. Truely these Colonians are no more to be condemned for attributing that adoration and worship unto these dumbe bones and rotten skulles, which is properly and only due to the invisible God creator of heaven and earth, who will be served in spirit and truth, and not with such blinde devotions that are seisoned with the leven of superstition: no more I say, are they to be condemned for these things, then for their superstitious prayers which I have observed written in some of their Churches. Especially in this Church of St. Ursula, whereof foure I wrote out, and brought them home with me into England, which I have here thought good to communicate to the reader, as well as the rest. Hoping that they will be so farre from corrupting any good christian that shall reade them, that they wil rather the more confirme him in the true religion of Christ, by observing the grosse vanities of the Papists. The first was this, which I saw written in a certaine table hanged upon one of the pillars.

Prayers to the Virgin Mary.

De Beatissimâ virgine Mariâ.

Hæc est præclarum vas paracleti Spiritus sancti, hæc est gloriosa civitas Dei. Hæc est mulier virtutis, quæ *contrivit caput Serpentis. Hæc est sole speciosior, lunâ pulchrior, aurorâ rutilantior, stellis præclarior. Hanc peccatores devotè adeamus, rea pectora tundamus, dicentes.

* This is a most impious and blasphemous speech. For it was not the Virgin Mary that brused the head of the Serpent, but only Jesus Christ the son of God.

338

OBSERVATIONS OF COLOGNE

Sancta Maria, Sancta Maria, clemens pia Domina nostra,
fac nos tuis precibus consortes cœlestis gloriæ. Versus.
In omni tribulatione & angustiâ nostrâ succurre nobis
beatissima Virgo Maria.

Oremus.

Famulorum tuorum quæsumus Domine delictis ignosce,
ut qui tibi placere de actibus nostris non valeamus, genitricis filii tui Domini Dei nostri intercessione salvemur ·
Per eundem Christum Dominum nostrum. Amen.

Here followeth a second prayer to the
Virgin Mary.

[p. 615.]

O Domina mea Sancta Maria, me in tuam benedictam
fidem, ac singularem custodiam, & in sinum misericordiæ
tuæ hodiè & quotidiè, & in hora exitus mei, & animam
& corpus meum tibi commendo: omnem spem meam &
consolationem meam, omnes angustias & miserias meas,
vitam & finem vitæ meæ tibi committo. Et per tuam
sanctissimam intercessionem & perpetua merita, omnia
mea dirigantur & disponantur opera secundum tuam
tuique filii voluntatem. Amen.

A second prayer to the Virgin.

In another side of the Church I read this prayer,
printed in a pretty little table hanged up at one of their
candlesticks together with other tables written in Dutch.

Oratio studiosi ad Sanctam Ursulam.

Ego me & parentes & consanguineos meos, omnesque
mihi benè faventes, tuæ intercessioni ô Sancta Ursula
commendo. Et rogo per virginitatem tuam ut nobis
fortitudinem in resistendis dæmonum insidiis, constantiam
in adversitatibus, prudentiam in actionibus nostris, consilium in rebus dubiis, mihi fœlicem progressum in studiis
meis à Domino nostro Jesu Christo impetrare digneris;
tuâque sanctissima intercessione nos delictorum catenâ
constrictos solvere, ac salutaria corpori ac animo per
nobilissimum sanguinem tuum, quem pro Christi amore
effundere non perhorruisti, quæso expostulare non inter-

A prayer to S. Ursula.

339

mittas : & adolescenti qui in honorem tuum hanc oratiun-
culam composuit, mihique in omnibus adversitatibus
succerrere digneris. Amen. Under the prayer this is
written with a pen. 1607. 17. Mensis Aprilis.

Church of the
Maccabees. Next I went to the Church of the Maccabees, in which
they report the Bones of that holy mother of the Maccabees and her seven sonnes doe lye, that were with such
most horrible and exquisite tortures punished by King
Antiochus before the incarnation of Christ, as it appeareth
at large in the seventh chapter of the second booke of the
Maccabees, where it is mentioned that the seven sonnes
[p. 616.] together with their mother had their tongues and the
Martyrdom of utmost parts of their bodies cut off by the commande-
theMaccabees. ment of King Antiochus, their skinne pulled over their
heads with their haire ; and lastly were fryed in a frying
pan, only because they would eate no swines flesh. Certainely this monument is very memorable, and worthy to
be seene by a curious traveller, if a man were sure that
these were the true bones of them. For truly for my
owne part I will confesse, I love to see these kind of
things as much as any man living, especially when I am
perswaded that there is no delusion. But indeed there is
so great uncertainty in these Papisticall reliques, that a
man cannot certainly tell which are true, and which are
false. Over the dore as I entred the Court that leadeth
to the Church, I observed the image of the mother and
her seven sonnes boyled in a cauldron, with the flames
of fire under it, and beneath the image this inscription is
written.

> Salomona vocor cocta sartagine,
> Cum liberis litor ignis aspergine,
> Agens mœstissimum Deiparæ typum.

Under another image also in the same front, this is
written.

> Unda Rheni rosea fit sanguinis madore,
> Corpora Virginea hìc ensis stant in ore,
> Dat Præsul Reinoldus Maccabeis sedem.

OBSERVATIONS OF COLOGNE

Againe, over the dore at the entrance of the Church it selfe, I read these two verses written in golden letters upon a ground of azure.

> Arca Virgineo priùs hìc imbuta cruore,
> Nunc Macabeorum corpora sacra tegit.

In the quire of the Church is the Monument of the mother and her seven sonnes behinde the high Altar, whose bones and skulles (they say) are kept in the same. The monument is made of wainscot, at the top whereof the image of King Antiochus is erected with Solomona and her seven sonnes, but one of the images of the seven is broken. Upon one side of the monument I read this inscription in golden letters. Diva Solomona cum septem suis filiis Maccabeis in hâc arcâ continetur. In another side this. Antiochus Rex septem fratres Maccabeos & matrem eorum martyrio interemit. Round about the Quire of the Church these sentences are written in golden letters. In one place this. O quám fragrantia hic redolent Martyrum opobalsama. Next this. O quám purpurei hìc spirant Virginum flores. In another place this. Hìc certè sunt candidis Lilia rosis mista. In another place this. Et prata spiritalibus vernantia gemmis. Hic vides serta quibus Dominus coronatur. In another place this. Ut in penitissimo pectoris tui recessu. Last this. Vivus tibi semper atque cælestis ignis exæstuet ô Colonia. Againe about the body of the Church this is written.

Monument to the Maccabees.

[p. 617.]

> Christo par decus atque habeat hoc Paracletus idem.
> Maxima dehinc sacro dabitur reverentia cultu
>   Reliquiis divûm cœlitibusque piis.
> Ecce Panomphæo dicata hæc sacra Tonanti,
>   Sacra profecto ædes sanguine tincta sacro.
> Ecce triumphales arcus superûmque triumphos,
>   Aptaque virgineo pulchra trophæa choro.
> Victor adest Christus, victrix est Ursula virgo,
>   Et Macabæorum palma decora Ducum.

341

In another place this.

Hìc Sanctis optata quies, optataque Tempe,
   Qui quondam herboso hoc procubuere solo.
Hi cœlo, terræ, pelago dominantur et auræ,
   Et summum norunt conciliare Deum.
Non igitur talis toto thesaurus in orbe,
   Exuperans Cræsi divitiasque Mydæ.

In another part of the Church under the historicall
Pictures of St. Ursula and other Virgins that were Martyred with her, this is written. Ursulanarum virginum
stragem hic piè et sincerè o viator venerator. In another
place this. Sacrum earundem sanguinem hoc Magdalenæ

[p. 618.] quondam * infusum sacello reverentèr colunto. In another place this. Insigne hoc Pugilum Christi polyan-

Many relics. drium puro corde exosculantor. Also I observed an
exceeding multitude of the Virgins bones laid within certaine yron lattises round about the Quire, and the body
of the Church ; and under them are erected their images
represented a little beneath their breast, and fairely gilt.

Lastly, I visited the temple of Saint Gereon, a holy
man that was martyred in this city, in the tenth persecution of the primitive church under the Emperour Dioclesian. Over the dore whereof at the first entrance this
is written in golden letters.

Templum Sanctorum.

Gereonis sociorumque ejuss ccc. xviii. Thebeorum Martyrum & Gregorii, sociorumque ejus ccc. lx. Maurorum
Martyrum.

Tombs of the In this Temple I saw many Tombes of Thebean Mar-
Thebean tyrs that were martyred with Saint Gereon, and of the
martyrs. Moores that suffered martyrdome with Saint Gregory.
These tombes are in the body of the Church : seven in a
Tombe, eight, ten in a Tombe, &c. with the pictures of
them in the outside, whose bodies are inclosed in the

---

* By this I gather that the holy Virgins were slaine in this very place
where the Church now standeth.

inside. Also there is one very great stony Tombe in a lowe vault or crypta, under the entrance of the Quire, and at the entry of the same vault there is an yron grate. In this Tombe lyeth the body of Saint Gereon, and many more of the Thebean Martyrs. In the same vault there is a taper alwaies burning. Also round about the Quire the whole history of his martyrdome and his associats is written in Latine in ancient cloth of Arras. And towards the end of the Quire the bones and skulles of the same Martyrs are inclosed within a frame of glasse on both sides of the Quire, their skulles being covered with pretty silken cases as those of the Virgins in the Church of Saint Ursula and the Macchabees. In the middest of each of these bones is the head of a blacke Moore placed, [p. 619.] made as farre as his breast, whereof the one representeth Saint Gregory; whom the other, I know not.

The histories of sacred and religious matters being ended, I will now descend to civill and secular matters · and will make mention of their Prætorium or Senate house, which they commonly call the Rathausz. Cer- *The Rathhaus.* tainly the outward workmanship of it is a thing of such gorgeous magnificence and admirable state that I preferre it both for the front, and for most of the outward worke, before any Senate house that ever I saw either in my owne country, or abroad: only the Prætorium of Padua excepted, which is commonly esteemed the fairest of Christendome. This of Colen is of a most lofty heigth, which maketh it seen a farre off, wholy composed of very elegant stone, & most excellently beautified with great store of faire images; also the curious workes in stone, the pinnacles, and other exquisite devices together with the delicate white toppe, doe yeeld a most pompous shewe. Hard by this goodly building which seemeth to be of some antiquitie, is lately erected another portly edifice as part of the Senate house, which doth marvailously adorne it. For besides other ornaments it hath a faire galery, and a fine walke beneath. The edge whereof is beautified with rich marble pillars, whose bases are exactly

343

wrought with many artificiall borders. Also to adde the more grace to the worke the pillers of the top are at both endes gilted. Moreover there is another thing which doth exceedingly garnish this beautifull structure. For whereas there are three severall fronts belonging to this building, each of them is decked with memorable histories touching the antiquities of this renowned city, which indeed doe worthily illustrate the place. In the fairest front of all, these two histories. First this.

[p. 620.]

M. Vipsanio L. F. Agrippæ, qui Octavii Imp. Aug. gener ejus in Pontif. ac Trib. pot, imperioque Collega factus & successor ab eo delectus, Senatum populumque Ubiorum trans fl. Rhenum in hanc citeriorem ripam traduxit, urbemque hanc auspicato opportunissimoque â primis fundamentis loco condidit; mœnibusque firmissimis cinxit, atque variis publicis operibus et illustribus monumentis ornavit. Cos. S.P.Q. Agripinensis post tot sæcula fundatori suo grati.

Next this.

But betwixt these two inscriptions there is a golden Lyon carved in stone, together with a certaine valiant Champion, who clapping his cloake about his arme, did very couragiously thrust his hand into his mouth, & slue the Lyon.

History of the slaying of a lion.

Therefore before I write the nexte inscription I will here adde a passing memorable history, which I have both heard in the Citie, and read in Munster, touching the man that slue the Lyon; which indeed is as worthy the reading as any thing I have written in my whole booke. It hapned about the yeare of our Lord 1260. that there was great dissention betwixt the Archbishop of Colen and the City: at what time it chanced also that two of the Canons of the Cathedrall Church that favored the Bishops faction, had a certaine Lyons whelpe, which they fed and brought up for the honour of the Bishop. Now whereas the said Canons bare a great spite and malice to the Consul of the city whose name was Hermannus Gryn, they invited him

344

one day very kindly to dinner under colour of friendship, and when he came to their house, shewed him this young Lyon, whome they kept hungry without meate some two or three daies before, and so forced him unawares and fearing no such matter, to approach neerer to the Lyons denne then it was fitte for him. Presently after this the Canons conveighed themselves out of the roome, and hav- [p. 621.] ing shut the dore waited without, still expecting when the Lyon would devoure the man. But the Consul being a man of a notable courage and stout spirit, when he sawe that he was by the treachery of these lewd Prelates brought to these extremes, either to be devoured by that mercilesse and fierce beast, or to fight manfully for his life, did put on a valiant resolution, verifying that speech of Virgil,

* Audentes fortuna juvat ————

Clapped his cloake about his left hand which he boldly thrust into the Lions mouth as he came gaping towards him, & with his right hand slue him, & so finally by this meanes escaped free from danger. Afterward he sent Officers for the two Canons with commandement to apprehend them, and to see them incontinently hanged. Which was accordingly performed. Having now mentioned this remarkable history of this valiant Colonian Champion (the like whereof I never read or heard of, saving Sampson, Daniel the Prophet, King David, Benaiah one of Davids three Worthies, Captaine Lysmachus in the time of Alexander the Great, and one of our English Kinges Richard the first surnamed Cor de Lyon) I will now at length after so long an introduction adde the second inscription which is this.

Flavio Valerio Constantino Max. Aug. P. F. Constantii F. Imp. invicto quod ad immortalitatem Imperii R. gloriam ac limitis summam utilitatem et ornatum factu difficilem lapideum pontem in

* Ænei. 9.

perpetuum exercitui cum liberet adversus Francos
ne in Galliam transirent. ipse heic
utramque Rheni ripam Agrippinensem quippè Franci-
Conjungendo muniens imposito quasi flumini in [camque
hostes jugo construxerit S. P. Q. Agrippinensis.

In another front that looketh towardes the East these two
histories are written.

First this.

Inscriptions   C. Julio Cæs.
on the East Quod Ubiorum Principes, Senatum, civitatemque eorum
front. Transrhenanam Amplam atque florentem finitima Sueorum
gente longè maxima Germanorumque omnium bellicosis-
sima injuriis belbi et obsidione pressam in amicitiam
fidemque S. P. Q. R. receperit, et exercitu Romano p
geminatos pontes Sublicios â se perquam celeritèr con-
fectos, ex Treviris trans Rhenum in Ubios Cn. Pompeio
et M. Crasso Cos. traductos liberarit, Senatus populusque
Ubiorum,

Next this.

C. Octavii Cæs. Imp. P. P. Augusti
Æternæ memoriæ.
Ob Principes, Senatum, populumque Ubiorum ejus aus-
piciis ex vetere transrhenanâ sede in hanc citeriorem
Rheni ripam per M. Agrippam generum,
orbe terrâ marique pacato
fœlicitèr traductos
Senatus Populusque
Ubiorum.

In the westerne front these two histories are written.

First this.

Imp. Cæsari F. L. Justinian P. F. Aug.

346

OBSERVATIONS OF COLOGNE

Gratiæ testandæ apud Fœderatos Quiritibus Agrippinen-
ses preclaris olim juris Italici propter perpetuam in
Rom. Imperium fidem beneficiis donatos, ideis
fortissimus religiosissimusque Imp. Uni
verso etiam legum corpore ad amplio-
rem justitiæ reique publicæ totius orbis reformandæ cultum
â se renovato, consignarit.
S. P. Q. Agripp.

Next this.   [p. 623.]

Imp. Cæs. Maximiliano Austrio Ferd. f. Philippi N.
Maximiliani.

Pronep. Frid. Abnep. Augusti Caroli v. Imp. Genero
Cum Otto primus Cognomento Magnus Imp. Germaniæ
insigniores Civitates ac Coloniensem imprimis liberas
fecisset, & qui eum sequuti sunt antiquis conservandis,
novis insuper privilegiis eam ornarint auxerintvè. Tu
verò potentissime Imp. omnium anteriorum Cæsarea
authoritate plenissime ea confirmaveris, pacem publi-
camque quietem patriæ pater difficillimo rerum statu
paraveris, ea propter gratæ mentis instinctum numini
majestatique tuæ cujus stirps longa antiquaque Impp.
serie consurgit, et invicta virtus sola pietate superata est.
S. P. Q. Agripp. hanc tabulam ære publico devotus col-
locari jussit. CIƆ. IƆ. Lxxii.

Under these histories round about the three fronts, the
heades of the twelve first Romane Emperours to Domitian, are carved with their titles round about them written
in gold. The lower part of this Prætorium is adorned *Lower part of*
with seven very beautifull arches, whereof five are made *the Rathhaus.*
in one rowe, and two at the sides. At the toppe of the
front, even in the middle of the same, the image of justice
is advanced in milke-white stone, with a sword in one hand
& a payre of scales in an other. At the ends of the toppe
the armes of the city are curiously presented, viz : the
Lyon and the Griphin, and betwixt them their scutchin,

347

which is a golden helmet. At the toppe of all, the Emperours armes the blacke spread eagle is erected, adorned with a golden Crowne, in regard the citie is imperiall.

University of Cologne.

Now I will make some short mention of their Universitie. For there is an Universitie in this citie: which was instituted in the yeare 1388. under Pope Urban. It

[p. 624.]

consisteth of three Colledges, whereof I saw the ancientest, and the Jesuites Colledge. But they are but meane buildings in comparison of the noble Colledges of our famous English Universities.

Deutz.

I observed a pretty towne on the other side of the Rhene called Teusch, which though I was not at it, but onely saw it afarre off, I will mention for two most memorable matters that I have heard and read of it. The one is, that it is reported to have bene first inhabited by ancient Tuisco otherwise called Teuto (whom I have before mentioned) the sonne of the Patriarch Noah by his wife Arezia; who being sent by his father into these parts of Europe, made his residence in the same place, which is said to derive his denomination of Teusch from this Teuto. Howbeit, I will not confidently avouch this to be true, though I depend upon the authority of a sufficient author Sebastian Munster. Otherwise I will not avouch it. The other, that there was an ancient castell built in that place by the Emperour Constantine, where there lay a garrison of souldiers for the defence of the Citie of Colen. I am the sooner induced to beleeve this, because it is verified by the testimony of Philip Melanthon, who writeth that there was a table found once in an ancient Monastery of Teuch, wherein there was an inscription that confirmed this matter.

I cannot write of any famous battels that have bene fought neere this Citie, as I have done before of those by Basil, Strasbourg, and Mentz: because I have neither heard nor read of any. Onely I can say that it was once much blemished by Attila King of the Hunnes, and a long time after that by the Normanes in the time of the Emperour Lotharius the second, who did much eclipse

348

the glory of it, and defaced many goodly buildings at the
same time that they sacked the towne of Bonna, as I have
before written.   But in steed of writing of worthy battels,
I will mention two famous wights that once lived in this [p. 625.]
citie, who by their excellent Martial discipline and renowned victories, will be eternized in Chronicles of fame
till the end of the world.   The one was Ulpius Trajan
that puissant Spaniard and the fourteenth Romane Em- *Two famous*
perour, who being adopted by Cocceius Nerva to succeed *warriors.*
him in the Empire, was sent for to this citie of Colen,
where he was then Captaine or Lieutenant of a Romane
legion.   The other was the victorious warrier and glorious
conquerour of the Saracens Carolus Martellus (of whom I
have before made mention in my notes of S. Denis) who
after the death of his father Pipin was imprisoned in this
citie, being a yong man, by the meanes of his stepmother
Woldruda.   But being by the mercifull providence of
God afterward released, he became the most fortunate
and valiant Martialist that was then in all the world.

Now were it expedient that I should make some relation of their magistrates & government.   But I hope
thou wilt pardon me, although I cannot satisfie thee in
those affaires of policy.   I would have thee consider that
I made my abode in Colen but two daies.   During which
space I hope thou wilt say I was not idle.

Here at the conclusion of this history of Colen I will
briefly mention one notable thing that I saw in this citie,
besides all the rest before mentioned.   It was my chance
to see the picture of our famous English Jesuite Henry *Henry*
Garnet, publikely exposed to sale in a place of the citie, *Garnet's*
with other things.   Whose head was represented in that *picture.*
miraculous figure imprinted in a straw, as our English
Papists have often reported.   A matter that I perceive is
very highly honoured by divers Papists beyond the seas.
Though I thinke the truth of it is such, that it may be
well ranked amongst the merry tales of Poggius the
Florentine.

Thus much of Colen.

349

[p. 626.]

I Departed from Colen in a boate downe the Rhene upon a Wednesday being the one and twentieth of September, about two of the clocke in the afternoone, after I had made my aboade there two daies, and came to a certaine solitary house nine miles beyond it, situate by the river side, about eight of the clocke at night, being *English fellow-travellers.* accompanied with foure English men whose names were Peter Sage, and James Tower Londoners, William Tassell a Cambridgeshire man. These three had bene at Franckford Mart. The fourth was one Richard Savage a Cheshire man, that came then from the University of Minychen in Bavaria; where he had spent some time in studie. The two later of these foure proceeded in their journey with me till we came to Flushing the farthest towne of Zealand, where I was imbarked for England, & there we parted companie. Also there was another in out boate, whose company I enjoied all the way betwixt Mentz and Colen, that ministred great delight unto me with his elegant learning. His name was Christopher Hagk, borne in Koningsperg the Metropolitan citie of Prussia, and a famous University. Also he was the sonne and heire of the high Consul of the citie. A sociable & pleasant Gentleman, and one that had bene a traveller for the space of a dozen yeares in the famousest regions of Christendome, as Germany, France, Italy, England, Denmarke, Poland, &c.

I departed from the foresaid solitary house about three of the clocke in the morning the two and twentieth of September being Thursday, and came to the town of Rees in Cleveland about seven of the clocke at night. This dayes journey consisted of thirty miles. The first *Dusseldorf.* towne that I came unto was Dysseldorp a faire towne of Cleve-land, situate hard by the Rhene, which is famous for two things, the one a magnificent Palace belonging to [p. 627.] the Duke: the other the residence of the Dukes Court here. I am sorry that I can speake so little of this Palace. For I tarryed but a quarter of an houre upon the shore, which shortnesse of time affoorded me no more leisure

350

then to survay after a superficiall manner some parts of the outside only. Yet as little as I viewed it, I observed it to be the most sumptuous building of any dwelling house that I saw in all the Netherlands. This Palace hath one singular commodity belonging to it. For a part of the Rhene is finely conveighed under it by certaine convenient vaults made for the same purpose. The Duke of this place is a Prince of great power and authority. For his titles are these: Duke of Juliers and Cleve-land, and Count of Ravensperg, and Ravestein. The greatest part of these Dukes have been buried in the Colledge Church of this towne of Dysseldorp, where I understand they are honered both with sumptuous monuments and elegant epitaphs. The religion of the * present Prince is Romish: he married the daughter of the Duke of Lorraine. I heard in the country that he wanted one principall thing to grace his Princely titles and ample dominions. For it was generally reported that he had not that pregnancy of capacitie as others have. A little without the towne wall I saw a certaine instrument that is very frequently used in these parts, called a crane, which serveth for the drawing up of vessels and such other things of any weighty burden, to the land from out of boates. I doe therefore name this instrument, because it was the most beautifull of that kinde that I saw in al Germanie.

Duke of Cleveland.

A beautiful crane.

When we were a few miles past beyond this towne, we glanced by the towne of Duysburg situate in Cleve-land, also hard by the Rhene. This towne is famous for containing the bones of that worthy man Gerardus Mercator borne in a towne in Flanders called Rupelmunda, who by the universall suffrage of all the learned is esteemed the most excellent cosmographer & mathematician (Ortelius only excepted) that hath flourished in the world these thousand yeares. For he hath written such exact and elegant geographical tables as will never suffer his name to be committed to oblivion.

Gerardus Mercator buried at Duisburg.

[p. 628.]

Betwixt Duysburg and the towne of Rhene Barke I

* I meane the same Prince that was then alive when I was there.

observed the lamentable tokens of the Belgicke warres three Churches very miserably battered and sacked, which was done by the souldiers of the Grave Maurice. About a mile before I came to Rhene-Barke I saw a certaine tower *Dinslaken.* in the towne of Dinslaking in the Province of Cleve-land, the walles whereof are said to be of such an exceeding thicknesse that no peece of Ordinance is able to pierce it, but it will reverberate the bullet, be it never so great. For I heard it very credibly reported that they are eighteene foote thicke. When I came to Rhene-Barke, which is a towne belonging to the Archduke Albert, and guarded by a garrison of his souldiers, there hapned this accident; our whole companie was stayed from passing any farther by certaine officers for the space of two houres, to our great terror and amazement, in so much that we could not be suffered to depart till we had been all convened before the Governor of the towne, who was a Spanish Gentleman, a man that used us more graciously than we expected. For after a few termes of examination he gently dismissed us. Here I saw one of their towers most grievously battered with shot, and many of their other buildings, which was done about a dozen yeares since by the Grave Maurices souldiers. I heard most tragicall *Two* newes of two Englishmen in this towne. For it was *Englishmen* reported unto me, that whereas two of them went into the *killed.* field to fight, the one being slaine by the other, he that killed his fellow was condemned by the Governor to receive this punishment; to be shot to death by a dozen of his countrymen. And to be first tyed to a post or some such thing with a paper pinned upon his breast, *[p. 629.]* having a blacke marke in the middle. So this was accordingly performed. But the offendour was so stout-hearted a fellow, that his countrymen were constrained to discharge two or three volleys of shot at him before they could throughly dispatch him.

After we were gone from Rhene-Barke, we passed by *Wesel.* the faire City of under Wesel, in Latin inferior Wesalia, which is so called for distinction sake, betwixt this and the higher Wesel before mentioned, in the Diocesse of the Archbishop of Trevirs. This City is in Cleve-land (which country was in former times inhabited by the ancient Tenctheri mentioned by Cæsar and Tacitus) and is esteemed the fairest city of the whole Province, though the City of Cleve be indeed the Capitall, and hath the principall name, in regard the Province hath her denomination from the same place; howbeit, it is reported to be inferior to Wesel. It was not my good hap to goe into it, but only to passe by it, yet I perceived that it yeeldeth a most elegant shew afarre off by meanes of her lofty towers, goodly walles, bulwarkes, and other stately buildings both publique and private. It is seated a pretty way within the land, and farther from the Rhene then the other Rhenish Cities and Townes are, even about some two furlongs in my conjecture. There is a pretty arme of the Rhene derived unto it in a faire channel that maketh a very commodious river called the Lippia, in which there lay a great multitude of ships when I passed by it. For it is a City of great trafficke, and very populous, as I heard.

I observed a little beyond Wesel on the same side of the Rhene that Wesel standeth, certaine trenches and rampiers in an open field, where the renowned Grave Maurice made his Rendevous with all his armie about some dozen yeares since, when he battered the towne of Rhene-Barke.

About some three miles from Wesel on the other side *Saint Truyen.* of the Rhene, I saw a faire towne called Saint Truyen, but indeede I could see but a little part of the towne, [p. 630.] saving their principall Church, which seemeth to be a beautifull building. This towne was once built upon a hill not farre off, but being there wasted and destroyed (for the ancient ruines of it are to be seene to this day) it was afterward built in a plaine, even there where it now standeth.

I arrived at the towne of Rees in Cleve-land about *Rees.* seven of the clocke at night, as I have before said. Of my arrivall there I will report one memorable thing.

c. c. iii   353   z

CORYAT'S CRUDITIES

Whereas the gates of the towne were locked before we came thither, presently after our arrivall we made all the meanes that might be to be admitted into the towne. But we were absolutely denied it a long time. Whereupon we went into one of the ships that lay at the key, determining to take a hard lodging there all night upon the bare boordes. No sooner were we in the ship but I beganne to cheare my companie as well as I could with *Consolation* consolatorie termes, and pronounced a few verses and *out of Virgil.* fragments of verses out of Virgil, tending to an exhortation to patience in calamities, as :

* Quicquid erit, superanda omnis fortuna ferendo est.

And,

§ Per varios casus & tot discrimina rerum
tendimus in patriam————————

And,

‡ ————————Dabit Deus his quoque finem.

And the same hemistichium that I spake joyfullie unto my selfe, when with much labour and difficulty I was come to the toppe of the first Alpine mountaine Aigubelette, as I entred into Savoy ·

† —— forsan & hæc olim meminisse juvabit.

A sympathetic But at last, the Burgo-master of the towne being touched *Burgomaster.* with a certaine sympathie of our misery (having himselfe belike at some time tasted of the like bitter pilles of adverse fortune, according to that memorable speech of Dido in Virgil :

[p. 631.] Non ignara mali miseris succurrere disco,)

was contented that the gates should be opened to admit us into the towne, but first he sent two souldiers to us with their muskets charged, to the end to examine us what we were, and so after a few termes of examination

* Ænei. 5. § Ænei. 2. ‡ Ibid. † Ibid.

354

they kindly conducted us to our inne, and that to our infinite comfort. For we were all most miserably weather-beaten and very cold, especially I for mine own part, who was almost ready to give up the ghost through cold. But when we came to our inne we were exceedingly refreshed with all things convenient for the comforting of distressed travellers. This towne of Rees belonged to the Duke of Cleve-land, and professeth the Romish religion as he did. It hath but one Church, wherein I observed a wonderfull *Church of* multitude of Papistical images & pictures, amongst the *Rees.* rest the images of St. Christopher and St. George of Cappadocia killing the dragon, and another of that royall Virgin the King of Ægypts daughtèr, whom he freed from the serpent. In the Churchyard I saw an exceeding company of stonie crosses infixed upon the graves of them that have been buried there, in which their names are written, and the yeare of the Lord wherein they died. Which is a custome much observed in many places of the Netherlands. The market place of the towne is very *The market* faire, being two hundred six and twenty paces long, and *place.* five and fifty broade. For I paced it over. Also the sides of it are adorned with two goodly rowes of bricke buildings, the ends whereof together with the sides are beautified with battlements according to the fashion of the German houses in divers other Cities and Townes, as I have before mentioned. But they use not halfe so much those kinde of little windowes in the outside of the roofes of their houses, as they doe in the cities of higher Germany, as I have before spoken. This market place is much graced with a faire towne house that standeth at [p. 632.] the east end. I observed one thing in this towne which I did not in any other towne in all Germanie, though I understand it is very frequently used in many townes of the Netherlands. For all the night a certaine fellow walked about the towne, and once every houre winded a *Hours sounded* horne. The like he did also hourely in the day time, *on a horn.* and sometimes he sounded a trumpet from a certaine place of the tower of the Church. I heard that this cus-

355

tome is continually used in this towne : so that they give
a certaine yearlie stipend to a fellow that executeth this
office.   I made my aboade in Rees all day the three and
twentieth of September being Friday, by reason that the
weather was so boysterous, and the Rhene so furious,
that there was no travelling upon the river without great
danger.   But the foure and twentieth of September being
Saturday I departed therehence about sixe of the clocke
Emmerich. in the morning, and came to Emricke a faire towne of
Cleve-land six miles therehence and situate by the
Rhene, about nine of the clocke the same morning.   In
this towne I saw nothing memorable (for indeede that little
time that I spent there I bestowed in the refection of my
body, that I had no leisure to walke abroade) and therefore I will let it passe without any farther mention but
only the name.   I departed therehence about noone the
same day, and came about three of the clocke in the afternoone to the City of Nimmigen in Gelderland, being nine
miles beyond it.   This dayes journey was but fifteene
miles.   In my journey betwixt Emricke and Nimmigen
Cleve. I saw the City of Cleve, in Latin Clivium, the Metropolitan of Cleve-land, situate afarre off from the Rhene,
a pretty way up in the country.   It seemeth to be a faire
City.   For it yeeldeth a beautifull shew afarre off.   Also
I observed one very memorable thing about six miles on
this side Nimmigen, a certaine sconce in an island of the
Rhene called Skinkel-sconce.   I heard that it is esteemed
[p. 633.] the strongest sconce of all Europe.   It belongeth to the
States, and standeth in a certaine little Island which was
converted to such an impregnable fortification by the rare
invention of a certaine Dutchman whose name was
Skinkel, from whome the fort hath his denomination.   It
hapned that this Skinkel was afterwards drowned in the
river Waell neere the city of Nimmigen.   The sconce is
joyned to the land on one side by a wooden bridge.
     But now before I begin to write of the city of Nim-
migen, I will make some mention of the country wherein
it standeth.   The Latine name is Geldria, but the vulgar

356

OBSERVATIONS OF GELDERLAND

Dutch Gelderland; one of the seventeen Provinces of *Gelderland* the Netherlands, and one of the eight united Provinces that belong to the States. In the East, it is bounded with Cleveland: In the West with Holland & Brabant. In the North with Frisland & a creeke of the German Sea. In the South with the country of Julia. It is said that the whole Province is so plaine, that there is not as much as one hill of any note to be seene in it. Againe, all this plain is so exceedingly furnished with abundance of wood, that there are few vacant places unwooded. Besides it is esteemed so fertile a Territory, that it bringeth forth all manner of commodities whatsoever, saving wine. For two thinges it is very memorable. For the admirable store of corne that it yeeldeth, and the goodly pastures and *Famous* meadowes for fatting of Cattel. For the which it is so *grazing* famous, that sometimes leane cattell are sent hither to *meadows.* grazing from the farthest confines of Denmarke. Also it is well watered with these three famous Rivers, the Rhene, the Maze, and the Wael, and so populous that it containeth twenty two walled townes, and three hundred villages. The ancient inhabitants of this country, many yeares before the incarnation of Christ, and after, were called Sicambri, which are mentioned by Cæsar and Tacitus: and they were so called either from a Queene called Cambra (as Munster writeth) or rather (as learned Peucer affirmeth) [p. 634.] quasi Sec Cimbri, that is, the Cimbri which dwelt neere the sea.

Some are of opinion that the ancient Menapii mentioned by Cæsar did once inhabite this Province. But I differ from them. For I take the Menapii to be those that inhabited the Territory about the city of Juliacum commonly called Gulick.

My Observations of Nimmigen.

THis Citie hath three names, in Latine two, Neomagus *Nimeguen.* and Noviomagus. But the vulgar name is Nim migen. It is the Metropolitan of Gelderland. And is of that antiquity, that it was built about 582. yeares before the incarnation of Christ by the ancient Sicambri.   It is situate neere the river Wahalis commonly called the Waell, which is one of the three mouthes of the Rhene wherewith he exonerateth himselfe partly into the Ocean, and partly into the river Meuse.   The Emperor Charles the Great was so delighted with the situation of this city that he did often keepe his Imperiall Court here, & built a very magnificent palace in the same, which stood a long time after his death, till the furious Normans invaded the City in the time of the Emperour Lotharius the second, who utterly destroied that palace with many other buildings

The market street. of the City.   The streets are very faire, especially one amongst the rest, which is the same that leadeth up to the market place from the gate neere the river Waell at the entrance of the towne.   But this streete is very uneven, being a continuall ascent till one doth enter the market place.   Againe it is much graced with two goodly rowes of beautiful buildings on both sides, being built all with bricke, and garnished with battlements, according to the

[p. 635.] German forme of building, as I have before often mentioned.   Their market place is very faire and spacious, paved all with bricke, and adorned with stately buildings on every side.   A little beyond their market place is their principal church.   You enter a pretty church before you come into the Churchyard, over the gate whereof these two sentences are written in golden letters.

Concordiâ parvæ res crescunt, discordiâ
magnæ dilabuntur.

Which sentence is taken out of Salust.   The other

Beata Civitas cujus Dominus spes ejus. 1606.

The Church. The Church it selfe is a very faire building, and is decked with many beautifull and great tables placed upon the walles in divers partes of the Church, wherein are written sentences of Scripture in golden letters.   Also it is beautified with a faire paire of Organs which have the blacke Spreadeagle the Emperours armes in it, in regard the Citie

358

is imperiall. Hard by the Church there is an ancient & magnificent building, which I think in times past was a religious house. But now I understand it is converted to a schoole. Upon one side whereof towards the Church are tenne buttresses, and in each space betwixt every couple of them is written one of the tenne Commandements all of them being comprehended in as many Latin verses. Likewise under this schoole there is a roome reserved for the bestowing of munition. The Prætorium or rather the Stadthouse (for so in all the Cities & townes of the Netherlands doe they call a Senate house, the word being compounded of Stadt, which in the Dutch tongue signifieth a towne, and house) is a very ancient & stately place, the front whereof is graced with many faire images. At one side of the towne neere to their key I observed an ancient Castell built with bricke, and invironed with a faire wall. Besides all these ornaments of the City already mentioned, there is one thing more that doth specially grace it. Even a faire front of building at the entrance of the city before you enter the first gate. Which front or series extendeth it selfe in a goodly length, and ministreth a notable ornament to that part of the city. The City is subject to the Empire, as I have already said (though indeed at this day it bee principally under the dominion of the States) unto which it payeth the least tribute of any imperiall City whatsoever. For that which they pay is nothing but a glove full of gunnepowder that they send once every yeare to the city of Aquisgranum otherwise called Aken, according to an ancient custome that they have observed these many yeares. The religion of the city is wholy Protestant. It is much given to traffique, and inhabited by many wealthy Merchants. When I was in Nimmigen, there was a great garrison of soldiers planted there that consisted of three thousand men of armes, who did continually watch and ward for the defence of the City. Againe this great company was divided into twenty other lesser companies, whereof each contained one hundred and fifty soldiers, of which three were Englishmen.

The Senate House.

[p. 636.]

A strange tribute.

359

In this city was borne one famous learned man, whom for his great learning sake (though indeed he were an *Peter Canisus.* Arch-papist) I will name, even Peter Canisius. He was the first Jesuite of Germany, and chosen Provinciall of the rest of the German Jesuites by Ignatius Loyola himselfe that Spanish soldier and first founder of the Jesuiticall family. After which time in Rome, Sicilie, and in divers Universities of Germany, especially Ingolstad, hee was publike reader of Divinity, & lastly at Friburg a fayre city of Switzerland, where he died the seventy seventh yeare of his age, and there lieth buried.

Thus much of Nimmigen.

[p. 637.] I Observed certaine things both in this Citie of Nimmigen and in other townes of the Netherlands, which I could not perceive in any place of high Germany. For it is their custome in the Innes to place some few peeces of browne bread hard by the guests trencher, and a little white *Eating customs* loafe or two. In many places also at the beginning of *in the* dinner or supper they bring some martlemasse beefe (which *Netherlands.* custome is used also in some places of the Grisons countrie, as I have before mentioned) and a good pestle of bacon to the table, before they bring any other thing. This I observed at Colen, Rees, and other places: at the ende of the meale they alwaies bring butter. One of their customes I much disliked, that they sit exceeding long at their meales, at the least an howre and halfe. And very seldome do they go to supper before seven of the clocke. In most places betwixt Colen and the farther end of the Netherlands even till I came to Vlyshingen commonly called Flushing the farthest towne of Zealand, I observed *Drinking* that they usually drink beare & not Rhenish wine, as in the *habits.* higher parts of Germany. For they have no wine in their country. This custome also I observed amongst those of Cleveland, Gelderland, and Holland, that whensoever one drinketh to another, he shaketh his fellow by the hand, and whensoever the men of the country come into an Inne to drink, they use to take a tinnen tankard full of

360

beere in their hands, and sit by it an howre together, yea sometimes two whole howres before they will let their tankards go out of their hands.

I departed from Nimmigen about eight of the clocke in the morning the five and twentieth of September being Sunday and came to a faire towne in Holland called Gorcom situate by the river Waell, about sixe of the clock at night. This daies journey was foure and twentie miles.

One thing I will here speake of the river Rhene that I have not before mentioned, that whereas he descendeth [p. 638.] prono or secundo cursu in all that long space betwixt the citie of Basil and this river of Waell, into the which together with two more that I have already named, he dischargeth himselfe : all barkes or boates that come downe thus far, do goe very easily, because it is with the streame : which is the reason that all passengers which descend do pay but a small price for their passage ; but on the contrary side all that ascend doe strive very painfully against the streame. So that all their vessels are drawen by *Boats drawn* horses with great might and maine. For this cause all *up the Rhine* passengers that ascend into the higher parts of Germany *by horses.* doe pay much more for their carriage than those that descend.

In my journey betwixt Nimmigen and Gorcom I passed by two pretty townes of Gelderland, situate by the river Waell, whereof the first is called Tiel, which is about *Tiel.* twelve miles beyond Nimmigen ; the second Bommel, *Bommel.* which is sixe miles beyond Tiel. This Bommel is the farthest frontier towne westward of Gelderland, and memorable for one thing. For I saw a great bullet sticke in the Tower of their Church, even about the toppe, which was shot by the enemy in the yeare 1574. which figures (1574) are subscribed in such great characters under the bullet, that a man may very plainly discerne them afarre off. From Bommel to Gorcom it is sixe miles. Also I observed another towne opposite unto Gorcom on the other side of the river, called Worcom.

Seeing this towne of Gorcom is in Holland, I will speake

a little of the country in which it is situate, before I make
Country of any more mention of the towne it selfe.   This country
Holland. was heretofore called Batavia, and the inhabitants Batavi,
which are mentioned by Cæsar and Tacitus.   They were
in times past accounted a very sottish & foolish people,
even as the Bœetians were amongst the ancient Græcians.
But in this age they deserve not to be so esteemed.   For
they are as ingenious both for al manuary arts, and also
[p. 639.] for the ingenuous disciplines, as any people whatsoever
in all Christendome : which a man that liveth amongst
them may easily perceive.   The name of Batavia was
commonly in use til the yeare of our Lord 860. at what
time there hapned such an exceeding inundation as overflowed a great part of the country, and did so scowre and
wash the very bowels of the earth, that it hath bene ever
since σομφώδης (as a learned author writeth) that is,
hollow and spungie.   For which cause the old name of
Batavia was afterward changed to Holland, which is so
called quasi hollow land, or quasi Hol-land.   For hol in
the Flemish tongue doth signifie as much as our word
hole.

My Observations of Gorcom.

Gorkum. I Shall doe this towne more wrong then I have done to
any other citie or towne of note in Germany, in which
I lay a whole night, and in no other respect but onely in
speaking so little of it, concealing the admirable beauty
thereof.   For I had not the opportunity to survey it
throughly according to my desire, because I came late into
it, & departed therehence something early the next morning.   The sweetnesse of the situation, the elegancy of
their buildings, the beauty of their streets, and all things
whatsoever in this town, did wonderfully delight me, in
so much that as soone as I entred into one of the longer
streets, me thought I was suddenly arrived in the Thes-
salian Tempe, or the Antiochian Daphne.   For indeed it
is a most elegant and sweet little towne, situate in a plaine,
hard by the goodly navigable river Waell.

362

OBSERVATIONS OF GORKUM

And I observed some of their streets to be passing beautifull, both for breadth and length. And they are *Streets paved with brick.* much graced by the fayre bricke pavier. For every streete is very delicately paved with bricke, which is composed after that artificiall manner that a man may walke there [p. 640.] presently after an exceeding shower of raine, and never wet his shooes. The buildings are all of brick, of a goodly heigth, and an excellent uniformity in most of the streets, the toppes rising with battlements. I observed that these kinde of prety buildings are of a just correspondency on both sides of the streets, which doe minister notable beauty to the towne. Their market place is very spacious and neatly paved with bricke like to the streets. At one side whereof there is a faire Stadt-house adorned with a beautifull turret, from the toppe of which I heard it credibly reported by a Gentleman of good note, a man may plainly perceive in a faire day two and twenty goodly walled townes, together with many faire villages and Gentlemens Palaces in the country. At their docke or key which is neare to one of their bridges, I observed a great company of prety ships and barkes also. Another of their dockes hath a faire bricke walke hard by it, without the gate of which walke I observed a certaine wooden image which presenteth the figure of a man as farre as the breast. This image is erected as a marke or bound to the end that no forraine barkes or other vessels may passe beyond it, which is lawfull for those only of the same towne and none else. The religion of the towne is Protestant. For it belongeth to the States.

I departed from Gorcom about seven of the clocke in the morning the six and twentieth of September being Munday, and came to the towne of Dort twelve miles *Dordrecht.* beyond it about ten of the clocke the same morning. In this space I observed one speciall thing. On both sides of the river Waell I saw a great company of little castels or Forts not above halfe an English mile distant asunder, which they call Ridouts, wherein presidiarie souldiers do lie for the defence of the country, fifty persons or thereabout in each. The like I observed also betwixt Nimmigen and Gorcom. I heard that this was the

occasion of building these Ridouts: because the enemie was wont heretofore to invade the States territories in the night time, and to take some Gentleman or speciall man prisoner, and to keepe him captive till he ransomed himselfe with a great summe of money. Hereupon for the security of the country, the States thought good to erect these little Ridouts. I observed another thing also betwixt Gorcom and Dort that moved great compassion in

Churches under water.

me. For I saw many Churches halfe drowned, all the upper part of the tower appearing very plainly above the water. There were heretofore faire Parishes belonging to these Churches, which were utterly defaced with the mercilesse furie of the angry God Neptune almost two hundred yeares since, as I wil hereafter more particularly declare, so that there is not the least token of them to be seene at this day. Moreover I saw a faire Castell drowned a little on this side Dort, which in former times belonged to a noble man of the country. It was seated in a faire towne, which hapned to be so overwhelmed with water at the same time, that the sea did so loose his raines of liberty to the destruction of the other townes, that there remayneth not the least stone thereof to be seene, saving only a part of the foresaid Castell that doth now belong to the towne of Dort, by which they enjoy certaine priviledges.

My Observations of Dort.

THis City in Latin is called Dordracum, but the common word is Dort, and some doe call it Dordrecht. It is a very famous, opulent, and flourishing towne, and memorable for many things, especially one above the rest

Dordrecht the maiden city of Holland.

which is worthy the relation. For it is called the Mayden City of Holland, (in which respect it may be as properly called Parthenopolis, as Naples is in Italie, and Maydenburg in Saxonie) and that for these two causes. First,

because it was built by a Maide, but none of the Citizens could tell me either the name of her, or the yeare of the

OBSERVATIONS OF DORDRECHT

Lord when the foundation was laid. Neither indeede can *Dordrecht founded by a maiden.*
I finde it in any historian that hath written of the Holland-
ish Cities. But certaine it is that a Virgin was the first
founder of it. For a monument whereof they have
pictured a beautifull Virgin in lively colours according to
the full proportion of her body, over the gate neare to
their haven at the first entrance into the towne. Which
picture is adorned round about with the armes of the
principall families of Holland. Besides, for a farther testimony of this matter they use to stampe the figure of a
maide upon one of their coynes that is called a Doit,
whereof eight goe to a Stiver, and ten Stivers do make
our English shilling. Secondly, because almighty God
hath priviledged this towne with such a speciall favour
and prerogative, as no City or Towne that I ever read or
heard of in all Christendome, saving only Venice. For
it was never conquered, though all the circumjacent Cities
and townes of the whole territorie of Holland have at
some time or other beene expugned by the hostile force.
The situation of it is very pleasant. For it standeth in a
prety island being invironed round about with foure rivers *Situation of Dordrecht.*
that make a confluent, which are the Mosa, the Waell,
the Linga, and the Merva; according to a pretty distich
that I have read of the same rivers, which is:

> Me Mosa, & Wahalis, cum Lingâ Mervaque cingunt,
>   æternam Batavæ Virginis ecce fidem.

But if I should relate how it came to passe that this plot
of ground was first converted to an island,

———— ———— *Quis talia fando
Myrmidonum Dolopumve, aut duri miles Ulysses
Temperet â lachrymis?

For indeede it is a most lamentable and tragicall matter to [p. 643.]
be spoken, and such a thing as cannot but move great
commiseration. For whereas a part of it was ever joyned
to the maine territorie of Brabant, till the yeare of our
Lord 1420. it hapned that these foure foresaid rivers

* Ænei. 2.

365

Brabant inundated by the sea A.D. 1420.

together with a part of the sea, did that very yeare upon the seventeenth day of April breake up their repagula, their bounds within the which they did ever soberly containe themselves till then, and made such a wofull inundation in the country, that I never read of the like in Christendome since the generall cataclysme in the time of the Patriarch Noah. For they overwhelmed sixteene faire Townes : some write there were no lesse then three-score and ten of them drowned. And they swallowed up at the least a hundred thousand persons with al their goods, cattels, and whatsoever else. The pittifull tokens whereof I saw in divers places of the country thereabout, namely certaine towers of Churches appearing above the waters, which belonged to those Parishes that were frequently inhabited with people till the time of that deluge

The buildings of this Towne, both publique and private, sacred and civill are very beautifull, being built all with bricke, and garnished with those kind of pretie battlements that are so much used in the Batavian Cities. Their streets also are of a notable length and breadth, in number many, and paved with bricke as those of Gorcom.

Mint built by the Earl of Leicester.

Besides other publike buildings of the towne I visited their mint, which was built by our famous Earle of Leicester, at the front whereof the Emperours armes are erected : above the which this word is written in golden letters, Moneta. And againe under that, Divo Carolo 5. Cæsari. Likewise there are eight Latine sentences written upon the front : foure on the one side of the armes, and

[p. 644.]

as many on the other. This is the first. Pax & tranquilla libertas. The second, Nomen pacis dulce est. The third, Pecuniâ vincere speciosum non est. The fourth, Pecunia mater belli. The foure on the other side are these. The first, Paci semper est consulendum. The second, Pace sublatâ leges esse non possunt. The third, Omnia pecuniâ effici possunt. The fourth and the last, Pecunia effectrix multarum voluptatum. After this I sawe a beautifull

366

OBSERVATIONS OF DORDRECHT

Palace called the Doole, which was likewise built by the *The Palace.* Earle of Leicester: it is a very magnificent building, in which the Grave Maurice his Excellencie doth use to lie whensoever he is commorant in Dort. Also there is an other faire house wherin his Excellencie doth sometimes repose himselfe, which is the signe of the Peacocke. In that place lay Marquesse Spinola the General of the Arch-dukes Armie, when he came thither from the Hage, a little before my comming to Dort. Their Stadt-house is a very faire building of a goodly height, and built all with square stone, which is rare to bee seene in Dort. There are foure Churches in the towne, whereof two belong to the Citizens; of which one is the fairest of them all, a building that seemeth to be of great antiquitie, but adorned with no worthy Monuments or Antiquities: onely it hath faire Tables hanged upon divers Pillars, wherein are written sentences of holy Scripture, like to those that I sawe in the great Church at Nimmigen. The third Church belongeth to the Englishmen, the fourth to the French. Out of those foure Rivers that inviron the *Many rivers in Dordrecht.* Towne round about, and make it an Iland, there are some pretie armes derived into the Towne, which doe make certaine inferiour rivers that are very commodious to the inhabitants. Over one of them that runneth through the middle of the towne, there are many pretie Bridges, but two especially very faire. Whereof one is of Timber, the fairest woodden Bridge that I saw in Germany, saving that of Heidelberg. For it is so broad that three Cartes may [p. 645.] passe joyntly together over it. On both sides of this bridge there lyeth great abundance of shippes. The other is of stone, the edges whereof are finely rayled with yron rayles contrived in curious workes.

For traffique I have heard that this towne doth more *Flourishing traffic.* flourish then any town of all Holland, saving famous Amsterdam. And the Merchants of the towne are said to be very wealthy. For heere is the principle Staple of Holland for all manner of Wines, especially the noble Rhenish Wine, from whence it is afterward transported into divers remote regions, as to England, &c. But the greatest part of it being first sophisticated in Dort with their &c. confections.

Manuary trades. The manuary trades of al sorts in this towne are commended for excellent. It was garded with five companies of presidiary soldiers when I was there, whereof one was English. For the Leager (this is the name of the States armie which doth use in the time of warres to lie abroad in the fieldes) was dissolved when I was in Holland, by reason that there was a truce betwixt the Archduke and the States, and it was distributed into many severall companies that were planted abroad in divers cities and townes for the common safety of the country

What excellent men for the ornaments of learning this towne hath bred I doe not remember, saving one whose *Gulielmus Lindanus.* name was Gulielmus Lindanus, who flourished about some forty yeares since. A man in his kinde very famous, though indeed a Papist. In this towne of Dort he was borne, but he spent the greatest part of his life afterward in Ruremunda a City of Gelderland, whereof he was bishop. This man also hath commended his name to posterity by his manifold workes, especially theologicall, as other learned men whome I have named in my description of some of the German Cities.

[p. 646.] Having now related some of the principall thinges of this noble towne, I will conclude my observations thereof, partly with mention of their religion, which is the Protestant. For Popery is cleane exterminated out of the towne; and partly with that memorable elogium that is commonly attributed unto it by all those that know it well, that it is the very Garden of Holland.

Thus much of Dort.

FRom this towne I once resolved to have directed my journey to a certaine memorable place not farre therehence that I might have communicated one notable thing ὥσπερ ἔν προσθήκης μέρει, by way of over-plus, to my friends & country as well as the rest, yea such a thing, as is the most monstrous and prodigious matter that was in any place of the whole world since the creation thereof. But my resolution was hindered by a certaine sinister chance. Yet I will make some relation of the matter as I have not only heard, but also read it in a good author. Though surely I feare least many will deeme it a meere exorbitant digression to write of those things either by reading or report which doe not fall within the compasse of my travels. There is a Monument extant in a certaine Monastery called Laudun neere the famous university of *Monastery of* Leyden in Holland, where a certaine Countesse called *Laudun.* Margarite was buried, who was the wife of one Hermannus Earle of Henneberg, the daughter of Florentius the fourth of that name, Earle of Holland and Zeland, and the sister of William King of the Romanes. This Countesse hapned to be delivered of three hundred sixty five children at one burden about three hundred and fourteene yeares since, even just as many as there are daies in the yeare. All which, after they were baptized by one Guido Suf- [p. 647.] fragan of Utrecht, the males by the names of Johns, & the females by the names of Elizabeths, died that very day that they came into the world : and were buried all together in one monument in the Church of the foresaid Monastery of Laudun, which is to this day shewed (as I have heard many worthy travellers report that were the eie witnesses of the matter) with a most memorable Latine inscription upon it, together with two brasen basons wherin all those infants were baptized. This strange history will seeme incredible (I suppose) to al readers. But it is so absolutely and undoubtedly true as nothing in the world more. The occasion of which miraculous and stupendious accident I will here set downe (seeing I *A miraculous* have proceeded thus farre in the narration of a thing that *accident.* I have not seene) because it may confirme the stronger belief in the reader. It hapned that a poore woman came a begging to the foresaid Countesse Margarite, bearing a twinne of young babes in her armes. But the Countesse was so farre from having any commiseration upon her, that she rather scornefully rejected her, affirming that it was not possible shee should have those two children by one man. The poore soule being much vexed in spirit through these injurious words of the Lady, pronounced

A bitter imprecation. such a bitter imprecation upon her, that she wished that God would shew a miracle upon the Lady, as well for a due revenge upon her that had so slandered her, as for the testifying of her unspotted honesty & chastity; she wished, I say, that God would shew this miracle, that the Lady might bring forth as many children at one burden as there are daies in the yeere; which indeed came to passe, according as I have before mentioned. For the Ladie in the fortieth yeare of her age was delivered of just so many upon a saturday about nine of the clocke in the morning, in the yeare of our Lord 1276. The truth of this most portentous miracle is confirmed not so much by that

[p. 648.] inscription written in a certaine table upon her tombe, as by sundry ancient Chronicles of infallible certainty both manuscript and printed. Pardon me I beseech thee (curteous reader) for this my boldnesse in reporting matters that were beyond the limits of my travels. Notwith-standing I have thought good to mention it in this place for a matter beyond all comparison remarkable of that kinde that ever was in the world, being induced to the commemoration of this history for these causes. First, because I heard very frequent speeches of it in the towne of Dort which I have last described, partly by Englishmen, and partly by other strangers. Secondly, because the fame of it had invited mee to have seen the place, if one disastrous impediment had not crossed me. Thirdly, because I am perswaded this history was never before written in our English tongue, till the History of the Netherlands was set forth in English since my arrivall in England from beyond the Seas, by that worthy traveller and thrise-worthy serjeant at Armes unto our Kinges most excellent Majesty, and most faithfull attendant quondam upon the right Worshipful Sir Edward Phillips lately the most illustrious speaker of the Parliament house, and now

Maister of the Rolles viz: Maister Edward Grimston.
Wherefore after this long digression I will now returne
againe to the discourse of my following travels.

I departed from Dort towards Zeland in a barke
the seven & twentieth of September being Tuesday about
noone, and lay the same night in a hard lodging of my
barke upon the water, about fortie miles beyond it: in this
space I observed these things. I sawe a goodly Towne
called Zirixee, in Latine Zirzæa, situate in an Iland whose
name is Scowen, on the right hand of my journey: this
Towne is commended for a beautifull place. But nothing
whatsoever hath so much graced it as the birth of that
admirable sweete Scholler, that worthy ornament of learn- [p. 649.]
ing Levinus Lemnius a Physition, who hath purchased *Levinus*
both himselfe and his Countrey eternitie of praise by his *Lemnius.*
elegant Booke De occultis naturæ miraculis, and other
excellent fruites of his ripe wit that are commonly read in
the world to the great benefit of the learned. In the same
Iland where Zirixee standeth, there is an other faire Towne
called Brewers Haven, and a Sconce called Bominee,
belonging to the States. On the other side of the river,
right opposite to Zeland, I observed two Ilands more,
whereof the one is called Tarnous, the other Targous.
But before I came towards those Ilands, I passed by a part
of Brabant where Bergenopzome standeth a little within
the Iland, which is said to be a very strong Towne that
belongeth to the States. Also I observed in this journey *A pitiful*
a great many high Towers in the water, which were here- *sight.*
tofore Parish churches, and belonged to some of those
Parishes that I have before spoken off, which were
drowned in the yeare 1420. I observed a speciall thing
in one side of the river as we passed forward in our
journey. Many Boores of the country laide a great deale
of strawe and earth uppon it at the edge of the banke,
to the ende to preserve the banke, that the water may not
eate and devoure the earth, and consequently breake into
the land to drowne it, as it hath done heretofore in many
other places thereabout.

371

I departed from the foresaid place where I lay all night upon the water, about seven of the clocke in the morning the eight and twentieth of September beeing wednesday, and came to a haven towne of Zeland called Armu, about sixe of the clocke at night. This daies journey was nine miles. The inhabitants of this Island were in former times called Mattiaci, which are mentioned by Cornelius Tacitus. As for the Island it selfe wherein this Towne, Middleborough, and Flushing stand, it is commonly called [p. 650.] Walcheren. In this towne of Armu I sawe nothing memorable but their Stadt-house. For it is but a little towne. Yet it is famous for one thing. For there al the Ships that come from Dort do arrive, as in a safe station, & therehence many a great fleete doth often launch forth into the Ocean Sea.

I departed from this towne of Armu about seven of the clocke in the morning the nine and twentieth of September *Flushing.* being thursday and Michaelmas day, & came to Vlissingen commonly called Flushing, a famous haven Towne of this Island Zeland, about two of the clocke in the afternoone. This dayes journey was but five little miles.

In my journey betwixt Armu and Vlissingen I passed through the beautifull Citie of Middleborough in Zeland, which is about a mile beyond Armu. But I cannot write the tenth part of it that this notable Citie deserveth. For I employed those fewe houres that I spent in the city otherwise than in matters of observation. Yet that little which I did observe I will relate. For I will not do this goodly Citie that wrong as to write so copiously of many other Cities, and nothing at all of her.

Middleburg. Middleborough hath her denomination from a Noble Roman Consul called Metellus, who is said to have bene the first founder of it. For some do call it in Latin Metelburgum quasi Metelliburgum, that is, the towne of Metellus. It is strongly walled, beautified with faire gates, goodly streets, and very stately buildings of bricke like to those of the townes of Holland. Their Market place also I observed to be a fayre and spacious thing, and

372

was exceedingly frequented with people the same day that I was there. Likewise their Stadt-house is a very ancient *Notable buildings.* and beautifull building, built all of free stone (which I observed to be as rare in Middelborough as I did before in Dort) and the front adorned with many goodly images that yeeld a delicate shew. I sawe their exchange also, which [p. 651.] is a very elegant little place, distinguished with faire walkes, neere to the which there is a pleasant grove. I visited likewise the house of our English Merchants, which is a faire building, having delicate gardens and walkes belonging to it. And I went to their fayrest Church, which is graced with a curious clocke, and with two monuments of great fame. But it was not my hap to see eyther of them. Whereof the one was of William Earle of *William Earl of Holland and Zealand.* Holland and Zeland, and afterward King of the Romanes, who being slaine by the Frisians about nine yeares after the beginning of his reigne, in the yeare one thousand two hundred fifty five, his bones were solemnly buryed in this Church about seven and twenty yeares after his death. The other is of that rare Schollar and learned Writer Adrianus Junius, who is famous for many notable workes that hee left behinde him as the true monuments of his pregnant witte, especially his ample Dictionary consisting of Greeke & Latine words. I observed also their Haven, which is a very convenient place, and was the receptacle of many goodly shippes when I was there.

Their religion is Protestant, answerable to that which the reformed Churches of England and Holland doe professe.

Thus much of Middelborough.

My Observations of Vlyshingen commonly called [p. 652.] Flushing, but in Latin Flissinga.

THe situation of this towne is very memorable. For *Situation of Flushing.* it is built in the forme of a pitcher, which is slender at both the endes, and wide in the middle. In regard whereof the name of the towne is derived from the Dutch

Flushing in form of a pitcher.

word Flessche, which signifieth a pitcher. For indeed he that shall rightly consider the forme of the building thereof, will say that it doth very neare represent the fashion of a pitcher. For I for mine owne part observed the site of it, and found it very correspondent to the mould of a pitcher, the endes being slender and the middle long Which is the reason that the inhabitants doe present the figure of a pitcher in their flagges & banners that are advanced at the tops of the mastes in their ships. The towne is not great: yet very faire, and beautified with many stately buildings, that are made all of bricke, according to the rest of the Zelandish and Hollandish cities. It is inhabited with many rich Merchants that have within these fewe yeares very much inriched themselves

A notable harbour.

by the art of navigation. Their haven is very strong, and it is a notable harbour of goodly ships. For I can say more of Flushing then of any other haven towne that I saw in my travels: that their haven contained such an exceeding multitude of ships, as I could not see the like in Venice it selfe, the Arsenall only excepted. For I heard that all those that I saw at Flushing were in number at the least two hundred.

The Stadthaus.

Their Stadthouse, that was newly building when I was there, is like to be a very magnificent worke. The front being raised to a notable heigth, and adorned with many

[p. 653.]

faire armes, scutchins, and other curious devices that doe exceedingly beautifie the same. Here I sawe those birds called Storkes that I have before mentioned in my observations of Fountaine Beleau.

Flushing garrisoned by the English.

This towne is garded with a garrison of English Souldiers, whereof one (who was a Gentleman) I saw very martially buried that day that I came into Flushing, with a dolefull beating of many drummes, and discharging of many volleys of shot. All the companies of souldiers in this towne are commanded by that right worshipfull and most worthy Knight Sir William Browne, who is Deputie Governour of this towne under that right honourable and illustrious Robert Sidney Viscount Lisle.

374

OBSERVATIONS OF FLUSHING

I received a very special courtesie in this towne both of the foresaid noble Knight, and of a certaine learned, godly, and religious Minister Mr. Pots, who is the Preacher of the towne (for it professeth the Protestant religion also as well as Middleborough) for the which they have perpetually bound me unto them in all officious respects of due observance till I cease to enjoy this common vital breath. Therefore tandem aliquando, with this thankfull commemoration of their names (since I have not as yet any other meanes to express my gratitude towards them, but only by this remembrance of them in my booke) I here adde ultimam coronidem, the full period and finall conclusion to my outlandish observations.

I made my aboade in Flushing all Friday being the last day of September, and departed therehence in a barke the first day of October being Saturday, about foure of the clocke in the afternoone, and arrived at the custome house *Arrival in* in London the third day of October being Munday, about *London.* foure of the clocke in the afternoone, after I had enjoyed a very pleasant and prosperous gale of winde all the way betwixt Flushing and London.

The distance betwixt Flushing and London is a hundred and twentie miles.

The number of Miles betwixt Venice and Flushing: in [p. 654.] which account I name only some of the principall Cities, as I have done before in the computation of the miles *Number of* betwixte my native Parish of Odcombe and Venice. For *miles between* it is needlesse to name all the particular miles betwixt all *Venice and* the cities and townes I passed through. Because it would *Flushing.* be a repetition of that which I have alreadie done.

Imprimis, betwixt Venice and the Inne before mentioned *Total of the* upon the toppe of the Mountaine Ancone, otherwise called *whole journey.* Montane de St. Marco, being the farthest bound of the Venetian Signiorie Westward, . . 174
Item, betwixt the Inne, and the City of Curia in
  Rhetia. 76

375

Item, betwixt Curia and Zurich the Metropolitan
    City of Switzerland.   55
Item, betwixt Zurich and Basil. .   .   .   40
Item, betwixt Basil and Strasbourg.   .   .   .   80
Item, betwixt Strasbourg and Heidelberg.   72
Item, betwixt Heidelberg and Franckford.   67
Item, betwixt Franckford and Colen.   .   92
Item, betwixt Colen and Nimmigen in Gelderland.   54
Item, betwixt Nimmigin and Dort in Holland.   34
Item, betwixt Dort and Flushing in Zeland.   53
           The totall is   .   .   797
Againe betwixt Flushing and London.   120
Againe, betwixt London and Odcombe.   106
The totall betwixt Venice and Odcombe.   .   1023
The totall betwixt Odcombe and Venice as I
    travelled over France is (as I have before
    written)   952
The totall of my whole journey forth and backe   .   1975

[p. 655.] THe Cities that I saw in the space of these five
      Moneths, are five and forty.   Whereof in
    France five.   In Savoy one.   In Italie
      thirteene.   In Rhetia one.   In Hel
      vetia three.   In some parts of
      high Germanie fifteene.   In
        the Netherlands
        seven.

FINIS.

376

POSTHUMA

FRAGMENTA

POEMATUM

GEORGII CORYATI

SARISBURIENSIS,

SACRÆ THEOLOGIÆ BACCALAUREI,

Quondam e sociis Novi Collegii in inclyta
Academia Oxoniensi,

Ac postea Ecclesiæ Odcombiensis in agro Somersetensi Ministri, ubi tandem Anno 1606.
extremum vitæ diem clausit.

LONDINI,
Anno Domini 1611.

Serenissimo P:.
Tito, id est.
Walliæ, D:.
Palatino Ce:
aureæ per ce

O:

rasores, qui me:
stringere atque su:
litdini tuæ rationes
in medium profer:
multos annos latu:
Primo, quoniam
Coryatus paulo a:
in juventute sua (:
contexuit, mecum :
ut (si illi supers::

—— D:
mihi indulgenter
penes me fuisse a:
vetustatis eruerem
plurimi mei qu:
familiares congen
munis hujus luci

Serenissimo Principi Henrico Christiani Orbis
Tito, id est, humani generis Deliciis, Principi
Walliæ, Duci Cornubiæ ac Rothsaiæ, Comiti
Palatino Cestriæ, Equiti splendidissimi ordinis
aureæ periscelidis, &c.

On sum nescius (Serenissime Princeps)
nonnullos mihi objecturos, supervacaneum
ac τὸ ἀπροσδιόνυσον opus me jam suscipere,
observationibus meis in regionibus exoticis
ista posthuma poematum Patris mei fragmenta quæ jam subsequntur, attexendo ;
nec deerunt fortasse aliqui nimis rigidi
censores, qui mordaculis suis sannis nomen meum per-
stringere atque sugillare non dubitabunt. Proinde Celsitudini tuæ rationes explicabo quibus fretus poemata ista
in medium proferre, & ex Cimmeriis illis tenebris quibus
multos annos latitarunt, in lucem edere mihi visum est.
Primo, quoniam pater meus piæ memoriæ Georgius
Coryatus paulo ante obitum suum de carminibus, quæ
in juventute sua (Musis faventibus ac propitia Minerva)
contexuit, mecum colloqui subinde solitus est, rogavitque,
ut (si illi superstiti esse

—— Divum pater atque hominum rex

mihi indulgenter concederet) pauca poemata sua quæ
penes me fuisse animadvertebat, tandem aliquando è situ
vetustatis eruerem, præloque mandarem. Secundo, quia
plurimi mei φιλομουσοὶ amici, tum consanguinei, tum
familiares congerrones, qui patrem meum, (dum com-
munis hujus lucis usura fruebatur) medullitus amarunt,

& jam fato defunctum nomen ejus gratissima quadam recordatione commemorare solent, instanter precibus suis me identidem sollicitarunt, ut posthuma ejus poemata typis excudi curarem.

Quare cum patris voluntati, tum amicorum postulatis morem gerens, Juvenilia ejus Celsitudini tuæ dedicare una cum itinerario meo ausus sum, Celsitudinemque tuam humillime oro ut sub Serenissimi nominis tui auspiciis ista qualiacunque poemata in vulgus emanare patiatur. Nec elogia quibus patris mei memoriam cohonestarunt atque illustrarunt duo celeberrimi scriptores, quorum unus in Germania natus erat, alter in patria mea Anglia, jam tacebo. Hic nimirum Jacobus Middendorpius in libro quodam quem de totius orbis Academiis conscripsit; ille autem, scilicet Joannes Casus Medicinæ Doctor; & Collegii Divi Joannis Præcursoris apud Oxonienses quondam socius, in elegantissimo libro suo quem Speculum Moralium inscripsit, charissimi patris mei nomen hujusmodi verbis citavit. Georgius Coryatus poeta Oxoniensis ita quondam cecinit, & statim uterque ista carmina ejus subjungit.

> Et duo sunt totum Gymnasia nota per orbem,
> Oxonium studiis florens, mihi dulcis alumna,
> Regis opus; tuaque (illustris Rex Cantaber) ædes
> Magnifice florens sacris Academia Musis.

Quae carmina quadraginta plus minus annis elapsis cum plurimis aliis de descriptione Angliæ, Scotiæ, & Hyberniæ, Serenissimæ Reginæ Elizabethæ beatæ memoriæ (jam cum cælicolis in cælesti Hierosolyma vitam angelicam agenti) nuncupavit. Sed ea cum duobus pene millibus versuum quos ἐν τῇ ἀκμῇ ætatis atque ingenii sui composuit, elegantibus sane ac â viris eruditis non parum laudatis, sive patris incuria, sive temporis injuria partim interiere ac extincta jacent, partim cariosis chartis adeo tineis edacibus corrosis sepeliuntur, ut omnis mihi spes præcidatur ullam illorum particulam in publicum emittendi. Quæ vero jam conquisivi, & in unum quasi

THE EPISTLE DEDICATORIE

corpus collegi, quum animo patris mei nomen ab oblivione vindicandi hoc susceperim, ut Manes ejus illud* poetæ usurpent,

> Non omnis moriar, multaque pars mei
> Vitabit Libitinam ;

Serenitatem tuam iterum enixissime obsecro, ut contra virulentos Momorum morsus, qui dente Theonino aliorum lucubrationes rodere solent, eadem ὑπερασπίζειν, ac pro pitio tuo patrocinio protegere clementissime dignetur.

Celsitudini tuæ

devotissimus deditissimusque

Thomas Coryatus Odcombiensis,

Peregrinans pedesterrimus.

Hora. Carmin. lib. 3. Od. 30.

[Exhortatio ad

Exhortatio ad Serenissimam Angliæ Reginam, Dominam Elizabetham, sexto sui regni anno, ut nubat.

O Virgo & Princeps, ô Regis filia, Regis
   Et soror, ô Regis Uxor ut esse velis.
Te tua forma, decus, virtus, pietasque, fidesque
   Hoc rogitant, patriæ ut perpetiare Patrem.
Sic tibi sic poteris, patriæ sic utilis esse :
   Angelicè in terris vivere posse rogant.
En tibi sic poteris, patriæ sic utilis esse
   Non poteris : patriam prole beare potes.
Si potes, ergo velis : Regalem sumito sponsum,
   Sic tibi, sic patriæ consule Virgo tuæ.
En Dæmon satagit, stimulat Caro, Mundus adurit,
   Sola potes tantis belligerare malis ?
Si modo sola potes, vestram sed respice gentem.
   Ne miserum Satanas devoret ore gregem.
Da deus hanc mentem, da nostra Principe dignum
   Et regem et Prolem : cætera jam dederas.
Tuque tui Princeps regimen sic dirige regni,
   Ut post hoc regnum cœlica regna petas.

In effigiem Reginæ.

P Allas, Juno, Venus, sophiâ, diademate, formâ,
   Corda, caput, vultus, imbuit, ornat, alit.

The English.

Pallas, Juno, Venus, with wisedome,
   Crowne, and comely hewe,
Thy heart, head, face, endewes, adornes,
   And deckes most fine to view.

382

Allusio ad illud Ovidii Metamorphoseos⎫Scripta
   in dictum patris Penei ad filiam⎬ad
   Daphnem.   ⎭Eandem.

S Æpè pater dixit, Generum mihi filia debes
     Sæpè pater dixit, Debes mihi nata Nepotes.
Sic pater Henricus : Generum mihi filia debes,
   Longaque debetur posteritas Proavis.
Nata potes regnare ? potes sine compare vitam
   Ducere ? & hac rarâ dote beata, mori ?
Ingenium, doctrina, fides ; huic consona doti
   Regnum, forma, decus, singula summa tibi.
Hisce tuo Patri non es virtutibus impar,
   Major at ille unâ est, & minor ipsa Patre.
Quod talem Patri licuit te cernere Prolem,
   Qualis adhuc Natæ non datur ulla suæ.
Sic minor & major, minor es tu, major at ille,
   Tu minor : hoc partu major at esse potes.

Alia allusio ad eandem.

D Ixerunt olim : Rex & Regina beati.
     At nunc plebs dicit, Tantùm Regina beata.
O utinam possent (si sint pia vota) sonare,
Sunt cum Prole suâ Rex & Regina beati,
Tunc essent omnes, simul omni ex parte beati :
Patria, Plebs, Princeps, Rex & Regina beati.

De novem literis Reginæ Nominis ELIZABETA.

D Ic cur literulas habet ELISABETA novenas ?
     An Musas quod amet ELISABETA novem ?
Est ita, sed ratio subit hâc tamen altera major,
   Te Musæ quòd ament ELISABETA novem.

GEORGE CORYAT'S POEMS

Ænigma ad eandem per eundem.

ANglia dicat Io, solenni ex more triumphans,
    Virgo parit, nobis ELISABETA parit.
An tibi quæ peperit virgo, peperisse videtur?
    Mater sola parit, virgoque nulla parit.
Anglica sola suos sentit Respublica fœtus,
    Concipit huic virgo commoda, virgo parit.

Prosopopeia ad Portam Palatii Episcopi Wintoni-
ensis, ut Reginæ aperiatur ad illius ingressum.

CLara bipartitas aperito Janua portas,
    Ut repetat Princeps interiora domus,
Mox ea majori fulgebit lumine dives
    Quâm micat Arctoo nobilis Ursa Polo.
Antè fuit fœlix multorum nomine Regum,
    Ut nunc est fœlix non tamen antè fuit.
Nam si Marte, fide, doctrinâ, stemmate, formâ
    Clarior ulla foret, clarior ista foret.
O nostri ut fuerit Cordis tam * Janua lata,
    Intrares tectum (Cor puto dulce) meum.

* Iste lepor refertur ad nomen ejus Cor-yate. Posteriori syllaba
scilicet yate, idem significante Anglicè quod Latinè janua.

Pro quinque minis tria verba scripta nomine
gratiarum actionis & valedictionis ad candem
per eundem.

SI mihi non parcis, non audeo dicere verbum
At mihi parce precor, sed tria verba tibi.

NUBE

Quod scripsi spero, quod spero postulo, Nube,
Sic tibi, sic patriæ consule Virgo tuæ.

VIVE

Sic vive ut vivas, sic regnum dirige Princeps,
Ut tibi sit proles, quæ tua regna regat.

VALE

Hoc tibi postremum dicetur carmine verbum,
Quod peto, quod rogito, quod precor, oro,

VALE.

De insignibus Angliæ ad eandem in Angliæ
descriptionem per eundem.

HInc Leo & inde Draco parmam qui sustinet, iste
Prudentes, validos denotat ille duces.
Qui pariter certant Domina sub Principe (cujus
Prælucent medio stemmata fixa loco)
Sustinuisse humeris Regalia Principis arma,
Ingenio iste suo, viribus ille suis.

[Præfatio in

Præfatio in librum Psalmorum, à Georgio Coryato Latine translatum, ad Serenissimam Angliæ Reginam D. Elizabetham de variis carminum generibus.

	Math. 16.
TU Deus atque tui divina potentia verbi	Tu
Es mihi, Christe etiam, non mihi Papa Petra.	Es
Petrus erat Christi tantùm firmissima Petra,	Petrus,
Et mihi Christe Petra es, & mihi Christe Petrus.	Et
Supra vel supèr hanc sat erit si struxero Petram,	Supra
Hanc statuit Dominus, noluit esse aliam.	Hanc
Petram Pontifices non hanc statuere, sed altram,	Petram
Ædificabo igitur quâm potero super hanc	Ædificabo
Ecclesiam mores, vitam, famamque fidemque	Ecclesiam
Nostram : Christe Petra es, non mihi Papa Petra.	Nostram.
Porta cui triplicem gestans in limine mitram	Porta
Inferni custos præsidet assiduus.	Inferni
Non huic vel duplici circundatus ense nocebit,	Non
Prævaleat summi spesque fidesque tui.	Prævaleat
Adversus Petram hanc sua tendunt retia Papæ,	Adversus
Illam sed Dominus proteget usque Petram.	Illam.

Sacræ tuæ Majestatis fidelissimus subditus devinctissimusque scholaris Oxoniensis.

Georgius Coryatus.

386

GEORGE CORYAT'S POEMS

Viridis Draconis Triumphus, in funere clarissimi
viri D. Gulielmi Herberti nuper Baronis Car-
difiensis, Comitisque Pembruchiensis, & regiæ
Aulæ Oeconomi primarii, ad æternam tanti viri
memoriam.

Spice Penbruchium specie viridante Dra-
conem
Lector, & auratum per colla virentia
Torquem,
Hamatosque ungues, oculosque, alasque
volucres,
Immanemque jubam, & formosos cor-
poris artus.
Hunc neque Phryxei custodem velleris olìm
Colchiacæ flevere nurus, neque Mala sororum
Servantem Hesperiis Alcides vicit in hortis.
Cynthius innumeris fixit Pythona sagittis,
Et tua servantem (Gradive) fluenta Draconem
Cadmeæ fixere manus : Hunc frangere nemo
Heroum, Divumve potest : non Aesone natus,
Non Jove, non profugas ab Agenore missus in oras.
Ipsa adeò quæ cuncta domat, legesque cruentas
Imponit rebus Mors implacabilis ortis,
Mors ipsa hunc solum superare nec ausa Draconem,
Nec potuit ; nam cum terris superesse vetaret,
Inseruit cœlo : nunc illic fulgidus ardet,
Quâ micat, & flexu voluentes dividit Ursas,
Aut ubi contortis Ophyuchia brachia spiris
Implicat, & longos ducit per inania tractus.
Solus enim soli didicit parere Leoni.
Hunc coluit, Regemque suum patienter adorans
Esse tulit : quem nec vis ulla, nex hosticus ensis,
Nec Jovis æthereo disjectum fulmen Olympo
Fregit adhuc, hunc una sui cultura Leonis
Perdomuit, Dominique feros procumbere fecit
Ante pedes : fulvum metuunt ita cuncta Leonem.

387

Sed nec inutilibus coluit tam grande tribunal
Obsequiis, ipsique adeo fuit utile tanto
Concessisse Duci, cujus tot martia gessit
Auspiciis, varias & fortia bella per oras.
  Capta sub Henrici primum Bullonia ductu
Vulgavit rutilis Herberti nomen in armis:
Regia quo fulvi mens inclinata Leonis
Conspicuo viridem promovit honore Draconem.
Protinus & celsum miles conscende caballum,
Ense caput feriens, auratis (inquit) in armis.
  Nec minus uxorem præclari stemmatis Annam
Despondet Regina tuam Catharina sororem,
Par tibi, par illi virtus, Par denique nomen.
Tres tulit ex ista virides celebresque Dracones
(Quot Leo Regalis magnos clarosque Leones)
Henricum comitem, Eduardumque, Annamque tenellam.
Junxit & hos vivens tædis illustribus omnes.
Et nunc cum charis vivunt confortibus omnes,
Atque diu multos peragant fœliciter annos.
Jam Leo grandævus vitales deserit auras,
Et charum catulis commendat voce Draconem.
Inde fuit Regum, Reginarumque per annos
Delitiæ multos, multo insignitus honore.
Octavo Henrico, Eduardo, Mariæ, Elizabethæ,
Et patri & natis charissimus omnibus unus.
  Nam simul Eduardus tener ille Leunculus Anglis
Prodit, ad acceptos aliquid Draco majus honores
Addit adhuc, multoque magis prorumpit in altum.
Rursus factus Eques magnusque Magister equorum.
  Quid referam positis tot prælia gesta trophæis?
Tot spolia? & ductos civili ex hoste triumphos?
Ut vigili occiduos sedaverit arte tumultus?
Horrendosque suo superârit Marte rebelles?
Magnum opus, & multo quæsitam sanguine laurum.
Hic sese in Gyros, & multa volumina torquens,
Terrificis altas quatiens clangoribus alas,
Claruit ante alios virtus generosa Draconis.
Hinc Baro Cardifios regali munere fasces,
388

Pembruchiumque Comes titulis adjungit honorem.
   Proh dolor, Eduardus fato succumbit, & ejus
Protinus ad Mariam volvuntur sceptra sororem.
Jamque iterum in patriæ grassatur viscera ferrum.
Evocat innumeros funesta ad bella Viatus,
Armatamque manum Londini ad mœnia ducit,
Præficit huic bello, & rebus Regina gerendis
(Nam quid agat?) viridem (spes hæc fuit una) Draconem.
Ille suum partes virus diffundit in omnes,
Ille per insanos ruit imperterritus hostes,
Confunditque viros, vincitque capitque Viatum.
   Quin aliud tractans Mariæ sub nomine bellum,
Quintinos forti perrupit milite muros,
Contudit & sævos pulchro certamine Francos,
Hispanus dum bella gerit : sic scilicet unus
Præripuit cunctis omni in certamine palmam.
   Nec dextram patulo frustrâ gerit ore cruentam,
Invictus, victorque potens. An segnior idem
(Elisabetha) tuos pugnasset miles in hostes,
Te nisi pace frui, tua mens, & qui tua servat
Regna Deus mallet : sub te quod vincere posset
Non habuit, seramque togam te ferre coactus
Edidicit regnante senex : neque prælia gessit
Ulla, nisi extremum hoc sæva cum morte duellum.
Quo tamen & victor (quod sæpius antè) triumphans,
Lætus, ovans, Superûm ad cœlestia tecta recessit.

Apostrophe ad Illustrissimum Henricum Comitem Penbruchiensem Gulielmi filium.

A T tu clare Comes, Comitis clarissime proles,
   (Henrice) huc flectas oculos, hos perlege versus.
Multa patris virtus animo, multusque recurset
Ejus honos, maneant infixi pectore vultus.
In te certa tui remanent vestigia patris,
Os oculosque Patri similes, moresque paternos
Egregiè reddis : superest ut comprecer unum hoc,
Ut patris exemplo discas parere Leoni.

Utque Pater, Patri Placuit, Catulisque Leonis,
Hujus ad exemplum sic te componere cures.
Quod facis, hoc semper facias: reverere Leonem,
Seu Leo, sive Lea est quæ nunc regit Elisabetha,
Semper erat viridi multùm propensa Draconi,
Et patris illa sui dilexit more Draconem,
Cujus præclaro solius munere factus
Oeconomos, Custosque Aulæ, Columenque Britannæ est,
Illa potest juvenem veteri præferre Draconi.
Illa agat: illa diu vivat, regnetque Britannis.
Atque diu vivat Draco Penbruchiensis eisdem,
Et parere Draco, discatque placere Leoni.

Tuus humillimus Sacellanus

Georgius Coryatus.

The same translated into English by the Author of the former.

THe Pembroke Dragon, greene of hue, good reader, here behold,
His scaled necke environed with glittering chaine of gold,
His hooked clawes, his piercing eyes, his winges prepar'd to flight,
His mighty crest, well favoured limmes, and body shaped right.
   'Twas not this Dragon whom the dames of Colchos did bewaile,
The keeper of the golden Fleece: not Hercules did prevayle
Against the same: it was not this which kept the Golden frute
In Hespers grove, Appollos sleight right cunningly did shute,
His thousand shafts, which Python pierst: yea Cadmus hand hath slain
Thy monstrous Dragon (mighty Mars) which kept Bœotian plain.

390

The Gods them.
earthy w.
Nor Æsons sonn.
to fight,
If fathers wr.
might,
So not despair
doth make
Against al
earth to t.
Death, death I say
throw,
Ye could it do: i
show,
To skies she se
whirling be
Or where sh.
appeares.
There as he stretu
beast.
The Lyon old, w^n
breast.
He only hath wel
ober,
That Kingly beast
swey.
Whom erst no fo-
enimies swe
Nor thundering Jo,
afearde,
Only the Lyon cau
So each thing bowes
His duties to so
His loyalty to such
First Bulleine won
race,
Brought Herbert
place,

The Gods themselves, the sonnes of God, no Imps of
    earthy wight,
Not Æsons sonne, not Jove his youth, not Cadmus (put
    to flight
By fathers wrath, Agenors ire) could quaile this Dragons
    might;
No not despightfull death, even she which cruell lawes
    doth make
Against al things, who al things tames, which shape in
    earth do take;
Death, death I say durst not presume this Dragons over-
    throw,
Ne could it do: for when on earth she bid him not to
    show,
To skies she sent his glistering ghost, twixt both the
    whirling beares,
Or where she wresteth Ophiucus armes, which there
    appeares.
Where as he stretcheth out his limmes nigh to the gentle
    beast,
The Lyon old, whose princely heart foreshineth in his
    breast.
    He only hath well learn'd the lore, the only Lyon to
    obey,
That Kingly beast he honoured still, yeelding to him the
    swey.
Whom erst no force could cause to creak, nor dint of
    enimies swerd,
Nor thundering Jove, with fiery flash might force to be
    afearde,
Only the Lyon caus'd to crouche, and fall before his feete:
So each thing bowes and bendes unto the Lyon, as is meete.
    His duties to so hye a throne were not employed in vaine,
His loyalty to such a Lord encreased much his gaine,
First Bulleine wone, where Henry was, and led the royall
    race,
Brought Herberts name for warly feates into a worthy
    place,

Whereby the Lyons Kingly minde inclined to advance
The Dragon greene to higher state, to more triumphant
  chance,
He stoutly strikes him with his sword, Arise my Knight,
  he saies,
Bestride thy horse, use gilded spurres, and weare the like
  alwaies.
  And likewise of a noble house, with him to lead his life,
O Katherine Queene, thy Sister Anne he doth espouse to
  wife.
In natures giftes a peere to thee, in virtues rare a peere,
And Parre by name, a meeter match, I deeme no time did
  heare.
Of her he leaves three Dragons green, three impes of
  worthy fame,
(The Lyon of the princely race, in number left the same)
Henry this Earle, and Edward eke with Lady Anne his
  deere,
All which he joinde to worthy mates, whiles that he lived
  here.
And now they live in happy state, each one both man and
  wife,
God graunt them many yeares to live, and lead a joyfull life.
  The Lyon old leaveth this ayre, there is no other choyce,
And to his yong, this Dragon green, commends with
  Kingly voice.
To kinges & queenes, from time to time, thus was he
  holden deare,
As by the honours he attainde, most plainly doth appeare.
To Henry eight, to Edward sixth, and to Elizabeth,
The father and the children all, he was beloved till death.
For when the little Lyon came (king Edward) to his reigne,
In honour more the dragon grew, he had a greater traine;
Made of the noble order Knight, (a Knight so was he
  twise)
And after maister of the Horse: thus did this Dragon rise.
  Of trophies pight for foughten fields, what should I here
  recite ?

The goodly spo:h
The Westerne ru
   cease,
And how those h
   to peace.
A deed worth pra:
   of blooi.
The Dragons curre
   him good.
He cast him there :
   he makes,
With grisly shrikes
   shakes.
For these explo:s
   where.
Both Baron of Car:
   brokes::re.
O rufull dar, K:
And Mary doth po
   roome;
And now anew er 1
Against the Quee::
   torle.
He leadeth forth ::.
The Queene dou: :
   generall.
The Dragon gree:
   hope rema::
He spits his ven::
   stainde.
Through thickest (
   he go,
The traytors tren
   Wyat tho.
An other batta:
   name,
S. Quintines wall
   and game.

The goodly spoiles, the triumphes got of civill foe by fight ?
The Westerne tumults how he quencht, to shew here do I
cease,
And how those furious rebels were by his force brought
to peace.
A deed worth praise, a palme not wonne without expence
of blood,
The Dragons curtesie shineth yet, the ground did feele
him good.
He cast him there in compasse wise, and folding wreathes
he makes,
With grisly shrikes his lofty wings amongst those ghests he
shakes.
For these exploits done in the West, tis knowne every
where,
Both Baron of Cardiffe was he made, & County of Pem-
brokeshire,
O rufull day, King Edward dies, his fatall time is come,
And Mary doth possesse the Crowne, his sister hath his
roome ;
And now anew by Wyats fetch, there gins a civill broyle,
Against the Queene he doth conspire with all his force and
toyle.
Hè leadeth forth his rebell route, even unto London wall,
The Queene doth make chiefe of this warre, & Captaine
generall,
The Dragon green. What should she do ? what other
hope remaind ?
He spits his venim round about, wherewith her foes are
stainde.
Through thickest of the enemies rout, without feare doth
he go,
The traytors tremble, he them o'errunnes, and taketh
Wyat tho.
An other battaile yet he fought under Queene Maries
name,
S. Quintines walles his soldiers shakt, and got the gole
and game.

And in the field the Frenchmen forst to flee before his face,
Whiles Philip war in France doth hold: this dragon had
    such grace,
That in each fight from all the rest, the palme he still did
    get,
And therefore in his open mouth the bloudy hand is set.
A Conquerour invincible; would he have bene more slacke
(Elizabeth) to fight for thee, and put thy enemies backe?
But that the God who rules the Realm, & eke thy heavenly
    minde,
Makes thee enjoy a quiet time? for thee he could not finde
Just cause to shew his manly heart. And now well smitte
    in yeares,
He learnes the quiet gowne to d'on, to him no warre
    appeares:
But this last fight with cruell death, to whome he yeeldes
    not yet;
His worthy Ghost with triumphes joy in starry sky is set.
And as in life for good successe, a triumpher he was,
So now with glee into the heavens, the Dragons sprite doth
    passe.

The conversion of the Triumph to the right
    honourable Henry Earle of Pembroke his
    sonne and heire.

BUt thou (my Country Lord) most worthy impe of
    counties race,
Henry my L. reade thou these lines, turne hitherward thy
    face.
An heape of Fathers haughty acts, and honours to thy
    minde
Presents themselves, his countenance in heart do thou fast
    binde.
The perfect signes of Pembrokes blood in thee do full
    remaine,
Thy face, thy eies, thy fathers looks, thy deeds shew his
    wordes plain.

394

One thing my Lord there resteth yet, which I do boldly
    crave,
That fathers lore thy lesson be, t'obey the Lyon brave.
And as the Sire pleasde the old, and all the Lyons seede,
By his example be thou prest therein eke to proceede.
Do as you do, prostrate before the Lyon lay you downe.
The Lyon, or the Lyonesse, which now doth beare the
    Crowne,
Was ever bent, and most propense unto the Dragon greene,
As King her father was his friend, so hee his friendly
    Queene.
Whose onely gift did him preferre to beare so high a
    port,
Lord Steward of her house, chiefe guide & guerdon of her
    Court.
She can exalt the Dragons impe, before the Dragon old,
And will I trust God graunt her life, long reigne over us
    to hold.
God grant the Pembroke Dragon may likewise live many
    a yeare,
That he may learne the Lyon well both for to love and
    feare.

        Your honours most humble Chaplayne,

          George Coryate.

Ad illustrissimum Comitem Oxoniensem.

CLare Comes, generis summum decoramen aviti,
    Insuper Angliaci magna Columna soli.
Da veniam tenui modulanti carmina plectro,
    Quòd nequit optatis verba referre sonis.
Te tua nobilitas commendat & inclyta virtus,
    Fortiaque eximii corporis acta tui.
Nil opis externæ quæris, nec carmina (quamvis
    Carmen amet quisquis carmine digna gerit)
Huc tamen adveniens cum Principe nobilis hospes,
    Carminibus nobis excipiendus eris.

GEORGE CORYAT'S POEMS

Tum quia Musarum tanto capiaris amore,
  Auribus his modulis occinit una tuis.
Tu velut hesterna cepisti carmina nocte,
  Hac quoque sic capias carmina nostra die.

                    Tuo Honori deditissimus,

                         Georgius Coryatus.

Ad illustrissimum virum Dominum Burghleium primarium Angliæ Thesaurarium.

SI locus hic superest, inter si gaudia tanta
   Admittunt tenues tua magna negotia Musas,
Omnis Pegasii properaret turba fluenti.
Hîc tibi gratificans, & nobile nomen adorans.
Ast licet hæ sileant, cytharâ tamen obstrepet una,
Olìm nominibus tibi devinctissima multis,
Hæc mea Calliope est, ne dedignere canentem.
(Inclyte vir) totam tibi quæ cum corpore vitam
Devovet, & gratam reddit testantia mentem
Carmina more suo, sed multo majus amore.
Obsequiis concede suis, concede Camœnis.
Scilicèt hisce mei Domini quòd sedibus hospes
Advenis, accepta Regina, proximus astas,
His mihi carminibus summo excipiendus honore.
Hoc superest magno profundam vota Tonanti,
Fœlix Nestoreos hìc quum superaveris annos,
Det tibi promissam super aurea sydera vitam.

                    T. H devotissimus

                         Georgius Coryatus.

396

GEORGE CORYAT'S POEMS

Ejusdem Carmina ad illustrissimos Oxoniensis &
Cantabrigiensis Academiæ Cancellarios D.
Robertum Dudleium Comitem Leicestrensem
& D. Gulielmum Cecilium Dominum Burgh-
leium, pronunciata in magna Aula Novi
Collegii Oxoniensis, Astronomicè.

SYdera qui lustrat, qui spherica corpora cernit,
   In sphæra geminos cernit is esse Polos.
Arcticus est alter, Polus est antarcticus alter,
   Hoc splendente Polo non micat ille Polus.
Nos tamen hîc geminos lucere videmus in urbe
   Hac nostra claros stelligerosque Polos.
En micat Oxonii Polus inclytus Oxoniensis,
   Dudleius nostri duxque decusque Poli.
Lucet & hac nostra Polus alter in urbe Cecillus,
   Ut videas geminos jam simul esse Polos.
Ille Polus noster studiorum stellifer Atlas,
   Hic Cantabrigii lucida stella Poli.
Quòd simul hanc nostram juncti venistis ad urbem,
   Quòd simul unus honor junxit utrosque Polos,
Accipite hæc simili simul ô pietate Patroni,
   Vivite fœlices atque valete Poli.

Clarissimo & honoratissimo Viro D. Gulielmo
Cecillo Baroni Burghlœo, ordinis Perisceledis Equiti aurato, Summo Angliæ Thesaurio, Regiæ M$^{ti.}$ à sanctioribus consiliis, &
Academiæ Cantabrigiensis Cancellario dignissimo, rheumate laboranti pharmacum, unde
ex morbo convaluit.

MUlta aliis alii, tibi semper reddimus unum
   Carmen, at est docto grata medela viro.
Carmine dii superi placantur crimine læsi,
   Carmen amat quisquis carmine digna gerit.
Fertur Alexandrum peteret quum morbus, Homeri
   Carminibus lectis convaluisse citò.

GEORGE CORYAT'S POEMS

Huc venio, & redeo, maneo, rogo, quærito, plango,
   Audio nil nisi te morbus iniquus habet.
Comprecor (ut prosim tibi) magni carmen Homeri
   Quo tu perlecto convaluisse potes.
Nunc tibi devotos morborum postulo divos.
   Nunc mihi Mercurium consuluisse rogo.
Iste jubet libros medicorum ut consulam, et illi
   Nec tibi, nec mihi se consuluisse negant
Hos repeto doctè promittit multa Galenus,
   Rheumatico certam datque Salernus opem.
Quos ego sic paucis conjunxi versibus, ut sint
   Auxilioque tibi, præsidioque tibi.
Perlege de morbo vestro breve carmen.   Homerus
   Juvit Alexandrum, te mea Musa juvet.

   1   2   3   4
Jejuna. vigila. caleas dape. tuque labora.

  5   6   7
Infundas calidum. Modicum bibe. comprime flatum.
  8
Hæc bene tu serva, Si vis depellere rheuma.

1 Jejuna.
Ejice Rheumaticos jejunans (optime) fluxus,
   Jejunare bonum est, sed macerare, malum.

2 Vigila.
Tu multum vigilas. & dormis rarò. quid inde?
   Vis dormire magis? & vigilare minus?

3 Caleas dape.
Teque dape, (ast calida) meque juvabis ope.

4 Tuque Labora.
Nonne labor studium multorum? lectio multa?
   Est labor ille animi, sit labor iste manus.

5 Infundas calidum.
Hoc liquet, ut frigus tanti sit causa doloris,
   Infusum calidum pellere rheuma potest

6 Modicum bibe.
Cuncta facis modicè, modicè comedisque bibisque,
   Quid juvat ut jubeam te modicum bibere?

398

Et flatus, ven
Naribus

Hæc benè s
Consule

Ad eundem

Q l'aru
  E
Munere
  Ast
Tum t
  Q
Pondere s
  Equ
Ast tibi
  Qua
Aurea nec posse
  Aurum
Aurea
  Atqu
Aurea nulla
  Ærea nam
Auro quando
  Æqua que

Eusdem ad e
& Musi
mentes.

S Icilid in
  Princi

* Sic dixit ill
Buchananum Sco

7 Comprime flatum.
Et flatus, ventusque nocent, tu comprime flatum,
   Naribus ut pulsus non ferat inde caput.
8 Hæc benè tu serva &c.
Hæc benè si serves, nec possis pellere rheuma,
   Consule tunc Medicos, namque Scholaris ego.

Ad eundem gratiarum actio pro 40 solidis á se illi
     dono donatis.

QUatuor ex vestra venerunt aurea dextra,
   Et data tu nostris versibus apta refers.
Munera carminibus tua sunt majora tenellis,
   Ast utinam verti versus in illa queat.
Tum tibi carminibus possem pergratus haberi,
   Quatuor atque darem terque quaterque tibi.
Pondere sed nequeunt, numero sed munera vestra
   Æquiparare queunt, parque referre pari.
Ast tibi ponderibus, nec mùnera versibus æqua,
   Quando referre mihi non datur ulla tibi.
Aurea nec possim tibi carmina ferre Cecili,
   Aurum nec cures, quando poeta refert.
Aurea tanta tibi quòd sint quot carmina Vati,
   Atque tua hæc dixit * Desipientis opes.
Aurea nulla tibi, sed tantùm, Carmina reddam.
   Ærea nam mea sunt, aurea nulla mihi.
Auro quando tuo mea carmina nulla referre
   Æqua queant, summus reddat id ipse Deus.

Ejusdem ad eundem querela pro Principe, Patria,
   & Musis, in Pseudocausidicos se injustè oppri-
   mentes.

SIcilidùm immortale decus Cecille Sororum,
   Principis, & Patriæ summa columna tuæ ·

* Sic dixit illustrissima tua uxor in carminibus suis ad Georgium
Buchananum Scotiæ poetam.

Suscipe pro regno, pro Musis, Principe, posco
  Provoluens pedibus paucula verba tuis.
Reginam, Regnum, Musas immanìter omnes
  Causidici spoliant, dilaniantque suas,
Decipulis legum, linguis venalibus, astu,
  Sumptibus immodicis, innumerisque malis.
Non peto Causidicos qui causas dicere verè,
  Sed qui pro lucro dicere falsa solent.
Lex bona, legis et est bonus usus. & optimus ordo
  Ast bona sæpè malus non bene tractat homo.
Hinc vis & lites, dolus & furor, impetus, ardor,
  Quum trahit ad mores optima quæque malos.
Quando trahit retrahitque viros ad devia legum,
  Ut Cacus Herculeos traxit ad antra boves.
Ast precor Alcides veluti superaverit illum,
  Hosce novos poteris exuperare Cacos
Alcidesque boves illos velut extulit antris,
  Sic nobis vestram ferre velitis opem.
Regnum fortè potest, sed Princeps fortitèr illos
  Legibus Angliacis exuperare suis.
Nos opis expertes Musæ flavæque monetæ,
  Imbelles, illis nil nisi præda sumus.
Qui potes, ergo velis miseras defendere Musas,
  Sub patrocinio sint maneantque tuo.
Fasnè nefasnè siet, jus, situè injuria juris,
  Non reputant, modò sic diripiantur opes.
Dicite, sed quales? Sapiens sic dixerat olim,
  Aurifluas, nullas Insipientis opes.
Ast utinam veras sapientum quærere gazas
  In cœlo inciperent, & nisi vera loqui,
Causidici falsi, qui leges munere torquent,
  Falsaque pro veris substituisse solent.
Hæc tibi Stellato venient dicenda Cubiclo,
  Hìc ubi Stella potens, tu Cynosura micas.
Intereà verò Musarum nobile Sydus,
  Unica Castaliis spesque salusque deis,
Noscere supplicibus petimus te vocibus ista,
  Et sine lege malis ponere posse modum.

400

Sicelidûm immortale decus Cicille sororum,
Principis & Patriæ summa columna, Vale.

T. H. deditissimus, devinctissimusque

Georgius Coryatus.

Sacræ Theologiæ Baccalaureus.

Ad illustrissimum virum D. Joannem Puckeringum Magni Sigilli Custodem.

INclyte qui regni suprema negotia tractas,
  Cujus & ingenio consilioque vigent,
Da veniam tenui modulanti carmina Musæ,
  Quod nequit optatis verba referre sonis.
Multa & magna tibi cupio proferre, sed obstat
  Hic dolor auditus debilitasque mei.
Ast tibi committo me, causam, pectora, vitam,
  Et pro judicio stentvè cadantvè tuo.
Plurima sæpè dedi Reginæ carmina, sæpè
  Hæc mihi munificê munera plura dedit.
Testis erit Dominus nunc Thesaurarius iste
  Inclytus Aonidum, magnus Apollo, Parens.
Et si vixisset, Dominus Dudleius esset,
  Oxonii Phœbus qui mihi semper erat.
Et si vixisset, nunc Walsinghamius esset,
  Clarus Eques, Dominæ Principis altra manus.
Hic mihi surreptas (qua tu nunc parte laboras)
  Principis assensu restituebat opes.
Sic age. Reginam, Patriam, Musasque juvato,
  Hinc tibi proveniet gloria, fama, decus.
Summe Pater totum qui torques numine cœlum,
  Reginam & regni sceptra tuere sui.
Et tibi perpetuam super aurea sydera vitam
  Det tibi perpetuus qui regit astra deus.

T. H. devotissimus

Georgius Coryatus

Sacræ Theologiæ Baccalaureus.

Reverendissimo in Christo Patri ac Domino D. Joanni Vitegifto Archiepiscopo Cantuariensi, totius Angliæ Primati ac metropolitano, Georgii Coryati in nomen ac cognomen suum et in librum illius adversus Thomam Cartwright, elogium atque Evangelica Ἀκροστιχίς.

FU|lget in æthereo veluti Sol aureus orbe,
  It|que reditque vias, pervolitatque Polum :
Ho|c agit Angliaco florens tua gloria Regno,
  Mo|mus ut injudeat, progreditura magìs.
Mis|sus ab excelso cœli Rectore supremi,
  Sus|picis hunc animo, pectore, voce Deum.
A|rdua divini reseras mysteria verbi,
  De|que tuo totus provenit ore Deus.
O|mnia, falsiloqui tollis deliria Vatis,
  Cu|ras ipse gregem, pellis et ipse lupum.
I|procul umbrisequax, procul ito tenebrio T. C.
  No|n potes in clara luce videre diem.
Men|te manuque tuâ destruxit mœnia Babel,
  Io|manu Nemrod concidit ipse sua.
An|non Nestoreos igitur tibi comprecer annos ?
  Nes|toreum quando pectus et ora refers ?
Vi|ribus humanis deus altior omnibus unus,
  Te|dedit, æthereas quo caperemus opes.
Gift|etenim Angligenis donum cognoscitur esse,
  Us|us et ô doni maximus esto Dei.

V. R. P. devotissimus

Georgius Coryatus.

402

GE'

Epitaphium
  Domini
  tempori .
  sis, ac
  Metr

Risus
  Perse
Romuleo C
(Quod
Sic erepta
Gaudet,
Persei cel
  Ora M
Saxa Deos
  Transtulit
Saxea facta
  Pallas ut in
Nunc viget A
  Inachides mot
Phorcis obit.
  Anglorum Pa
Pallada sic nostra
  Perseus horre
Ergo Pater, Præs
  Christi athleta
Andromedes capi
  Scilicèt ex vict
Terruit excelsos o
  Os tetrum in su
Mitra triplex
  Supremum infe
Seu Draco multo
  (Monstrum ho
Ille sacro Domin
  In Phlegetont
At tu summe P.
  Es cum syder

GEORGE CORYAT'S POEMS

Epitaphium Reverendissimi in Christo Patris ac
  Domini D. Joannis Piersei, seu potius nostri
  temporis Persei, Episcopi quondam Sarisburiensis, ac postea Archiepiscopi Eboracensis, &
  Metropolitani ejusdem, Mecœnatis sui optimi.

TRistis ut Andromede monstris objecta marinis
    Perseiâ erepta est inviolata manu
Romuleo Christi subjecta Ecclesia monstro
  (Quod fera terribilis dicitur esse maris)
Sic erepta tuæ divinæ robore dextræ
  Gaudet, & in laudes occinit ista tuas.
Piersei celsus perrupit spiritus oris
  Ora Medusæi sanguinolenta Papæ.
Saxa Deos quondam, truncos quæ numina fecit,
  Transtulit & vivos in fera saxa viros:
Saxea facta tuâ nunc squalet Bestia voce,
  Pallas ut in clypeo Gorgonis ora geris.
Nunc viget Andromede florens Ecclesia Christi,
  Inachides vicit, perdomuitque feram.
Phorcis obit, clypeo Pallas caput intulit altum
  Anglorum Pallas, Regia virgo, caput.
Pallada sic nostram Capitis veneramur honore,
  Perseus horrendæ quod dedit iste neci,
Ergo Pater, Præsul, Præco sanctissime Perseu,
  Christi athleta potens, perdomitorque Papæ;
Andromedes capias gratantia carmina nostræ,
  Scilicèt ex victa læta trophæa fera.
Terruit excelsos olim quæ Bulla Monarchas,
  Os tetrum in superos impia verba tonans.
Mitra triplex duplices geminans cum clavibus enses,
  Supremum inferni, Cerbereumvè caput.
Seu Draco multorum Capitum, teterrima pestis
  (Monstrum horrendum, ingens, quod solet esse Papa)
Ille sacro Domini percussus flamine verbi
  In Phlegetontæa jam Styge monstra parit.
At tu summe Pater terris surrepte, triumphans
  Es cum sydereo nobilis umbra Deo.

Epitaphium Reverendissimi in Christo Patris ac
Domini D. Joannis Juelli Episcopi Sarisburiensis, Mecœnatis sui optimi.

Julius Austriacos Cæsar cum vicerat Anglos,
 Fertur ad occiduas castra locasse plagas :
Et fundasse suo de nomine Cæsaris urbem
 Sive Sarisburiam Cæsareamvè voces.
Julius abscessit, rexitque hanc jure Juellus,
 Angliaci nuper maxima Gemma soli.
Quo neque vir melior quisquam, neque Episcopus alter
 Doctior, aut vitâ purior ullus erat.
Hoc sua testantur pulchrè monumenta laborum,
 Proque Dei scripti relligione libri.
Queis nunquam scripsit quisquam meliora, locutus
 Nèc magis Hyblæo verba referta favo.
Fulminat in vitia : in veræ pietatis amantes
 Spargit Evangelica singula plena fide.
Chara Deo imprimis, cunctis mortalibus æqua
 Vita fuit, nullis mens pia fracta malis.
Mortalis vitæ pertæsus, & æthera scandens,
 Evolat ad superas inclyta Gemma domos.
Ergo Juelle vale rutilo preciosior auro,
 Angliaci nuper fulgida Gemma soli.

Aliud Epitaphium in eundem.

Buccina, Pastor, Eques, sonuit, pavit, superavit,
 Christum, Anglos, Papam, voce, labore, manu.

The English.

A Trumpet, Shepheard, Knight, did sound, feed, overcome,
 Christ, England, Pope, with voice, labour, hand.

GEORGE CORYAT'S POEMS

Epitaphium in lectissimam fœminam D. Annam
   Clifton, D. Joannis Clifton Equitis uxorem,
   sepultam Baringtoniæ in agro Somersetensi.

A N A equitis conjux Joannis Clifton, & A N N A
   N ata Patris Domini Montegli, gloria, lume N
   N ec non vita viri dum vixit, nobile lume N
A N N A hæc in partu periens hìc conditur   A N N A.

Ad clarissimum virum D. Eduardum Dierum
   optimè de se meritum.

DUm tibi carminibus cupio pergratus haberi,
   Hæc subiit mentem sollicitudo meam.
Multa an pauca darem, seu prorsus carmina nulla,
   An alio possem gratior esse modo.
Multa jubent (præclare) tibi me scribere multa,
   Purus amor, probitas, officiumque meum.
Sin tibi multa darem, culparem carmina multùm,
   Sic melius multò, si tibi nulla darem.
Sin tibi nulla darem, meritò tibi nullus haberer,
   Nec memor officii dicerer esse mei.
Quid faciam quæro? numero, vel pondere justo,
   Carmina tu modulo dimetiare tuo?
Si numero; non multa fero, sin pondere, multa,
   Etsi pauca tibi, sint modo grata, feram.
Ac si me logices non multùm regula fallat,
   Nec tibi multa fero; nec tibi nulla tamen.
Accipe perplacida gratissima carmina fronte,
   No alio possum gratior esse modo.
Gratulor adventum vobis cum Principe lœtum,
   Et cum nobilium (chare Diere) choro.

Epicedium D. Richardi Worselii clarissimi Ar-
   migeri, Insulæ Vectensis olim Præfecti.

URsula Worselium cur deflet sponsa maritum?
   Quidvè gemunt raptum nati duo pignora Patrem?
Quidvè suum Dominum famuli toto agmine plangunt?
Quid lachrymis luget populus Vectensis obortis?

Quidvé suum Phœbum Musæ lachrymentur ademptum?
Cur ego? cur tantos gemitus? cur fundo querelas?
Nonne gravis dolor est quum tot moriuntur in uno?
Vir, Pater, & Dominus, Rector, Philomusus, amicus?

Epitaphium ejusdem, Parentum ejus, clarissimi
Equitis & Dominæ, Jacobi & Annæ Worseliæ,
matris suæ etiam Parentum D. Joannis Lee,
Equitis clarissimi, & illius Dominæ Annæ,
duorum etiam filiorum ejusdem Richardi Pulu-
ere bombardico sublatorum: Octo nimirum
hominum in una Ecclesiæ superiori parte tumu-
lis quatuor inclusorum, octo versibus compre-
hensum.

EN pia Worselii lapis hic tegit ossa Richardi,
  Insula Præfectum quem gemit ista suum.
Quem pater adversâ Materque aspectat in urnâ,
  Matris & in media spectat uterque parens.
Ad latus hìc nati pueri duo, sorte perempti
  Præpropera, infesti pulveris igne jacent.
Fœlices omnes, vel quos sors dira coegit
  Tristia funestis claudere fata rogis.
    Vester affinis summè devinctus & devotus
      Georgius Coryatus composuit, & posuit.

Epitaphium Clarissimi Viri Gulielmi Awberii,
civilis juris Doctoris, Vicarii Generalis Archiepiscopi Cantuariensis, & supplicum libellorum
Reginæ Elizabethæ Magister.

HIc situs Awberius, Legum Clarissimus ille
  Doctor & Interpres, jusque piumque docens:
Ille fori judex quum Cantuariensis obivit
  Munus, & eximie præstitit illud onus:
Supplicibus præfectus erat, summisque Libellis
  Principis Elisabeth, queis bene functus, obit.
Quid referam ingenium, mores, vitamque probatam,
  Consilium, studium, judiciumque suum?

406

GEORGE CORYAT'S POEMS

Quid genus & proavos & maxima nomina dicam?
    Prædia quid vel opes enumerare juvat?
Vel sua turritis surgentia mœnia saxis?
    Tecta domus miris ædificata modis?
Non bona fortunæ deerant, non corporis, artis
    Mentis & egregiæ vis sibi magna fuit.
Testis erit Princeps, proceres, populique Britanni,
    Quos coluit studiis, officiisque suis.
Præcipue testis sit munificentiæ & auri
    Supplicibus precibus pauper inopsque suis.
Nam veluti Princeps est clementissima, sic is
    Supplicibusque favens simplicibusque fuit.
Charus erat toti populo, procerumque catervæ,
    Reginæ imprimis, Principibusque viris.
Audiit Oxonii superantem se sua Princeps,
    Tunc admirata est ingeniumque suum.
Quum tot Pandectas, quum tanta volumina legum
    Tam citò tam subito volveret ore suo.
Sic cum vixisset, famamque decusque parasset
    Eximium, vitæ jam satur, astra petit.
Atque animam Domino reddens, corpusque sepulchro
    Awberius, nomen liquit in orbe suum.

Epitaphium Trium Clarissimorum Armigerorum
    sepultorum Londini in proxima Ecclesia West-
    monasteriensi, D. Rowlandi Vaughan nuper
    Sereniss. Reginæ Angliæ D. Elizabethæ cor-
    poris Armigeri: D. Joannis Vaughan ejusdem
    Reginæ in partibus Borealibus à Consiliis, ac
    D. Gulielmi Vaughan ejusdem Rowlandi filii,
    D. Gulielmi Cecilli, Equitis inaurati, ʾD.
    Burghleii, totiusque Angliæ D. Thesaurarii,
    nuper clarissimi charissimique servi.

CErnite tres uno conclusos funere claros,
    Et consanguineos, conspicuosque viros.
Armigeros omnes: Rowlandus at Armiger unus
    Corporis Elisabet Principis hujus erat.

Principis & corpus sic defendebat, ut armis
　　Hoc vivo est ausus perdere nemo suis.
Pòst miseri sacrum statuerunt perdere corpus,
　　Vertit in authores sed Deus arma suos.
Vertat & usque precor, Reginam protegat usque
　　Talibus Armigeris, cœlitibusque suis.
Armiger excellens Joannes nomine Vaughan
　　Et pius, et prudens, & venerandus homo.
Ergo à consiliis regni Borealibus hujus,
　　Inclyta consiliis præstitit acta suis.
Ergo tibi charus Domina ô clarissima Knevet,
　　Conjugii junxsti quem tibi jure virum :
Tam benè qui vixit mortis benè finiit horam,
　　Hic etiam adversa parte sepultus adest.
Hic Gulielme jaces Rowlandi maxima proles,
　　Spes patriæ, ac patrui, spes quoque primi Patris.
Quem citò præreptum præclara insignia, virtus
　　Inclyta, mens fœlix, cælica vita beant.
Et si forma viros commendet ut aurea virtus,
　　Huic Phæbi facies, corpus Alexis erat.
Nobilibusque viris si laus placuisse, Cecillo
　　Est tua laus Domino perplacuisse tuo.
At Rowlande Pater, Joannes Patrue Vaughan
　　(Quos priùs hic tumuli condecoravit bonos)
Nunc charo juncti nato, claroque nepoti
　　In supera æterni vivitis ârce Dei.

　　　　　　　　　　　　G. C.

Index

Abbeville, Thomas Coryat at, I. 160; gallows at, 160.

Abdua, river at Cremona, I. 257.

Abraham, ancestor of the Magi, II. 325.

Achmet, Sultan, and the defence of his empire, I. 212.

Acrostic on Thomas Coryat by Ben Jonson, I. 19.

Actors in Venice, I. 386.

Adige river at Verona, II. 17, 154; overflowings of, 18.

Adinheim, Eberhardus, bishop of Spires in Coryat's time, II. 249.

Adolph of Nassau, thirty-third German Emperor, II. 235.

Adolphus, archbishop of Cologne, epitaph and monument of, II. 332.

Adrian, Emperor, and Justinus, I. 209.

Adrian, Pope, and Charles the Great, I. 235.

Adula, spring of the Rhine at, II. 176.

Ænus, river in Rhaetia, II. 64.

Agnes, wife of Andrew, king of Hungary, II. 147.

Agnes, first wife of Emperor Arnolphus, II. 225.

Agnes, Empress, wife of Henry III., II. 234.

Agricola, Rodolphus, praise of, by Erasmus, II. 227; epitaph of, by Barbarus, 228.

Agrippa, Marcus Vipsanius, and Cologne, II. 312.

Agrippa, Sibylla, prophecy of, II. 259.

Agrippina, wife of Germanicus Caesar, and Cologne, II. 312.

Aiguebelette, the first Alp in Savoy, seen by Thomas Coryat, I. 215; his ascension of, 216.

Aiguebelle, near the Aiguebelette mountain, I. 215, 219.

Aix in Province, Court of Parliament, I. 179.

Aken, Nimeguen's tribute to, II. 359.

Alaric, king of the Goths, in Italy, I. 305.

Albanus, martyr at Mayence, II. 282.

Albert, Archduke, at La Fere, in Picardy, I. 156.

Albert, duke of Austria, at Zürich, II. 108.

Albert, emperor and king of the Romans, slain by John, duke of Swabia, II. 144.

Albertus, statue of, at Padua, I. 279.

Albertus, Austriacus, and the death of Adolph of Nassau, 1298, II. 235.

Albis, river in Saxony, I. 237.

Alboin, first king of the Longobards, I. 236, 238; at Verona, II. 21, 28; death of, at Verona, 38.

Alciat, epigram of, I. 229.

Alcuin and the Sorbona, I. 171; schoolmaster of Charlemagne II. 169.

Aldobrandini, Cardinal, ambassador of the Pope to Charles Emanuel, Duke of Savoy, I. 231.

Alemannia, etymologies of, II. 178.

Alemannus, surname of Hercules, II. 179.

Alexander III., Pope, and Frederick Barbarossa at Venice, 1166, I. 349.

Alexandria, body of St. Mark the evangelist brought from, 810, I. 354.

Allapiazza, Thomas Coryat at, II. 61.

Alley, Peter, panegyric verses on Thomas Coryat by, I. 75-76.

Allobroges, people of Vienna, I. 218.
Alphonsus, king of Castella, pretendant to the empire of Germany, II. 266.
Alsatia, description of, II. 180.
Altorf university, in Germany, II. 307.
Amadeus, first duke of Savoy, 1415, afterwards Pope Felix V., I. 218.
Amandus, first bishop of Strasburg, II. 193.
Ambigatus, king of the Celts, I. 241.
Ambrose, earl of Bergamo, II. 56.
Amerbachius, Joannes, and his sons, learned men of Basle, II. 171.
Amiens, Thomas Coryat at, I. 161; Scaliger's verses on, 161; surprise of, by the Spaniards, 1597, 165.
Amphitheatre at Verona, description of, II. 19 f.
Amsterdam, Hugh Broughton at, II. 175.
Anacharsis, travels of, I. 128.
Anafectus, Panluccius, first duke of Venice, c. 700, I. 418.
Ancone mountain, Mezolt near, II. 61; distance from to Chur in Rhaetia, 375.
Andernach, battle of, 776, II. 37; birthplace of Guinterius, 195; battles of, 306.
Andrew, king of Hungary, II. 147.
Angelus, Politianus, epistles by, I. 393.
Anna, Empress, monument of, at Basle, II. 159.
Anne, Queen, wife of James I. of England, her picture in Venice, I. 426.
Antennacum, see Andernach.
Antenor, Padua built by, I. 138, 270; epitaph of, 271.
Antiquities of Germany, II. 82.
Antoninus, Marcus Aurelius, the philosopher, and the city of Amiens, I. 161; the seventeenth Emperor of Rome, II. 200.
Antoninus Pius, and the City of Amiens, I. 161.
Antoninus, Verus, and the fourth persecution of the Christians, I. 207.
Antonio, fellow-traveller of Thomas Coryat, I. 228.
Ἀποδημουντόφιλος, panegyric verses on Thomas Coryat by, I. 22-26.
Aponus, Petrus, statue of, at Padua, I. 280.

Aquileia, in Emperor Martian's time, and Attila, I. 305; Cardinal Grimannus, patriarch of, 321; Hermolaus Barbarus, patriarch of, II. 228.
Aquinas, Thomas, and Corpus Christi day, I. 176.
Arar (Latin name of river Saône), I. 205; II. 154.
Archidapifer, meaning of, II. 224.
Arezia, Tuisco, son of Noah, and, II. 178.
Argentina, Roman name for Strasburg, II. 184.
Arians, Bartholomew, bishop of Vicenza, and the, II. 5.
Ariovistus, king of the Germans, battle of Julius Caesar against, at Basle, II. 172.
Aristotle, travels of, I. 128.
Armoury of the Duke's Palace at Venice, I. 345.
Armoury of Zürich, II. 100.
Armu in Zeeland, Thomas Coryat at, II. 372.
Arnolphus and the siege of Verona, II. 37; at Bergamo, 900, 56.
Arnolphus Malus, son of Emperor Arnolphus, II. 225.
Arola river, II. 144; Solodure on, 154.
Arsenal of Venice, description of, I. 358.
Asimo, first bishop of Chur, 452, II. 89.
Athanasius, bishop of Spires, c. 610, II. 249.
Athenaeum, meaning of, I. 296.
Athesis river, see Adige.
Attalus, martyr at Lyons, I. 207.
Attila at Lyons, I. 204; at Cremona, 260; at Padua, 273; in Italy, 305; in Vicenza, II. 12; in Verona, 21; at Brescia, 47; at Bergamo, 56; at Basle, 171; at Strasburg, 183; at Spires, 251; at Worms, 263; at Cologne, 348.
Augst, see Augusta Rauracorum.
Augusta, name of many cities, I. 230.
Augusta Rauracorum, built by Munatius Plancus, II. 152.
Aurelian, battle of, with the Germans near Mayence, II. 280.
Ausonius, verses on Milan by, I. 240-241.
Austin, William, panegyric verses on Thomas Coryat by, I. 83-86.

INDEX

Autharus, third king of the Longo-bards, I. 235.

Awbrey, William, epitaph of, by George Coryat, II. 405-406.

Aymon, last earl of Savoy, I. 218.

Bacchara, on the Rhine, II. 299.

Bacchilio, river of Vicenza, II. 3, 154.

Baden, Thomas Coryat at, II. 137; on the Limacus, 154.

Baden, Lower, Thomas Coryat at, II. 197; marquisate of, 199; Hochberg, title of the marquesses of, 200.

Badley, Richard, panegyric verses on Thomas Coryat by, I. 107-110.

Bajazet, and Tamberlane, I. 349, note.

Baker, William, panegyric verses on Thomas Coryat by, I. 79-80.

Balaam, ancestor of the Magi, II. 325.

Ball, Lord, of Bagshot in Hampshire, customs of, II. 303.

Balthasar, third wise king, offers myrrh, II. 326.

Barbarus, Hermolaus, patriarch of Aquileia, Agricola's epitaph by, II. 228.

Bardo, abbot of Fulda, cathedral of Mayence finished by, II. 271.

Barocius, Vicentius, praetor of Bergamo, II. 53.

Bartholomew, bishop of Vicenza and the Arians, II. 5.

Basil, see Basle.

Basle, bishop of, and Zürich, II. 108; death of Huldricus of Palma at, 146; Thomas Coryat at, 152; etymology of, 153; on the Rhine, 154; cathedral of, 156; university of, founded by Pius II., 170; Attila at, 171; Council of, 1431, 172; distance from, to Strasburg, 376.

Bassano, owner of Livy's house, I. 282.

Bassanum near Trent, I. 273.

Bastard, Thomas, panegyric verses on Thomas Coryat by, I. 78.

Bat, Swiss money, II. 107.

Batavia, former name of Holland, II. 362.

Baths of Baden, description of, II. 139-143; discovered in 160, 200; number of, 201.

Battles fought near Cremona, I. 259.

Beatrix, wife of Frederick Barbarossa, II. 235.

Beauvoisis, province of, I. 167.

Bede, Venerable, II. 169; Alcuin, scholar of, I. 171.

Belford, Master, secretary of Sir Henry Wotton, I. 376.

Bellicure, archbishop of Lyons, I. 204.

Bellovesus, son of Ambigatus, king of the Celts, I. 241.

Bembo, Cardinal, monument of, in Padua, I. 287.

Benacus Lake, I. 264.

Beratterius, Nicolas, and the pillars of St. Mark's Place in Venice, I. 324.

Berberomagum, see Worms.

Berengarius, Duke of Friuli, II. 56.

Berengarius, Prince, at Verona, II. 28.

Bergamo, subject to Venice, I. 420; Thomas Coryat at, II. 48-60; Scaliger's verses on, 49; cathedral of, 49-53; church of the Augustinian friars in, 54; Attila at, 56; Arnolphus at, 56.

Bergen-op-zoom in Brabant, II. 371.

Bericus, hill near Vicenza, II. 3.

Berne, city of, against Zurich, II. 108; Kiningsfelden Monastery, possession of, II. 143.

Bertha, wife of Henry IV., II. 234.

Bessarion, Cardinal, his library at Venice, I. 321.

Betsa, Venetian tin coin, I. 423.

Bevelaqua, La, Thomas Coryat at, I. 269.

Bibliander, Theodorus, learned man of Zurich, II. 98, 111.

Bibliotheca by Gesner, I. 394.

Bing, see Bingen.

Bingen on the Rhine, II. 209; Thomas Coryat at, 295.

Biron, marshall of, at Amiens, I. 166.

Blandina, martyr at Lyons, I. 207.

Blood, rain of, in Brescia, II. 46.

Boars' heads on houses in Baden, II. 137.

Bodin, praise of the Germans by, I. 132; II. 76.

Bollanus, Dominicus, senator of Venice and bishop of Brixia, monument of, I. 382.

Bominee, Sconce in Scowel Island, II. 371.

Bommel, on the Waal, II. 361.

Bonamicus, Lazarus, of Padua, I. 298.

CORYAT'S CRUDITIES

Bonifacius, English bishop of Mayence, II. 274.

Bonn, description of, II. 309.

Bononia, Carolus Quintus and the Pope at, I. 340.

Bonus, Joannes, first dweller on the Rialto, I. 304.

Booksellers' Street in Frankfort, II. 291.

Boppard, description of, captured by King Richard of England, II. 304.

Boquinus, Petrus, preacher at Heidelberg, II. 229.

Borromeo, Cardinal, his monument in Milan, I. 244.

Boson, king of Province or Provence, II. 38.

Bouillon, Duke of, master of the horse of the king of France, I. 193.

Bouillon, Godfrey, duke of, and the first crusade, 1094, II. 238.

Boulogne, Thomas Coryat at, 1608, I. 157; gallows at, I. 158.

Bourbon, monument of the Cardinal of, at St. Denis, I. 185.

Brabant inundated by the sea, 1420, II. 365.

Bragadino, Antonius, at the siege of Famagusta, I. 421.

Brandenburg, Marquess of, and Rugia Island, I. 237.

Brandus, Sebastianus, learned man of Basle, II. 171.

Braves, Venetian bandits, I. 413.

Brembana Valley, Brembus river in, II. 61.

Brembus river in Brembana Valley, II. 61.

Brenes, M. de, ambassador in Constantinople, I. 211.

Brennus, Gaulish chief, in Verona, II. 17.

Brenta river, near Padua, I. 270.

Brescia, subject to Venice, I. 420; Thomas Coryat at, II. 40; Scaliger's hexastichon on, 41; cathedral of, 43; Attila at, 47.

Bressa, see Brescia.

Bretueil, Thomas Coryat at, I. 167.

Brewers Haven in Scowen Island, II. 371.

Briare, Thomas Coryat at, I. 196.

Bridge over the Mincius, I. 266.

Bridge, wooden, at Mayence, built by

Charles the Great, 813, II. 281; destroyed by fire, 823, 281.

Bridges in Paris, I. 171; in Venice, 312; in Dordeecht, II. 367.

Brisac on the Rhine, II. 176.

Brixia, see Brescia.

Brondolo, haven of Venice, I. 304.

Brooke, Christopher, panegyric verses on Thomas Coryat by, I. 56-57.

Brooke, Kiningsfelden Monastery near, II. 139; Thomas Coryat at, II. 150.

Brothers, the four Albanian, statues of, in Venice, I. 331.

Broughton, Hugh, supposed conversion of, II. 175.

Browne, Sir William, deputy governor of Flushing, II. 374.

Brule, Albertus de, carving done in St. George's Church by, I. 383.

Brun, William Tell at, II. 102.

Bruschus, river in Strasburg, II. 183.

Bucentoro, the, Venetian ship, I. 359.

Bucer, Martin, reformer in Strasburg, II. 194; reformed preacher, 335.

Buelerus, Marcus, of Zurich, friendly to Thomas Coryat, II. 95, 97, 109; Thomas Coryat's epistle to, 130-134; his epistle to Thomas Coryat, 135-136.

Buffolero in Lombardy, Thomas Coryat at, I. 237.

Bullinger, Henry, learned man of Zurich, II. 98, 109, 111; manuscripts of, 110; Coryat's epistle to, 127-130.

Burdeaux, in Aquitaine, Court of Parliament, I. 179.

Burghley, William Cecil, Lord, George Coryat to, II. 395 f.

Burials, strange, in Venice, I. 393.

Bursa College, at Heidelberg, II. 227.

Busbequius, Augerius, German writer, II. 85.

Butterflies, great swarms of, in Savoy, I. 223.

Byrsa river at Basle, II. 153, 155.

Cadmus, Thebes built by, I. 138.

Caesar, Julius, travels of, I. 138; battle of, against Ariovistus, king of the Germans at Basle, II. 172; and the institution of the Roman prefects in Gaul, 282.

Calais, Thomas Coryat at, 1608, I. 152; sands of, 153; description of, 155;

INDEX

captured by the Spanish, 156 ; distance from, to Paris, 301.

Calepine, Ambrose, Augustinian friar in Bergamo, Latin Dictionary by, II. 54.

Camerarius, Joachimus, of Heidelberg, Jacobus Micyllus of Strasburg, to, II. 215.

Camp, village in Valtulina valley, II. 62 ; Thomas Coryat at, 65.

Campegius, Symphorianus, his Latin tract on Lyons, I. 214.

Campian, Thomas, panegyric verses on Thomas Coryat by, I. 73.

Campion, Edmund, picture of, in the College of Jesuits at Lyons, I. 210.

Campus Martius, in Zürich, II. 105.

Canal, Grand, at Venice, I. 306.

Canareio, quarter in Venice, I. 306.

Candia or Crete, subject to Venice, I. 421.

Candianus, Thomas, consul of Padua, I. 305.

Candolchin, Thomas Coryat at, II. 65, 67.

Canisius, Peter, learned man of Nimeguen, II. 360.

Capitano, military head of the forces in the land cities subject to Venice, I. 420.

Capito, Wolfangus Fabricius, reformer in Strasburg, II. 194.

Capra, Earl Odoricus, palace of, in Vicenza, II. 9, 11.

Carew, Sir Francis, gardens of, II. 24 36.

Carinthia, Meinhard, duke of, II. 144.

Carolostadius, Andreas, Protestant reader of Basle, II. 167.

Carolus Calvus, see Charles the Bald.

Carolus Magnus, see Charles the Great.

Carolus Martellus, see Charles Martel.

Carolus Quintus, see Charles V.

Carrarius, Francis, and Verona, II. 29.

Carteromachus, Scipio, of Padua, I. 298.

Cartwright, Thomas, II. 401.

Casa, Joannes, bishop of Beneventum, II. 110.

Casaubon, Isaac, and Thomas Coryat, I. 180.

Casimires, family name of the Count Palatines, II. 225.

Casimirian College at Heidelberg, II. 227.

Cassandra, picture of, in Venice, I. 393.

Cassels, Prince Mauritius and the Persian ambassadors at, II. 84.

Castella, haven of Venice, I. 304 ; quarter in Venice, 306.

Castiglione, or Castilion, Balthasar, poet and orator, 1529, I. 268.

Castles of Verona, II. 19.

Castriot, see Scanderbeg.

Cathedral Church of Basle, II. 156 ; monument of Erasmus in, 158 ; of Bergamo, 49-53 ; of Brescia, monuments of, 43 ; of Chur, built by bishop Thello, 770, 88 ; of Cologne, 314 ; description of, 315 ; of Mayence, founded by Willigisus, bishop, c. 1011, 271 ; pulpits in, 273 ; of Spires, Robert Turner on, 233 ; S. Bernard's salutation to the Virgin in, 236-237 ; of Strasburg, founded by Clodoveus, 508, 185 ; of Verona, 31 ; S. Zeno's monument in, 33 ; of Worms, 256.

Catti, ancient warlike people, II. 301.

Cenis, see Senis.

Cethura, ancestress of the Magi, II. 325.

Chambery, capital city of Savoy, I. 217.

Chambre, la, see La Chambre.

Chapineys used in Venice, I. 400.

Chapman, John, panegyric verses on Thomas Coryat by, I. 72-73.

Chappel de la Royne, Thomas Coryat at, I. 195.

Charenton, Protestant preachers at, I. 185.

Charité la, Thomas Coryat at, I. 198.

Charles the Bald, king of France, monument of, at St. Denis, I. 183, 268 ; and the Normans, 197 ; death of, at Mantua, 267; at Verona, 778, II. 37; at Andernach, 776, 37; Ludovicus king of Italy, grandson of, 39 ; battle of, with Lewis II. at Andernach, 306.

Charles the Great (Charlemagne), Sorbonne founded by, 796, I. 171 ; in Italy, 230 ; and Pope Adrian, 235 ; at Verona, II. 28; and the siege of Verona, 37 ; tower in Zurich, 98 ; and the ecclesiastical affairs of Germany, 261 ; crowned king of France at Worms, 769, 264 ; wooden bridge built at Mayence by, 813, 281.

Charles Martel, monument and epitaph of, at St. Denis, I. 184; imprisoned at Cologne, 349.

Charles IV. German Emperor, II. 292.

Charles V. King of France, first Dauphin, 1364, I. 194.

Charles V. of Spain, battle between Francis I. and, I. 230, 255; and the Pope at Bononia, picture of, at Venice, 340; statue of, in the Senate House of Worms, II. 262.

Charles, son of Empress Anna, monument of, at Basle, II. 159.

Charles, Duke of Burgundy, and the Swiss at the battle of Granson, 1476, I. 192; and the Swiss, II. 103.

Charles Emanuel, present Duke of Savoy, I. 231.

Chatillon, admiral of France, and the Mount Falcon gallows, I. 170.

Chiavenna, Thomas Coryat at, II. 65.

Chiliades by Erasmus, II. 227.

Chioggia, haven of Venice, I. 304.

Chiquinie, Venetian coin, value of, I. 389; gold coin, 422.

Chondomarius, king, prisoner of Julian the Apostate, II. 193.

Christian II. Duke of Saxony, benefactor to Chur, II. 90.

Chur, or Curia, principal town of Rhetia, II. 63; Thomas Coryat at, 87-92; past history and description of cathedral of, 88-89; confederation of, 1419, 1424, II. 90; distance from, to Zurich, 376.

Church, cathedral, of Amiens, description of, I. 162; cathedral of Milan, description of monuments in, 244; cathedral of Paris, 172; of Nevers, 198; cathedral, at Turin, 231; of the Augustinian friars in Bergamo, II. 54; of Madonna Miracoloso in Venice, 365; of the Maccabees, in Cologne, 340; Maria Antiqua, in Verona, 27; of Middleborough, monuments of, 373; of Rees, 355; of S. Albanus at Mayence, 281; S. Anastasia, in Verona, 34; of S. Barbara, in Mantua, I. 266; S. Bartholomew's, in Frankfort, II. 289; S. Catherine's in Oppenheim, 268; of S. Felix and S. Regula built by Clodoveus, king of France at Zurich, 97; Greek, S. George's description

of, I. 367; ceremonies in, 368; of S. Gereon, and the martyrs, relics in Cologne, II. 342; of S. Justina in Padua, I. 288; of S. Mary in Vicenza, II. 10; S. Mark's in Venice, I. 347; S. Paul's in Venice, 385; of S. Peter in Zurich, II. 99; of S. Ursula in Cologne, 337.

Churches in Lower Baden, II. 199: in Calais, ceremonies in, I. 153; in Cologne, II. 314; of Dordrecht, 367; of Heidelberg, 209; in Lyons, I. 208; of Mayence, II. 270; in Milan, description of, I. 242, 247, 254; at Spires, II. 233; S. Anthony's, in Padua, I. 286; S. John and Paul in Venice, description of, 361.

Cicero, travels of, I. 129.

Ciconia, Pascalis, Duke of Venice, Palma castle built by, 1593, I. 421.

Cimerica, Sibylla, prophecy of, II. 259.

Cirinus, king of Liguria, Bergamo built by, II. 49.

Claraval in Burgundy, S. Bernard, abbot of, II. 236.

Clarke, Josias, Anagram, on Thomas Coryat by, I. 82.

Claudia, mother of Constantius Chlorus, buried at Spires, II. 231.

Claudius, Flavius, Emperor, and the battle near Lago di Como, II. 40.

Clavel, William, panegyric verses on Thomas Coryat by, I. 35-36.

Clermont, Thomas Coryat at, I. 167; dynasty of the counts of, 168; council of, in France, 1094, II. 238.

Cleve, capital of Cleveland, II. 353, 356.

Cleveland, Duke of, titles of, II. 135.

Clifton, Anna, epitaph of, by George Coryat, II. 404.

Clock of Strasburg, description of, II. 187.

Clodoveus (Clovis), king of France, and the church of S. Felix and S. Regula at Zurich, II. 97; and the bishops of Worms, c. 500, 260.

Cloister of S. Felix and S. Regula church, monuments of, II. 98.

Cloisters in Basle cathedral, II. 160.

Coblentz by the Mosella and Rhine, II. 154.

Coblenz, etymology of, description of, II. 305.

INDEX

Cocharus, river, tributary of the Neckar, II. 208.

Coctiae, Alps, from king Coctius, I. 225.

Coctius, king, victor of the ancient Gauls, I. 225.

Colen, see Cologne.

Coleon, Barthelmew, of Bergomo, captain of the Venetians, I. 420; picture of, in Venice, 361; monument of, in Bergamo cathedral, II. 50.

Colmaria in Alsatia, II. 181.

Cologne by the Rhine, II. 154; council of, 348, 260; S. Maternus, first apostle of, 310; Scaliger's verses on, 311; founders of, 312; description of, 313; cathedral and churches of, 314; the Magi, and the other saints in, 329; bishopric of, 334; S. Ursula's church in, 337; Maccabees' church in, 340; university of, 348; Attila at, 348; distance from, to Nimeguen, 376.

Colonia, see Cologne.

Colossus, stone, near Mayence, erected by Drusus Nero, II. 276.

Como, Lago di, or Lacus Larius, description of, II. 40.

Companies, city, in Venice, I. 389.

Condé, Prince of, at Fontainebleau, I. 195.

Confederation of Switzerland, 1316, II. 103; of Rhaetia, 90.

Conrad II., Emperor, surnamed Salicus, cathedral of Spires founded by, c. 1030, II. 233.

Conrad the Wise, monument of, in Worms, II. 267.

Consilio di Dieci, in the palace of the duke of Venice, I. 340; after the Roman Decemviri, I. 418.

Constantine, Emperor, cross of, kept in Brescia, II. 44; at Chur, 354, 88.

Constantius Chlorus, founder of Spires, II. 231.

Contareno, Thomaso, Podestà of Padua, I. 294.

Contarens, Cardinal, *Commonwealth of Venice* translated into English, I. 3.

Contarenus, and the public schools of Germany, I. 135.

Copernicus, Nicolaus, his statue on the Strasburg clock, II. 188.

Corbet, Richard, panegyric verses on Thomas Coryat by, I. 70-71.

Corfu, or Corcyra Island, subject to Venice, I. 421.

Cornelius, Marcus, bishop of Padua, I. 293.

Corpus Christi ceremonies in Paris, described by Thomas Coryat, I. 176-178, 182.

Corvinus, Messala, Roman orator, II. 150.

Coryat, Rev. George, *Posthuma fragmenta poematum* of, II. 377-407.

Coryat, Thomas, dedicatory epistle to Henry, Prince of Wales, by, I. 1-6; his epistle to the reader, 7-15; character of, by Ben Jonson, 16-18; acrostic on, by Ben Jonson, 19; verses by, 120; Carolus Wimier of the Praemonstratenian Order and, 161; his epistles to Gaspar Waserus, II. 113-121; answer of Gaspar Waserus to, 122-123: his epistle to Rodolphus Hospinianus, 123-126; his epistle to Henry Bullinger, 127-130; his epistle to Marcus Buelerus, 130-134; answer of Marcus Buelerus to, 135-136; to the Prince of Wales, 379.

Cosmography by Munster, I. 421; II. 109.

Cotton, Rowland, panegyric verses on Thomas Coryat by, I. 32-33.

Courtesans in Venice, I. 401-409.

Courtney, Edward, Earl of Devonshire, buried in Padua, I. 287.

Courts of Parliament in France, I. 179.

Cranfield, Lionel, panegyric verses on Thomas Coryat by, I. 63-64.

Crema, see Cremona.

Cremona, Scaliger's verses on, I. 257; besieged by the French, 260; subject to Venice, I. 420.

Crescens, first apostle of Mayence, II. 274.

Crocodile, stuffed in Padua, description, of, I. 290.

Cross of Emperor Constantine in Brescia, II. 44.

Crown, iron, of the Lombard kings at Modoetia, I. 252; of thorns, of Christ, II. 4.

Cumana, Sibylla, prophecy of, II. 258.

Cunegunda, wife of Henry II. the saint, II. 225 note.
Cunimundus, father of Queen Rosamund, II. 38.
Cups, wooden, used in Switzerland, II. 67.
Curia, see Chur.
Curio, Caelius Secundus, I. 232 ; epitaph of, at Basle, II. 164, 165.
Curio, Leoni, son of, epitaph of, at Basle, II. 165.
Curtabatus, Joannes, and Thomas Coryat at Mezolt, II. 62 ; at Chiavenna, 65.
Cuttenbergius, Joannes (Gutenberg), printing invented by, 1440, II. 277.
Cuve on the Rhine, II. 300.
Cyprus Island, sometime subject to Venice, I. 421.
Cyrus, travels of, I. 135.

Dagobert, king, monument and epitaph of, at S. Denis, I. 183 ; bishopric of Strasburg founded by, c. 630, II. 193 ; and the heathen temples in Spires, II. 251.
Dalburgius, Joannes, counsellor to Ludovicus and afterwards bishop of Worms, II. 228, 267.
Danube, Trajan's bridge over the, I. 309.
Dasypodius, Conradus, architect of the clock of Strasburg, II. 187.
Daulus, Zenus, consul of Padua, I. 305.
Dauphin or Dolphin, origin of the title of, I. 194.
Davis, John, panegyric verses on Thomas Coryat by, I. 101-107.
Decemviri, Roman, model of the " Consilio di Dieci," I. 418.
Decius, Emperor, and the seventh persecution of the church, II. 33 ; and Philippus Arabs, II. 37.
Delph in Holland, death of William Prince of Orange at, II. 225.
Delphica, Sibylla, prophecy of, II. 258.
Delphinus, Dionysius, bishop of Vicenza in Coryat's time, II. 12.
Denmarke, king of, Venetian gentleman, 1425, I. 415.
Desensan, Thomas Coryat at, II. 39.
Desiderius, last king of the Longobardes, I. 235 ; nunnery at Brescia built by, 750, II. 45.

Deutz, on the Rhine, etymology of, II. 348.
Dialogue, by Josias Simlerus Tigurinus, I. 394.
Diana's temple in Spires, II. 250 ; demolished by Dagobert, 251.
Dictionary, Latin, by Ambrose Celepine, II. 54.
Dier, Edward, George Coryat to, II. 404.
Digges, Dudley, panegyric verses on Thomas Coryat by, I. 31-32.
Dijon in Burgundy, Court of Parliament, I. 179.
Dion Cassius, Greek author, I. 309.
Dionet, king of Britain, father of S. Ursula, II. 336.
Disertinum, abbot of, and the confederation of Rhetia, 1424, II. 90.
Dodo, Petrus, captain of Padua, I. 293.
Doit, Dutch coin, II. 365.
Domitian, Emperor, and the flies, I. 268.
Domo or Cathedral in Italy, I. 295.
Donato, Leonardo, Duke of Venice, I. 309, 418.
Dones, John, panegyric verses on Thomas Coryat by, I. 71.
Donne, John, panegyric verses on Thomas Coryat by, I. 37-39.
Doole, palace of Dordrecht, built by the Earl of Leicester, II. 367.
Dordrecht, Thomas Coryat at, II. 363 ; maiden city of Holland, 364 ; situation of, 365 ; churches of, 367 ; distance from, to Flushing, 376.
Dorso Duro, quarter in Venice, I. 306.
Dotrula, prefect, Lombard tyrant, I. 235.
Dourlans, Hernand Teillo, governor of, I. 165.
Dover, distance from, to Calais, I. 301.
Drayton, Michael, panegyric verses on Thomas Coryat by, I. 97-98.
Drepanum, haven in Sicily, I. 284.
Dress worn in Venice, I. 398 ; by women, 399 ; of gentlewomen in Bergamo, II. 55 ; of the Swiss in Zurich, 105-106 ; of women in Strassburg, 192 ; of Helvetians, 173.
Drinking in Germany, II. 174 ; in the Netherlands, 360.

INDEX

Drusus Nero, and the stone Colossus near Mayence, II. 276 ; battles of, 280 ; death of, at Bingen, 296.

Ducatoon, silver coin in Venice, I. 422.

Durand, M., Protestant preacher at Charenten, I. 185.

Dusseldorf in Cleveland, Thomas Coryat at, II. 350.

Duysburg in Cleveland, Gerardus Mercator buried at, II. 351.

Dysseldorp, see Dusseldorf.

Earthquakes at Basle, 1346, 1356, II. 171.

Eberhardus, Duke of Franconia, battle of Otho the Great with, at Andernach, II. 307.

Ecclesiastical History, by Eusebius, I. 207.

Edwards, Thomas, *Monostiches* by, quotation from, II. 56.

Egilolphus, fourth King of the Longobards, I. 260 ; at Mantua, 267.

Election, Mode of, in Venice, I. 419.

Elizabeth, Empress, Kiningsfelden monastery founded by, 1408, II. 144.

Elizabeth, Queen, George Coryat in praise of, II. 381-384.

Elizabeth, wife of Rupertus, Duke of Bavaria, II. 212.

Emley, Laurence, panegyric verses on Thomas Coryat by, II. 99-101.

Emmerich, Thomas Coryat at, II. 356.

Engers, on the Rhine, II. 306.

Episcopius, Nicolaus, printer of Basle, II. 172.

Erasmus of Rotterdam, monument of, in the cathedral of Basle, II. 158 ; praise of Rodolphus Agricola by, II. 227.

Eretinus, river of Vicenza, II. 3.

Ergovia, II. 96.

Eridanus, see Po.

Erythraea, Sibylla, prophecy of, II. 258.

Eselerus, Hortmannus, prefect of Zurich and Thomas Coryat, II. 100.

Essenbach, Walterus de, and the murder of Emperor Albert, II. 145 ; death of, 146.

Este in the Signiory of Venice, I. 269.

Etlingen, antique town near Baden and Turlowe, II. 203.

Eucherius, disciple of S. Denis, I. 169 ; shrine of, 185.

Eugenius IV., Pope, and the Council of Basle, 1431, II. 172.

Euphrates, Archbishop of Cologne, deposed by the Council of Cologne, 348, II. 260.

Europaea, Sibylla, prophecy of, II. 259.

Eusebius, bishop of Caesarea, his account of the martyrs of Lyons, I. 207 ; *Ecclesiastical History of*, II. 168.

Eustorgius, bishop of Milan, and the bodies of the Magi, II. 329.

Exchange of the merchants in Paris, description of, I. 172; of Venice, 312 ; of Bergamo, II. 53 ; at Frankport, 292.

Ezzelinus, tyrant of Padua, I. 273 ; at Verona, II. 29.

Fairs in Frankfort, II. 290, 292.

Faletrus, Albertus, consul of Padua, I. 305.

Famagusta, or Salamis Island and the Turks, I. 421.

Families, noble, in Venice, I. 414.

Fans, used in Italy, I. 256.

Farnaby, Thomas, *alias* Bainrafe, panegyric verses on Thomas Coryat by, I. 82-83.

Fastrada, fourth wife of Charles the Great, 783, II. 264 ; death of, at Mayence, 281.

Feasts, religious, in Venice, I. 388.

Felix V., Pope, formerly Amadeus, 1st duke of Savoy, I. 218 ; and the council of Basle, 1431, II. 172.

Fenton, William, panegyric verses on Thomas Coryat by, I. 73-74.

Ferdinandus Primus Caesar, statue of, in the Senate House of Worms, II. 262.

Ferivarius, John, travels of, I. 129.

Ferroe monte, Franciscus de, work of, in Bergamo Cathedral, II. 52.

Ferry, description of a, in Italy, I. 233.

Field, James, panegyric verses on Thomas Coryat by, I. 115-116.

Fights, street, in Venice, I. 413.

Firtle, German measure, II. 219.

Flessinga, see Flushing.

Florentus IV., Earl of Holland and Zeland, II. 369.

Flugius, Joannes, bishop of Chur in Coryat's time, II. 89.

Flushing, or Ulissingen in Walcheren Island, drinking habits of, II. 360, 372; etymology of, 374; distance from, to London, 375-376.

Foelix, see Felix.

Fontainebleau, Thomas Coryat at, I. 185; forest of, 186; palace of, 187; gardens of, 188.

Fontigo, the, in Venice, description of, I. 384.

Food in Venice, I. 395.

Forest, Black, or Nigra Sylva, the Neckar's source in, II. 208.

Forest, Ottonica, near Heidelberg, II. 209.

Forks, used in Italy, I. 236.

Fracastorius, Hieronymus, of Padua, I. 298.

Francis I., battle between, and Charles V. near Turin, I. 230; prisoner at Pizighiton, 255.

Franckendal, Thomas Coryat at, II. 252.

Frankfort, Scaliger's verses on, II. 287-288; Thomas Coryat at, 288-293; description of, 288 f.; election of the King of the Romans at, 289; fairs at, 290, 292; distance from, to Cologne, 376.

Frederick I., Barbarossa, II. 235; at Padua, 1170, I. 273; and Pope Alexander III. at Venice, 1166, 349.

Frederick II., and the town and tower of Turlowe, II. 205; Count Palatine, and the Popish church, 1546, 226; Emperor, marriage of, with Isabella, daughter of King John of England, at Worms, 1235, 266.

Frederick III., Emperor, picture of, in the Senate House of Worms, II. 261; death of, at Lintz, 1493, 307.

Frederick IV., Count Palatine, manuscript book by the great-grandfather of, kept in Heidelberg library, II. 211.

Frederick, Duke of Austria, and the Swiss Confederation, II. 103.

Freebooters, near the Rhine, II. 308.

Fregosius, Janus, monument of, in S. Anastasia's church in Verona, II. 34.

Friburg, city of, against Zürich, II. 108.

Frisius, Joannes Jacobus, learned man of Zürich, II. 111.

Frisius, Nicolaus, at Spires, II. 251.

Frobenius, Hierome, printer of Basle, II. 166, 172.

Frobenius, John, printer of Basle, II. 172.

Frogs, used as food in Italy, I. 258; in Rhaetia, II. 64; lake of, at Zürich, 96.

Fuder, German measure. II. 219.

Fulco, Earl of Anjou, travels of, I. 138.

Fulda, abbey of, founded by Bonifacius, II. 274.

Fulgosus, Raphael, of Padua, I. 298.

Funerals in Verona, II. 36.

Furca mountain, spring of the Rhodanus at, I. 205.

Furstenberg, wines of, II. 299.

Fuscarus, Duke of Venice, I. 334; and the King of Denmark, 1425, I. 415.

Gabriel, archbishop of Philadelphia, and Thomas Coryat, at Venice, I. 369.

Galeatius, Joannes, Viscount of Milan, and Verona, II. 29.

Galleys, Venetian, I. 359; and slaves in Venice, 414.

Gallows at Boulogne, description of, I. 158; at Abbeville, 160; at Clermont, 168; on Mount Falcon, 170; of alabaster in Venice, 330; at Rheinfelden, II. 151; near Frankfort, 287; near the Rhine, 308.

Garda, see Benacus.

Garden of Earl Leonardus Walmarana in Vicenza, description of, II. 6.

Gardens of Fontainebleau, I. 188.

Gardo, see Benacus.

Garnet, Henry, picture of, at Cologne, II. 349.

Gaspar, second wise king, offers frankincense, II. 326.

Gattamelita, and the reducing of Padua to the signiory of Venice, 1402, I. 274; statue of, 286; of Narnia, renowned captain of the Venetians, 420.

Gazet, Venetian tin coin, I. 422.

Gelderland, province of the Netherlands, II. 357.

Gemusaeus, Hieronymus, professor at Basle, II. 171.

Genebria, learned woman of Verona, II. 39.

Genepe, Guil... in Cologne, II. ...

Genet, M. de ...

Calais, and ...

Geographie, by ...

Gesburga, wife ...

Germany, ...
I. 8; praise ...
Leo's ...
turrets and ...
155; praise ...
Thomas Cor...
178, 311; ...
Sebastian's ...

Gemersheim, Cx... Hapsburg ...

Gessner, C...
Zürich, on Pers...
Attraction by ...

Gletto, the... Ver...
1. 502; in Ver...

Goth, daughter...
France, wife ...

Galeberus, Duke... Lor...
near Anderna...

Glareanus, Henr...
Basle, II. 171.

Glass, Venetian, I. ...

Godard, mountain...
mountain, II. 1...

Godbey, Duke of Bo...
first Crusade, 1...

Golden Lyon, The...
at Lower Bacer... ...

Godolias, desc...

Gonzaga, Vicen...
1. 231; palace ...

Gonzaga, Will...

Gonzaga, II. S.

Goocker, Henry...
Thomas Cor...

Goncom, see G...

Gorcia, Mech...

Gorizium, on the W...
at, II. 361; bear... of
Gospel of S. Mark...
313.

Gothofredus, D oc...
in Heidelberg, II...

Goths in Piedmont, I...

Gowns worn by the Ve...
I. 397.

Granson, battle of, Sv...
191.

INDEX

Genepe, Gulielmus de, monument of, in Cologne, II. 334.

Genet, M. de la, deputy-governor of Calais, and Thomas Coryat, I. 152.

Geography, by Ptolomaeus, II. 256.

Gerbirga, wife of Gislebertus, II. 307.

Germany, universities in, number of, I. 8 ; praise of, by Bodin, 132 ; Pope Leo's ambassadors in, 133 ; Contarenus and the public schools of, 135 ; praise of, by Bodin, II. 76 ; Thomas Coryat's description of, 178-311 ; etymology of, 179 ; George Sidenham's verses on, 181-182.

Germersheim, death of Radolph of Hapsburg at, 1291, II. 235.

Gesnerus, Conradus, learned man of Zurich, on Petrus Aponus, I. 280 ; *Bibliotheca* by, 394 ; II. 98, 111.

Ghetto, the, in Venice, description of I. 370 ; in Verona, II. 31.

Gisela, daughter of Lotharius, king of France, wife of Conrad II., II. 234.

Gislebertus, Duke of Lorraine, drowned near Andernach, II. 307.

Glareanus, Henricus, professor at Basle, II. 171.

Glass, Venetian, I. 387.

Godard, mountain, highest Alpine mountain, II. 176.

Godfrey, Duke of Bouillon, and the first Crusade, 1094, II. 238.

Golden Lyon, Thomas Coryat's inn at Lower Baden, II. 202.

Gondolas, description of, I. 313.

Gonzaga, Vicentius, Duke of Mantua, I. 231 ; palace of, 265.

Gonzaga, William, father of Vincentius Gonzaga, II. 8.

Goodier, Henry, panegyric verses on Thomas Coryat by, I. 28.

Gorcom, see Gorkum.

Goricia, Meinhard, Earl of, II. 144.

Gorkum, on the Waell, Thomas Coryat at, II. 361 ; beauty of, 362.

Gospel of S. Mark, kept in Venice, I. 355.

Gothofredus, Dionysius, civil lawyer in Heidelberg, II. 230.

Goths in Piedmont, I. 230.

Gowns worn by the Venetian nobility, I. 397.

Granson, battle of, Swiss at, 1476, I. 192.

Gratarolus, Gulielmus, famous preacher of Bergamo, II. 60 ; learned man of Basle, 171.

Gratian, Emperor, II. 153 ; and the name of Amiens, I. 161 ; Germans defeated by, near Strasburg, II. 193.

Graveling, M. de Rosne, governor of, I. 156.

Gregory VII., or Hildebrand, Pope, and the golden crown of Rodolphus, Earl of Rheinfelden, II. 151 ; deposed by the fourth Council of Worms, II. 265.

Grenoble, or Gratianopolis, in Dolphinie, Court of Parliament, I. 179.

Griffin, George, panegyric verses on Thomas Coryat by, I. 101.

Grimanno, Marino, Duke of Venice in Thomas Coryat's time, I. 309 ; in Coryat's time, his picture, 425.

Grimannus, Cardinal, patriarch of Aquileia, I. 321.

Grimston, Edward, history of the Netherlands by, II. 371.

Grisons, see Rhaetia.

Gritti, Peter, Venetian palace of, II. 15.

Groninga, Rodolphus Agricola, born at, II. 227.

Gruterus, Janus, bibliothecary or librarian of the Palatine library, II. 210, 230.

Gryn, Hermannus, and the slaying of the lion, in Cologne, II. 344.

Grynaeus, Joannes Jacobus, of Basle, works of, II. 168.

Grynaeus, Simon, of Basle, II. 168.

Gualterus, Rodolphus, learned man of Zurich, II. 98, 111.

Guard, French, I. 191.

Guasto, Albertus, Marquess of, and the arsenal of Venice, I. 358 ; his opinion on Venice, 427.

Guasto or Waste plot in Italy, II. 2.

Guerilio, last archbishop of Worms, deposed by Pepin, king of France, II. 260.

Guerilius, Joannes, stationer in Venice, friend to Thomas Coryat, I. 367.

Guido, Duke of Spoleto, II. 56.

Guinterius, Joannes, learned man of Strasburg, II. 195 ; born at Andernach, 306.

Guise, Duke of, his brother, and Thomas Coryat at Lyons, I. 213.

Gulick, see Menapii.
Gulielmus, bishop of Worms in Coryat's time, II. 257, 261.
Gunterus, Earl, competitor of Charles IV. for the German empire, II. 292.
Gyfford, John, panegyric verses on Thomas Coryat by, I. 67-69.
Gymnosophist, meaning of, I. 58, note.

Habspurg, John of, prisoner at Zurich, 1350, II. 108.
Habspurg, Rodolphus de, II. 147.
Hagk, Christopher, Coryat's fellow-traveller, II. 350.
Hair, dying of the, in Venice, I. 401.
Halles, salt mines at, II. 144.
Halswell, Robert, panegyric verses on Thomas Coryat by, I. 67.
Harrington, John, of Bath, panegyric verses on Thomas Coryat by, I. 27.
Hartmannus, son of Empress Anna, II. 159 note.
Harvests, two in Italy, I. 268 ; in Germany, II. 206.
Hassia, Landgraviat of Germany, II. 301 note.
Hatto, archbishop of Mayence, history of, 914, II. 297.
Haunschildt, George, scholar of Hermannus Kirchnerus, I. 122.
Health, bills of, required to travel into Italy, I. 214.
Hedio, Gaspar, reformer in Strasburg, II. 194.
Heidelberg by the Neckar, II. 154 ; Scaliger's verses on, 207 ; etymologies of, 208 ; churches of, 209 ; distance from, to Frankfort, 376.
Helena, town near the Pyrenees, II. 91.
Helena, Empress, and the bodies of the Magi, II. 329.
Helenopolis, see Frankfort.
Hellespontia, Sibylla, prophecy of, II. 258.
Helmichildus and Queen Rosamund, II. 38.
Helvetia, see Switzerland.
Henneberg, Margarite, wife of Hermannus, Earl of, II. 369.
Henricpeter, Sebastian, printer of Basle, II. 172.
Henry II., King of France, and the Louvre, I. 173.

Henry II., the Saint, German Emperor, II. 225.
Henry III., king of France, and the Order of the Holy Ghost, I. 193 ; at Venice, 1574, I. 309 ; testimony of, 338 ; Venetian gentleman, 1574, 415.
Henry III., the Black, German Emperor, cathedral of Spires finished by, II. 233 ; son of Conrad II., II. 234 ; and the third Council of Worms, 1051, II. 265.
Henry IV., King of France, at Rouen, I. 165 ; death of, 168 ; his picture in Venice, 425.
Henry IV., the elder, Emperor of Germany, son of Henry III. and Agnes, II. 234 ; and the fourth Council of Worms, 1076, II. 265.
Henry V., the younger, Emperor of Germany, son of Henry IV. and Bertha, II. 234 ; and the fifth Council of Worms, 1122, II. 265.
Henry VII., Emperor of Germany, and John of Swabia at Pisa, II. 146.
Henry, Prince of Wales, dedicatory epistle to, by Thomas Coryat, I. 1-6 ; his picture in Venice, I. 426 ; Thomas Coryat to, II. 379.
Henry, last Earl of Baden, 1180, II. 138.
Heraclea, town of, dwelling-place of the first Dukes of Venice, I. 418.
Herbert, William, George Coryat in memory of, II. 386 f.
Herborne, John Piscator at, II. 195.
Hercinia or Nigra Sylva, Wiesa's spring from, II. 155.
Hercules, travels of, I. 135.
Hercules, Alemmanus, surname of, II. 179.
Hermannus, first Marquess of Baden, 1153, II. 200.
Hermenstein Castle, near Coblenz, II. 306.
Hervagius, Joannes, printer at Basle, II. 172.
Hildegardis, Lady, daughter of king Ludovicus, II. 99.
Hildegardis, S., nun at Bingen, friend of S. Bernard, 1180, II. 296 ; works of, 297.
Hildegardis, wife of Charles the Great and mother of Ludovicus Pius, II. 282.

INDEX

Hinderhove, or baths of Baden, II. 139-143.

Hippolytus, Lord President of the Princes' Chancery Court, verses dedicated to, II. 221-223.

History, Ecclesiastical, of Eusebius, II. 168.

Hochberg, title of the Marquesses of Baden, II. 200; Otto, Marquess of, death of, II. 148.

Hoestenius, Henry, printer of the university of Leyden, II. 221.

Holland, Hugo, panegyric verses on Thomas Coryat by, I. 43-49; friend of Thomas Coryat, 425.

Holland, meaning of, II. 362.

Honorius, Emperor, 409, I. 305.

Horses of the King of France at Fontainebleau, I. 190; used to draw boats on the Rhine, II. 361.

Hortmannus, last earl of Kyburg, 1260, II. 138.

Hoskins, John, panegyric verses on Thomas Coryat by, I. 58-61.

Hospinianus, Rodolphus, learned man of Zurich, II. 95; Thomas Coryat's epistle to, 123-126.

Hotoman, Francis, epitaph of, at Basle, II. 162-164.

Houses, Venetian, I. 307; at Spira, description of, II. 232.

Hughes, Richard, panegric verses on Thomas Coryat by, I. 119.

Humbertus, Bishop, and the stone bridge over the Arar, I. 205.

Iaxus river, tributary of the Neckar, II. 208.

Illa, river in plain of Strasburg, II. 183.

Imbert, or Hubert, Dauphin of Viennois and Philip VI., 1328, I. 194.

Ingelheim Palace, Charles the Great at, II. 217; Court at, 265.

Intuergi, people dwelling formerly in Palatinate, II. 224.

Irenaeus, first bishop of Lyons, I. 209; II. 168.

Irene, Empress, and the sacred images, I. 368.

Irenicus, Francis, historiographer, born at Etlingen, II. 203.

Irmengardis, first wife of Ludovicus Pius, II. 293.

Isabella, daughter of King John of England, marriage of Emperor Frederick II. with, 1235, II. 266.

Isella, branch of the Rhine, II. 177.

Isingrius, Michael, printer of Basle, II. 166, 172.

Isota Nigarola, learned woman of Verona, II. 39.

Italians, courtesy of, to foreigners, II. 13.

Italy, Thomas Coryat in, I. 227, 428.

Jackson, John, panegyric verses on Thomas Coryat by, I. 96.

Jacobus, Cardinal, epistle from Angelus Politianus to, II. 177.

James I., King of England, his picture in Venice, I. 425, 426.

James, Thomas, Librarian of the Bodleian Library at Oxford in Coryat's time, II. 211.

Jason, travels of, I. 132.

Jesuits' College at Lyons, description of, I. 209; in Chambery, 217; at Turin, 232; in Spires, II. 249.

Jews in Venice, description of, I. 372.

Joan, Pope, born at Mayence, II. 282.

Joannes Baptista, bishop of Bergamo, palace of, II. 53.

John, Don, and the battle of Lepanto, I. 289, 344.

John, Duke of Swabia, and the murder of Emperor Albert, II. 144; punishment of, 146.

John, earl of Habspurg, prisoner at Zurich, 1350, II. 108.

Jonson, Ben, character of Thomas Coryat by, I. 16-18; acrostic on Thomas Coryat by, 19.

Jones, Inigo, panegyric verses on Thomas Coryat by, I. 64-65.

Jovius, Paulus, study of, on Lago di Como, II. 64.

Jucundus, bishop of Paris, I. 171.

Judith, Countess, wife of Hermannus, Marquess of Baden, II. 200.

Juelli, John, bishop of Salisbury, epitaph of, by George Coryat, II. 403.

Julian the Apostate, Ammanianus Marcellinus, soldier of, II. 153; battle of, with some German kings, near Strasburg, 360, 193; Mayence bridge, built by, 280.

Junius, Adrianus, monuments of, in Middleborough Church, II. 373.

Junius, Francis, learned man of Heidelberg, II. 229.

Jura Mountain, Byrsa's spring from, II. 155.

Justinian, I., Emperor, c. 550, I. 273.

Justinus, Emperor, and Narses, I. 237.

Justinus, martyr at Lyons, I. 209.

Justus, Augustinus, palace of, in Verona, II. 35.

Keinperger, Jonas, head of the Jesuits in Spires and Thomas Coryat, II. 249.

Kelsterbach, on the Rhine, II. 287.

Kemerer, Eckenbertus, founder and first abbot of Franckendal monastery, c. 1119, II. 252.

Kicherman, Bartholomew, philosopher at Heidelberg, II. 230.

Kigele, Joannes, architect in Worms, II. 262.

Kingman, Robert, Englishman settled in Strasburg, II. 183.

Kings, the Three, of Cologne, II. 315; images of, 317; history of, Latin, 318-325; English, 325-330.

Kiningsfelden, monastery of, near Brooke, II. 139; Thomas Coryat at, 143; possession of Berne, 143; meaning of name, II. 144.

Kintzgus, river, in plain of Strasburg, II. 183.

Kirchnerus of Marpurg, Hermannus, orations by, I. 4, 11, 122-148; in praise of travel in Germany, II. 71-86.

Knighthood, orders of, I. 193.

Koningsperg, birth-place of Christopher Hagk, II. 350.

Kyburg, Earls of, and the Swiss confederation, II. 103; and the earldom of Baden, 138.

La Bevelaque, Thomas Coryat at, I. 269.

La Chambre, Thomas Coryat at, I. 223.

La Charité, Thomas Coryat at, I. 198.

Ladenburgum, palace of, residence of the bishops of Worms, II. 257.

La Fere, in Picardie, Archduke Albert at, I. 156.

Lahnstein on the Rhine, II. 305.

Langres, Voga Hill, near, I. 171; spring of the Mosella at, II. 305.

Larius, Lacus, or Lake Como, meaning of name of, II. 65.

Lasnebourg, or Lanslebourg, Thomas Coryat at, I. 224.

La Tour du Pin, Thomas Coryat at, I. 215.

Laudun, Monastery of, Margarite of Henneberg, buried in, II. 369.

Lauredanus, Leonardus, Duke of Venice, tomb and epitaph of, I. 362.

Lauredanus, Peter, Duke of Venice, 1568, I. 361.

Lavaterus, Ludovicus, learned man of Zurich, II. 98, 111.

Lecca, branch of the Rhine, II. 177.

Leicester, Earl of, mint of Dordrecht, built by, II. 366; the Doole, built by, 367; George Coryat to, 396 f.

Lemnius, Levinus, learned man of Zirixee, II. 371.

Leo, Pope, his ambassadors to Germany, I. 133.

Leo III., Greek Emperor, and the sacred images, I. 368.

Leo IX., Pope, and the third council of Worms, 1051, II. 265.

Leopold, Duke of Austria and the Swiss confederation, II. 103; and the murderers of Emperor Albert, 146; wars and death of, 148.

Lepanto in Greece, Don John of Austria, at the battle of, I. 289, 344.

Lewis II. of Germany, battle of Charles the Bald with, at Andernach, II. 306.

Lewknor, Ludovic, panegyric verses on Thomas Coryat by, I. 27-28.

Lezere, lake or river in Savoy, I. 205, 221.

Library of Mayence, II. 279; in Holy Ghost Church, Heidelberg, 209.

Libyca, Sibylla, prophecy of, II. 259.

Liege, death of Henry IV. at, 1106, II. 234.

Lieutenant of the Castle, of the land cities, subject to Venice, I. 420.

Limacus river at Baden, II. 137; Zurich on, 154.

Lime tree, description of a, in Basle, II. 169.

Lindanus, Gulielmus, learned man of Dordrecht, bishop of Ruremunda, II. 368.

Linga river, near Dordrecht, II. 365.

Lingelsemius, Doctor of Civil Law at Heidelberg, and Thomas Coryat, II. 214, 230.

Liniago, in the signiory of Venice, I. 269.

Lintz, on the Rhine, death of Frederick III. at, 1493, II. 307.

Lio, castle for soldiers of Venice, I. 388.

Lippia, river, at Cleve, II. 353.

Lipsius, Justus, friend of James Gruterus in Heidelberg, II. 210.

Lir Lake, near Splugen Mountain, II. 67.

Litenawe, Thomas Coryat at, II. 196.

Liver, Venetian coin, value of, I. 389 ; silver coin, 422.

Livy, three statues of, at Padua, I. 275, 277, 278 ; his house, 281-285.

Loches, Lodowic, Duke of Milan, prisoner at, 1500, I. 239.

Lodi, Thomas Coryat at, I. 254.

Lodowic, Duke of Milan, and the Swiss and French armies at Novara, 1500, I. 239.

Loire, river in France, I. 197.

Loiseau de Tourval, Jean, panegyric verses on Thomas Coryat by, I. 111-113.

Lombardy, past history of, I. 237; fertility of, 238.

London, distance from, to Dover, I. 301 ; Thomas Coryat's return to, II. 375 ; distance from, to Odcombe, 376.

Longinus, first exarch of Ravenna and Queen Rosamund, II. 38.

Longobards in Piedmont, I. 230; past history of the, 237.

Longolius, Christopher, of Padua, I. 298.

Lotharius, Emperor, and the Normanes, I. 197.

Loure, see Louvre.

Louvre, description of the palace of, I. 173.

Loyola, Ignatius, founder of the Jesuits, II. 360.

Lucerne, an ally of Zürich, II. 108 ; on the Ursula, 154.

Lucie Fesina, near Padua, I. 300, 304.

Lucius III., Pope, monument of, in Verona Cathedral, II. 32.

Ludolphus, son of Otho the Great, battle of, with his father II. 280 ; death of, 281.

Ludovica, wife of Frederick IV., Count Palatine, II. 225.

Ludovicus II., surnamed Germanicus, Emperor, and the second council of Worms, 868, II., 265, death of, at Frankfort, 293.

Ludovicus Pius, Emperor, and the first Council of Worms, 829, II. 265 ; death of, at Mayence, 282.

Ludovicus, king of Italy, grandson of Charles the Bald, II. 38.

Ludovicus, Count Palatine, 1319, II. 212 ; and Joannes Dalburgius, his counsellor, 228.

Ludovicus, dauphin of France (afterwards Louis XI.) and the Helvetians, near Basle, II. 173.

Lugarda, wife of Conrad the Wise II. 267.

Lutetia, meaning of, I. 171.

Luther, Martin, and the Wittemberg university, II. 194.

Lycosthenes, Conradus, professor at Basle, II. 171.

Lycurgus, travels of, I. 135.

Lycus, river in Rhetia, II. 63.

Lyons, Thomas Coryat at, I. 202-214 ; Julius Caesar Scaliger's hexastichon on, 203 ; Pontius Pilate's exile and death at, 207 ; distance from, to Turin, 301 ; on the Arar and Rhodanus, II. 154.

Macaronicon, by John Donne, I. 39.

Maccabees, martyrdom of the, II. 340.

Magantia, Alexander, work of, in Vicenza, II. 12.

Magi, see Kings of Cologne.

Magnentius, Emperor, proclaimed at Chur, II. 91.

Magnus, statue of, in Verona, II. 28.

Maine, river, at Frankfort, II. 284.

Malomocco, haven of Venice, I. 304 ; dwelling-place of the first Dukes of Venice, near, I. 418.

Malta or Melita, S. Paul and the viper at, I. 412.

Mammea, mother of Alexander Severus, death of, at Mayence, II. 281.

Mandevile, Sir John, 'English Ulysses,' I. 303.

Manes, the heretic martyr in Persia, I. 363.

Mannus, son of Tuisco, II. 179.

Mantua, Vicentius Gonzaga, Duke of, I. 231 ; Thomas Coryat at, 261 ; Scaliger's verses on, 262 ; birth-place of Virgil, 263.

Marcellinus, Ammanianus, soldier of Julian the Apostate, II. 152 ; on the etymology of Palatinate, II. 224.

Marcomirus, king of France, and Cologne, II. 313.

Marcus Aurelius, see Antoninus.

Margarita, Æmiliana, monastery, built by, near Venice, I. 387, 406.

Margarite, wife of Hermannus, earl of Henneberg, buried in Laudun monastery, II. 369.

Maria Antiqua, church in Verona, II. 27.

Maristella, Thomas Coryat at, II. 136.

Market place of Brescia, II. 43 ; at Chur, 91 ; in Verona, 29.

Maron, a guide or conductor in Italy, I. 226.

Marot, French poet, I. 31 note, 42 note.

Marpurg, university of, II. 71.

Martin, Richard, sonnet to Thomas Coryat by, I. 39 ; quotation from a letter of, to Thomas Coryat, 239 ; letter from, to Sir Henry Wotton, 1608, 377-379.

Martock Manor, near Odcombe, in Somersetshire, II. 203.

Martyr, Peter, the Vermilian, learned man of Zurich, II. 98.

Martyrs of Lyons, history of, by Eusebius, bishop of Caesarea, I. 207 ; of Brescia, II. 46 ; of Zurich, 97 ; at Mayence, 282 ; Theban, buried in S. Gereon's Church, Cologne, 342.

Mary, Virgin, picture of, by S. Luke, the Evangelist, kept in Venice, I. 355.

Masauc, Earl of, and the confederation of Rhetia, 1424, II. 90.

Mattiaci, former inhabitants of Zeeland, II. 372.

Maturus, martyr at Lyons, I. 207.

Maurice of Orange, commander of the Netherland armies, II. 225 ; towns sacked by, II. 352.

Mauritius, Prince, at Cassels, and the Persian ambassadors, II. 84.

Maurocenus, Francis, last bishop of Brescia in Coryat's time, II. 43.

Maurocenus, Vincentius, Venetian knight, monument of, I. 382.

Maurus, Rabanus, abbot of Fulda, II. 275.

Maximilian I., Emperor, and Verona, II. 29.

Maximilian II., statue of, in the Senate House of Worms, II. 262.

Maximinus and the murder of Alexander Severus at Mayence, II. 281.

Maximus, bishop of Turin, 420, I. 232.

Mayence, II. 154 ; prefect of, and the city of Worms, II. 263 ; description of, 269 f.

Maze, river in Gelderland, II. 357.

Medicis, Katharine de, description of her monument at S. Denis, I. 184.

Megander, Gaspar, learned man of Zurich, II. 111.

Meinhard, Earl of Tyrol and Goricia, II. 144.

Mejus, Octavianus, Protestant preacher in Chiavenna, II. 65.

Melancthon, Philip, his opinion on the etymology of Alemannia, II. 179 ; reformed preacher, 335 ; on Deutz, 348 ; verses on the river Maine, 285.

Melchior, first king, offers gold, II. 326.

Meleager, epigram of, I. 229.

Melissus, Paulus, poet and knight Palatine at Heidelberg, II. 230.

Menapii, former inhabitants of Gelderland, II. 357.

Meniana, or Italian terrace, I. 307.

Mentz, see Mayence.

Mercator, Gerardus, buried at Duysburg, II. 351.

Merceria, street in Venice, I. 328.

Mercury's temple in Spires, II. 250 ; demolished by Dagobert, 251.

Merva river, near Dordrecht, II. 365.

Metellus, Middleborough founded by, II. 372.

Mezolt, near Ancone Mountain, II. 61.

Micyllus, Jacobus, learned man of Strasburg, II. 195 ; of Strasburg, to Joachimus Camerarius of Heidelberg, 215.

Middleborough in Walcheren island, II. 372 ; founded by Metellus, 372 ; church, 373.

INDEX

Milan, Dukedom of, Spanish possession, I. 239.

Milan, Scaliger's verses on, Thomas Coryat at, I. 240; history of the foundation of, 241; Roman emperors in, 251; governors of, 253; distance from, to Padua, 301; in Emperor Martin's time, and Attila, 305.

Milberg Castle at Baden, II. 199, 206.

Mimlingus river, tributary of the Maine, II. 285.

Mincius river, I. 264.

Mint of S. Mark's in Venice, description of, I. 332; of Dordrecht, built by the Earl of Leicester, II. 366.

Mirandula, birth-place of Joannes Picus, I. 261.

Misnia, Theodorus, Marquess of, and Frederick Barbarossa, 1166, I. 350.

Mithridates, travels of, to Cappadocia, II. 74.

Mocenigus, Duke of Venice, and Henry III., King of France, 1574, I. 415.

Modena, Duke of, I. 231.

Modoetia, iron crown of the Lombard kings at, I. 252.

Moenus river, see Maine.

Mogonus, see Maine.

Moguntia, or Moguntiacum, see Mayence.

Molino, Clarissimo of Venice, I. 293.

Molinus, Peter, Protestant preacher at Charenton, I. 185.

Momford, Thomas, panegyric verses on Thomas Coryat by, I. 77-78.

Monasteries at Amiens, I. 164; at Milan, 246; of Benedictine monks in Padua, description of, 287; of Benedictines in Venice, 380; at Lyons, 210; built by Margarita Æmiliana, near Venice, 387, 406; of Camaldulenses, near Verona, II. 16; in Verona, 35; of Carthusian monks at Coblenz, 305; of Dominicans in Vicenza, 4; of Kiningsfelden, near Brooke, 139; Thomas Coryat at, 143; possession of Berna, 143; monks and nuns, founded by Empress Elizabeth, 147.

Money, Venetian, I. 422.

Monostiches by Thomas Edwards, quotation from, II. 56.

Monsferratus, marquesses of, kings of Italy, I. 230.

Montacute, Sir Edward Philippes of, II. 310.

Montargis, Thomas Coryat at, I. 196.

Montigny, M. de, Protestant preacher at Charenton, I. 185.

Montmelian, strong castle at, I. 219.

Montmorency, M. de, high constable of France, I. 169.

Montrescut, Porte de, at Amiens, I. 166.

Montreuil, Thomas Coryat at, I. 158; description of, 159.

Monuments in Holy Ghost Church, Heidelberg, II. 212; in Spires cathedral, 233; to bishops of Spires, in the cathedral, 246-247.

Moore, Dr., in Padua, and Thomas Coryat, I. 299.

Morata, Olympia Fulvia, learned Italian woman at Heidelberg, II. 229.

Morbinio in Rhetia, II. 63.

Mosa river, near Dordrecht, II. 365.

Mosbach, George Eucharius, architect in Worms, II. 262.

Mosella, the, II. 154; spring of, at Langres, 305.

Moulins, description of a fair at, I. 201.

Mountebanks, I. 267; in Venice, 409.

Mount Falcon, near Paris, gallows on, I. 170.

Mowse Turn, in the Rhine, II. 298.

Munatius Plancus, cities founded by, I. 203.

Munster, Sebastian, *Cosmography* by, I. 421; II. 109; quotation from, 152, 153; professor at Basle, 171; learned man of Heidelberg, 229; on Deutz, 348; etymology of the word Spires, 232; *Cosmography* and the Jesuits of Spires, 249.

Murano, fabrication of Venetian glass at, I. 387.

Music, beautiful, in Venice, I. 390.

Musto, Paulo Æmilio, and the epitaph of Antenor, I. 271.

Naha river, tributary of the Rhine, II. 295.

Nancy, battle of, between Charles, Duke of Burgundy and the Swiss, 1477, II. 103.

Narses, Eunuch, and the coming of the Longobards in Italy, I. 237; Padua repaired by, c. 550, I. 273.

Naupactus, see Lepanto.

Neccarus, see Neckar.

Neckar river, at Heidelberg, II. 154, 208.

Nemetes, Spires inhabited by people called, II. 231.

Nemetum, see Spires.

Neobourg on the Rhine, II. 176.

Neomagus, see Nimeguen.⅛

Netherlands, Thomas Coryat in the, II. 311-376; eating customs in the, 360; overfloodings of, 364.

Nevers, Thomas Coryat at, his description of, I. 198-200.

Nevill, Henry, of Abergavenny, panegyric verses on Thomas Coryat by, I. 26.

Nicaea, council of, in Bithynia, I. 368.

Nicoletis, Joannes, friend of Thomas Coryat in Vicenza, II. 13.

Nicrus, see Neckar.

Nilus, crocodiles in, I. 291.

Nimeguen by the Wahalis, II. 154; Thomas Coryat at, 357; distance from, to Dordrecht, 376; founder of Worms, 256.

Ninus, king of the Assyrians, II. 183, 256.

Noah, Tuisco, son of, and Arezia, II. 178.

Norimberg, the Pegnetius river at, II. 285.

Normanus at Cologne, II. 348.

Notre-Dame of Paris, see Church.

Novalaise, in Piedmont, I. 225.

Novara, first city of the dukedom of Milan, I. 239; battle between French and Swiss at, 1500, 239.

Noviomagus, see Nimeguen.

Nunneries, at Amiens, I. 163; at Brescia built by King Desiderius, 750, II. 45; at Zurich, founded by Ludovicus, king of Germany, 853, 99.

Odcombe, distance from, to London, I. 301; to Venice, II. 376.

Olevian, Gaspar, preacher at Heidelberg, II. 229.

Olivet, representation of Mount, in the cloister of Spires cathedral, II. 248.

Ome, German measure, II. 219.

Operinus, Joannes, printer of Basle, II. 172.

Oppenheim, near Worms, II. 266; death of Rupertus, king of the Romans at, 268; S. Catherine's Church in, 268.

Ostriches, description of, I. 190.

Otho, Viscount of Milan, his single combat with Volucis, I. 245.

Otho the Great, battle of, with his son Ludolphus, II. 280; with Eberhardus, at Andernach, 307.

Owen, John, epigram and distichon on Thomas Coryat by, I. 74.

Padua, built by Antenor, I. 138, 270; Scaliger's decastichon on, description of, 270; past history of, 273; monuments of, 281; distance from, to Venice, 301; in Emperor Martian's time, and Attila, 305; subject to Venice, 420; Lord Wentworth and Thomas Coryat at, II. 1.

Padus, see Po.

Page, Samuel, panegyric verses on Thomas Coryat by, I. 76-77.

Pajellus, Livius, orator of Vicenza, II. 8.

Palace of the Viscounts of Milan, description of, I. 245; of the Dukes of Mantua, 265; of Padua, description of, 274; of the bishop of Padua, 293; of Earl Leonardus Walmarana in Vicenza, II. 4, 5; of Odoricus Capra, 9, 11; of the Scaligers, at Verona, 25; of Count Augustinus Justus in Verona, 35; of Brescia, 41; palaces of Brescia, 46; of the bishop of Bergamo, 53; of the prince at Heidelberg, 214; of the bishop of Worms, 257.

Palaces in Venice, I. 308; of the Duke of Venice, 318; description of, 333.

Palatinate, Lower, Heidelberg, metropolitan city of, II. 207.

Palatine princes, titles of, II. 223; etymology of, 224.

Palavicino, Sir Horatio, II. 62.

Palaeologus, Constantine, last Christian Emperor of Constantinople, his opinions on Padua, 1453, I. 274.

Palladio, Andrea, architect of Vicenza theatre, II. 9.

Palma Castle in Forum Julii, Venetian possession, I. 420.

Panicke, Italian ...
Pannonia, the L...
Pantaleon, Henr...
physician of ...
epitaph of at ...
Panninus, O...
Joan, II. ...
Papia, capital of ...
258.
Parens, David ...
Heidelberg, II. ...
Paris, Thomas C...
Scaliger's verse...
distance f...
the Sequana ...
Participius, A...
builds the ...
I. 335.
Paul, Friar, of the ...
360.
Paulus, statue of ...
Pavia, I. 238; C...
I. 41, I. 255.
Pavy, see Pavia.
Pawlet, John, of ...
panegyric verses ...
by, I. 62.
Parton, John. ...
Thomas Cory...
Peacham, Henry, ...
Thomas Coryat by ...
Pearch, measure ...
Peel, Antony, hanged ...
Pegnetius river, tribut...
II. 285.
Pelicanus, Conrad ...
Heidelberg, II. ...
Pepin, King, and S. Ze...
in Verona cathedra...
ment of, 33; and th...
affairs of Ger...
residence of, at Wor...
Persica, Sibylla, proph...
Peschiera, Venetian ...
Petrarch, Francis, ca...
295; his library le...
of Venice, 321.
Petrengo, Vincent...
Friar of Bergam...
Coryat, II. 57.
Peucerus, Gaspar, ...
of Sabaudi, I. 218...
word Spires, II. 2...
logy of Palatine, ...

INDEX

Panicke, Italian corn, I. 234.

Pannonia, the Longobards in, I. 237.

Pantaleon, Henry, philosopher and physician of Basle, at Baden, II. 142 ; epitaph of, at Basle, 162.

Panuinius, Onuphrius, friar, and Pope Joan, II. 282.

Papia, capital of the Longobardes, I. 238.

Pareus, David, professor of divinity in Heidelberg, II. 230.

Paris, Thomas Coryat at, I. 170-182 ; Scaliger's verses in praise of, 170 ; distance from, to Lyons, 301 ; on the Sequana, II. 154.

Participitius, Angelus, Duke of Venice, builds the palace of the Dukes, 809, I. 333.

Paul, Friar, of the Order of Servites, I. 380.

Paulus, statue of, at Padua, I. 279.

Pavia, I. 238 ; Charles V. and Francis I. at, I. 255.

Pavy, see Pavia.

Pawlet, John, of George Henton, panegyric verses on Thomas Coryat by, I. 62.

Payton, John, panegyric verses on Thomas Coryat by, I. 29.

Peacham, Henry, panegyric verses on Thomas Coryat by, I. 113-115.

Pearch, measure, II. 24.

Peel, Antony, hanged in effigy, I. 168.

Pegnetius river, tributary of the Maine, II. 285.

Pellicanus, Conradus, learned man of Heidelberg, II. 229.

Pepin, King, and S. Zeno's monument in Verona cathedral, II. 33 ; monument of, 33 ; and the ecclesiastical affairs of Germany, 260 ; of France, residence of, at Worms, 764, 264.

Persica, Sibylla, prophecy of, II. 259.

Peschiera, Venetian fort at, II. 39.

Petrarch, Francis, canon of Padua, I. 295 ; his library left to the Senate of Venice, 321.

Petrengo, Vincentius de, Dominican Friar of Bergamo, and Thomas Coryat, II. 57.

Peucerus, Gaspar, on the etymology of Sabaudi, I. 218 ; etymology of the word Spires, II. 232 ; on the etymology of Palatine, II. 224.

Pfaltz, castle in the Rhine, II. 224.

Phaesulae, near Florence, I. 305.

Philip Augustus, and the Louvre, c. 1214, I. 173.

Philip II., king of Spain, his picture in Venice, I. 425.

Philip VI. of Valois, King of France, and the title of Dauphin, 1328, I. 194.

Philip, twenty-fourth German Emperor, son of Frederick Barbarossa and Beatrix, II. 235 ; Strasburg taken by, 1200, II. 193.

Philip, Count Palatine, and the palace of Heidelberg, II. 217.

Philippes, Sir Edward, master of the rolls, II. 310.

Philippus Arabs, first Christian emperor, death of, at Verona, II. 37.

Phillips, Robert, panegyric verses on Thomas Coryat by, I. 30-31.

Phillips, Sir Edward, Thomas Coryat's patron, I. 317 ; II. 370.

Phrygia, Sibylla, prophecy of, II. 258.

Picardy, province of, I. 157.

Pickeney, see Picquigny.

Picquigny, in Picardy, Thomas Coryat at, I. 160, 164.

Picus, see Mirandula.

Piersey, John, bishop of Salisbury, archbishop of York, epitaph of, by George Coryat, II. 402.

Pisa, in Etruria, Henry VII., emperor of Germany at, II. 146.

Piscator, Joannes, learned man of Strasburg, II. 195,

Pius II., Pope, epitaph by, II. 166-167 ; university of Basle founded by, 170.

Pizighiton, Francis I., king of France, prisoner at, I. 255.

Plancus, Munatius, Augusta Rauracorum built by, II. 152 ; statue of, in Basle, 156.

Plato, travels of, I. 128 ; travels of, to Egypt, II. 74.

Plinius Secundas, elogium of, in Como, II. 64.

Plutarch, quotation from, I. 251, 321.

Po, or Padus, or Eridanus, river in Turin, I. 230.

Podestà, Magistrate, ruling the land cities subject to Venice, I. 419.

Poggios, the Florentine, II. 81, 143, 349.

Polanus, Amandus, a Polensdorf of Basle, II. 167.

Politianus, Angelus, epistle from, to Cardinal Jacobus, II. 177.

Polma, Huldricus de, and the murder of Emperor Albert, II. 145 ; death of, at Basle, 146.

Polycarpus, bishop of Smyrna, I. 209.

Polyodopolis, Attila's name for Strasburg, II. 184.

Pompey, travels of, I. 138.

Ponds, carp, at Fontainebleau, I. 187.

Pontanus, Ludovicus, at the council of Basle, 1439, II. 166.

Pont de Beauvoisin, Thomas Coryat at, I. 215.

Pont de Nieullet, at Calais, I. 156.

Ponte de Rialto, description of, I. 309.

Pontius Pilate, exile and death of, at Lyons, I. 207.

Poole, Henry, panegyric verses on Thomas Coryat by, I. 29-30.

Portraits in palace of Augustinus Justus, II. 35.

Posthuma fragmenta poematum of George Coryat, II. 377-407.

Pots, Mr., preacher at Flushing, II. 375.

Praepositura, sacked by freebooters, II. 309.

Praetorium of Vicenza, description of, II. 3.

Prefects, Roman, instituted by Julius Caesar in Gaul, II. 283.

Prettigoia, confederation of Rhaetia, signed at, 1470, II. 90.

Prince Royall, the English ship, I. 359.

Prison, State, in Venice, I. 357.

Procurator of S. Mark, dignity in Venice, I. 419.

Prosdocimus, first apostle of Padua, I. 293 ; first apostle of Vicenza, II. 13.

Psalms, preface to a book of, translated by George Coryat, II. 385.

Ptolomaeus, *Geographie* by, II. 90.

Puckering, John, George Coryat to, II. 400.

Pulpit in Spires cathedral, II. 244-246.

Pulpits in Mayence cathedral, II. 273.

Punishments in Switzerland, II. 107.

Pythagoras, travels of, to Italy, II. 74.

Quin, Walter, panegyric verses on Thomas Coryat by, I. 54-56.

Radagisus, king of the Goths in Italy, I. 305.

Ragatz in Switzerland, II. 92.

Ramus, Peter, quotation from, II. 84.

Rapperswyl, John of Habspurg at, II. 108.

Rathaus in Cologne, description of, II. 343.

Ravilliacke, murderer of Henry IV., I. 168.

Rees, Coryat at, II. 350 ; church of, 355.

Regius, Raphael, of Padua, I. 298.

Ramagan, sacked by freebooters, II. 309.

Rezuns, Baron of, and the confederation of Rhetia, 1424, II. 90.

Rhaetia, geographical divisions of, II. 63 ; Thomas Coryat at, 63-70, 87-88 ; confederations of, 90

Rhaetus, king of Tuscia, and the name of Rhetia, II. 63.

Rheinfelden city, Thomas Coryat at, II. 151.

Rhenanus, Beatus, on the etymology of Palatinate, II. 224.

Rhene-Barke, Thomas Coryat at, II. 352.

Rhenes in Little Britaine, Court of Parliament, I. 179.

Rhine, at Basle, II. 153 ; Thomas Coryat on, 176 ; cataract or waterfalls on the, 302 ; bishoprics on the left side of the, 335 ; river in Gelderland, 357.

Rhine Valley and River, II. 68, 87.

Rhodanus river, I. 205 ; II. 154.

Rialto, Joannes Bonus, first dweller of the, in Venice, I. 304 ; Ponte de, 309 ; or Exchange of Venice, 312 ; temporary dwelling-place of some Dukes of Venice, 418.

Rice-bank at Calais, I. 155.

Richard I., king of England, elected Emperor of Germany at Worms, II. 266 ; and the tolls and taxes in Germany, 295 ; Boppard town captured by, 304.

Richlindus, wife of Eckenbertus Kemerer, first Abbess of the Franckendal monastery, II. 252.

Richmond, Robert, panegyric verses on Thomas Coryat by, I. 50-54.

Ridouts, or forts near the Waell, II. 363.

Risus river, II. 14...
Rivole, or R....
I. 227.
Robertellus, Fr....
Roch Melon or M... tain near N....
Rodolph, e....
II. 144.
Rodolph II. s....
House of W....
Rodolphes, Coc....
II. 167.
Rodolphus, L....
Rheinfelder...
Rodolphus, Ex....
the Roman..., II. 1...
Emperor, ...
Turlowe, 225...
Romans, travel... 74.
Rooke, George...
friend, I. 27...
friend at P....
Rosamund, Q....
Rosne, M. de ....
I. 156.
Rotenburg, the T....
285.
Renis in Norman... men, I. 179.
Row, Sir Henr... London, II. 2.
Row, Thomas, a... Franklin, in ...
Rowland, and the C... S. George's ....
Roy, M. de la. Fr....
Thomas Corvat...
Rudiger, bishop o....
Rufach in Alsatia.
Rufinus, II. 168.
Rugia Island, ... I. 227.
Rupelmunda, burh... II. 351.
Rupertus, duke of nunnery of Zur...
Rupertus, the elder church of the Ho the university. He II. 212, 227 ; tom death of, at Oppe... Ruremunda, Lind... II. 368.

INDEX

Risus river, II. 144.

Rivole, or Rivoli, Thomas Coryat at, I. 227.

Robertellus, Francis, of Padua, I. 298.

Roch Melow or Molom, high mountain near Novalaise, I. 225.

Rodolph, eldest son of Emperor Albert, II. 144.

Rodolph II., statue of, in the Senate House of Worms, II. 262.

Rodolphus, Count Palatine, 1209, II. 212.

Rodolphus, Duke of Swabia, Earl of Rheinfelden, II. 151.

Rodolphus, Earl of Hapsburg, king of the Romans, II. 138 ; 32nd German Emperor, 235 ; and the conquest of Turlowe, 205.

Romans, travels of, to Marseilles, II. 74.

Rooke, George, Thomas Coryat's friend, I. 272 ; Thomas Coryat's friend at Padua, II. 1.

Rosamund, Queen, II. 38.

Rosne, M. de, governor of Graveling, I. 156.

Rotenburg, the Tuberus river at, II. 285.

Rouen in Normandy, Court of Parliament, I. 179.

Row, Sir Henry, Lord Mayor of London, II. 293.

Row, Thomas, and Thomas Coryat at Frankfort, II. 293.

Rowland, and the Cleft Rock, near S. George's, I. 227.

Roy, M. de la, French Protestant, and Thomas Coryat, I. 180.

Rudiger, bishop of Spires, II. 231.

Rufach in Alsatia, II. 181.

Ruffinus, II. 168.

Rugia Island, and the Longobards, I. 237.

Rupelmunda, birthplace of Mercator, II. 351.

Rupertus, duke of Alemanny and the nunnery of Zurich, II. 99.

Rupertus, the elder, founder of the church of the Holy Ghost, and of the university, Heidelberg, c. 1346, II. 212, 227 ; king of the Romans, death of, at Oppenheim, II. 268.

Ruremunda, Lindanus, Bishop of, II. 368.

Rusticus, disciple of S. Denis, I. 169 ; shrine of, 185.

S. Albanus Church at Mayence, II. 281.

S. Ambrose, bishop of Milan, and Theodosius I., I. 242.

S. André, Thomas Coryat at, I. 223.

S. Anthony of Padua, I. 286.

S. Apollinaris, bishop of Ravenna, first apostle of Brescia, 119, II. 46 ; near Basle, 172.

S. Barnabas, Milan converted to Christianity by, I. 244 ; first apostle of Bergamo and Milan, II. 49.

S. Barthelmew, martyr in Albania, I. 363.

S. Bartholomew's Church in Frankfort, II. 289.

S. Bernard, abbot of Claraval in Burgundy, his salutation to the Virgin, II. 236-237 ; his letter to the Bishop of Spires about the first Crusade, 1094, 238 ; translation of his letter to the Bishop of Spires, 239-244 ; friendship of, with Hildegardis, 296.

S. Brixe, Thomas Coryat at, I. 168.

S. Croce, quarter in Venice, I. 306.

S. Denis, first apostle of the Gauls, I. 169 ; shrine of, near Paris, Thomas Coryat at, 169, 182, 185.

S. Erasmo, haven of Venice, I. 304.

S. Georges in Italy, Thomas Coryat at, I. 227.

S. Geran, Thomas Coryat at, I. 201.

S. Gereon, martyr in Cologne, II. 342.

S. Gewere, on the Rhine, II. 301 ; merry custom at, 302.

S. Goar, see S. Gewere.

S. Gregory, martyr in Cologne, II. 342.

S. Jean de Maurienne, Thomas Coryat at, I. 223.

S. John Baptist's Day in Piedmont, I. 234.

S. John's village in the Brembana Valley, Thomas Coryat at, II. 61.

S. Lewis, king of France and the bishop of Vicenza, II. 4.

S. Liew, Thomas Coryat at, I. 168.

S. Luke's monument in Padua, I. 288.

S. Marco Mountain, see Ancone Mountain.

S. Marco, quarter in Venice, I. 306 ; market-place of, description of, 314 ; piazza of, description of, 323.

429

S. Mark, the evangelist, patron of Venice, his body brought from Alexandria, 810, I. 354.

S. Mary's Church in Vicenza, II. 10.

S. Maternus, first apostle of Strasburg, II. 193; first apostle of Cologne, 310, 334.

S. Michael Monastery, near S. George's, I. 228.

S. Paul and the viper in Malta, I. 412; place in Venice, 385.

S. Polo, quarter in Venice, I. 306.

S. Reinoldus, archbishop of Cologne, II. 331.

S. Saphorine de Lay, Thomas Coryat at, I. 201.

S. Stephen, first martyr, tomb of, in Venice, I. 381; place in Venice, games played in, 385.

S. Truyen, on the Rhine, II. 353.

S. Ursula, history of, II. 336; church of, in Cologne, 337.

S. Zeno, bishop and patron saint of Verona, II. 32; monument of, in Verona Cathedral, 33.

Saba, Queen of, ancestry of, II. 325.

Sabaudi, people of Savoy, etymology of the name, I. 218.

Sackfield, Thomas, Dorsetshire-man, settled in Frankfort, II. 291.

Sage, Peter, Coryat's fellow traveller, II. 350.

Sala river in Saxony, I. 237.

Salamis, see Famagusta.

Salt mines at Halles, II. 144.

Salust, quotation from, I. 421.

Samia, Sibylla, prophecy of, II. 258.

Sanctus, martyr at Lyons, I. 207.

Sangona, Latin name of river Sone I. 205; Thomas Coryat at, 268.

Sansovinus, Jacobus, statues of the tower of S. Mark, made by, I. 328.

Santo, see Anthony's Church.

Sapor, King of Persia, and Emperor Valerian, I. 349 note.

Sarbini, Arnaldi, bishop of Nevers, 1592, I. 200.

Sariana, Torellas, and the antiquities of Verona, II. 21.

Sartorius, Joannes Antonius, and Thomas Coryat, I. 256, 258.

Sarum, Thomas Coryat at, I. 293.

Sassam in Rhaetia, II. 68.

Savage, Richard, Coryat's fellow-traveller, II. 350.

Savoy, Thomas Coryat in, I. 215-227; a dukedom, 218; family of the Duke of, 231.

Saxenhausen in Frankfort, II. 288.

Scaliger, Antonius, 1596, 29.

Scaliger, Con Grande, II. 29.

Scaliger, Canis Signorius, statue of, II. 28.

Scaliger, Joannes Galeatius, 1596, II. 29.

Scaliger, Julius Caesar, his verses on Amiens, I. 161; his hexastichon in praise of Paris, 170; of Lyons, 203; his octostichon, on Turin, 229; his verses on Milan, 240; decastichon on Cremona, 257; his verses on Mantua, 262; decastichon on Padua, 270; verses on Venice, 301; verses on Vicenza, II. 2; verses on Verona, 16; palace of the, 25; monuments of the, 27; hexastichon on Brescia, 41; verses on Bergamo, 49; verses on Heidelberg, 207; verses on Frankfort, 287-288; verses on Cologne, 311.

Scaliger, Mastinus, statue of, in Verona, II. 27.

Scanderbeg, George Castriot, King of Servia and Epirus, statue of, at Venice, I. 360.

Sconenberg, Earl of, at the Frankfort fair, II. 291.

Scory, John, panegyric verses on Thomas Coryat by, I. 36.

Scowen island, in the Netherlands, II. 371.

Seine river, or Sequana, I. 171; II. 154.

Sempach, battle of, between Leopold, Duke of Austria, and the Swiss, II. 148.

Senate House of Worms, II. 261.

Seneca, quotation from, I. 204; works of, II. 210.

Senis Mount, I. 222.

Sequana, see Seine.

Serrarius, Nicholas, Jesuit of Mayence, II. 175, 274, 279.

Severus, Alexander, Emperor, slain at Mayence, II. 281.

Seward, John, Laurence Whitaker's epistle to, I. 149.

Sheep in Rhaetia, II. 64.

INDEX

Sian in Piedmont, Thomas Coryat at, I. 233.

Sibyllae, prophecies of the, II. 257.

Sicambri, former inhabitants of Gelderland, II. 357.

Sidenham, George, his verses on Germany, II. 181-182.

Sidney, Robert, Viscount Lisle, Governor of Flushing, II. 374.

Sigismund, Emperor, and the Earldom of Baden, II. 138 ; and the Dukedom of Savoy, I. 218 ; and the Council of Basle, 1431, II. 172.

Simlerus, Josias, treatise by, II. 91 ; learned man of Zurich, 98, 111.

Singers, Venetian, I. 391.

Skinkel-sconce, in an island of the Rhine, II. 356.

Slade, Samuel, of Merton College, praised by Archbishop Gabriel, I. 370.

Sleidanus, Joannes, learned man of Strasburg, II. 195.

Smaragdus, second exarch of Ravenna, I. 235.

Smith, Nicholas, panegyric verses on Thomas Coryat by, I. 98.

Smyrna, Polycarpus, Bishop of, I. 209.

Socrates, II. 168.

Sol, Venetian coin, value of, I. 389 ; tin coin, 423.

Solodure on the Arola, II. 154 ; one of the three oldest cities in Germany, II. 183.

Solodurum, see Solodure.

Solomono, mother of the Maccabees, II. 341.

Solon, travels of, to Asia, II. 74.

Sone (Saône) river, or Arar, or Sangona, I. 205.

Sophia, Empress, and Narses, I. 337.

Sorbona, founded by Charles the Great, 796, I. 171.

Sorverden, Frederick, Comes de, arch of Cologne, II. 331.

Spanivellis, Thomas of, friend of Thomas Coryat in Vicenza, II. 13.

Speronus, Speronius, statue of, at Padua, I. 321.

Spira or Spier, see Spires.

Spira river at Spires, II. 232.

Spires, II. 147 ; confluence of the Rhine and Neckar near, 209 ; Thomas Coryat at, II. 231-251 ;

churches of, 233 ; cathedral of, 233 ; Attila at, 251 ; death of Adolph of Nassau near, 1298, 235 ; Attila at, 251.

Splugen, town and mountain, Lir Lake near, II. 67.

Stadthaus of Flushing, II. 374 ; of Nimeguen, 359.

Stangi, Henry de, scholar of Hermannus Kirchnerus, II. 71.

Statues in the Duke's Palace in Venice, I. 321 f ; of learned men in Verona, II. 27.

Steinbach, Ervinus of, II. 182 ; architect of Strasburg tower, 186.

Stilico, Consul, and Radagisus, I. 305.

Stiver, dutch coin, II. 365.

Stones, huge, in Savoy, I. 221.

Storks, description of, I. 189 ; at Flushing, II. 374.

Strangwayes, John, panegyric verses on Thomas Coryat by, I. 34-35.

Strasbürg in Alsatia, II. 180-194 ; bishop of, and Zürich, 108 ; Attila, 183 ; cathedral, 185 ; bishopric of, 193 ; distance from, to Heidelberg, 376.

Strigelius, Victorinus, professor at Heidelberg, II. 229.

Stuckius, Joannes Gulielmus, II. 98, 100, 111, 195.

Suetonius, I. 307.

Suevia, see Swabia.

Suicardus, Joannes, archbishop of Mayence in Coryat's time, II. 275.

Sungovia, or Sequania in Switzerland, II. 152.

Sunnazarius, Jacobus, reward bestowed by Venice on, I. 301.

Susa, Thomas Coryat near, I. 227.

Sutclin, John, panegyric verses on Thomas Coryat by, I. 64.

Swabia, Wimpina in, II. 208.

Swice, prefect of, and William Tell, II. 101 ; at the help of Zurich, 108.

Swiss at the battle of Granson, 1476, I. 192.

Switzerland, Thomas Coryat in, II. 92 f ; boundaries of, 92 ; origin of the name of, 103.

Sydenham, George, panegyric verses on Thomas Coryat by, I. 65-67.

Sylla river, in Switzerland, witches' ashes thrown in, II. 107.

Sylvius, Æneas, see Pius II.
Synagogues in the Ghetto, description of, I. 371.

Taberna, see Zabernia.
Tacitus, on Baden, II. 137; quotation from, 177; his account of the foundation of Cologne, 312.
Tamberlane, Bajazet and, I. 349, note.
Tarara, Thomas Coryat at, I. 202.
Tarentinus, Architus, wooden pigeon of, II. 188.
Targous island, in the Netherlands, II. 371.
Tarnous island, in the Netherlands, II. 371.
Tarquinius Priscus, I. 138, 241.
Taruisium, see Treirsa.
Tassell, William, Coryat's fellow-traveller, II. 350.
Tassilo, king of Bavaria, condemned by king Pipin, 764, II. 264.
Taylour, Thomas, galley-slave in Venice, I. 414.
Teillo, Hernand, governor of Dourlans, I. 165; Amiens surprised by, 166.
Telina, see Valtulina.
Tell, William, history of, II. 101 f.
Tenctheri, former inhabitants of Wesel, II. 353.
Tesino, see Ticino.
Teusch, see Deutz.
Teutonia, etymologies of, II. 178.
Theatre of Vicenza, II. 7, 9; at Verona, 25.
Thebes, built by Cadmus, I. 138.
Thello, Bishop, and the cathedral of Chur, 770, II. 88.
Themistocles, travels of, I. 138.
Theodoret, II. 168.
Theodosius I., S. Ambrose, bishop of Milan, and, I. 242.
Theonestus, companion of S. Albans, II. 282.
Theseus, travels of, I. 135.
Tholosa, in Languedoc, Court of Parliament, I. 179.
Thomannus, prefect of Zurich, and Thomas Coryat, II. 109.
Tiber, overflowings of, II. 19.
Tiburtina, Sibylla, prophecy of, II. 259.
Ticino, river, I. 235.
Tiel, on the Waell, II. 361.

Tigurinus, Josias Simlerus, Dialogue by, I. 394.
Tigurum, see Zürich.
Tilt-yard at Whitehall, II. 24.
Tinctoretus, see Tintoretto.
Tintoretto, pictures in Venice by, I. 342, 344.
Titian, pictures of, in Padua, I. 287; statues by, in Venice, 333.
Tò 'Oρòs-ὀξù, panegyric verses on Thomas Coryat by, I. 81.
Torture, public, in Venice, I. 392.
Tossana, Thomas Coryat at, II. 67, 87.
Totila, 5th king of Ravenna, I. 289.
Tour du Pin, see La Tour du Pin.
Tower of St. Mark in Venice, description of, I. 325; of Vicenza, II. 4.
Tower, James, Coryat's fellow-traveller, II. 350.
Trajan, Emperor, at Cologne, II. 349; his bridge over the Danube, I. 309.
Trapezuntius, George, Greek orator, II. 150.
Treasurer of the land cities subject to Venice, I. 420.
Treasures of the French kings at S. Denis, I. 182.
Trebeta, son of Ninus, king of the Assyrians, II. 183.
Trebeta, Prince, founder of Mayence, II. 270.
Tremellius, Emanuel, I. 374; preacher at Heidelberg, II. 229.
Tremoville, commander of the French at the battle of Novara, 1500, I. 239.
Trent, Bassanum, near, I. 273.
Trevirs, one of the three oldest cities in Germany, II. 183; founded by Prince Trebeta, 256; Strasburg, subjected to, 193.
Trevisa, subject to Venice, I. 420.
Triboces, former inhabitants of Alsatia, II. 183.
Triphone, the Jew, and Justinus, I. 209.
Trithemius, John, and the writings of Bishop Maximus, I. 232.
Triumphus Bavaricus, by Robert Turner, II. 233.
Trontz, confederation of Rhetia, 1424, signed at, II. 90.
Truccessius, Gebhardus, archbishop of Cologne, II. 335.

Tuberus river, II. 285.
Tuetanes, lord of, Tuilleries, palace, Tuisco, son of Noah, 178; and, 348.
Tun, Great, of, Turegum, see Zürich.
Turgovia, II. 95.
Tune, illness of, 209; Sion, story of, Milan, 351.
Turlowe, II. 195; Turner, R. 348.
Turner, Robert, by, on Syon, Tyre, limit of, II. 15.
Two Storks, II. Coryat at, II. 15.
Tyrol, Membara, 52.

Uberwinter, or Coryat at, II. 344.
Ulm, founders of Unopolis, see Constance.
Ulsingen, see Fluntern.
Ulmo, Thomas Coryat, Utrechingen, see Fluntern.
Underwald, or Switzerland, II. 101, 108.
Universities in Germany, of Basle, II. of Heidelberg, 273; of Wittenberg, at, 154.
Urban II., Pope, 1094, II. 258.
Urban IV., Pope, Christ day, II.
Urban VI., Pope, founded by, 1368.
Urn, or Uranus, II. 108.
Ursinus, Zacharias, berg, II. 229.
Ursula river, Lucerne.
Usumcassanes, presents to the, I. 336.

INDEX

Tuberus river, tributary of the Maine, II. 285.

Tuetanes, lord of Tuetonia, II. 178.

Tuilleries, palace of the, I, 175.

Tuisco, son of Noah and Arezia, II. 178 ; and the foundation of Deutz, 348.

Tun, Great, of Heidelberg, II. 218.

Turegum, see Zürich.

Turgovia, II. 96.

Turin, illness of Thomas Coryat at, I. 229 ; Scaliger's verses on, 229 ; history of, 230 ; distance from, to Milan, 301.

Turlowe in Baden, Marquisate of, II. 199 ; Thomas Coryat at, 203 ; conquered by Emperor Rodolph, 205.

Turner, Robert, *Triumphus Bavaricus* by, on Spires Cathedral, II. 233.

Turre, limit of Vicenza and Verona, II. 15.

Two Storks, inn at Zürich, Thomas Coryat at, II. 107.

Tyrol, Meinhard, Earl of, II. 144.

Uberwinter, on the Rhine, Thomas Coryat at, II. 307.

Ubii, founders of Cologne, II. 311.

Ubiopolis, see Cologne.

Ulissingen, see Flushing.

Ulmo, Thomas Coryat at, II. 61.

Ulyshingen, see Flushing.

Underwald, or Sylvania, in Switzerland, II. 101 ; at the help of Zurich, 108.

Universities in Germany, I. 8 ; II. 76 ; of Basle, II. 170; of Cologne, 348; of Heidelberg, 226; of Mayence, 279 ; of Wittenberg, Martin Luther at, 194.

Urban II., Pope, and the first Crusade, 1094, II. 238.

Urban IV., Pope, and the Corpus Christi day, I. 176.

Urban VI., Pope, university of Cologne, founded by, 1388, II. 348.

Uri, or Urania, in Switzerland, II. 101, 108.

Ursinus, Zacharius, preacher at Heidelberg, II. 229.

Ursula river, Lucerne on, II. 154.

Usumcassanes, king of Persia, his presents to the Signiory of Venice, I. 356.

Utrecht, death of Conradus II. at, II. 233 ; death of Henry V. at, 1125, 235.

Vadianus Glareanus, panegyric verses on Thomas Coryat by, I. 86-95, 116-119.

Valentinian, Emperor, II. 153.

Valerian, Emperor, and Sapor, king of Persia, I. 349 note.

Valerius, Albertus, bishop of Verona in Thomas Coryat's time, II. 32.

Valerius Brobus, Emperor, II. 179.

Valtulina Valley, II. 62.

Vangionum, see Worms.

Vaughan, Rowland, John, and William, epitaph of, by George Coryat, II. 406-407.

Vegetius, on the army of ancient Rome, I. 212.

Venice, Signiory of, Padua added to, by Gattamelita, 1402, I. 274 ; Gulf of, 303.

Venice, description of, I. 301-428 ; a 'maiden city,' 415 ; government of, 417 ; possessions of, 420 ; Coryat's departure from, II. 1 ; distance from, to Ancone mountain, II. 375.

Venus's temple in Spires, demolished by Dagobert, II. 251.

Vercellis in Piedmont, S. John Baptist's day in, I. 234.

Verona, subject to Venice, I. 420 ; Scaliger's verses on, Thomas Coryat at, II. 16 ; description of, 17-40, 154.

Veronne, forest of, near Abbeville, I. 160.

Verses, panegyric, on Thomas Coryat, I. 22-121.

Vespasianus, Flavius, Roman prefect at Mayence, II. 283.

Vic, M. de, governor of Calais, 1608, I. 152.

Vicenza, subject to Venice, I. 420 ; Scaliger's verses on, II. 2 ; description of, 3 ; Attila at, 12 ; on the Bacchilio, 154.

Vicetia, see Vicenza.

Victor, archbishop of Worms, and the Council of Cologne, 348, II. 260.

Vienna, inhabited by Allobroges, I. 218.

Vincentia, see Vicenza.

Vineyards and wine houses in Savoy, I. 219 ; in Piedmont, 233.

Virdungus, Joannes, mathematician in Heidelberg, II. 229.

Virgil, at Cremona, I. 260 ; his verses on Mantua, 262 ; Mantua, birth-place of, 263 ; quotation from, II. 176.

Virginius, Rufus, Roman prefect at Mayence, II. 283.

Visdossein, M. de, governor of Calais, I. 156.

Voga, hill in Burgundy, I. 171.

Voitlandia, Maine river rises in, II. 284.

Volucis, Otho, Viscount of Milan, his single combat with, I. 246.

Vopiscus, Flavius, historiographer, II. 183.

Voragine, Jacob de, and the legend of S. Denis, I. 169.

Vorpillere, Thomas Coryat at, I. 214.

Vulteius, travels of, I. 130.

Wael, river, in Gelderland, II. 357.

Wahalis, Nimeguen by the, II. 154 ; branch of the Rhine, 177.

Walanus, first bishop of Basle, 704, II. 172.

Walastat in Switzerland, Thomas Coryat at, II. 91, 93.

Walcheren island, towns in, II. 372.

Walks, vaulted, in Padua, I. 298.

Walmarana, Earl Leonardus, palace of, in Vicenza, II. 4.

Wan, Joannes de, last bishop of Basle, 1365, II. 172.

Warner, Michael, builder of the great tun of Heidelberg, II. 219.

Wart, Rodolphus de, and the murder of Emperor Albert, II. 145 ; death of, 146.

Wasalia, Joannes de, learned man of Wesel, II. 301.

Weserus, Gaspar, of Zurich, II. 100 ; Thomas Coryat's epistles to, 113-121 ; epistle from, to Thomas Coryat, 122-123.

Watchman in the Netherlands, II. 355.

Weda, Hermannus Comes a, arch-bishop of Cologne and the Reform, II. 335.

Wentworth, Mary, monument of, at Calais, I. 154.

Wentworth, Lord, Thomas Coryat and, at Padua, II. I.

Wernerus, martyred child in Wesel, 1287, II. 300.

Wernharius, first bishop of Worms, in the time of Charles the Great, II. 261.

Wesel, Higher, Thomas Coryat at, II. 300.

Wesel, Under, in Cleveland, II. 352.

Wheel, Tormentor's, near Boulogne, I. 159.

Whippings, public, at Lyons, I. 213.

Whitaker, Laurence, panegyric verses on Thomas Coryat by, I. 40-43 ; Elogie of Coryat's Crudities, 149.

Whittelbach, Otto Palatine of, Emperor Philip murdered by, 1208, II. 235.

Wiesa river at Basle, II. 153, 155.

William, Earl of Holland and Zeland, monuments to, in Middleborough, II. 373.

William, Prince of Orange, father of Ludovica, wife of Frederick IV., II. 225.

Willigisus, bishop, founder of the cathedral of Mayence, c. 1011, II. 271.

Willingus, Joannes, preacher at Heidel-berg, II. 229.

Willoughby, student in Padua, and Thomas Coryat, I. 299.

Wimier, Carolus, of the Praemon-stratenian Order, and Thomas Coryat, I. 161.

Wimpina in Swabia, II. 208.

Windows, French, I. 197 ; of Lyons, 204 ; size of, in Rhaetia, II. 69.

Wines, variety of, in Venice, I. 424.

Wirtemberg, Earl of, and Zurich, II. 108.

Wisdom, College of, at Heidelberg, II. 227.

Witches burnt in Zürich, II. 107.

Wittemberg, University of, Martin Luther at, II. 194.

Woldruda, wife of king Pipin, II. 349.

Wolphangus, Count Palatine, 1558, II. 212.

Wolphius, Joannes, printer of Basle, II. 172.

Worcom, on the Waell, II. 361.

INDEX

Wormacia, see Worms.
Worms, Joannes Dalburgius, bishop of, II. 229; Thomas Coryat at, 252-268; description of, 255 f.
Worsley, James and Anne, epitaph of, by George Coryat, II. 405.
Worsley, Richard, epitaph of, by George Coryat, II. 404-5.
Wotton, Sir Henry, English ambassador in Venice, I. 272, 332; praised by Archbishop Gabriel, 370; letter from Richard Martin to, 377-379.

Xylander, Gulielmus, philosopher in Heidelberg, II. 229.

Yaxley, Robert, panegyric verses on Thomas Coryat by, I. 34.

Zabarella, Francis, of Padua, I. 298.
Zabernia, or Taberna, seat of the bishops of Strasburg, II. 193.
Zamolxis, travels of, I. 128.
Zanchius, Hieronymus, famous preacher of Bergamo, II. 60.

Zani or Zanus, Sebastianus, Duke of Venice, 1166, I. 349; and his betrothal to the sea, 1174, 359.
Zante island, or Zacynthos, I. 320.
Zanus, Petrus, Duke of Venice, and the lions of S. Mark's, I. 348.
Zara, subject to Venice, I. 421.
Zebenico, subject to Venice, I. 421.
Zedechias, Jewish physician, 872, I. 267.
Zeno, Joannes Baptista, Cardinal, his tomb in S. Mark's Church, Venice, I. 351.
Zirixee, in Scowen island, II. 371.
Zogno, Thomas Coryat, II. 61.
Zollern, John, Earl of, death of, II. 148.
Zuinggerus, professor of Greek at Basle in Coryat's time, II. 170.
Zuinglius, pastor of Zurich, II. 109, 111.
Zürich, II. 96; lake of, II. 94; history of, 94; description of, 95-112; Thomas Coryat leaves, 136; on the Limacus, 154; one of the three oldest cities in Germany, 183; distance from, to Basle, 376.

CORYAT'S CRUDITIES

The following list of Errata is reprinted from the original edition.

ERRATA.

In the first Oration of Kirchnerus for plency read plenty, ibid. for contained r. contemned. ibid. for matters r. manners. pag. 16. lin. 30. for hairse r. haire. p. 21. l. 4. for hore r. horse. p. 23. l. 14. for videt r. vidit. p. 29. l. 14. for subdio r. sub dio. p. 35. l. 15. for preambulating r. perambulating. p. 58. l. 31. for from r. to. p. 63. l. 17. for prestin r. pristin. p. 136. l. 33. for remited r. remitted. p. 149. l. 35. for attentator r. attentato. p. 161. l. 16. for Vinetia r. Venetia. p. 162. l. 24. for twenty r. twentieth. p. 163. l. 16. for fourty r. forty. p. 167. l. 6. for breath r. breadth. p. 202. l. 33. for ratriæ r. patriæ. p. 206. l. 17. for is r. it. p. 257. l. 27. for shall r. shalt. p. 271. l. 30. for maner r. manners. p. 308. l. 16. for sounded r. founded. p. 312. l. 21. for Sariana r. Saraina. p. 297. l. 17. for Lordships r. Mannors. p. 385. l. 3. for sacers r. sakers. In the last line of one of the pages of my latin Epistle to Buelerus for connere r. continere. p. 397. l. 19. for afterwaed r. afterward. p. 419. l. 16. for wood r. forrest. p. 422. l. 7. for ipsam r. ipsum. p. 438. l. 1. for opposing r. opposed. p. 467. l. 18. for Cassia r. Hassia. p. 492. l. 9. for Saronie r. Saxonie. p. 495. l. 2. for who read which. p. 509. l. 14. for of r. or. p. 522. l. 30. for in r. of. p. 539. l. 30. for canot r. cannot. p. 573. l. 3. for Princedomes r. Principalities. p. 578. l. 3. for beuatifull r. beautifull. p. 581. l. 34. for slave r. slue. p. 561. l. 13. for nobis r. novis. p. 603. l. 35. for inumerable r. innumerable. p. 621. l. 13. for ength r. length. p. 623. l. 24. for to r. two. p. 622. l. 6. for belbi r. belli.

Other faults there are also in the booke at the least halfe a hundred (I beleeve) unmentioned in this place, which I intreate thee to winke at, and to expect a truer Edition, which I will promise thee shall make recompence for the errors now past.

GLASGOW: PRINTED AT THE UNIVERSITY PRESS BY ROBERT MACLEHOSE AND CO. LTD.

Lightning Source UK Ltd.
Milton Keynes UK
UKOW06f1859250816

281532UK00017B/479/P